ROUTLEDGE LIBRARY EDITIONS: GERMAN HISTORY

Volume 4

THE SCHELDT QUESTION

THE SCHELDT QUESTION
To 1839

S. T. BINDOFF

NEW YORK AND LONDON

First published in 1945 by George Allen & Unwin Ltd.

This edition first published in 2020
by Routledge
52 Vanderbilt Avenue, New York, NY 10017

and by Routledge
2 Park Square, Milton Park, Abingdon, Oxon OX14 4RN

Routledge is an imprint of the Taylor & Francis Group, an informa business

© 1945 S. T. Bindoff

All rights reserved. No part of this book may be reprinted or reproduced or utilised in any form or by any electronic, mechanical, or other means, now known or hereafter invented, including photocopying and recording, or in any information storage or retrieval system, without permission in writing from the publishers.

Trademark notice: Product or corporate names may be trademarks or registered trademarks, and are used only for identification and explanation without intent to infringe.

British Library Cataloguing in Publication Data
A catalogue record for this book is available from the British Library

ISBN: 978-0-367-02813-8 (Set)
ISBN: 978-0-429-27806-8 (Set) (ebk)
ISBN: 978-0-367-22928-3 (Volume 4) (hbk)
ISBN: 978-0-367-22939-9 (Volume 4) (pbk)
ISBN: 978-0-429-27771-9 (Volume 4) (ebk)

Publisher's Note
The publisher has gone to great lengths to ensure the quality of this reprint but points out that some imperfections in the original copies may be apparent.

Disclaimer
The publisher has made every effort to trace copyright holders and would welcome correspondence from those they have been unable to trace.

THE SCHELDT QUESTION

to 1839

by

S. T. BINDOFF

With a Foreword by
Professor G. J. RENIER

LONDON, GEORGE ALLEN & UNWIN LTD

FIRST PUBLISHED IN 1945
All rights reserved

To
PIETER GEYL

PRODUCED IN COMPLETE CONFORMITY
WITH THE AUTHORIZED ECONOMY
STANDARDS

PRINTED IN GREAT BRITAIN BY
THE WOODBRIDGE PRESS, LTD.
ONSLOW STREET, GUILDFORD

CONTENTS

	PAGE
Foreword by Professor G. J. Renier	vii
Preface	viii

INTRODUCTION
The River Scheldt and the " Scheldt Question " - - 1

PART ONE: ORIGINS, 1200-1572

CHAPTER
1. *To the Close of the Fourteenth Century*
   - (i) The Scheldt-Honte Delta - - - - - - 6
   - (ii) Navigation in the Delta - - - - - - 15
   - (iii) Political Jurisdiction over the Delta - - - - 17
   - (iv) The Tolls - - - - - - - - - 21
     - (a) *The* Geleiden *on Scheldt and Honte* - - - - 23
     - (b) *The Toll of Iersekeroord* - - - - - 29

2. *The Fifteenth Century*
   - (i) The transformation of the Honte-Wielingen - - - 32
   - (ii) Antwerp, Middelburg and the Honte - - - - 35
   - (iii) The union of the delta-lands under the Dukes of Burgundy - 36
   - (iv) The Middelburg Staple - - - - - - - 39
   - (v) The Tolls - - - - - - - - - 40
     - (a) *The* Haringtol - - - - - - - - 40
     - (b) *The* Geleiden - - - - - - - - 43
     - (c) *The Toll of Iersekeroord* - - - - - - 46

3. *The " Golden Age "*
   - (i) The Lower Scheldt - - - - - - - - 62
   - (ii) The " Watch " on the Honte - - - - - - 64
   - (iii) The Middelburg Wine-Staple - - - - - - 74

PART TWO: THE CLOSURE, 1572-1780

4. *The Eighty Years' War*, 1572-1648
   - (i) To the fall of Antwerp, 1572-85 - - - - - 82
   - (ii) The war, 1585-1648 - - - - - - - 85
   - (iii) The Twelve Years' Truce, 1609-21 - - - - - 93
   - (iv) The Evolution of Articles XIV and XV of the Treaty of Münster - 100

5. *The Münster Regime,* 1648-1780
   (i) The Evolution of the Regime on the Scheldt, 1648-80 — — — 108
   (ii) "Third States" and the Closure, 1648-80 — — — — 116
   (iii) The Closure under International Guarantee, 1680-1780 — — — 129

PART THREE: THE REOPENING, 1780-1839

6. *The End of the Closure,* 1780-1830
   (i) The Austro-British Campaign against the Closure, 1780-85 — — 138
   (ii) The French Revolution and Napoleon — — — — — 143
   (iii) The Settlement of 1814-15 — — — — — — — 146
   (iv) The Years of the Union, 1815-30 — — — — — — 154

7. *The Belgian Revolution and the Treaty of November 1831*
   (i) The Belgian Revolution and the " Bases de Séparation " — — 156
   (ii) The Eighteen Articles and the Ten Days' Campaign — — — 167
   (iii) The Twenty-Four Articles and the Treaty of November 1831 — — 174

8. *The Theme of Lord Palmerston*
   (i) The background of the Theme — — — — — — — 183
   (ii) The Theme and its Reception — — — — — — — 190
   (iii) The Motive and Significance of the Theme — — — — 199

9. *The Convention of May 1833 and the Treaties of April 1839*
   (i) The Coercive Measures and the Convention of May 1833 — — 204
   (ii) The Negotiation of 1833 — — — — — — — — 210
   (iii) The Treaties of April 1839 — — — — — — — 219

APPENDIX

A list of the principal works on the Scheldt Question to 1839 — — — 231

Index — — — — — — — — — — — 232

MAPS

The Scheldt-Honte Delta in the late Thirteenth Century — — *- facing* 9
The Scheldt Estuary in the early Seventeenth Century — — *- facing* 96
The Scheldt Estuary in the early Nineteenth Century — — *- facing* 151

FOREWORD

As adviser of the Dutch Government in London on literary publications I drew the attention of my Minister, Mr. E. N. van Kleffens, to Mr. S. T. Bindoff's work on the river Scheldt. After a careful reading of the typescript Mr. van Kleffens pronounced in favour of its publication at the expense of the Dutch Government. In taking his decision he disregarded the fact that Mr. Bindoff advances several theses that are not consonant with the official view taken by the Dutch when the Scheldt question was a live issue. The Minister was animated solely by the desire to secure the publication of a scholarly and objective study of Netherlands history by a British expert.

As the appointed teacher of Dutch History in the University of London I welcome the appearance of a first-rate work on the subject in which I specialise, written by a former student of my friend and predecessor, Professor Pieter Geyl.

G. J. RENIER.

PREFACE

IT was once said that the Irish Question would never be settled until the English had learned some history and the Irish had forgotten some. In much the same way, the "Scheldt question" is likely to remain a live issue until both the Dutch and the Belgians have forgotten a good deal of its history. For the "Scheldt question" is one of those international controversies of which the current difficulties are continually aggravated by the rankling memories of the past. That being so, it may be argued that to write a book which rakes over the old embers is to render a disservice both to the present and to the future, and that the only proper treatment for these "old, unhappy, far-off things" is decent burial. This argument might have carried some weight a generation ago, when, as part of the aftermath of the First World War, feeling on the subject ran very high in Holland and Belgium. But to-day, in the more sympathetic atmosphere engendered by their common ordeal, Dutchmen and Belgians are little disposed to squander energy upon an issue which, however large it may once have loomed, now appears insignificant beside the problems which they have to face and solve in common. If neither country has forgotten, or is likely to forget, the "Scheldt question", each sees it in a new perspective which robs it of much of its ugliness; and a sober chronicle of its earlier phases, seen through the eyes of a neutral observer, is unlikely to upset this new objectivity.

Even if it were otherwise, the historian would not let himself be dissuaded from striving to satisfy the curiosity about the past which is his *primum mobile*. Of this curiosity, this urge to know, the present book may fairly claim to be a direct product. It originated in the study of British policy in the "Scheldt question" between 1814 and 1839, which I submitted for the Master's Degree of the University of London in 1934.[1] That study included a long introduction on the earlier history of the "question", based upon the existing literature; and it was my dissatisfaction with the conventional picture thus derived which afterwards led me to push my own inquiry further and further back, until it reached the point at which this book begins. My search was of necessity limited, owing to other claims upon my time and interest, almost exclusively to the field of printed material,[2] of which, however, thanks to generations of painstaking editorial labour, there proved to be an immense bulk, much of it evidently ignored by earlier students of the subject. I am only too conscious, however, of the gaps in my list of sources, as well as of the many points upon which further work needs to be done. The different parts of the book are therefore of very

[1] "Great Britain and the Scheldt, 1814-1839". See below, p. 156 *n* 1.
[2] The occasional use of MS. sources will be found noted among the references.

unequal standard in respect of the amount and character of the research involved, although not, I hope, in respect of the handling of the material itself. While Part Three is based almost entirely upon unpublished, and largely unused, archive material, and Part One upon a fairly exhaustive study of the medieval documents in print, Part Two (the detailed work for which had mostly to be done in war-conditions) rests far more upon secondary sources and, I doubt not, is correspondingly weaker. But I trust that, taken as a whole, the book will be adjudged to have justified itself as an attempt to trace the subject over a long period.

Its appearance, in these difficult times, is due chiefly to the generosity of the Dutch Government. In particular, I wish to express my gratitude to His Excellency Dr. E. N. van Kleffens, Netherlands Foreign Minister, who did me the honour of reading the book in typescript.

My debt to my old master, who introduced me to the study of Netherlands history and who taught me most of what I know about it, I have tried to express by dedicating this book to him. While writing it, I feared that the dedication might prove to be to his memory, but happily he has been spared the fate of so many of his brother-intellectuals. May this token of admiration and affection from an earlier pupil mingle with those of many new generations of his students. To his successor in the Chair of Dutch History in London, my colleague and friend, G. J. Renier, I owe much, not merely in the production of this book, but over the whole range of our common work and interests, and I wish to express my gratitude to him in this place. I must also thank the officials of the many archives and libraries in which I collected material, and especially of those in Holland and Belgium, where, as a young and unknown student, I was received with so much courtesy and given so much help. (To the Belgian archivist who warned me not to do as many men had done and "drown myself in the Scheldt", I express the hope that I have sufficiently heeded his injunction.) Part Three of this book owes much to my utilisation of the Palmerston Papers; the late Lord Mount-Temple kindly granted me access to these and took a personal interest in my discoveries among them.

Many friends have contributed, in many and various ways, to the making of this book, and I thank them all. I will name only the two ladies, Mrs. Marion Plant and Miss J. D. I. Tyson, who laboured with such care to produce the maps, and Miss Pauline Strange, who collaborated with them. The person to whom this book owes most of all has expressed a wish not to be mentioned in this preface; I respect her wish. And finally, I think it fitting to associate this volume with the kindly folk among whom it was written during my war-time sojourn in their Principality, and I therefore date this preface from
      Bethesda,
         Caernarvonshire.
                S. T. B.

INTRODUCTION
The River Scheldt and the " Scheldt Question "

THE river Scheldt[1] rises in France, in the department of the Aisne, between Le Catelet and Belcour, and the first sixty miles of its course lie in French territory. Becoming navigable at Cambrai, where it is linked with the Somme and Oise by the St. Quentin canal, the river flows north-east through Bouchain and Valenciennes and is joined by the Scarpe at Mortagne shortly before crossing the Belgian frontier. In Belgium the Scheldt first follows a northerly course by way of Tournai and Oudenaarde to Ghent, where it receives its most important tributary, the Leie (Lys), and thence turns sharply to the east to pass through Dendermonde to Antwerp. Dendermonde and Rupelmonde, as their names imply, mark the junctions with the Scheldt of the Dender, which comes from the south through Aalst, and of the Rupel, a river which, deriving from the Senne, Dijle, Demer, and the two Nethes, links the Scheldt with a network of waterways radiating across Brabant into Hainaut, Namur, Liége and Limburg. At Antwerp the Scheldt swings back to its northerly course and some twelve miles below the city it crosses the Dutch frontier. Two miles beyond the frontier, opposite Santvliet, the river turns sharply to the west and broadens into a wide estuary, bounded on the north by the Zeeland islands of Zuid-Beveland and Walcheren and on the south by the coast of Zeeland-Flanders. Beyond Flushing, the southernmost point of Walcheren, this estuary widens out into the North Sea. The mouth of the Scheldt consists of alternating banks and channels; the most important channel, the Wielingen, hugs the Belgian coast as far as Zeebrugge before losing its identity in the sea.

It is a far cry from the infant Scheldt at Cambrai to the noble river at Antwerp, still more to the majestic expanse of water between Santvliet and Flushing. The transformation of the river only begins below Ghent and is due almost entirely to the remarkable influence of the tides, which reach as high as the Flemish capital. In its hundred-mile course from Cambrai to Ghent the Scheldt increases but little in size, and the navigable waterway is limited by the many locks. But below Ghent, and still more below Dendermonde, where the last bridge crosses the river, it gains rapidly in volume. At Mariakerke, just below Dendermonde, the incoming tide, bringing more than 100

---
[1] French: *Escaut;* Dutch: *Schelde.*

times as much water as the river itself, swells its width from 200 to 275 yards, and at Hemiksem, near Antwerp, from 360 to over 600 yards, while between Santvliet and the sea the estuary stretches more than three miles across at high water. The accompanying increase in depth is such as to give a minimum of 23 and a maximum of 33 feet of water at the quays of Antwerp and as much as 100 feet in parts of the fairway below Santvliet.

The marked difference in the size of the Scheldt above and below Ghent means that, in respect of its navigation, the Scheldt is not one river but two. This is reflected in a change of name, the navigable waterway from Cambrai to Ghent being officially styled the Upper Scheldt (*Haut-Escaut, Boven-Schelde*) and the river from Ghent to the sea the Lower Scheldt (*Bas-Escaut, Beneden-Schelde*) or Maritime Scheldt (*Escaut-Maritime, Zee-Schelde*).[1] The commercial navigation of the Upper Scheldt is performed by ships limited in size by the locks to a maximum of 450 tons; it is thus essentially an interior navigation. By contrast, the navigation of the Lower Scheldt is pre-eminently maritime, for the river bears comfortably all but the largest ocean-going ships up to Antwerp. The port of Ghent no longer depends for its maritime navigation on the Scheldt by way of Antwerp, but on the canal joining it with the Scheldt estuary at Terneuzen; since this canal was deepened in 1900-11 to nearly 30 feet it has made Ghent accessible to ships of 10,000 tons. Thus above Antwerp the largest ships normally using the river are those of up to 1350 tons which pass along it and the Rupel between Antwerp and Brussels.

The navigability of the Upper Scheldt is largely the result of human effort. As early as the fifteenth century improvements were made to the river between Ghent and Tournai,[2] but before the construction of the locks at Tournai in 1670 boats could hardly pass above that point. The canalization of the river between Valenciennes and Cambrai, projected in the seventeenth century, was hindered by the recurrent wars and was only completed in 1782. The last great improvement, the linking of the Scheldt with the Somme and Oise by the St. Quentin canal, had also been planned as early as 1614, but was not begun until the middle of the eighteenth century and would not have been finished in 1809 but for the vigour imparted to the work by Napoleon. The eighteenth century saw great progress made on

---

[1] This division is as old as the mid-seventeenth century. On the map in Sanderus's *Flandria Illustrata* (Cologne, 2 vols., 1641-4) the river above Ghent is called " Schelde " and below Ghent " neer Schelde ".

[2] Pinchart, A., *Inventaire des Archives des Chambres des Comptes*, IV (Brussels, 1865), 349.

the Belgian part of the Upper Scheldt in straightening the waterway and in building barrages and locks; these works, and the industrial development which accompanied them, gave a great stimulus to the navigation of the Upper Scheldt across the Franco-Belgian frontier.

On the Lower Scheldt Nature herself has been the great improver. We have seen that the river below Ghent owes its size, not to any great increase in the volume of water coming down, but to the tides which thrust themselves up to that point. This phenomenon is largely the outcome of the changes which took place in the estuary below Sahtvliet towards the close of the Middle Ages. Before that time the Scheldt was protected from heavy tidal action by the configuration of the delta through which the river found its way to the sea; it was natural forces which transformed this delta and thus created the Lower Scheldt as a highway of maritime navigation. Moreover, this highway has improved, rather than deteriorated, with the passage of time, and only recently has the growing size of the ships seeking to use it called for the use of artificial means to supplement the natural clearing action of the tides.[1]

Why has the navigation of this river given rise to an international "question" which has persisted through more than three centuries down to our own day?

Reduced to its simplest terms, the "Scheldt question" is the product of three facts of history. The first is that since the end of the fifteenth century Antwerp has been, potentially if not actually, one of Europe's greatest seaports; the second, that since the year 1585 (with one short interval) a political frontier has separated Antwerp from the mouth of the Scheldt, which is its gateway to the sea; and the third, that the state whose territory is thus interposed between Antwerp and the sea was long dominated by economic interests in greater or less degree hostile to those of Antwerp.

Many factors, geographical, political, and economic, contributed to the rise of Antwerp to commercial pre-eminence in the sixteenth century. The town already enjoyed exceptional advantages of location before the transformation of the Lower Scheldt gave it direct communication with the sea. Placed at the lowest point on the river secure from serious flooding—an inestimable advantage during the two centuries of great inundations from 1377 to 1570—Antwerp possessed in the rivers radiating south and east from the Scheldt excellent lines

---

[1] A useful symposium, historical, hydrographical and economic, on Antwerp and the Scheldt will be found in the *Bulletin de la Société Royale de Géographie d'Anvers*, LVII (1937), 105*ff*.

of communication with the immediate hinterland of Brabant, Hainaut and Liége, and beyond them with the plain of Northern France and the valleys of the Maas and Rhine. Between these broad lands and the great delta of Scheldt-Maas-Rhine, the meeting-place of medieval Europe's principal trade-routes, Antwerp was one of the natural links. What the Scheldt, that is, the new maritime waterway created in the fifteenth century, enabled Antwerp to do was to add to its role of an inland port that of a seaport, and this at a time when the volume of overseas trade to be handled was rapidly increasing. It was the combination of the two roles, and the addition of a third, that of a money-market, which developed out of them, that gave Antwerp its unique position in sixteenth-century Europe.

Antwerp did not long enjoy the benefit of uninterrupted communication with the sea. The present-day map of the Scheldt shows the river traversed at two points by state-boundaries, the Franco-Belgian frontier which crosses it just below Mortagne, 63 miles from its source, and the Belgo-Dutch frontier at Santvliet, 43 miles from its mouth. This political trisection of the river has persisted throughout the greater part of the modern period. From the end of the sixteenth century, when the separation of the Northern and Southern Netherlands became an accomplished fact, until the year 1794, the three riparians of the Scheldt were France, the Southern Netherlands (first Spanish, then Austrian), and the Dutch Republic. The French conquest of the Southern Netherlands inaugurated a period of sixteen years (1794-1810) during which there were two riparians, France and the Batavian Republic (afterwards the Kingdom of Holland), and this was in turn followed by the brief and unique interlude when Napoleonic France, having annexed the Kingdom of Holland, possessed the river in its entirety. The return to the triple division was also accomplished in two stages; from 1814 to 1830 France, confined to her old limits, shared possession with the Kingdom of the Netherlands, and the advent of an independent Belgium in 1830-31 added a third riparian and established the present situation.

If we compare these political divisions with the natural division of the river at Ghent we shall see that neither the Upper nor the Lower Scheldt lies within the territory of a single state. Of the first, 40 miles belong to France and 58 to Belgium; of the second, 69 are Belgian and 43 Dutch. (Belgium and Holland also share the Ghent-Terneuzen canal, of which 11 miles lie in Belgian and $8\frac{1}{4}$ in Dutch territory.) Thus the international navigation of the Scheldt is to-day, as it has been for more than two centuries, of two distinct kinds, the interior navigation across the Franco-Belgian frontier and the maritime navigation across the Belgo-Dutch. Of the first of these we shall have little to say, since it has never given rise to any major dispute between the countries concerned, much less to an international question; its chief interest lies in the fact that at one decisive moment in Scheldt history its regulation was confused with that of the Lower Scheldt, with far-reaching consequences. It is the international navigation of the Lower Scheldt, and especially of the waterway between Antwerp and the sea, which has occasioned so much trouble. The political frontier which divides this part of the river dates from the separation of the Northern and Southern Netherlands towards the close of the sixteenth century; it was after Parma's reconquest of Antwerp in August 1585 that the military frontier between the warring provinces came to traverse the Scheldt by a line which, with but slight modification, marks the present Belgo-Dutch frontier. The circumstances in which this frontier originated were also largely responsible for the hostility, born of economic jealousy, which led the United Provinces to keep the Scheldt " closed " that is, to prohibit maritime navigation on the river, so long as they retained their control of it. Out of the situation thus created there developed the " Scheldt question ".

It might therefore appear that we need go no further back than the second half of the sixteenth century to trace the origins of that question. This has, indeed, been the usual starting-point for its study, and since it was only then that the three factors which go to make up the question came fully into play the modern " Scheldt question " may be said to date from that period. But this does not mean that there was no " Scheldt question " before that time. On the contrary, most of the elements in the situation after the outbreak of the Revolt were already present, although in a somewhat different and more rudimentary form, during the fifteenth and early sixteenth centuries, and the result was an anticipation of the " question " which is both of interest in itself and of importance as a background to the later history. This earlier " question " is the subject of Part One of this book, which covers the period between the thirteenth century and the outbreak of the Revolt. Parts Two and Three deal with the " Scheldt question " proper, from the fall of Antwerp in 1585 to the establishment of the existing regime on the river by the treaties of 1839.

PART ONE
ORIGINS, 1200—1572

CHAPTER ONE

To the Close of the Fourteenth Century

IF we wish to find an earlier starting-point than the conventional year 1572 from which to begin our inquiry into the history of the "Scheldt question" we shall have little or no hesitation in choosing the closing years of the fourteenth or the opening years of the fifteenth century. For it was then that the waterway which has since provoked so much controversy first came into existence, and manifestly there could be no "Scheldt question" before there was a "Scheldt". The present chapter, which covers the two centuries preceding this epochal change, is therefore to be regarded in the light of an introduction, designed to furnish a background to the two chapters which follow, just as they in turn form a background to the remainder of the book. One of the chief fascinations of history is its continuity, and there are some features of even the contemporary "Scheldt question" which are not to be wholly understood without a knowledge of events which took place in the thirteenth century.

(i) *The Scheldt-Honte Delta.*

The complex network of waterways which in the Middle Ages surrounded the islands of the Scheldt-Honte delta (and which, although much reduced in extent and simplified in pattern by centuries of reclamation, still does so) is of comparatively recent origin. At the opening of the Christian era the whole of this delta region was dry land, intersected only by minor channels. Bounded on the north by the broad estuary of the Rhine-Maas (*Ostium Helinium*) and on the west by the North Sea, this region was not separated by a waterway of any size from the Flemish plain to the south, of which indeed it formed the northernmost angle, but it was divided from the land to the east, the later Toxandria and modern North Brabant, by a considerable river. This river was the Scheldt, which, if Cæsar's evidence is to be relied upon, then held a northerly course down to its junction with the Maas at the head of that river's wide estuary.[1]

---

[1] *Bellum Gallicum*, VI, 33. See Hettema, H. Jr., *De Nederlandsche wateren en plaatsen in den Romeinschen tijd* (The Hague, 1938), 82-3. Whether or not Cæsar was right, it is clear that the Scheldt in the past conformed to the general rule by which all Netherland rivers have tended to shift their principal outlet from north to south, and that therefore the theory once put forward (and surprisingly adopted by Prims, *Geschiedenis van Antwerpen* (Antwerp, 1927-), I, pp. 3*ff*, and plate 4) of a former outlet of the Scheldt north of Ghent in the neighbourhood of the present Braakman is quite untenable.

It was in the third or fourth century A.D. that there took place the great invasion of the Netherlands coast by the sea which wrought widespread and lasting changes along almost its whole length. Nowhere save in the region of the Zuider Zee were its effects so marked as in the lands bordering the Lower Scheldt. Here the incoming sea engulfed wide tracts of land and converted what remained into a mosaic of islands set in a waste of waters. To the south the inundation penetrated into Flanders far beyond the line of the present Scheldt estuary, but on the east the Scheldt, that is, the original river running north into the Maas, marked the limit of its progress. The sea did not, it is true, keep all that it had taken, for the inundation was followed by a fairly rapid drying out of considerable stretches of shallow water. But some hundreds of years passed before the inhabitants of the delta, whose ancestors had fled before the oncoming waters to their *terpen*, or mound-refuges, first ensured the safety of the existing islands by ringing them about with dykes, and then, turning from defence to attack, began to recover ever-growing areas. These operations, begun on a small scale in the eighth and ninth centuries, culminated in the great outburst of activity in the twelfth and thirteenth, when very large areas were reclaimed.

Since it is at this point that the documented history of the Scheldt begins, we may pause to review briefly the state of the delta at that time.[1] Of the waterways composing the delta, the one which has undergone the least change in the last seven hundred years is the Scheldt between Antwerp and its junction with the Honte at Hontemuide. In the thirteenth century, however, the Scheldt between these limits must have been a considerably smaller river than it is to-day, since the penetration of the tides from its estuary was far less powerful and sustained than the thrust of the present tides through the Honte.[2] It was, moreover, a less "disciplined" river. Of the numerous streams which in earlier centuries had joined it on

---

[1] I wish to acknowledge my great indebtedness to the work of Dr. A. A. Beekman in the *Gescheidkundige Atlas van Nederland*, especially in the map of Zeeland in 1300 and the accompanying text (*Holland, Zeeland en Westfriesland in 1300. Blad VI*, and text III. Zeeland, The Hague, 1921), although, as will be seen, I find myself compelled to differ from Dr. Beekman on some points. The most useful study of the historical geography of the Scheldt-Honte is E. Cambier, "Etudes sur les transformations de l'Escaut et de ses affluents au nord de Gand pendant la période historique", in *Bulletin de la Société Royale Belge de Géographie*, 31me année (1907), 40-91, 126-70, 252-88, 349-83.

[2] Prims has suggested that before the transformation of the Honte at the end of the fourteenth century high water at Antwerp was about one metre lower than it normally is at the present time. "De grondgeschiedenis van het oude Antwerpsche gebied sinds de bewoning", in *Bulletin de la Société Belge d'Etudes Géographiques*, III (1933), 33.

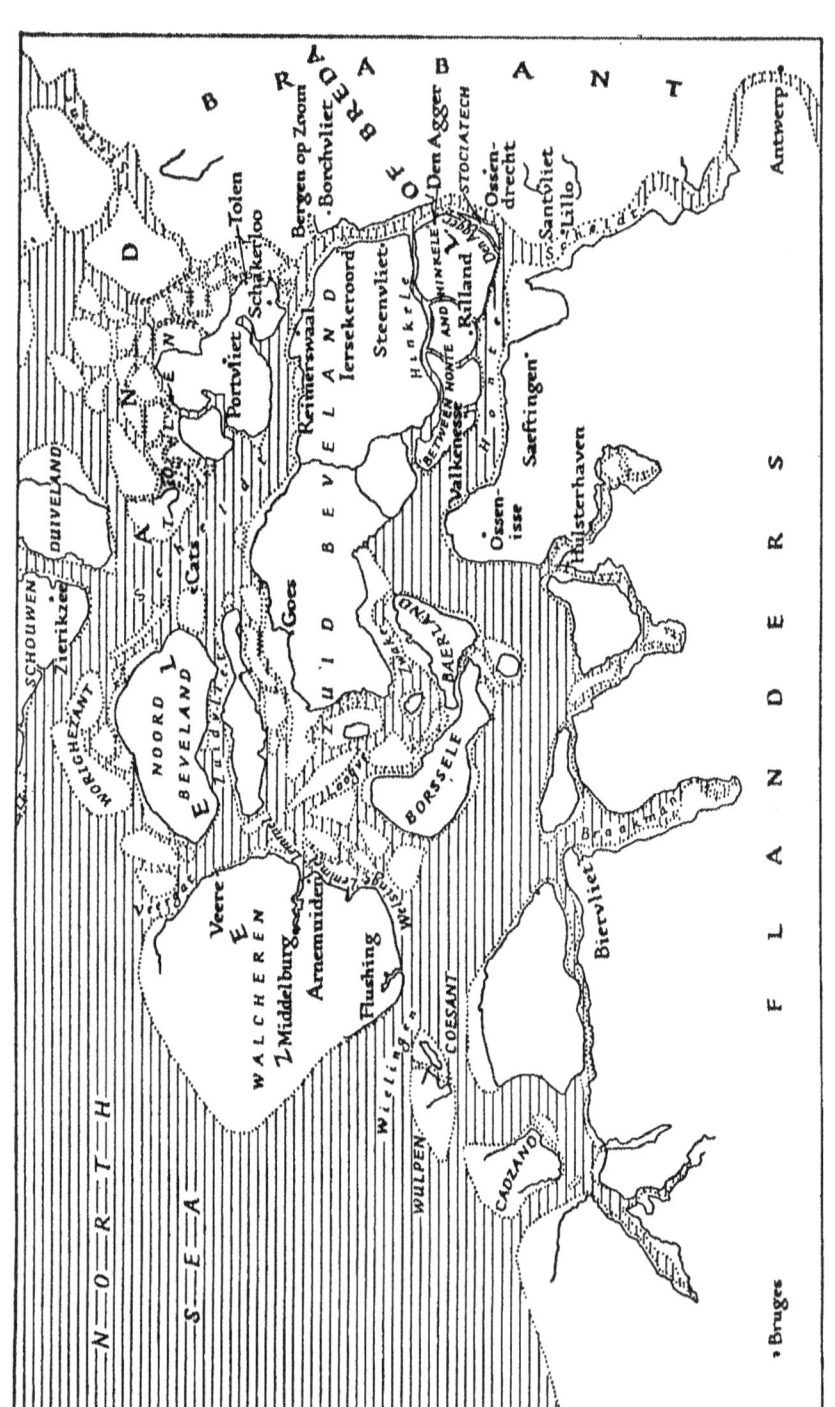

THE SCHELDT-HONTE DELTA IN THE LATE THIRTEENTH CENTURY.

——— Main dykes.   ······ Limits of undyked or inadequately dyked land which was periodically inundated.

both banks[1] some remained to absorb their share of each incoming tide; the dykes, too, stood for the most part further back, leaving a wider foreshore to be covered at high water. Thus dissipated, the tides coming up the Scheldt could scarcely have carved out and kept clear a channel as deep and broad as the present one below Antwerp. At the lower end of this stretch of the Scheldt lay the junction of the river with the Honte. It is possible that at an earlier period there had been no such junction.[2] But the use of the name Hontemuide from the middle of the twelfth century[3] suggests that there was a connecting channel here, at least at high water, from that date; a century or more later this channel was certainly navigable.

Beyond Hontemuide the Scheldt flowed north between the edge of the Brabant *diluvium* and the now almost totally submerged east coast of Zuid-Beveland. In size and character this stretch of the river must have closely resembled that above Hontemuide. The low lands on the left bank were dyked during the thirteenth century, but on the Brabant side the raised edge of the *diluvium,* along which lay the early villages,[4] must long have formed the real river "bank". Here, too, the Scheldt was joined by numerous minor channels. Of those on the left bank, two claim our attention. The first is the Hinkele, a channel running westwards from the Scheldt at Hinkelenoord across Zuid-Beveland and joining the Honte near the village of Die Warde. The triangular "island" bounded by the Scheldt, Honte, and Hinkele was known as the "land between Honte and Hinkele" (*tusschen Honte en Hinkele*). This "island" was itself subdivided by channels which crossed it from north to south. The easternmost of these channels, leaving the Scheldt-Honte junction at Hontemuide and running roughly parallel with the Scheldt, rejoined the river some distance south of Hinkelenoord; known as Den Agger, a name also borne by a neighbouring village, this channel thus formed for a short distance an

---

[1] Hasse, G., "Hydrographie primitive au nord d'Anvers", in *Bulletin de la Société Royale de Géographie d'Anvers,* LIV (1934), 334-43.
[2] But the conclusion to this effect drawn by Smallegange (*Nieuwe Cronyk van Zeeland,* I, 156-7) and repeated by Engelenburg ("Bijdragen tot de hydrographie en morphologie der Zuidelijke Zeegaten en Riviermonden in Nederland", in *Tijdschrift der Kon. Nederlandsch Aardrijkskundig Genootschap,* 2de serie, VII (1890), 314) is based upon an erroneous identification of "Scaftekynspolre", mentioned with lands in Zuid-Beveland in a charter of 1345 (Van Mieris, *Charterboek,* II, 691) with Saeftingen on the Flemish side of the Honte. "Scaftekynspolre", more correctly, "Schachtekijnspolder", was in Zuid-Beveland, not far from Ierseke (*Nomina Geographica Neerlandica,* VII (1930), 152).
[3] Kluit, A., *Historia Critica Comitatus Hollandiae et Zeelandiae* (Middelburg, 1777-80), II, i (*Cod. Dipl.*), 170-2. Goetschalckx in his edition of the *Oorkondenboek der Witheerenabdij van S.-Michiels te Antwerpen,* I (Eekeren-Donk, 1909), 20, dates this document 5 April, 1148/9.
[4] Weijers, M., "De Hooge Rand van Bergen op Zoom", in *Tijdschr. Kon. Nederl. Aardrijksk. Genootsch.,* 2de serie, LIII (1936), 833-44.

alternative route to the Scheldt. The long and narrow island between the Scheldt and Den Agger, the most easterly portion of the land " between Honte and Hinkele ", bore the name of Stociatech.[1] Of the creeks on the Brabant side, the only one which needs to be mentioned is that which gave access from the Scheldt to the town of Bergen-op-Zoom, situated, like the villages to the south of it, on the raised edge of the *diluvium*.

From its junction with this creek, opposite Bergen-op-Zoom, the Scheldt turned westwards and, beyond Reimerswaal, broadened into a sea-arm bounded on the north by the islands of Tolen, Duiveland and Schouwen and on the south by the two Bevelands and Wolfardsdijk. Across its seaward end stretched the island of Worighezant (Orizand), separated from Schouwen to the north and Wolfardsdijk to the south by the two channels which together formed the mouth of the Scheldt. In the thirteenth century the network of islands and waterways between Reimerswaal and the sea formed a bulwark against the penetration of a heavy tide into the Scheldt, so that the river was little, if at all, broader at Reimerswaal than at Antwerp. But with the progressive dyking of these islands and blocking of the lateral channels the tidal thrust into the narrow Scheldt grew stronger and the river began to widen and deepen. So there began, soon after 1300, the new process of change which was eventually to transform the map of the Scheldt below Hontemuide.

When we turn to consider the waterway connecting the Scheldt at Hontemuide with the sea between Walcheren and Cadzand we are faced with a problem of nomenclature. All previous writers appear to have taken it for granted that during the Middle Ages this waterway was known throughout the whole, or at least the greater part, of its length as the Honte.[2] This is, I believe, a quite unwarrantable assumption. The question of the scope of the name " Honte " was

---

[1] This statement is based upon the inference that the triangular area shown at the junction of Honte and Scheldt on the pictorial map of the late fifteenth century (see below, p. 60 and *n* 3) and labelled there " Stockachte de plate " represents the remains of the island described in the text and shown in Beekman's map of Zeeland in 1300 after the changes of the fourteenth and fifteenth centuries. We read in 1429 of " Stocachte, daer de Honte und de Scheld scheiden " (*Die Recesse und Andere Akten der Hansetage von 1256-1430*, VIII, 426). The description in the " Sommen Receuil van de gerechtigheid der stad Antwerpen . . . op de rivier en den stroom der Schelde ", drawn up in 1662, of " Stockachter " as " wezende bij Bergen-op-Zoom " (Prims, Fl., *Inventaris op het archieffonds van handel en scheepvaart . . . Aanhangsel: inventaris op den bundel Jurisdictie op de Schelde*, 29-30) may reflect the difficulty of locating Scotiatech after it had disappeared, a difficulty which has persisted to the present day.

[2] Cf., for example, Beekman's statement that it " heette over zijn geheele lengte de Honte " (" De Heidensee ", in *Tijdschr. Kon. Nederl. Aardrijksk. Genootsch.*, 2de serie, XLI (1924), 360).

first raised in 1468 in the course of an important lawsuit over the Duke of Burgundy's right to levy a toll upon the waterway so named.[1] The defendants in the case, the Duke's Procureur-General and the lessees of the toll, who were interested in restricting the meaning of the name, argued that " le flux et strom de la Honte failloit, et perdoit son nom au lieu appellé Hulsterhavenen "[2] and that the remainder of the waterway to the sea was not comprised in the name. To this the plaintiffs, the deputies of Brabant and Flanders, replied (again theory harmonized with interest)

que la dite riviere de la Honte et le fleux d'icelle prenoit commencement depuis la dite riviere de l'Eschault devant Chavetingues,[3] en venant tout au long de la coste de Flandres par devant la Neuze,[4] Hulsterhavene et aussi joingnant Biervliet et l'isle de Cadsant, jusques en la dite mer, où elle prenoit fin . . . et que avec ce, il n'estoit aucunement soustenable, que la dite riviere de la Honte preinst fin au dit lieu de Hulsterhavene . . . veu qu'il convient, que icelle riviere, qui tousjours d'un coste costie la dite conté de Flandres, prendre vuydenge et yssue en la mer, ou aultrement fauldroit dire que ce feust ung sacq. . . .[5]

The fact that the deputies won the case implies that the Duke's Council, before whom it was heard, accepted their interpretation of the name Honte. In the circumstances, this is not surprising. For by 1468 the Honte certainly did " prendre vuydenge et yssue en la mer ", in other words, it formed a continuous and clearly-defined waterway between Hontemuide and the sea. The deputies' contention that this waterway must bear the same name throughout its length was thus an eminently reasonable one. Confirmed half-a-century later by the verdict of the Great Council of Mechlin,[6] this use of the name Honte became universal and was never again questioned.[7]

Nevertheless, I believe that the defendants who argued for a restrictive use of the name had history on their side. It would, indeed, be strange if their argument, so little in accordance with conditions in their own day, had not had some justification from the past. Their contention that the name Honte rightly belonged only to the waterway stretching from opposite Hulsterhaven eastwards to Hontemuide is in fact borne out both by thirteenth-century definitions of the Honte as the channel bordering the land " between Honte and

---

[1] See below, p. 53.
[2] See map facing p. 9.
[3] Saeftingen.
[4] Terneuzen.
[5] First printed in Marshall, E., and Bogaerts, F., " Navigation de l'Escaut sous la maison de Bourgogne ", in *Bibliothèque des Antiquités Belgiques* (Antwerp, 1833-5), I, 143-4; most recently in Unger, *Tol van Iersekeroord* (below, p. 29 n 3), 24.
[6] See below, pp. 58ff.
[7] But see below, p. 105 n 1.

Hinkele"[1] and by the complete absence of evidence suggesting that the name was then used with any wider connotation. But the most striking confirmation of the correctness of their view is furnished by the well-known statement in the Mechlin verdict of 1504 that before its transformation in the early fifteenth century the Honte had been " petite, estroitte et peu profonde ". Ever since Blanchard conclusively demonstrated that in the Middle Ages the central portion of the waterway separating Flanders from Zeeland (which he, like others, called the Honte) must have been at least as wide as the corresponding part of the present Western Scheldt,[2] this description of the " little narrow " Honte has been a stumbling-block to historians. Beekman tried to explain a Honte which was at once broad and narrow by depicting it as a wide but shallow expanse of water encumbered by sandbanks and shoals between which passed the " narrow " channel or channels of the description.[3] But there is no call for such ingenuity once it is accepted that when the men of 1504, doubtless drawing upon oldest living memory, described the Honte as having once been small and narrow, they were, albeit unconsciously, using the name in its older and restricted sense; for all that we know of the Honte in this sense before about 1400 warrants the description, whereas the waters to the west of it as certainly did not.

There are grounds, then, for thinking of the medieval waterway between Hontemuide and the sea as consisting, not of a continuous recognizable channel bearing a single name throughout, but of a wide and irregularly-shaped central expanse of water narrowing at each end to well-defined channels. The easterly of these channels, separating the land " between Honte and Hinkele " from the Flemish lands of Ossenisse and Saeftingen, was the Honte; the corresponding westerly channel, or probably channels, passing between the islands of Walcheren, Wulpen, and Cadzand to join the open sea beyond, early acquired the name of the Wielingen.[4] Between the two lay a broad expanse of water stretching from the heavily-indented Flemish coast to the south

[1] In 1283 the *geleiders* of Valkenesse speak of the waters " contra Valkenesse que Honte vulgariter appellantur " and in 1284 the *geleiders* of Rilland similarly define the waters opposite Rilland as the Honte. Valkenesse and Rilland both lay " between Honte and Hinkele ". Van den Bergh, *Oorkendenboek*, II, 216, 233-4.
[2] Blanchard, R., *La Flandre* (Paris, 1906), 170ff.
[3] " De Heidensee ", in *Tijdschr. Kon. Nederl. Aardrijksk. Genootsch*, 2de serie, XLI (1924), 362.
[4] The origin and connotation of the name Wielingen have been the subject of a controversy between Dutch and Belgian historians arising out of the political dispute of 1920, but as this controversy has little bearing on the subject of this book I do not propose to enter into it. For a Dutch view, see Brugmans, H., *The Wielingen* (The Hague, 1920), and for a Belgian view De Visscher, C., and Ganshof, F. L., " Le différend des Wielingen ", in *Revue de droit int. et de lég. comparée*, I (1920), 293-328.

across to the Zeeland islands of Walcheren and Zuid-Beveland. If Baerland and Borssele, which to-day, joined to Zuid-Beveland, confine the Western Scheldt to a relatively narrow channel swinging south-west to skirt them, then appeared rather as islands set in this expanse of water than as part of its northern coast, the area covered at high-water must have been nearly as broad as it was long. Would the thirteenth-century Fleming or Zeelander have recognized, beneath the apparent contrast between this wide water and the narrow Honte, an essential unity entitling them to a common name? Even the present Western Scheldt is far less obviously a single broad estuary to those passing along it than when studied on a chart; and seven hundred years ago there were no maps or charts to correct the visual impression made upon the beholder.

If this central expanse did not originally share the name Honte, had it a name of its own? There is one name relating to the Zeeland waters which has puzzled Dutch historians since the eighteenth century: it is "Heidensee". This name occurs for the first time in the treaty of 1168 between Holland and Flanders, where Zeeland west of the Scheldt (*Zeeland Bewester-Schelde*) is defined as "inter Scheld et Hiddenzee"; used in this way, either in conjunction with the Scheldt, or in conjunction with "Bornesse" to mark the limits of Zeeland as a whole, the name appears in many thirteenth-century documents and as late as 1495 the Keur or Charter of Zeeland employs it in this sense. Of the many suggestions put forward to explain "Heidensee" the most widely supported is that it was the name of the waterway between Hontemuide and the sea, or at least of part of this waterway; and on the face of it this seems the likeliest explanation. The Heidensee clearly marked the southern limit of Zeeland, and since Zeeland proper has always been bounded on the south by the waterway in question, the identification of the two follows naturally. Dr. Beekman, however, dissented strongly from this view and basing himself upon two sixteenth-century maps in which the name appears declared that Heidensee was the name of the short channel which until the fourteenth century separated the islands of Wulpen and Coesant.[1]

Any detailed discussion of this problem would be out of place here, but it may be pointed out that the central expanse of water between Zeeland and Flanders has a strong claim to be regarded as the

[1] "De Heidensee", in *Tijdschr. Kon. Ned. Aardrijksk. Genootsch*, 2de serie, XLI (1924), 359-68. To the review of the various interpretations of the name given by Beekman may be added that of the seventeenth-century historian Butkens; on the map of Brabant facing p. 17 of Butkens' *Trophées de Brabant*, I (The Hague, 1724), the waterway between Hontemuide and the sea is labelled "La Honte ou Hedinse".

original Heidensee. Not only was it large enough to be called a "sea",[1] but both its size and position made it an unmistakable boundary between Zeeland and Flanders. Moreover, the same circumstances which later resulted in the extension of the name Honte to this sheet of water would also explain the gradual disappearance of the name Heidensee. Dr. Beekman's main objection to such an interpretation is that the use of this broad water as a boundary would have left unsettled the question of jurisdiction over the boundary itself. This jurisdiction he is convinced belonged to Zeeland, and one of his arguments in favour of the location of the Heidensee on the southern edge of the waters dividing Flanders from Zeeland is that it confirms this view. Since, for reasons to be given later,[2] I believe this view to be mistaken, I cannot agree with this part of his reasoning, while his own alternative seems to me to suffer from serious objections, notably the insignificance of the channel in question, which cannot be urged against the suggestion made above.

Although I believe that there is a strong case for applying the name Heidensee to the area of water lying west of the Honte, I do not propose to use the name in discussing it; instead, while reserving the names Honte and Wielingen to the channels leading east and west from it, I shall continue to refer to the "central expanse" or "central area", and use the composite name "Honte-Wielingen" to denote the entire stretch of water from Hontemuide to the sea.

Of the numerous waterways which communicated with the Scheldt and Honte-Wielingen to form the delta three alone need mention. The first is the waterway which, passing east of the islands of Noord-Beveland and Walcheren, linked the Scheldt near Cats with the Wielingen off Flushing; it was made up of a series of channels, of which the most important bore the names of Zuidvliet, Lemmel and Welsinge. This waterway was crossed, midway along its length, by another, which ran in a north-west to south-east direction from the sea between Noord-Beveland and Walcheren to pass between Zuid-Beveland and Borssele and meet the Honte where it merged into the central expanse of the Honte-Wielingen; the channels composing this second waterway were known as the Veergat, Looyve and Zwake. Thirdly, there was the complicated system of channels linking the Scheldt near Bergen-op-Zoom with the Striene and through the Striene with the Maas and Rhine. These were all that remained of the old

---

[1] It was so called by Melis Stoke in 1302. See his *Rijmkroniek* (ed. Brill, W. G., *Hist. Genootsch. Werken*, N.S., 40, 42, Utrecht, 1885), ii, 185.

[2] See below, pp. 20-21.

course of the Scheldt.¹ In the thirteenth century the most important of them were the Striene itself, the Vosvliet, which ran northwards from the Striene past Portvliet, and the Heentrecht or Eendracht, joining Striene and Scheldt and continuing north into the maze of islands which made up the Lordship of Putten.

(ii) *Navigation in the Delta.*

By the opening of the thirteenth century there was probably no part of the Scheldt-Honte delta which did not share in the water-borne traffic of the region. The rivers and creeks were the natural highways of the delta, along which was carried by far the greater part of the local trade and of the growing volume of traffic from overseas. But among these numerous waterways it is possible to distinguish three or four which in the thirteenth and fourteenth centuries constituted the " main routes " through the delta. Of these the most important— but from the present standpoint the least interesting—was the "Hanse route " linking Bruges, the commercial metropolis, with Holland and through Holland with West and North Germany and the Baltic. This route passed across the delta in a direction roughly parallel with the sea-coast, but keeping " binnen dunen ", that is, inside the outer line of islands (Walcheren, Noord-Beveland and Schouwen) along the various channels connecting the Wielingen first with the Scheldt and further north with the Maas.² Several old-established towns lay along this route : Zierikzee, Cats and Goes all stood directly on it, and Middelburg had connection with it through Arnemuiden; and it was commanded, at the northern edge of the delta, by the Count of Holland-Zeeland's toll-house of Geervliet.³

In its passage across the fringe of the delta this route was crossed by two others running at right-angles to it, that is, from north-west to south-east. The first followed the river Scheldt from its estuary between Noord-Beveland and Schouwen up past Reimerswaal and Bergen-op-Zoom to Antwerp and so into the heart of Flanders; the other entered from the sea through the Veergat, continued along the Looyve and Zwake between Zuid-Beveland and Borssele and thence through the Honte to Hontemuide, where it joined the Scheldt route. Of the two, the Scheldt route must always have been the more important, chiefly because of its more commodious waterway

---

¹ See above, p. 6.
² Here I follow J. G. Nanninga, " De Handelsweg door Holland in de dertiende eeuw ", in *Bijdr. voor Vaderl. Gesch.*, VI, ii, 94-108, as against Dr. H. J. Smit's " sea-route " theory.
³ See below, p. 30.

and of its greater convenience as a link between the Hanse route and the south-eastern corner of the delta; between Bergen-op-Zoom and the sea a number of channels served to maintain this connection. The early rise of towns along this route—below Antwerp there stood, besides many villages, Bergen-op-Zoom, Reimerswaal, Portvliet and Tolen—was at once a cause and an effect of the growth of traffic on it. By contrast, after Veere itself, which was really a sea-port serving the Hanse route, the Zwake-Honte route was devoid of towns. Moreover, when in the fourteenth century the traffic from England and the West began to outstrip the Hanse traffic, it too adopted the Scheldt as an easier and safer, though somewhat longer, route than the already shrinking Zwake.

If neither of these routes could compare in importance with the route to Bruges, they carried sufficient traffic, even in the thirteenth century, to make the local tolls (*geleiden*) upon them a matter of interest to the neighbouring magnates and their feudatories, while early in the fourteenth the Count of Holland-Zeeland would find it expedient to extend his toll of Geervliet to the Scheldt. At first this traffic must have been of a predominantly local character; besides the fish and the salt which the waterways themselves yielded, the produce of the countryside and of local industry would have provided the principal regular cargoes, as indeed they continued to do after 1400.[1] But to these local goods there was added an increasing volume of foreign commodities which left the main stream of international trade at the seaward edge of the delta and travelled up to the Brabant fairs. Unlike the local trade, which was more or less continuous throughout the year, this international trade was periodic, and its commodities were the great staples of medieval trade, English wool, later giving place to cloth, Rhenish wine, timber, grain and metals from North Germany and the Baltic, and wines and luxury foodstuffs from France, Spain and the Mediterranean.

If the Scheldt and Honte thus bore a growing volume of these goods neither could yet accommodate the sea-going ships which brought them from the lands of their origin.[2] It was the small craft engaged in the local trade which, receiving their cargoes from the sea-going ships in one of the roads or harbours lying inside the outer line of islands, carried them through the delta to their destinations. This feature of the navigation of the delta was of the utmost importance,

---

[1] See below, pp. 46-7.
[2] The only important exception to this was the Venetian galleys, which from the early fourteenth century came up the Scheldt as far as Antwerp.

for it meant that, although the trade from overseas was concentrated along certain routes and converged upon certain focal points, many towns and villages shared in the business of carrying it. Thus the rise of the Brabant fairs, and above all those of Antwerp, stimulated trade and shipping throughout the delta to a far greater extent than when international trade had concentrated more exclusively on Bruges.

(iii) *Political Jurisdiction over the Delta.*

At the opening of the fourteenth century the lands of the Scheldt-Honte delta were divided politically in two ways: by the frontier of the Empire, and by the boundaries of the feudal states.

The Scheldt was itself the frontier of the Empire from near its source down to Ghent. But below Ghent the Imperial boundary forsook the river, continuing north along the line of the Braakman into the Honte-Wielingen, which it then followed westwards to the sea; thus the whole of the Scheldt-Honte delta lay within the Empire.[1] The Imperial authority over these waterways was represented down to the early fourteenth century by the *advocatio fluminis* claimed by the Dukes of Brabant. What little evidence remains to substantiate this claim has been collected by Prims, who concludes that " in the thirteenth century and before, the Dukes of Brabant, as Margraves of the Empire, exercised the Imperial *advocatio,* with the duty of ensuring law and order on the Scheldt . . . from Vortvuremuiden to the sea ".[2] But after 1300 this *advocatio* sank to an empty title, and it had probably never counted for much in practice; it certainly did not affect the levy of tolls on the river.

The Duke of Brabrant was one of the three feudal rulers who from the opening of the fourteenth century held the lands bordering the Lower Scheldt and Honte-Wielingen; the other two were the Count of Flanders and the Count of Holland-Zeeland. From the map on p. 8, which shows the distribution of their territories, it is clear that the Scheldt was the boundary first between Brabant and Flanders, and then, below Hontemuide, between Brabant and Zeeland, and the Honte-Wielingen the boundary between Flanders and Zeeland. But this distribution was a simplification of the earlier position, in which a fourth ruler, the Lord of Breda, had held a block of territory lying on

---

[1] Whether or not the Imperial suzerainty over the land of Waes was, as Lot has suggested (in *Bibl. de l'Ecole des Chartes,* LXXXIV (1910), 5-32), a mid-thirteenth-century usurpation, the actual position thereafter was that described in the text.

[2] *Geschiedenis van Antwerpen*, II, i, 41. Vortvuremuiden (sometimes Borburemuiden or Borbure) marked the confluence of the Vliet with the Scheldt, about six miles above Antwerp, near the present Hemiksem.

both sides of the Scheldt below Hontemuide. The Lordship of Breda had disappeared as a semi-independent principality before 1300, but not without leaving its mark upon the jurisdiction over the waterways of this locality.

From the opening of the thirteenth century down to 1357 the Scheldt between Rupelmonde and Hontemuide separated the territories of the Duke of Brabant and the Count of Flanders. Since both claimed that the river itself lay within his jurisdiction there were continual disputes between them, only terminated in 1336 when the Count secured recognition of his right " partout sur le stroom de l'Escaut . . . si avant que nef peut flotter ", but with reservations which left the Duke certain rights of economic value, including the levy of the toll of Antwerp. But in 1357 Louis de Male, Count of Flanders, and his wife Margaret, second daughter of John III of Brabant, whose death had provoked a succession struggle, received Antwerp and the right bank of the Scheldt down to Santvliet (opposite Hontemuide) as their share of the Brabant heritage, and the Scheldt thus became a Flemish river. It remained so until 1406, when Anthony of Burgundy rejoined Antwerp and the adjacent territory to Brabant and thus restored the earlier position.[1]

Of greater interest are the changes in jurisdiction over the next stretch of the Scheldt, from Hontemuide to Bergen-op-Zoom, which followed upon the elimination of the Lordship of Breda. In the late twelfth century the Lord of Breda had held the whole of the right, or east, bank of the river from Santvliet to below Bergen-op-Zoom and had in addition exercised certain rights, the precise nature or extent of which is not clear, in the land " between Honte and Hinkele " on the opposite bank. It was clearly in virtue of his strategic position at the junction of Scheldt and Honte that the Lord of Breda acquired his toll-rights on these waterways.[2] But, placed between the two rising powers, Brabant and Holland-Zeeland, he could not maintain his position. In 1190, or soon after, Godfrey van Schooten, Lord of Breda, accepted the suzerainty of Brabant in respect of his territories east of the Scheldt, and although the Lordship for some time retained its identity (in 1287 it was divided into two, the barony of Breda and the lordship of Bergen-op-Zoom), its former rights on the Scheldt

---

[1] Duvivier, Ch., " L'Escaut est-il flamand ou brabançon?", in *Académie Royale de Belgique, Bulletin de la Classe de Lettres*, 1899, 721-68; for conflicting modern interpretations see H. van Werveke in *Bijdragen tot de geschiedenis*, XXI (1930), 224-36, and Fl. Prims in *Versl. en Mededeel. der Kon. Vlaamsche Akademie*, 1931, 889-964.

[2] See below, pp. 23-4.

passed to the Duke of Brabant.[1] It was not the Duke, however, but the Count of Holland-Zeeland who supplanted the Lord of Breda in the territory west of the Scheldt. Count Dirk VII's renunciation, in his treaty of 1200 with Henry I of Brabant,[2] of any claim to the Lordship of Breda (a renunciation which preluded or accompanied the assertion of Brabant suzerainty over it) did not prevent his successors from pursuing a policy of steady encroachment upon the Breda position in the land " between Honte and Hinkele ".[3] Raas van Liedekerke, who under the settlement of 1287 succeeded to the smaller barony of Breda, still retained some rights in this territory, but in 1312 he sold " al dat goede ende heirscepe tusschen Honte ende Hinkele " to William III of Holland-Zeeland.[4] Thereafter, Brabant and Zeeland faced one another across this stretch of the Scheldt.

Zeeland was not to prove, however, nearly so aggressive a co-riparian of Brabant as did Flanders higher up the river. The fact that this stretch of the river does not appear to have provoked any conflict of jurisdiction may, of course, only mean that the evidence has disappeared. But the circumstances in which the Dukes of Brabant secured their ascendancy over the Lordship of Breda (and possibly their former exercise of the Imperial *advocatio*) may explain why they were successful in asserting their claim. The earliest explicit statement of this claim dates from about 1400, and is as follows:

Dit is des Hertoghen van Brabant herelicheit ende der stadrecht van Antwerpen. Dat is te weten dat onse Here die Hertoghe van Brabant heeft op die Schelt ende op die Eendrecht, dat beghint te Vosvlietzhille ende strect totter Borburemuyden . . . ende al dat hierbinnen leeght dat houdt men te leen vanden Marcgrave van Antwerpen, dat is die Herthoghe van Brabant, ende wat binnen dese vours. palen ghevalt, vlotens sceps, van over-daden . . . ende mesdaden dat is die Herthoghe of syn gheweldicht Schouteit sculdich te berechten tAntwerpen in die Vierscare.[5]

---

[1] Kleyn, A. G., *Geschiedenis van het land en de heeren van Breda* (Breda, 1861), *passim*. I was unable to use the doctoral dissertation by W. Moll, *De rechten van de heer van Bergen-op-Zoom* (Groningen, 1915), which might have enabled me to clear up some of these obscurities, but I have used Dr. Moll's publication of documents, " Middeleeuwsche rechtsbronnen van het platteland der Heerlijkheid Bergen op Zoom " in *Verslagen en Mededeelingen der Vereeniging tot uitgaaf der bronnen van het Oud-Vaderlandsche Recht*, 7de deel (1924), 11-145.

[2] Verkooren, A., *Inventaire des Chartes et Cartulaires des Duchés de Brabant et de Limbourg et des Pays d'Outre Meuse* (Brussels, 1910-23), I, 9-10; Van den Bergh, L.Ph. C., *Oorkondenboek van Holland en Zeeland* (Amsterdam, 1866-73), I, 113.

[3] The process is well illustrated in the *Cronica et Cartularium Monasterii de Dunis* (Société d'Emulation pour l'etude de l'histoire et des Antiquités de la Flandre, 3 vols., Bruges, 1864-7).

[4] Van Mieris, F., *Groot Charterboek der Graven van Holland, van Zeeland en Heeren van Vriesland* (Leiden, 1753-6), II, 128.

[5] First published in Marshall, E., and Bogaerts, F., *Bibliothèque des Antiquités Belgiques*, I, 32; the above extract follows the version in *Antwerpsch Archievenblad*, XXV, 348-9.

The remainder of the Scheldt, from just below Bergen-op-Zoom to the sea, has always lain wholly in Zeeland and therefore been under the undisputed jurisdiction of the Count of Holland-Zeeland. This part of the river was, indeed, also a boundary, for it divided Zeeland into its two administrative divisions of "beooster Schelde" and "bewester Schelde"; between these, however, there was no conflict of jurisdiction.

We come finally to consider the question of jurisdiction over the Honte-Wielingen, of which the southern or left bank was Flemish and the northern Zeeland territory (that is to say, after the elimination of the Lord of Breda from the land "between Honte and Hinkele"). We have it on the weighty authority of Dr. Beekman that the Honte-Wielingen has always formed part of the territory of Zeeland, in other words, that the Flemish-Zeeland frontier has always followed the southern shore of this waterway. This was indeed the verdict of the Great Council of Mechlin in 1504, which has since become the staple item of evidence in support of this view.[1] But Beekman's thesis appears to me to rest upon two unwarranted assumptions. The first of these, that the waterway between Flanders and Zeeland has since the Middle Ages always borne the character of a single channel known throughout its length as the Honte, has been challenged above; and if the view there put forward is accepted, it makes equally inadmissible the second assumption, which is that evidence of jurisdiction over any part of these waters can legitimately be adduced as evidence of jurisdiction over the whole. On the contrary, in treating of the jurisdiction over these waters in their older form we must consider the component parts separately and regard any conclusion as valid only for the part to which it relates.

The first part to be considered is the Honte. There is a good deal of evidence about toll- and other rights on the Honte in the thirteenth and fourteenth centuries, and nearly all of it suggests that the jurisdiction over this channel pertained exclusively to the rulers of its northern bank, that is, originally to the Lord of Breda and afterwards to his successor the Count of Holland-Zeeland.[2] Indeed, in 1413 the Duke of Brabant recognized the Count's jurisdiction here, a weighty testimony in view of the Duke's former claim to the Imperial *advocatio*.[3] But for all that, the Zeeland claim did not pass unchal-

---

[1] See below, pp. 60-61 and *n* 1.
[2] The main items of evidence bearing out this conclusion are mentioned below, pp. 24-5.
[3] Van Mieris, *Charterboek*, IV, 235-6. That the Honte lies in Zeeland is also clearly recognized in the Antwerp petition of 9-10 Aug. 1395 to the Duke of Brabant preserved in the "Clementynboek" (*Antwerpsch Archievenblad*, XXV, 278-80).

lenged. From the fourteenth century, and probably earlier, the Count of Flanders was claiming jurisdiction over the so-called "Flemish river" (*Vlaamsche Stroom*). This was defined in 1409 as ' si avant que l'eaue de la mer ceurre et desceurre vers Flandres ",[1] that is to say, it covered all tidal water touching Flemish territory and thus included the Honte-Wielingen. That this was, in its application to the Honte, no mere trumped-up claim is shown by the fact that certain of the local tolls (*geleiden*) on the Honte were held as fiefs of Flanders[2] and that in 1370 the Council of Flanders could hear a suit arising out of them.[3] Flanders continued to press this claim throughout the fifteenth century, and it was not finally disposed of until the Mechlin verdict of 1504.

If the Honte thus became as early as the fourteenth century the subject of conflicting claims by its riparians, there is no good evidence that either Zeeland or Flanders at the same time made any claim to jurisdiction over the remainder of the waters which separated their territories. The earliest Zeeland claim to jurisdiction over the central area appears to date from the establishment on it about 1420 of a " watch " of the toll of Iersekeroord, and over the Wielingen from the first years of the fifteenth century; while on the Flemish side the definition of the "Vlaamsche Stroom " as including all these waters is of about the same date, and there is no earlier evidence—as there is in the case of the Honte—of any attempt to make it a reality. The significance of this simultaneous development of interest is clear enough when we remember that it coincides with the transformation of the Honte-Wielingen into an important shipping-route, that is to say, into a waterway whose jurisdiction could be a lucrative matter. Conversely, its neglect before that time is to be explained by its relative unimportance and also perhaps, in the case of the central area, by the practical difficulty of exercising jurisdiction.

(iv) *The Tolls*.

In the thirteenth and fourteenth centuries navigation in the Scheldt-Honte delta was subject to two groups of tolls, those levied on the passage of ships and their cargoes along its various waterways and those imposed at the ports where these ships loaded or discharged.

---

[1] Gilliodts van Severen, L., *Inventaire des archives de la ville de Bruges* (Bruges, 1878-85), IV, 41, 731, and *n* 1.
[2] See below, p. 25.
[3] De Pauw, N., *Bouc van der Audiencie. Acten en Sentencien van den Raad van Vlaanderen in de XIVe eeuw* (Ghent, 1901-3), I, 21, 46, 52, 83.

With this second group, the port tolls, we are only concerned in so far as they came to be used as weapons in the economic warfare between the leading towns of the delta; for the most part, however, their interest is a domestic, not an inter-provincial or international one.[1]

The tolls on navigation are themselves divisible into two types according to their origin. The first type bore the name of *geleiden* (Latin *conductus*), which, as it is scarcely translatable, may conveniently be retained.[2] The medieval *geleide* was an arrangement whereby users of a particular route were required to pay toll to the local feudal magnate ostensibly in return for protection against maltreatment while passing through his territory; it appears to have originated in Central Europe and to have spread to the West in the twelfth century,[3] and clearly it had not long been established there before it degenerated into an ordinary toll in exchange for which the trader got nothing but the right to proceed on his way. It is, however, to the original character of the *geleide* that we should probably ascribe the feature which chiefly distinguished it in practice from the toll proper (*teloneum*), namely, its division into fragments held by different individuals or families; for almost from its inception the *geleide* had doubtless been subdivided among the holders of riparian fiefs, upon whom, if upon anyone, would have fallen the duty of protecting passing ships.

The second type of duty, the toll proper (*tol, teloneum*), was distinguished both in theory and practice by a unity which was lacking in the *geleide*. The toll was never a payment for services rendered but a payment in recognition of territorial rights; and since, in the Netherlands, the rights in question remained with the feudal prince, the Duke or Count, the toll remained with him also. Although in theory granted, or at least recognized, by the Emperor, from whom all authority over waterways within the Empire derived, the toll was in practice an attribute of the growing sovereignty of the feudal prince. As a tax upon trade the toll had, of course, a much greater future

---

[1] For the toll of Antwerp in the thirteenth and fourteenth centuries see Prims, *Geschiedenis van Antwerpen*, II, ii, 148-178.

[2] The nearest English equivalent is "safe-conduct", but this has retained its original meaning, whereas *geleide* quickly lost it.

[3] Fiesel, L., "Woher stammt das Zollgeleit", in *Virteljahrschrift für Soziale- und Wirthschaftsgeschichte*, XIX (1926), 385-412. The earliest reference to a *geleide* in the Netherlands occurs in the treaty of Bruges, of 7 March 1167, between the Counts of Flanders and of Holland-Zeeland. Van den Bergh and De Fremery, *Oorkondenboek van Holland en Zeeland*, second revised edn. by Obreen, H. G. A. (The Hague, 1937-), I, no. 185, p. 94.

than the *geleide,* but during this early period it is the *geleide* which is the centre of interest.

(a) *The* Geleiden *on Scheldt and Honte.*

The earliest indisputable evidence of the existence of a *geleide* on the Scheldt below Antwerp dates from the early thirteenth century. On 25 February 1213 the Duke of Brabant confiscated the rights of the previous holders of the *teloneum navium per Strynam et Scaldam,* together with their fiefs of Schakerloo and Ossendrecht, on account of their maltreatment of shippers, and granted one-half of the yield of the toll, as well as the forfeited lands, to Godfrey Lord of Breda, reserving the other half to himself. In return the Lord of Breda and his mèn were to ensure the peace of the waterway as far as the Duke's *conductus* extended. How far this was is not clearly stated, but the mention of Scheldt and Striene, as well as of Schakerloo and Ossendrecht,[1] suggests that it stretched from the neighbourhood of Hontemuide to the point where both sides of the waterway became Zeeland territory.[2]

That the duty in question, although called a *teloneum,* was in reality a *geleide,* is clear both from the terms of the grant and from what we know of the Brabant *geleide* as it developed during the next two centuries. It also appears fairly certain that this *geleide* had belonged independently to the Lords of Breda during the second half of the twelfth century,[3] and that the transaction of 1213 by which Godfrey of Breda received the moiety of it as a fief of Brabant represented a stage in the decline of the Lordship to a dependent position. From that date, however, it was the Duke of Brabant who exercised the *conductus* over the Scheldt, and later definitions of the Brabant *conductus,* notably that of 1400,[4] state its limits in terms which agree substantially with those of 1213. Moreover, the evidence relating to the administration of the *geleiden* on the Scheldt during the fourteenth century leave no doubt that they are descended from this earlier *teloneum.* This evidence comes mainly from the entries of *water-leenen,* that is, shares in the Scheldt *geleiden,* occurring in the registers

---

[1] See map facing p. 9.

[2] Van den Bergh, *Oorkondenboek,* I, 135-6; Marshall and Bogaerts, *Bibliothèque des Antiquités Belgiques,* I, 33-34.

[3] The principal evidence for this is the grant of free *conductus* made by Henry van Schooten, Lord of Breda, to the abbey of Ter Does in the third quarter of the twelfth century, and confirmed by his son Godfrey about 1204 (Kleyn, *Geschiedenis van Breda,* 99-100), both without reference to the Duke of Brabant.

[4] Quoted above, p. 19.

of Brabant feudatories compiled between 1312 and 1350.¹ The places with which these *waterleenen* are invariably associated in the registers (only four out of twenty-five have no place-name added) all lay on the Scheldt, or in one case on the Honte, within territory formerly part of the Lordship of Breda, and we cannot doubt that each separate *geleide* listed there is a portion of the whole *teloneum* of 1213, or that the subdivision is the result of a century of subinfeudation. That process had indeed begun before 1213, when the *geleiden* had been in the hands of the tenants of Schakerloo and Ossendrecht, both bordering the river; since then the number of fiefs to which shares in the *geleiden* had become attached had increased to seven. But whereas in 1213 the Lord of Breda had become tenant-in-chief of the *geleide* as a whole, a century later the separate *geleiden* were all held directly from the Duke of Brabant. Precisely how this change had come about we cannot say; but it meant the final extinction of the interest of the Lordship of Breda in these *waterleenen*.

The Duke of Brabant did not, however, take over or succeed to the sum total of the rights formerly exercised by the Lords of Breda over the waterways adjoining their principality. In the second half of the thirteenth century we hear of *geleiden* on the Honte which are held by liegemen of Breda;² these *geleiden*, associated with the villages of Rilland, Valkenesse and Den Agger in the land "between Honte and Hinkele", lay outside the limits of the Brabant *conductus*. Already before 1300 the Count of Holland-Zeeland had established some measure of control over them,³ and when in 1312 Raas van Liedekerke sold his rights in this territory to Count William III his " tolne ofte geleede op die Honte " passed with them.⁴ The boundary between this group of *geleiden* and those pertaining to Brabant did not, as might have been expected, coincide with the division between Scheldt and Honte, for one of the Brabant *geleiden*, that of Santvliet, stretched some distance along the Honte.⁵ But this is a minor complication which does not alter the central fact that by the early fourteenth century the *conductus* on Scheldt and Honte originally exercised by the Lords of Breda had been split into two parts, one consisting of the group of

---

¹ Galesloot, L., *Le livre des feudataires de Jean III, Duc de Brabant* (Brussels, 1865).
² Van den Bergh, *Oorkondenboek*, II, 139, 216; 303.
³ Floris V confirmed the toll-freedom granted to the abbey of Afflighem by the holders of the *geleide* of Rilland in 1284. *Ibid.* II, 217, 246.
⁴ See above, p. 19.
⁵ This is clear from the many references to this *geleide* as lying " on the Honte and the Scheldt " (for example, in the *Livre des feudataires*, II, 115). The explanation appears to be that the *geleide* of Santvliet had absorbed that of Den Agger, possibly because the channel of that name might otherwise have given opportunity to shippers to evade payment (see above, pp. 9-10).

geleiden on the Scheldt held from the Duke of Brabant, the other of the two *geleiden* on the Honte held by or from the Count of Holland-Zeeland, and that these were entirely independent of one another.

There was yet a third group of *geleiden,* those on the Honte held from the Count of Flanders. This was almost certainly of independent origin. The usual assumption that all the Honte *geleiden* were dependent on fiefs lying on the Zeeland side is disproved by the fact that in 1338 William IV forbade all those who levied " tolne ende gheleide " on the Honte, " whether settled within or without our territory ", to do so in future without his consent.[1] It is not clear just whom this was aimed at, but in so far as it was an attempt to assert exclusive control over the Honte *geleiden* it was not in the long run successful, for when in 1479 Maximilian and Mary of Burgundy conveyed their own shares in the " haringe and geleyde vander rivieren vander Honte " to the town of Antwerp, it is explicitly stated that they owned part of these as Counts of Flanders.[2] There appears to be so little evidence about these Flemish *geleiden,* however, that we may legitimately infer that they were not of much importance, although we cannot doubt their existence.

By the fourteenth century, when evidence about the other *geleiden* has become much fuller, they were clearly regarded by the feudal princes primarily as a source of revenue, which they might yield either directly, when the prince kept any part of them in his own hands,[3] or—and this was more usual—indirectly, when he granted them as fiefs and received feudal incidents from them.[4] The prince always retained, however, the power of exempting individuals or groups from their payment, and this power was freely used; in the thirteenth century it was religious houses which chiefly benefited, in the fourteenth secular groups, especially towns. Of the town-exemptions the most

---

[1] First printed by Marshall and Bogaerts in *Bibliothèque des Antiquités Belgiques,* I, 41; most recently by Prims in *Antwerpsch Archievenblad* (2de reeks), VIII (1933), 58. It is possible that the Flemish rights which provoked trouble between the inhabitants of " Rulant " (that is, Rilland, not the " land of Ryen " as suggested by Saint-Genois) and the *châtelain* of Saeftingen in 1296 were rights of *geleide.* Saint-Genois, J. de, *Inventaire analytique des Chartes des Comtes de Flandre* (Gent, 1843-6), no. 876, p. 256.

[2] Mertens, F. H., and Torfs, K. L., *Geschiedenis van Antwerpen* (Antwerp, 1845-53), III, 591-2. See below,

[3] The Count of Holland-Zeeland appears to have drawn some revenues in this way from the Honte *geleiden* in the fourteenth century. See Hamaker, H. G., *De Rekeningen der Grafelijkheid van Zeeland onder het Henegouwsche Huis* (*Hist. Genootsch. Werken,* 29-30, Utrecht, 1879-80), I, 211, 218, 438; II, 181.

[4] Apart from the *Livre des feudataires* (see above, p. 24 *n* 1), the chief printed source for the history of the Brabant *waterleenen* in the fourteenth century is the accounts of the *receveur* of Antwerp, extracts from which have been published by Fl. Prims in *Bijdragen tot de geschiedenis,* XXV (1934), 47-51.

important in the light of future developments was that enjoyed by Antwerp with respect to the *geleiden* on the Honte; this was confirmed by the well-known arbitral decision of November 1276, by which Antwerp ships and goods were declared free and the *geleide* on foreign goods in Antwerp ships was fixed at 5s. 3d. Flemish.[1]

We have seen that at first the holders of the various *geleiden* into which the *conductus* soon came to be divided were those whose lands bordered the waterway. Doubtless at this stage of development each individual or group maintained his own collector at an appropriate spot and a ship traversing the waterway would be required to pay something to each collector. It is probable that mutual convenience would in any case have led in course of time to the consolidation of several collecting-posts into one and the division of the proceeds on some agreed basis. But the evolution of the system of tenure must also have contributed to this result. Already in the later thirteenth century the normal arrangement seems to have been for each *geleide* to be held, not by an individual, but by a family group.[2] As soon as these family holdings came to be split up among the several members they quickly lost all trace of their original unity. The fragments into which each *geleide* was thus broken soon acquired the character of marketable assets, to be sold, mortgaged or given away, or from another point of view that of investments for surplus capital, and an increasing number of them came into the hands of people who had no connection with the original grantees and whose interest was simply that of the modern shareholder. Well-to-do Antwerpers were early prominent among these " rentiers ".

These developments led to a series of changes in the organization of the *geleiden*. In the first place, the value of these fragments or shares had to be computed in terms of a unit, for the fractions earlier adopted ("bruedergedeelte" or one-half, "zustergedeelte" or one-third) were only appropriate to the family stage. The unit adopted was the *haring* or herring, and eventually all the shares in all the *geleiden* came to be expressed as a number of *haringen*. It is not difficult to understand the origin of this system of valuation; not only were herring at all times one of the most frequent cargoes in the delta, but the *geleide* must often have been levied, at least in its early stages,

---

[1] Van den Bergh, *Oorkondenboek*, II, 139. The privilege was again confirmed by Count William IV of Holland-Zeeland in 1343 by a charter which has been most recently published by Prims in *Antwerpsch Archievenblad* (2de reeks), VIII (1933), 66.

[2] This is most clearly illustrated by the names of the holders of the Honte *geleiden* appearing in the documents of 1276, 1283, 1284 and 1290. Van den Bergh, *Oorkondenboek*, II, 139, 216, 233-4, 303.

not in money but in kind, so that its yield would often be most easily expressed in terms of herring, and the value of shares in it calculated in the same way.[1] The use of the term *haring,* and of the derivative *haring-geld* as a synonym for *geleide,* has led some writers to regard the *geleide* as a duty solely on herring, similar to those levied in various parts of the delta.[2] But all the evidence goes to prove that from the first the *geleide* was a duty levied on ships and on cargoes of every kind, and that it was merely the preponderance of herring which led to its adoption as a unit.

But each share had not only to be computed as a fraction of the whole, its holder had to be paid his proportion of the receipts, and it was doubtless this necessity which led the holders of the *geleiden* to combine forces in a single system. How early they did so we do not know, but we have a clear insight into the arrangement in force on the Scheldt towards the close of the fourteenth century. By that time the number of separate *geleiden* on the river had been reduced, by consolidation, to three, those of Lillo, Santvliet and Borchvliet.[3] The *geleiden* were actually collected, however, at two places only: those of Lillo and Santvliet at Slooceters on the west bank of the Scheldt near Steenvliet,[4] and that of Borchvliet at Betkensveer, probably in the near neighbourhood.[5] From the record of agreements made between those interested in the *geleiden* and the towns of Amsterdam and Haarlem in 1395 and 1396[6] we get a picture of how the *geleiden* were collected at these two points. There were two rates of payment: the full *geleide* of 34 new Burgundian groots (including one groot for *bakengeld*[7])

---

[1] On this point see below, p. 28.

[2] For the Flemish *haringtol* see below, pp. 40-43. Under the name of " tiende visch " a herring-toll was in operation at several of the delta towns.

[3] This statement is based upon a comparison of the many descriptions of the fourteenth-century *geleiden* contained in the sources mentioned; space forbids the presentation of any of the detail.

[4] As " slooxseters " (not " tlooxseters " as read by Denucé) it appears on the late fifteenth-century map of the Scheldt discussed below, p. 60, and reproduced by J. Denucé in *De Loop van de Schelde van de Zee tot Rupelmonde in de XVe eeuw* (Antwerp, n.d.).

[5] The name does not appear on the map mentioned in the preceding note, but this map shows " Tveer " between Slooceters and Iersekeroord, which may have been the same.

[6] The Amsterdam agreement is printed in *Handvesten . . . der Stad Amstelredam* (A'dam, 1748), I, 68, and by Prims (with some misreadings, *e.g.* " hofdragers " for " botdragers ") in *Antwerpsch Archievenblad* (2de reeks), VIII (1933), 139-41; the two Haarlem agreements in *Handvesten . . . aan de stad Haerlem . . . verleend* (Haarlem, 1751), 55-7. For Antwerp's intervention in a dispute of 1391 between the *geleiders* and Haarlem see an entry in the Clementynboeck for 6 Nov. 1391 (*Antwerpsch Archievenblad*, XXV, 249-50).

[7] *Bakengeld,* or beacon-money, was a small addition to *geleide-geld,* ostensibly towards the upkeep of the beacons marking the waterway.

was payable on goods (except beer) of more than £13 value, and the half *geleide* of 17 groots on goods of less value and on all cargoes of beer. Goods worth less than three shillings went free, but the ships carrying them paid the same as empty ships, namely two groots. An important exception to the general rate was made in the case of herring. Where a ship carried both herring and other goods, the *geleider* had the choice of levying the *geleide* on the herring or on the other goods, and whichever he chose the rest of the cargo went free. The *geleide* on 1½ lasts (that is, 18 tons) of herring or more was fixed at 20 groots and 333 herring, and on less than that amount at 10½ groots (including one groot for *bakengeld*) and 166 herring. In all cases the *geleide* due was to be paid in two parts, two-thirds at Betkensveer and one-third at Slooceters, "unless [the *geleiders*] shall hereafter agree to collect it in one ship at one place to assist the trader".

It is impossible to say how far the terms of these agreements represent a deviation from the normal. But since groups of foreign merchants were increasingly securing such agreements, they are probably not untypical of the general practice. It is clear that by this time the bulk of the *geleide* was collected in money; the yield would, of course, vary with the volume of traffic and the value of each share fluctuate accordingly. But already in the first half of the fourteenth century these values (presumably based on the average yield) were expressed in monetary terms; thus the "Livre des Feudataires" adds the annual value, varying from £1 gr. to £11 gr.[1] to a number of its entries of *waterleenen*. While this monetary value would be the basis of dealings in these shares, the actual income due to each share out of the proceeds of any given period continued to be reckoned in terms of *haringen*. If we may assume that the total value of the three Brabant *geleiden* amounted to the 333 *haringen* of the full *geleide,* then the proportion due to each share, expressed in the same unit, is easily calculated. Not until the fifteenth century, however, is it possible to determine the monetary equivalent of the *haring* and thus to state with some precision the monetary value of a share consisting of a given number of these units.[2]

While there is no such detailed evidence of the organization of the *geleiden* on the Honte, its main features are clear enough. The three *geleiden* of the thirteenth century had been reduced by the close of the fourteenth to two, those of Rilland and Valkenesse,[3] and both were

[1] That is, Flemish pounds of 240 groots.
[2] See below, p. 45.
[3] For the probable explanation of the disappearance of the third (Den Agger) see above, p. 24 *n*. 5.

collected at a single point on the waterway. The rate of 5s. 3d. Flemish adopted in the " arbitral decision " of 1276 had developed into a standard rate for all " unfree " cargoes,[1] and there appears to have been no " half-geleide ", as there was on the Scheldt, for goods of less than a specified value, an omission which was later to become a grievance with foreign merchants.[2]

(b) *The Toll of Iersekeroord.*

If the rulers of Brabant, Flanders and Holland-Zeeland all participated in the system of *geleiden* on the Scheldt-Honte delta, only one of them, at least before 1400, drew additional revenue in the form of a toll on any of these waterways. This was the Count of Holland-Zeeland, and the toll in question was the toll of Iersekeroord, better known by its later name of toll of Zeeland.

The earliest reference to this toll dates from 1321,[3] and several documents relating to it during the next forty years confirm its permanent existence from that date. In 1341 occurs the first of the long series of leases of the toll, and from 1346 there are regular entries of receipts from it in the accounts of the Treasurer (*Rentmeester*) of Zeeland bewester Schelde. The establishment of the toll of Iersekeroord may thus be ascribed with fair certainty to the early years of the fourteenth century. It was not in origin an independent toll, but a branch or watch (*wacht*) of the toll of Geervliet. The relationship was thus explained by the Procureur-General of the Count of Holland-Zeeland in the course of the lawsuit of 1468 already mentioned,[4] when he declared that the Count

avoit droit de tonlieu une fois en l'eaue doulce, duquel la chief garde est scituee à Gorinchem et plusieurs autres gardes, scituees en autres lieux, . . . et une fois en l'eaue salee, duquel droit la chief garde est scituee et assise à Geervliet et les autres branches, scituees en autres lieux, comme Yersekerhoirt et autres, et que à cause des dits tonlieux le dite conte povoit mettre ses gardes en chacune des dites eaues où bon lui sembloit, par ce que incontinent par l'atouchement de l'eaue, tant salee comme doulce, et strom du conte le droit de tonlieu est deu, en paiant lequel tonlieu en l'une des dites gardes, les navieurs sont frans es autres gardes. . . .[5]

---

[1] See the tariff in force in 1396, in Höhlbaum, K., and others, *Hansisches Urkundenbuch* (11 vols., Halle, Leipzig and Munich, 1876-1916), V, no. 245 (1), p. 130-1.
[2] See below, p. 44.
[3] Unger, W. S., *De Tol van Iersekeroord. Documenten en rekeningen, 1321-1572* (Rijks Geschiedk. Publ., Kleine Serie 29, The Hague, 1939), no. 1, p. 1. Dr. Unger has lain all students of the subject under a debt of gratitude by this magnificent collection of documents; he has also given the most reliable brief account of the toll in his contribution to the *Etudes d'histoire dediées à la mémoire de Henri Pirenne* (Brussels, 1937), 351-6.
[4] See above, p. 11, and below, pp. 53-4.
[5] Unger, no. 21, p. 21.

The toll of Geervliet, granted by Frederick Barbarossa to Count Floris III in 1179, was confirmed to his son and successor Dirk VII by the Emperor Henry VI in 1195.[1] The rate of duty was then fixed at five per cent *ad valorem* up to a maximum of five marks on cargoes of 100 marks or upwards in value. Geervliet lay on the Bornesse, the waterway which, separating the territories of Voorne and Putten, formed the boundary between the counties of Zeeland and Holland, to which those two territories respectively belonged. It was thus well placed on the route from Holland by the interior waters to the Scheldt-Honte delta and its proceeds must early have formed a useful addition to the Count's revenues.

Although the toll of Iersekeroord was still officially regarded as a watch of the toll of Geervliet as late as the mid-fifteenth century, it had already in practice become an independent toll. Thus the provisions for the leasing of the Holland and Zeeland tolls drawn up about 1415 speak of the toll of Geervliet and its watches and the toll of Iersekeroord and its watches and clearly regard them as separate.[2] But their former connection continued to be reflected in the rule that payment of either exempted from the other.

It is now generally accepted that the tollhouse of Iersekeroord lay on the eastern coast of Zuid-Beveland, opposite Bergen-op-Zoom, in the part of the island submerged by the inundation of 1532.[3] It was at this point that the many routes through the waters of Zeeland bewester Schelde converged on the Scheldt, so that the toll was well placed to intercept both the traffic passing south from Holland and that entering the Scheldt from the sea. The establishment of the toll may itself be regarded as an indication of the growth of traffic along these routes, and especially that coming in from the sea, for the traffic from Holland would have been at least partly covered by the original toll of Geervliet.

It may safely be assumed that the toll of Iersekeroord was from the first based upon the five per cent rate of the toll of Geervliet,[4] but apart from that we can say little or nothing about its character or

[1] Van den Bergh, *Oorkondenboek*, I, 107.
[2] Van Mieris, *Charterboek*, IV, 355.
[3] This was finally established by Dr. Z. W. Sneller (*Walcheren in de vijftiende eeuw*, 18-24); for the various alternative suggestions see Unger, intro., x. The engineer, A. Hollestelle claimed to have located the remains of the tollhouse submerged in 1530 in the course of a submarine investigation early this century (*De Honte en het eiland Borssele* (Tholen, 1907), 30). The suggestion that Tolsende in Zuid-Beveland derives its name from the toll (which Dr. Unger appears to countenance) has been rejected on etymological grounds: see *Nomina Geographica Neerlandica*, II, 183.
[4] This was certainly the basis of the toll at a later date; see the Ordinance of 19 Nov. 1519 in *Recueil des Ordonnances des Pays-Bas . . . 1506-1700*, I, 714; also in Unger, no. 47, p. 100.

incidence during its first century, since the earliest detailed account of its proceeds dates only from 1418[1] and the earliest tariff only from 1444.[2] Nearly all the evidence from before 1400 relates either to the leasing of the toll or to grants of exemptions from it. The terms of the earliest known lease, taken in December 1341 by Jan Scenairt for seven years at an annual rent of £20 gr., suggests that the Count had previously levied the toll directly through his own collectors.[3] The toll was again leased in 1348 and 1358,[4] and although the next recorded lease is that to Claes van Borssele in 1393,[5] the figures of receipts suggest that there had been others during the interval. These figures,[6] generally for a year but sometimes for longer or shorter periods, show a notable increase from their commencement in 1346 to the end of the century; whereas the annual rent of the earliest lease (1341-8) was £20 gr., the average annual yield between 1398 and 1402 was about £60 gr. But between these dates the figures at times soared and at others slumped. Wars and other disturbances would account for some of these fluctuations, while changes in the location of the various foreign "staples", with resultant changes in the volume of trade to be taxed, would also have affected the yield.[7]

Besides the many general exemptions from tolls granted to towns and religious bodies, there were some specific exemptions from the toll of Iersekeroord granted during this period. The exemption of Bergen-op-Zoom for the period of its Pinxten market in 1327 is the oldest known grant of toll-freedom to a Netherlands town.[8] Reimerswaal secured the same privilege for ships coming from Brabant and Flanders to its "jaarmarkt" in 1355,[9] and Brouwershaven was confirmed in 1351 by William V in the exemption granted to it by the Empress.[10] The difficulty of reconciling these exemptions with the periodic leasing of the toll at a fixed rent is reflected in the clause of the lease of 1358 providing that during its term no one who did not previously enjoy exemption should be allowed it.[11]

[1] Unger, no. 2, pp. 166ff. See below, p. 46.
[2] Ibid., no. 16, p. 12. See below, pp. 50-1.
[3] Ibid., no. 3, p. 2.
[4] Ibid., no. 5, p. 3, 151 n 4.
[5] Not included by Unger; printed in Hogendorp, F. van, *Disputatio Historico-Politica Inauguralis de Flumine Scaldi Clauso* . . . (Leiden, 1827), 40 n 41.
[6] Unger, 151-2.
[7] See, for example, the clause in the van Borssele lease on the possibility that the English staple might move to Middelburg.
[8] Unger, no. 2, p. 1, and n 2.
[9] Fruin, R., *Rijks Archief-Depôt in de Provincie Zeeland. Het Archief der Stad Reimerswaal* (The Hague, 1897), 22.
[10] Visvliet, J. P. van, ed., *Inventaris van het Oud Archief der Provincie Zeeland* (3 vols., Middelburg, 1874-80), III, no. 554, p. 174.
[11] Unger, no. 5, p. 3; Van Mieris, *Charterboek*, III, 64.

CHAPTER TWO

The Fifteenth Century

THE development of navigation in the Scheldt-Honte delta down to the end of the fourteenth century was largely shaped by three sets of conditions. Physical factors confined maritime navigation to the fringe of the delta and concentrated its interior navigation along the routes formed by the Scheldt and, to a smaller and diminishing extent, the Honte-Zwake; economic conditions (in part a product of these physical factors) made Bruges, lying at the seaward edge of the delta, its commercial metropolis and retarded the development of the ports on the landward side; and finally, the distribution of the delta-lands among the feudal rulers determined the political conditions, and among them the fiscal burdens, under which the navigation of these waterways was conducted. During the first half of the fifteenth century all three sets of conditions underwent a remarkable change. The physical transformation of the waterways, prepared before 1400, began to have a notable effect on their navigation from soon after that date. Hardly less important was the political union of the delta-lands achieved by the Dukes of Burgundy before the new century had run a third of its course. Both these developments in turn gave a great stimulus to the more gradual change by which commercial pre-eminence passed from the seaward to the landward edge of the delta, from Bruges to Antwerp. If the first of these changes created the modern Lower Scheldt, the others provided the setting for the first version of the " Scheldt question ".

(i) *The transformation of the Honte-Wielingen.*

It was no sudden transformation which gave the Scheldt-Honte delta its modern shape. If contemporary observers of the changes of the early fifteenth century, which marked the most important stage in the process, tended to depict it in catastrophic terms, that was because they associated it with the great inundations of the time. Those disasters were certainly the most spectacular manifestations of the natural forces at work in the delta. Between 1375 and 1425 there were four major inundations (1377, 1394, 1404 and 1421), besides many on a smaller scale, and they were to be repeated at more or less regular intervals during the next two centuries.[1] But these periodic floodings

---

[1] A brief survey will be found in Torfs, K. L., *Historische Schets der Watervloeden in België en Holland* (Antwerp, Brussels and Ghent, 1850). Special study has recently

of the delta-lands and the more lasting changes which were at the same time being made in the shape and size of the waterways are to be regarded not as cause and effect but as twin results of the operation of a single force, the force of the tides.

We have seen that the medieval Scheldt and Honte-Wielingen were protected from heavy tidal action both by the islands which partially blocked their openings to the sea and by the existence of numerous lateral channels which absorbed some of the incoming water. Neither of these conditions was, however, to remain unchanged. The thirteenth and fourteenth centuries saw a continuation of the large-scale drainage-schemes begun before 1200; one by one the minor waterways were blocked and the larger ones confined within closer limits. But every reduction of the area open to tidal penetration meant a corresponding increase in the strength of the currents running through it, and these currents must have thrust with mounting force into the various "bottlenecks" of the delta, including those formed by the Scheldt in the neighbourhood of Reimerswaal and by the Honte. Had the total volume of water in movement remained approximately the same the increase of pressure would have been gradual and measures might have been taken to meet it; we must, indeed, imagine that such a gradual increase was already taking place in the thirteenth and fourteenth centuries, and that the occasional inundations of that period were at least partly due to it. But in the second half of the fourteenth century, owing to the widening of the sea-openings (*zeegaten*), the volume of water entering (which may also have been growing steadily for a century or more) underwent a rapid increase. The high tide which was the immediate cause of the inundation of 1377 produced its first and most lasting effects on the *zeegaten*, and the wider openings thus created were then exposed to the scouring effect of normal tidal action.

It was thus a combination of these two factors—the over-rapid progress of reclamation and the widening of the sea-mouths—which produced the inundations. But since every inundation meant a temporary re-expansion of the water-area, they are more likely to have checked than to have promoted the widening and deepening of the main channels. It was the regular action of the tides, reinforced by the enlargement of the *zeegaten*, which was the main agent in this process. The waterway which underwent the most notable change

been made by G. G. Dept of the inundation of 1404 (*Etudes d'histoire dédiées à la mémoire de Henri Pirenne* (Brussels, 1937), 105-24, and *Bulletin de la Société Belge d'Etudes Géographiques*, VII (1937), 24-35), and by A. A. Beekman of that of 1421 (*Geschiedkundige Atlas van Nederland. De Bourgondische Tijd* (1915), 63-94).

was the Honte-Wielingen. If what most impressed contemporaries (and those of succeedings generations who echoed them) was the enlargement of the two formerly narrow channels of the Honte and the Wielingen, a no less significant change must have been taking place in the expanse of water between them. The first effect of the inundations was to make this expanse even larger and more shapeless than before;[1] but when it was reduced to something like its former limits, not only did its breadth more closely match the greater breadth of the Honte and Wielingen, but through it there ran one or more deep channels which, extending eastwards through the Honte into the Scheldt and westwards through the Wielingen into the sea, formed a new continuous waterway between Antwerp and the sea.

The evidence of near-contemporaries that these changes had taken place by about 1430 must not be taken to mean that they had fully worked themselves out by that date; just as they had been slow to prepare, so they would take long to complete. This is borne out by what we know of the navigation of the new waterway during its first century of existence. Throughout that time it was used mainly by small craft plying between the waters south and west of Middelburg, the so-called "road of Walcheren", and the ports of Brabant, notably Antwerp. For the most part the sea-going ships which entered the delta by one or other of the *zeegaten* came no further than the "road of Walcheren", where their cargoes were transhipped to the smaller vessels which carried them south across the Wielingen to Bruges, south-east along the Honte to Antwerp or Bergen-op-Zoom, or north-east through the channels which led to the Rhine and Maas.[2] This restriction of the Honte to the role of an interior waterway doubtless reflects the continued limitations of its navigable channel. But that these limitations were disappearing is shown by the growing use of the Honte by sea-going ships during the second half of the fifteenth century; doubtless it was the smaller type of ship which first navigated the Honte direct from the sea, while the "great ships" ventured no further than their accustomed anchorage. None the less the change was of capital importance, for it marked the opening of Antwerp's career as a seaport and with it the fulfilment of the first of the conditions which were soon to give rise to the "Scheldt question".

If the new waterway had not yet appropriated the name "Scheldt" it had taken over that of "Honte". The extension of the name from the easternmost channel to the whole waterway must have begun

---

[1] This is well illustrated by the map in Blanchard, *La Flandre*, 181.
[2] Sneller, *Walcheren in de vijftiende eeuw*, ch. 5 and 6.

almost as soon as the original Honte, from being one reach of the old Honte-Zwake-Looyve route, came to be part of the new route, that is, during the first quarter of the fifteenth century. By the middle of the century the new usage was well-established, and in 1468-9 it was given official approval.[1] Thereafter, until it was superseded first by " Western Scheldt " and then by " Scheldt ", the name Honte was always used to denote the entire waterway from Hontemuide to the sea, and it is in this sense that I shall use the name throughout the rest of this book.

(ii) *Antwerp, Middelburg and the Honte.*

" Antwerp owes the Scheldt to God and everything else to the Scheldt ". While in the long run Antwerp was to benefit enormously by the creation of the Scheldt estuary, it is by no means easy to assess the importance of its contribution to the rise of the town in the fifteenth century. (A similar problem arises in connection with the simultaneous decline of Bruges, which is partly to be attributed to a comparable change, the decay of the Zwin.) The fact that Antwerp had largely attracted the foreign merchant communities away from Bruges before the enlargement of the Honte had gone far enough to allow of direct navigation from the sea suggests that the decisive factors are to be sought elsewhere. None was perhaps more important than the liberal outlook which characterized the citizens and government of the town and which contrasted so sharply with the reactionary exclusiveness of its declining rival, and nowhere was that liberalism more apparent than in the two great fairs, the " Pinxtenmarkt " or Pentecost Fair in the spring and the " Bamismarkt " or St. Bavo's Fair in the autumn, the twin peaks of the town's business year. (Together with the two fairs at Bergen-op-Zoom which began in February and May, these were the " four markets " so famous in the history of the delta.) Social and political considerations also enter into the question; not only was Antwerp fortunate in escaping the worst evils of civil strife and of foreign invasion in the course of a troubled century, but it maintained, with occasional lapses on both sides, good relations with its new rulers, the Dukes of Burgundy.

There is no need to describe here the steady growth of Antwerp's trade during the period.[2] For us the chief interest lies in the way in which this trade was handled in its movement along the Scheldt and Honte. We have seen that at first the adoption of the new route

[1] See below, p. 54.
[2] This has been done most recently by Prims in his *Geschiedenis van Antwerpen*, VI, ii and VII, ii. Prims challenges, among other things, the tradition of Antwerp's " liberalism ".

brought little or no change in the organization of this traffic; both the local trade, which continued to provide the bulk of the cargoes throughout the year, and the international trade which periodically converged on the fairs were carried by the same small vessels plying between Antwerp and the ports and anchorages at the seaward edge of the delta. It was this local and transit-trade which gave the delta its underlying economic unity; in particular it linked the fortunes of Antwerp and Middelburg. So long as the " great ships " continued to anchor in the " road of Walcheren " and to unlade their cargoes into river-vessels for transport along the Honte the shippers and traders of Middelburg, and to a certain extent those of all the delta-ports, were likely to be kept busy. Not that Middelburg was satisfied with the benefits thus derived. While the transit-trade was in full vigour Middelburg was fighting hard against both Antwerp and Bergen-op-Zoom for the succession to Bruges as the " mart town " of the Netherlands. But unlike Bergen-op-Zoom, a town for which the ultimate triumph of Antwerp could only mean stagnation, Middelburg could rely on a steady flow of business even though the greatest rewards went elsewhere.

The real threat to Middelburg arose from the encroachment upon this transit-trade of direct trade between Antwerp and the sea, which created no such demand for the services of the Zeeland town. Although the maritime navigation of the Honte developed only slowly during the fifteenth century, the danger must have been early apparent and it doubtless helped to stimulate the jealousy of Middelburg for Antwerp which was so marked a feature of the end of the period. In particular, it was this new development which lent such importance to the fifteenth-century battle over the " watch " of the toll of Iersekeroord on the Honte, which will form the chief subject of this chapter.

(iii) *The union of the delta-lands under the Dukes of Burgundy.*

If there appears to be a certain inevitability about the geographical and economic changes in the Scheldt-Honte delta during the first half of the fifteenth century, the political unification of the delta-lands which accompanied them was in large measure due to the blind operation of chance. Not that the Dukes of Burgundy, who achieved this unification, did so in a fit of absence of mind; on the contrary, they pursued it with the abundant vigour and the lack of scruple which characterized their line. But the combination of circumstances which enabled them to realize it with such relative ease and in so short a time was in the highest degree exceptional.

It was Philip the Bold who by his marriage in 1369 with Margaret, heiress of Louis de Male of Flanders, first secured a footing in the Netherlands for his family. Louis was then also in possession of Antwerp and its adjacent territory,[1] and these passed with Flanders to Philip and Margaret on his death in 1384. But Philip was already planning to secure the succession to the whole of the Brabant heritage. In 1390 he persuaded the old Duchess Johanna, his wife's sister, to vest the succession in his family, and on her death in 1406 his second son Anthony became Duke of Brabant, to which Antwerp was then reunited. Anthony was killed at Agincourt and was succeeded by his son John IV. Philip had meanwhile concluded the two marriage-alliances which were designed to add Holland-Zeeland (as well as Hainaut, with which the two counties already had a personal union) to the family territories; they were the marriages of his daughter Margaret with William, afterwards Count William VI, and of his son John (the Fearless) with William's sister, also named Margaret. Of the first marriage there was born an only daughter, the celebrated Jacoba of Bavaria, who in 1417 succeeded her father in the two counties; of the second, a son Philip, known as Philip the Good.

John the Fearless, who succeeded Philip the Bold in Burgundy and Flanders in 1404, completed the matrimonial triangle between the three principalities by securing the marriage of his niece Jacoba with his nephew John IV of Brabant. This marriage was childless and in 1422 Jacoba separated from her husband and without waiting for an annulment contracted a union with Humphrey Duke of Gloucester. This rash step gave Philip the Good, since 1419 Duke of Burgundy and Count of Flanders, his opportunity to occupy, first Hainaut, and then, after two years of war (1426-8), Holland-Zeeland. By the Pacification of Delft of 3 July 1428 Jacoba recognized Philip as governor of Holland, Zeeland and Hainaut, while herself retaining the title of Countess and certain revenues, including the toll of Iersekeroord. The title she forfeited in 1433 by her last marriage, with Frank van Borssele, of the well-known Zeeland family; her death shortly afterwards left Philip undisputed master of the three counties. Since he was already Duke of Brabant, the younger branch of the family having come to an end in 1430, the year 1433 saw Flanders, Brabant and Holland-Zeeland for the first time acknowledge a common ruler, who was also the ruler of Hainaut, Limburg and Friesland; on this territorial foundation there was to be built up, during the next century, the Burgundian-Netherlands state.

[1] See above, p. 18.

Coming when it did, the political unification of the delta-lands was of prime importance for their economic development. It spared them not only a perpetuation of the dynastic wars of the previous regime, with their inevitable accompaniment of violence and pillage on the waterways, but also from serious embroilment in the last phase of the great struggle between England and France. Moreover, with political unity and commercial progress there went a relaxation of the social tension which had underlain the internal conflicts of the previous century. Outside Flanders, which had least to gain from the new conditions, such conflicts became the exception rather than the rule. What was true in general also applied to the particular case of the navigation of the Honte. The Burgundian union made little or no difference to the internal structure of the individual principalities; within each the Duke ruled by the same title and exercised the same rights as his predecessors. Thus in Zeeland Philip the Good and his successors continued to levy the toll of Iersekeroord, just as in Flanders they levied the *haringtol*.[1] Moreover, since the administration of these tolls remained in the hands of officials or lessees whose principal aim was to make them yield as much as possible, an aim which could not but commend itself also to the rulers, the new regime had the effect rather of increasing than reducing the weight of these taxes upon trade. But this is not to say that Antwerp, which in general stood to gain most from Burgundian rule, in this particular respect was the loser by it. If the first impression made by the story of the "battle of the Honte" is that the advent of a common ruler weakened instead of strengthening the position of Brabant as against Zeeland, of Antwerp as against Middelburg, this impression will not survive a consideration of the character of that "battle" and of the weapons with which it was fought. Under the old regime it would have entailed wholesale confiscations, embargoes and reprisals, and probably have culminated in regular warfare; under the new the main theatre of operations was the Duke of Burgundy's Council, later the Great Council of Mechlin,[2] the chief engagements were lawsuits, and the deadliest weapons the charters of privilege with which each party sought to confound the other. The coming of the Dukes of Burgundy may have extinguished neither the "liberties" of each principality nor the desire to use them, as of old, against its neighbours; it did allow the resulting conflicts to be resolved "by the force of argument instead of by the argument of force". In that fact lies the main difference between the "Scheldt question" of the fifteenth century and that of the seventeenth.

[1] See below, pp. 40-43.
[2] Established by ordinance of Dec. 1473. Pirenne, *Histoire de Belgique*, II, 400.

(iv) *The Middelburg Staple.*

The first attempt to interfere with the free movement of trade entering the delta by the new Wielingen route was made at the very beginning of the fifteenth century. On 5 February 1405 William VI of Holland-Zeeland instructed the magistrates of Middelburg not to allow any goods to be transhipped off the coast of Walcheren unless they had first been brought into Middelburg and there paid a duty which was to be shared between himself and the town. In justification of this order he explained that goods brought from Flanders and elsewhere which were transhipped in the "road of Walcheren" escaped the payment of toll, to his own loss and to the prejudice of his town of Middelburg.[1]

It is clear that the cargoes in question were those which entered or left the delta by way of the Wielingen and that the bulk of them was being shipped to or from Flanders. For their transhipment from seagoing to river-craft, or vice versa, the "road of Walcheren" would be the obvious place. The Count's declaration that these cargoes were liable to his toll thus involved the claim that the "road of Walcheren", if not the Wielingen itself, was Zeeland territory. That this claim was novel and likely to be challenged, not an old and well-established one, is suggested both by the indirect way in which it was advanced and by the adoption of a roundabout method of exercising it instead of the simpler method of erecting a toll.[2] The Flemish counter-claim, based on the definition of the "Vlaamsche stroom" as including all tidal water touching Flemish territory, was already in existence,[3] and in the *haringtol* the Count of Flanders had, like the Count of Holland-Zeeland, a financial inducement to make this claim effective.

William VI's decision to exercise his claim, not by means of a toll, but by granting Middelburg a right of staple over cargoes brought into the "road of Walcheren", must have given great satisfaction in that town. But in practice the staple failed to yield the advantages expected. For a quarter-of-a-century Middelburg appears to have succeeded in enforcing it, but from about 1430 the town adopted the practice of making "compositions" with foreign shippers who wanted to take their goods elsewhere, and when in 1433 Philip the Good, newly become Count of Holland-Zeeland, formally sanctioned this practice

[1] Printed in Unger, W. S., *Bronnen tot de geschiedenis van Middelburg in den landsheerlijken tijd* (Rijks Geschiedk. Publ., 54, 61, 75, The Hague, 1923-31), III, no. 121, p. 50; also printed and fully discussed by Z. W. Sneller in his *Walcheren in de vijftiende eeuw*, 26ff, on which this section is largely based.
[2] *Ibid.*, 27.
[3] See above, p. 21.

and fixed the rate of composition at five per cent the attempt to divert trade forcibly to Middelburg broke down.[1] Thereafter the *cancelioengeld* accruing from this compromise became merely a form of local toll, and even this disappeared shortly after 1460.

To the historian of the Scheldt, therefore, this attempt to erect a Middelburg staple is of less importance for what it achieved than for what it implied in the matter of jurisdiction and for the use later made of it as a precedent. Since it operated in its original form only until the early 1430's, that is, before the development of the Honte as a direct route to Antwerp, it cannot to any extent have affected that city's trade.[2] But when revived a century later it would assume a much more serious aspect[3] and ultimately it would be made to serve as a basis for the closure of the river.[4]

(v) *The Tolls.*

(a) *The* Haringtol.

The 'thirties of the fifteenth century, which saw on the one hand the decline of the Middelburg staple and on the other the rise of the " watch " of the toll of Iersekeroord on the Honte,[5] were also memorable for the sharp struggle over the *haringtol* on the Scheldt.

In the autumn of 1434 Philip the Good placed an armed vessel, usually referred to as the " hulk ", on the Scheldt above Calloo[6] to enforce the payment of *haringtol* by ships coming up the river. This action so incensed the Antwerpers that on 2 March 1435 they sent an expeditionary force down the Scheldt which seized the hulk and brought it to Antwerp, where it was beached near St. Michael's Abbey. When Philip sent commissioners to Antwerp to ask the meaning of this act of violence the magistrates refused to discuss the matter with them and demanded that the Duke should come in person. Philip's reply was to institute a blockade of the town, cutting it off from all intercourse with Brabant and Flanders. For seven weeks the town held out, but then the magistrates sent a deputation to the Duke to receive his terms; these were such that the town hesitated long before accepting them, but there was really no choice and on 26 December 1435 they were embodied in a settlement. The magistrates were re-

---

[1] Unger, *Bronnen*, III, no. 160, p. 78; Sneller, *op. cit.*, 42*ff*.
[2] But the episode of 1436, when an English ship bound for Antwerp was held up at Middelburg, suggests that it might have done so if continued. *Ibid.*, 35.
[3] See below, p. 75.
[4] See below, pp. 120-122.
[5] See below, p. 45.
[6] Calloo lay on the left bank of the river about 8 miles below Antwerp.

quired to make a public apology to the Duke and in token of submission to lay the town gate on the ground at his next visit; the town was to pay a fine of 40,000 Philippus gulden, 10,000 of which were to be applied to the fortification of Antwerp castle; finally, the hulk was to be restored to its place on the river by 15 July 1436, " sans préjudice des pales et droit du pays de Brabant et de la cause principale." For his part the Duke undertook to appoint commissioners " selon le contenu de l'article des lettres de son entrée " to investigate the legality of the toll. The settlement also dealt with certain other questions at issue between the parties, notably the question of the Honte, but these were subsidiary to the main issue of the *haringtol*.[1]

This *haringtol* was described in 1507 as

le tonlieu des herens, appelle en thyoys *den harinck tol van Calloe oft tsheerenghelt* . . . lequel tonlieu pour ce que cest ung tonlieu et domaine de Flandres, lon est acoustume prendre et receuoir et leuer deuant ledit Calloe, et illec mettre vng batteau ou nauere a tout estandars et enseignes, armoyes des armes de notre tresredoubte Seigneur, ouquel se soulloient tenir les commis a receuoir icellui tonlieu,

and it was then provided that

nulz marchans, mariniers ne autres . . . pourront, quant ilz auront passe pardeuant icellui Calloe, deschargier, pacquier ne despacquier vendre, transporter ou alliener aucun herenck, que preallablement ilz nayent paye contente et satisfait iceulx fermiers ou commis dudit tonlieu, pour le droit dicellui montant, pour chacun last deux solz six deniers gros, monnoie de Flandres, ou du moins auoir congie et licence diceulx, a paine de fourfaire le batteau ou nauire entierement ayant mene ledit herenck, et tous les biens et marchandises estans en icelluy.[2]

The *haringtol* was thus a Flemish, not a Brabant, toll, and unlike the *geleide*, with which it has sometimes been confused, it was levied solely on herring. There appears to be little or no evidence of its existence before 1400, but in the first quarter of the fifteenth century it was being levied on herring brought into all the principal Flemish ports, and from 1424 at least on herring brought into Flanders by way of the Scheldt.[3]

It was this extension of the *haringtol* to the Scheldt which aroused the hostility of Antwerp. Although in theory the toll was levied only on herring carried into Flanders, in practice it would have been im-

---

[1] Prims, *Geschiedenis van Antwerpen*, VI, i, 105-115.
[2] Mertens and Torfs, *Geschiedenis van Antwerpen*, III, 598-9.
[3] The accounts of the tonlieu of Biervliet for 1410-13 include the *haringtol*, as do those of other Flemish ports (Pinchart, A., *Inventaire des Archives des Chambres des Comptes*, IV, 12, 53-7). In 1424 the town of Ghent recognized the Count's right to levy it on herring arriving in Flanders by the Scheldt (Le Glay, A., *Inventaire Sommaire des Archives Départementales antérieures à 1790 . . . Nord. Archives Civiles. Série B. Chambre des Comptes de Lille*, I, 340).

possible to differentiate between these and cargoes bound for Brabant without ruining the toll through evasion. The renewal in 1423-4 of negotiations between Brabant and Flanders on the subject of the "seigneurie de la Stroem" may have been prompted by Antwerp's objection to the *haringtol*.¹ Nothing seems to have come of these, but when in 1430 the Count of Flanders became also Duke of Brabant Antwerp took the opportunity to lay its grievance before the new ruler in whose name the toll was levied and received his promise, incorporated in the "Joyous Entry" to which he swore on 5 October 1430, that the toll should be suspended for four years and that a commission should inquire into its legality.² The four years' suspension expired in October 1434 without the inquiry having been held,³ and Philip straightway reimposed the toll and, evidently foreseeing resistance, stationed the hulk at Calloo. It was this which provoked Antwerp into the act of rebellion which was to cost the town so dear.

Antwerp completed its payment of the fine in August 1436 and four years later the magistrates purchased the right to re-erect the town gates, removed in 1436. With this the episode terminated. Of the inquiry promised in the settlement nothing more is heard; presumably it went the way of its predecessor of 1430. It is not, indeed, until 1467 that the *haringtol* itself reappears. The "Joyous Entry" of Charles the Bold of 12 July 1467 contained a reference to it almost identical with that in Philip the Good's of 1430.⁴ Two months later the town of Antwerp took a four years' lease of the *haringtol*, previously leased to a group of farmers, and undertook to pay the same rent as they were paying. Charles on his part promised to hold an inquiry "selon la forme et teneur des lettres de Son Entrée" into the legality of the toll. If the investigation proved it illegal, Antwerp was to be quit of its obligation for the rent of the lease from the date of the decision, but if no decision were reached during the four years "ledit tonlieu demourra en tel estat quil estoit auant la date de cestes, et mesdits [sic] Seigneur en sa possession dicellui comme deuant".⁵

All this is so reminiscent of the earlier promises that it raises a suspicion whether the transaction may not have been more formal than

---

¹ *Ibid.*, 338.
² On the "Joyous Entry" (*Joyeuse Entrée, Blijde Inkomst*) sworn to by the Dukes of Brabant on their succession see Poullet, E., *Histoire de la Joyeuse Entrée de Brabant* (Brussels, 1863); Philip the Good's is printed in Anselmo, A., *Placcaeten, Ordonnantien, Landt-Chartres . . . van Brabandt* (Antwerp, 1648-1774), I, 152*ff*.
³ This is clear from the wording of the clause about it in the settlement of Dec. 1435. See above, p. 41.
⁴ *Ibid.*, 168*ff*.
⁵ Mertens and Torfs, *Geschiedenis van Antwerpen*, III, 585-7.

real, a suspicion which is only deepened when we read in the "Joyous Entries" of both Philip the Fair (9 September 1494) and Charles V (April 1507) provisions identical with that in Charles the Bold's.[1] But the fact that on 14 July 1469 Charles appointed Gillis Spruyte, the nominee of Antwerp, as receiver of the toll certainly suggests that the town was then collecting it according to the lease of 1467.[2] It is clear that the *haringtol* continued to be levied in Flanders during the remainder of the century,[3] and presumably the same is true of the toll of Calloo. It did not, however, remain in the possession of Antwerp, for when in August 1507 the Antwerp magistracy obtained its removal from Calloo to their own town, together with the jurisdiction over disputes arising out of it, it was again in the hands of private lessees, whom the town promised to assist in the work of collection.[4]

(b) *The* Geleiden.

The *geleiden* on Scheldt and Honte appear to have undergone no significant change during the first three-quarters of the fifteenth century. They remained split up into numerous shares which descended from generation to generation or were sold and acquired like other forms of property.[5] The progress made before 1400 towards consolidating the various *geleiden* into groups for purposes of collection was also maintained, but there is no clear evidence that the process was carried any further. It is also difficult to establish how far the change in the relative importance of the two waterways as trade-routes affected the yield and therefore the value of the different groups. The *geleide* of Santvliet, which covered both the Scheldt and the Honte, would have remained unaffected, but the *geleide* of Borchvliet on the Scheldt might have been expected to suffer, and that of Rilland on the Honte to have profited, by the change. The fact that in the course

---

[1] That of 1494 in *Placcaeten van Brabandt*, I, 179*ff*; that of 1507 in *Recueil des Ordonnances des Pays-Bas* . . . *1506-1700*, I, 10*ff*.

[2] Mertens and Torfs, *Geschiedenis van Antwerpen*, III, 588-9.

[3] The accounts for Biervliet and other Flemish ports mentioned above (p. 41 *n* 3) are evidence of this; there is also a *mémoire* of 1492 on the *haringtol* (*Inventaire Sommaire des Archives Départementales antérieures à 1790* . . . *Nord. Archives Civiles, Série B. Chambre des Comptes de Lille*, I, 2º partie, 357).

[4] Mertens and Torfs, *Geschiedenis van Antwerpen*, III, 598-600.

[5] Much information on the descent of Brabant *waterleenen* in the fifteenth century is contained in Galesloot, L., *Inventaire des Archives de la Cour Féodale de Brabant* (2 vols., Brussels, 1870-84), especially among the extracts from the register of *Leenbrieven* covering the years 1396 to 1477 (I, 123*ff*). Holdings in the Zeeland *geleiden* on the Honte are illustrated in the calendars of collections of family muniments acquired during this century by the Rijksarchief in Zeeland and published in *Verslagen omtrent 's Rijks Oude Archieven*, XXV (1902), 297*ff*, XXIX (1906), 243*ff*, and XXXIX (1916), ii, 170, 194, 195.

of the century interest became focussed on the Honte *geleiden* doubtless reflects their growing importance.

It was the Honte *geleiden* which were the subject of an outburst of complaints and disputes during the third quarter of the century. The Hanse merchants protested that the rate had been at least doubled, and that this rate was levied in full no matter how small the value of the goods concerned.[1] The monotonous reiteration, often in identical words, of these complaints suggests that they quickly became stereotyped and are therefore perhaps not to be taken at their face value. But whether or not the *geleiders* were as extortionate as they were painted, there can be little doubt that, with the development of large-scale international trade in the delta, the tolls which they exacted were felt to be increasingly unjustified and burdensome. Although the foreign merchants tended to blame Antwerp for this state of affairs, there was nothing that the town could do beyond adding its own remonstrances to theirs so long as the *geleiden* remained in private hands and were subject only to the somewhat remote control of the Duke of Burgundy.[2] It was to overcome this difficulty that the town at length decided to acquire a controlling interest in the *geleiden* by a large-scale purchase of shares. When this decision was taken we do not know, but it is clear that Antwerp seized the opportunity of the temporary collapse of the ducal power which followed the death of Charles the Bold to secure the government's approval and cooperation.

By letters patent of 25 May 1479 Mary Duchess of Burgundy and the Emperor Maximilian her consort authorized Antwerp to acquire for an annual rent the shares of " divers private persons living in Brabant, Flanders and Zeeland " in the " haringe ende geleyde " of the Honte with a view to relieving merchants of part or the whole of its payment. The Duchess and Emperor themselves held two shares in the *geleide*, one of 21⅓ *haringen* as Count and Countess of Flanders and the other of 42 *haringen* as Count and Countess of Holland-Zeeland; these they now conveyed to Antwerp in exchange for an annual rent of 48 stuivers per *haring*. The magistrates were also required to nominate a " man living and dying " to represent them, upon whose death they were to pay a relief of £10 " parisis "[3] in respect of each

---

[1] *Hansisches Urkundenbuch*, VIII, no. 1255 (3), p. 767; IX, no. 426 (1), p. 283, no. 566 (6), p. 448; *Hanserecesse von 1431-1476* (7 vols., Leipzig, 1876-92), V, no. 724, p. 520; VII, no. 40 (4), p. 111.

[2] Cf. Antwerp's promise in the agreement of 4 May 1468 to use its influence with the *geleiders*, *Hansisches Unkundenbuch*, IX, no. 453 (4), p. 310.

[3] The £ Paris was equivalent to 20 groots Flemish, that is, it had one-twelfth of the value of the £ Flemish.

of the ducal shares.[1] Since the magistrates, in announcing this transaction to the Chamber of Holland at The Hague a week later, were able to report that they had already rented nearly all the private holdings,[2] they had obviously prepared the ground thoroughly before approaching the government. Whether the town eventually succeeded in persuading all the private holders to surrender their shares we do not know, but clearly the transaction of 1479 marked the end of the old system.

The rate of 48 stuivers, or 96 groots Flemish, a year at which Antwerp purchased the ducal shares is the earliest precise monetary equivalent of these units which I have found. If it can be taken as roughly equal to the average annual yield of a single *haring* it furnishes a basis for estimating the value of shares in the *geleiden*. When, for example, in 1443 Jan Ruychrock, counsellor of Philip the Good, gave his daughter Mary 96 *haringen* in the *geleide* of the Honte as a wedding-present, he was endowing her with nearly £40 Flemish a year. (This calculation necessarily ignores the probable increase in yield, and therefore in value, of the Honte *geleide* resulting from the growth of traffic between 1443 and 1479.) This is the largest single share recorded; the smallest, also acquired by Ruychrock in 1441, would on the same reckoning have been worth about ten shillings Flemish a year.[3]

The transaction of 1479 applied only to the *geleide* on the Honte, but there are grounds for believing that at some later date Antwerp similarly acquired the outstanding shares in the Scheldt *geleiden*.[4] This is the more likely since the *geleiden*, whether on Honte or Scheldt, ceased to provoke complaint or dispute. The explanation is not, as might have been expected, that the town abolished those which it acquired, for even in its wealthiest days it was still collecting enough from them to leave a substantial balance after the rent-charge had been paid.[5] But the phenomenal growth of trade which took place during the half-century following 1479 would clearly have enabled the town to meet this fixed rent-charge out of *geleiden* levied at a progressively

---

[1] The patent is printed in Mertens and Torfs, *Geschiedenis van Antwerpen*, III, 589-94.

[2] *Ibid.*, 595-7.

[3] *Verslagen omtrent 's Rijks Oude Archieven*, XXIX (1906), 262, 267.

[4] The chief of these grounds is the high degree of probability that the holdings on which Antwerp was paying rents in 1549-50 (see following note) included those previously held in the *geleide* of Borchvliet, that is, on the Scheldt alone.

[5] The town's accounts for 1549-50 contain a detailed statement of the holdings on which the town was paying rent and the names of the holders, as well as the yield of the *geleiden* during that year. The accounts are printed in *Antwerpsch Archievenblad*, I (1864), 17ff.

reduced rate; and it is doubtless owing to this fact, and to the other concessions which the town would have been able and ready to make, that the *geleiden* under their new administration ceased to give trouble and therefore faded into obscurity.

(c) *The Toll of Iersekeroord.*

Both in intrinsic importance and in the extent of their repercussions the tolls so far discussed were eclipsed by the toll of Iersekeroord.

The leading features of this toll as it operated at the beginning of the fifteenth century are well illustrated by the extant accounts for the year 1418.[1] The toll was then, as it was to remain throughout the century, in the hands of a lessee.[2] His account is divided into two parts, the first recording the day-to-day receipts throughout the year at the toll-house itself, the proceeds of the "watches", of the ferries (*veeren*), and of the subsidiary toll on ships (*roertol*), and the administrative and other expenses incurred, and the second the receipts from the four markets, two at Antwerp and two at Bergen-op-Zoom.[3] The relative importance of the "daily" and "market" receipts is reflected in the totals: of the total yield for the year of about £214, the "daily" proceeds at the toll-house accounted for £78, and those of the "watches," ferries and *roertol* for £36, while the four markets yielded £100. Well might the lessee note on his accounts for 1415-16: "It is well known that the toll of Iersekeroord depends on the four markets at Antwerp and at Bergen".[4] During these markets, by a mutually convenient arrangement, the toll was collected at the town itself.

Since the accounts furnish a practically complete list of the cargoes contributing to the toll, it is possible to construct from them a tariff of the rates then in force. This tariff is in general agreement with the part-tariff of 1444,[5] but where they differ the later tariff is invariably the higher. Moreover, although owing to the large and growing number of exemptions from the toll this list cannot be accepted as completely representative of the trade of the delta, it provides valuable

---

[1] Unger, 166-217.

[2] The names of the lessees of the toll, as far as they are known, are given in connection with the figures of the yield of the toll from 1346-7 to 1572 in Unger, 151-64. The lessee from 1416-18 was Lourijs van Overvest. Down to 1470, when the first of a series of ordinances was issued governing the lease of the toll, it was governed by the general regulations for the leasing of all the Holland-Zeeland tolls; the regulations of 18 Oct. 1415 are printed in Van Mieris, *Charterboek*, IV, 355.

[3] See above, p. 35.

[4] Smit, H. J., *Bronnen tot de geschiedenis van den handel met Engeland, Schotland en Ierland* (Rijks Geschiedk. Publ., 65-66, The Hague, 1928), I, i, no. 943, p. 583.

[5] See below, p. 50.

evidence of the general nature of that trade. Detailed analysis would be out of place here, but it may be said that the principal commodities contributing to the "daily" receipts, that is, the commodities which were dealt in throughout the year, were: peat (accounting for 100 out of the total of 442 separate cargoes listed), grain (52), salt (47), fish (28) and fruit (19), with wine, wool, cloth, and hides appearing less often. These were clearly the staple items of the more or less continuous local trade. By contrast, wool, cloth and "mercerie" were the main items contributing to the "market" receipts, together with a great variety of other commodities which formed the staples of international trade.

The Count of Holland-Zeeland might well have been envied his power to levy tribute on this trade, but the yield of his toll was continually threatened in two ways: by a temporary reduction in the volume of trade, or by a decline in the proportion which bore its share of the toll. At a time when the purely economic factors were making for a regular increase in the trade of the delta, setbacks were in the main due to political causes. There were continual claims for compensation from the lessees on account of wars and trade embargoes;[1] these claims illustrate a feature of the toll already noticed, namely, its growing dependence upon the periodic shippings by the foreign trading communities, especially the English, to the fairs of the delta-towns. But even when conditions were normal the lessee had to beware the other chief threat to his bargain, a loss of revenue arising from the fact that a portion of the trade was escaping payment. Shippers and traders might escape payment in one of two ways: by purchasing their freedom from the Count, or by adopting one of the various devices for evading the toll.

Already before 1400 there had been a number of grants of exemption.[2] The first half of the fifteenth century saw the continuance of this practice which, while in the long run adverse to the prince's fiscal interests, yielded hard-pressed treasuries ready cash or saved them from having to meet debts. The lessees of the toll covered themselves by the insertion in the lease of a clause compensating them for loss arising from such grants. But it was not only the lessees who claimed this protection. From the time of their union under the House of Burgundy the states and towns of the delta showed themselves extremely jealous of their privileges and strove to prevent their common ruler from extending them to his other possessions. Holland and Zeeland were particularly anxious that Brabant should not profit from the

[1] Many of these are reproduced in the footnotes in Unger, 152*ff*.
[2] See above, p. 31.

new connection to secure toll-privileges. Thus in 1425 one of their conditions for their support of John IV of Brabant against Jacoba was his promise not to grant any such privileges without their consent.[1] Twenty years later Philip the Good's confirmation of the privileges, including freedom from tolls in Holland and Zeeland, granted to Bergen-op-Zoom by Albert of Bavaria in 1395, provoked the towns of Holland and Zeeland into demanding a confirmation of the promise of 1425. This the Duke gave in 1452; but his successors likewise failed to keep it.[2]

For merchants and shippers who had failed to secure exemption there was always the possibility of achieving the same end by evasion. All the usual devices such as false claims to toll-freedom, fraudulent declarations, concealment of goods, and, of course, the bribery of officials, were in constant use; but these do not distinguish the toll of Iersekeroord from any of its contemporaries. There was, however, another and far more significant form of evasion, the use of the new route by way of the Honte to "by-pass" the toll-house. This practice is generally thought to have originated in the last quarter of the fourteenth century, chiefly on the ground that in 1387 Antwerp successfully asserted the right of its citizens to use the Honte provided they had no foreign goods on board against an attempt by the lessees of the toll to compel them to use the Scheldt and to pay toll at Iersekeroord.[3] There are, however, two qualifications to be made to the conclusion usually drawn from this episode. The first is that the "Honte" mentioned here was almost certainly the short channel west of Hontemuide originally so named, and that since this channel, as part of the route Honte-Zwake-Looyve, had long provided an alternative route to the Scheldt, its use in 1387 was no novelty. The second is that the case did not raise the general issue of the evasion of the toll by the use of this route, since the Antwerpers claimed to be free on the Honte by virtue of old custom explicitly recognized in 1276 and 1343.[4] What was doubtless new in 1387 was the volume of foreign goods passing up to Antwerp which, having entered the delta by one of the *zeegaten*, had not passed the toll of Geervliet and which, if not taken up the Scheldt, would have paid no toll in Zeeland.

[1] Van Mieris, *Charterboek*, IV, 753.
[2] Smallegange, M., *Nieuwe Cronyk van Zeeland* (Middelburg, 1696), 329; Cornelissen, J., *Uit de geschiedenis van Bergen-op-Zoom in de 15de eeuw* (The Hague, 1923), 62.
[3] The extract from the Antwerp "Clementynboek" reporting this case was first printed by Marshall and Bogaerts in the *Bibliothèque des Antiquités Belgiques*, I, 45ff; a better text is given in *Antwerpsch Archievenblad*, XXV, 169-71.
[4] See above, p. 26 and *n* 1.

It was in the first quarter of the fifteenth century that the progressive improvement of the Honte (in its new and extended meaning) and the growth of trade from the West, to which it offered the greatest attraction, caused the " by-passing " of the tollhouse to assume serious proportions. In 1431 the lessee reported that the yield of the toll had greatly suffered " because the merchants for the most part send their goods upwards, and bring goods down again, by way of the Honte·'".[1] To meet this situation the Count and the lessees could either attempt to force all ships bound for Brabant to take the Scheldt route (as they had tried to do in 1387), or they could allow shippers to choose their own routes and establish a chain of subsidiary toll-points or *wachten* on those routes to enforce payment. They chose the second course, and from about 1410 they began to set up the necessary " watches ". The first was at Cats, on the waterway linking the Scheldt with the western Honte; after a stormy period during which this " watch " was first shifted to Arnemuiden and then suppressed, it reappeared at Cats and by the middle of the century had been reinforced by other " watches " along the same waterway and at the *zeegaten*. When Middelburg leased the toll of Iersekeroord in 1470 there were " watches " at Middelburg, Veere, Arnemuiden, Cats and Flushing, besides one outside Bergen-op-Zoom.[2]

Meanwhile a similar development had been taking place on the Honte. The Count's first attempt to bring traffic passing along the southern fringe of his territory within the scope of his toll-system took the form of the grant of a right of staple to Middelburg;[3] but when in 1433 Philip the Good virtually put an end to this experiment, it was only to replace it by the new one of a " watch " on the Honte. This had, indeed, already been tried (there was a " wachte in die Honte " in 1418 which brought in about £20),[4] but Philip the Good brought a new vigour to the campaign against evasion which entitles his ordinance of 13 October 1433 to be regarded as the real beginning of the " battle of the Honte ". After describing how " shippers from England, from France, from our lands of Brabant, Holland and Zeeland, as well as others " were taking advantage of the new route, he ordered all his officials in Holland and Zeeland to assist the toll-collectors to levy on all traffic using the Honte the same toll that it would have paid on

---

[1] Unger, 154 *n* 6. The same complaint had been made the year before. *Ibid.*, 154 *n* 5.
[2] There are many references to these " watches " in Unger's *Tol van Iersekeroord* and in his *Bronnen tot de geschiedenis van Middelburg in den landsheerlijken tijd*, and an account of them in Sneller's *Walcheren in de vijftiende eeuw*.
[3] See above, pp. 39-40.
[4] Unger, 184.

passing the toll-house of Iersekeroord.[1] Shortly afterwards the lessee, Nicolas Ruychrock, re-established the "watch" on the Honte, that is, he stationed one or more ships on the waterway, probably in the neighbourhood of Hontemuide, to collect toll from passing vessels.

The result was a crop of detentions and confiscations, followed by years of negotiation for an "accord". To the Hanse merchants, who led the opposition, the dispute was only part of the general economic war waged during these years between them and Holland-Zeeland. This was brought to a close by the treaty of Copenhagen of August 1441, which provided that outstanding grievances, and among them the new "watch", should be referred to representatives of the six "Wendish" towns and of five Netherlands towns, one of these being Antwerp. Antwerp had already sought to intervene in the dispute over the "watch" (witness the reference to it in the agreement of December 1435 on the *haringtol*),[2] and doubtless the town now took an active part in organizing the campaign within Brabant against it. The result of this campaign, and of the continued protests of the Hanse, was that in December 1443 Philip the Good ordered the suspension of the "watch" pending an inquiry into its legality.[3] This did not, however, mean that all trade on the Honte was automatically free from payment of toll, but rather that the ground was cleared for new arrangements. In March 1444 the Hanse representative at Bruges was in negotiation with the lessee for such an arrangement,[4] and six months later he secured it as part of a general agreement on the liability of the Hanse to the toll. During a three-year period (that is, concurrently with a new lease) Hanse merchants were to enjoy a tariff considerably below the general tariff. They were also allowed to ship their own goods to and from Antwerp along the Honte provided that these were coming from or going to the "Eastland" and that no breaking of cargo took place in Zeeland, but their goods or ships bound to or from England or the West were to pay toll according to the reduced tariff.[5]

The introduction of this Hanse tariff and of the accompanying concession coincided with the drawing-up of a new general tariff and of two other special tariffs, one for the citizens of Kampen, who with

---

[1] Unger, 5-6.
[2] See above, pp. 40-41.
[3] This document is omitted by Dr. Unger, although a reference to it occurs in the decision of the Great Council of 1468 included in his collection (p. 20); it appears in Marshall and Bogaerts, "Navigation de l'Escaut sous la maison de Bourgogne", in *Bibliothèque des Antiquités Belgiques*, I, 129-31.
[4] *Hanserecesse 1431-1476*, III, 62.
[5] Unger, no. 16, pp. 12-15.

those of Utrecht and Stavoren had long enjoyed a reduction of the toll to the " hundredth penny ", that is, one per cent *ad valorem*,[1] and another for the English merchants.[2] The English tariff was one of the series of grants, culminating in the " statute " of 1446, which marked the ending of the recent trade-war between England and the Netherlands; like the others it represented a substantial reduction of the general rate, and it also included a grant of exemption from payment at two of the " watches ", Cats and Goes. In later years, when, after another period of embargo, the English were readmitted to the Netherlands on the terms which they had enjoyed in 1446, they claimed that these included their freedom from the " watch " on the Honte.[3] While there appears to be no evidence that they did in fact secure this concession in 1446, they may have secured one of less but still of far from negligible value. In the course of the proceedings before the Great Council of Mechlin in 1504 the Count's Procureur-General stated that it was Jan de Bock who, on leasing the toll of Iersekeroord in 1450, began the practice of collecting what was due to the " watch " on the Honte " sur le Werf de nostredicte ville dAnvers, pour la commodité des marchans ".[4] Jan de Bock in fact first became a lessee in 1444,[5] and it is therefore possible that the transfer of the collection to Antwerp was part of the reorganization which followed the suspension of 1443; it would certainly have facilitated the arrangement then made with the Hanse. In that case, the English claim that in 1446 they had not been the subject to the " watch " on the Honte would have been true to the extent that their ships were not stopped, as they were in 1496, in their passage of that waterway but could continue to Antwerp and pay the toll due there.

The transfer of the collection to Antwerp, while it doubtless eased the situation, did not solve the problem. Nothing came of the inquiry promised in 1443, and it was left to the States of Brabant and Flanders to raise the issue of the legal validity of the " watch " in the first of the two " leading cases " to which it gave rise. The immediate background of this case was the fresh series of incidents which followed Philip the Good's new drive against evasion inaugurated by his ordinance of 4 April 1456. Under this all ships, whether free or not, were

---

[1] *Ibid*, no. 14, p. 11. Entries in the accounts for 1418 (see above, p. 46) show that they were then already paying at this rate.
[2] Smit, *Bronnen*, I, i, no. 1325, pp. 856-7.
[3] See below, p. 57.
[4] I take this quotation, as all others from the decision of 1504 (see below, p. 58), from the copy preserved in the Antwerp town archives, of which the archivist, Fl. Prims, kindly supplied me with a photostat. *Ff*. 11*v*-12.
[5] Unger, no. 12, p. 6.

to stop and be examined at the toll-points and all goods passing to and from Brabant through Zeeland were to pay toll " as if they had passed our toll-house of Iersekeroord."[1] If the latter provision could not fail to provoke a new conflict with the Hanse, the former was a challenge to the privileged towns. Moreover, it is almost certain that with this ordinance there was reintroduced the practice of collecting at least part of the toll on the Honte itself.

Following the detention of a number of Antwerp shippers in 1464 and 1465 the town brought an action against the lessees of the toll which came to hearing before the Great Council on 17 April 1466. The town rested its case on the ancient privilege of its citizens, confirmed in 1276 and 1343, to navigate the Honte freely unless they were carrying foreign goods, when they were to pay only 5s. 3d. Flemish;[2] this right the lessees had violated both by subjecting Antwerp ships and goods on the Honte to toll and by levying more than the maximum duty on foreign goods in Antwerp ships. The Procureur-General of Holland, appearing for the lessees, replied by asserting the Count's right to demand toll from all ships and goods traversing the Zeeland waters and with this object to establish " watches " where he pleased, including the Honte, on which he had recently placed " plusieurs gardes ". Both parties having been heard " bien au long ", the court ordered them to deliver their arguments in writing by 8 May and announced that the Duke would appoint four commissioners, two from Holland and two from Brabant, to report on the matter by 1 August. Pending a decision Antwerp ships and goods were to go free on the Honte, but a register of them was to be kept so that if the lessees won the case they could collect the toll due.[3]

The case still stood thus—we have no explanation of the delay—when Philip the Good died on 15 June 1467. The States of Brabant seized the opportunity of the " Joyous Entry " of his son Charles the Bold to shift the question on to a broader basis by petitioning against the levy of any toll on the Honte as being " au grant prejudice du bien publique des dicts pays et subgiez de Brabant, et contre les franchises et libertez anciennes d'icellui pays ". Charles promised to consider and answer this petition before he took his leave of the Duchy, and for once he was as good as his word. On 2 August 1467 he issued letters patent suspending the levy of toll upon the Honte until further order, but without prejudice to his rights or to the suit between

---

1 Summarised in Unger, 27 *n* 1.
2 See above, p. 26 and *n* 1.
  Marshall and Bogaerts, *loc. cit.*, 131-4.

Antwerp and the lessees.¹ Yet within a few months, and before either judgement had been given in this suit or the promised inquiry had been carried out, the lessees had re-established the "watch" on the Honte and had arrested the ship of an Antwerp citizen, Gerard Pels. This infringement of the "surceance" of August 1467 brought the deputies of the towns of Brabant and of the four "members" of Flanders into the field, and on 14 July 1468 the matter came again before the Great Council.

Although on this occasion all that the Council had to decide was whether or not the arrest of Pels' ship had contravened the "surceance", both parties appear to have regarded it as a "test case" involving the main question of the validity of the "watch" on the Honte. As far as Pels was concerned the Procureur-General justified the action of the lessees on two grounds: that his ship had been arrested "hors la dite riviere de la Honte en l'eaue et jurisdiction du dit conte de Zellande", and that the arrest was only an execution of a previous one from which he had escaped. On the general question of the validity of the "watch" the Procureur-General restated the Count's right and added the description of the enlargement of the Honte, and the consequent necessity of a "watch" on it to preserve the toll, which has been so often quoted.

The Procureur-General's definition of the Honte, supported by the testimony of one of the lessees, Henry Janszoon van Wissenkerke, as stretching only as far as Hulsterhaven was strenuously opposed by the deputies, who maintained that the name applied to the entire waterway between Hontemuide and the sea. The significance of this conflict of view for the earlier history of the name has already been discussed.² The deputies denied the Count's right, either by strict title or by prescription, to levy any toll on the Honte and went on to demonstrate that the Procureur's argument that the toll became due "incontinent par l'atouchement de l'eaue" would logically entitle the Court to toll at any place to which the salt water of Zeeland, mingling with the fresh waters of the rivers, might be carried, for example Antwerp or Mechlin. In any case the Honte was not Zeeland territory, it belonged to the Count of Flanders. This claim the deputies supported by the additional argument that

ce que la dite riviere a gaigné par alluvion, inondacion ou aultrement en largeur et parfondeur, elle la gaignie sur la terre et coste de Flandres, où est presentement la droite parfondeur, flux et strom par où passent les dits navires.

¹ *Ibid.*, 135-6.
² See above, p. 11.

They denied that the navigation of the Honte was something new; ships had used it without payment " de tel et si long temps, qu'il n'est memoire du contraire" and had thus acquired a prescriptive right. They concluded with a warning as to the evils which would flow from the maintenance of the " watch " on the Honte, " car par ce moien l'execercité de la marchandise seroit fort diminuee, sur quoy les dits pais de Brabant, Flandres, Hollande et Zellande sont principalment fondez ".[1]

The Great Council's decision, which was announced, after a further investigation by commissioners,[2] by letters patent of 8 September 1469, dealt solely with the arrest of Pels' ship, which it declared had been made in contravention of the " surceance " of August 1467.[3] Although this decision left untouched the larger question to which so much of the argument in the case had been addressed, it did settle, at least by implication, the subsidiary question of the scope of the name Honte; by rejecting the Procureur-General's plea that Pels' ship had been arrested, not on the Honte, but on the waters west of it the Council tacitly accepted the deputies' contention that the name Honte applied to the entire waterway between Hontemuide and the sea. Moreover, the decision was of great practical significance for the future of the " watch " on the Honte in that it made the legal re-establishment of this " watch " dependent on the termination of the " surceance " of 1467, that is, on the completion of the promised inquiry, of which there was little prospect. In the upshot the " watch " was not re-established for nearly twenty years, and then without the legal condition having been satisfied, so that it could again be challenged. Finally, if the proceedings had not settled the main issue, they had at least clarified it, and both parties profited by the experience to sharpen their weapons for the next and last great legal contest.

The final phase of the " battle of the Honte ", which opened in 1496, was both provoked and embittered by the political and economic changes of the preceding years. In 1494 Philip the Fair assumed the government of the Netherlands and straightway set himself to reassert the ducal authority which the seventeen years of civil strife since the death of Charles the Bold had gone far towards destroying. One of the most urgent problems was that of finance. On 6 May 1495 Philip issued his great Reform Edict, designed to assist the government in

---

[1] Unger, no. 21, pp. 20-26.
[2] Besides hearing evidence, the commissioners caused to be made " par maniere de figure une veue de lieu ", that is, a representation of the waterways similar to that made at the close of the century. See below, p. 60 and *n* 3.
[3] Marshall and Bogaerts, *loc. cit.*, 148-159.

resuming many sources of revenue now either worthless or yielding far less than their true value. Among the items dealt with were the ducal tolls, including the toll of Iersekeroord; the existing leases were to be respected, even though the rents fell far short of the proper figures, but on their expiry the tolls would be publicly auctioned under regulations framed to ensure the maximum rents.[1]

When this edict appeared the toll of Iersekeroord was leased by the town of Middelburg. Middelburg, in partnership with Veere, had taken its first lease of the toll in 1470. On the expiry of this lease in 1475, the toll had reverted to individual lessees, but on 23 July 1486 Middelburg had taken a new ten-year lease, which thus had little more than a year to run after the issue of the edict.[2] This lease fully deserved the strictures which the edict contained: the rent was £2000 of 40 groots a year, that is, between one-half and two-thirds of what Middelburg and Veere had paid in 1470-5.[3] It is true that, except in 1489, when the yield was abnormally large, the receipts would not have justified a higher rent, for during the ten years of the lease they averaged only £372 (against a rent of £333), compared with the average of £843 for the years 1471-5. But while this meagre yield was partly attributable to trade-wars, especially those with England, for which the ducal government had to share the responsibility, the general relaxing of administrative control and the increased facilities for evasion which the disturbed conditions of the period offered probably had more to do with it.

What happened to the " watch " on the Honte during this quarter-of-a-century is not altogether clear. In the course of the proceedings before the Great Council of Mechlin in 1496-1504 the Procureur-General reviewed its history during these years, but his evidence must be treated with some reserve as that of an interested party. His assertion, for example, that during the lease of 1470-5 Middelburg and Veere " commecterent leurs wachtes et firent lever le thonlieu sur le Werf dudict Anvers, comme avoyent faict leurs predecesseurs "[4] is difficult to reconcile with the verdict of 1469 and is not borne out by the evidence of the accounts of the toll for those years.[5] We are, how-

---

[1] Kluit, A., *Historie der Hollandsche Staatsregering* (Amsterdam, 1805), V, 380*ff*.
[2] Unger, 155-6.
[3] From 1465 the rent of the toll was expressed in the £ of 40 groots and must therefore be divided by six for comparison with the earlier figures, for example, those cited above, p. 31, and with the actual receipts as recorded in the Middelburg town accounts.
[4] *Ff*. 13-13*v*.
[5] The very occasional appearance in the accounts for 1472-3 of the receipt of toll from ships using the Honte hardly constitutes evidence to the contrary. Unger, pp. 267, 322, 325.

ever, on safer ground with his statement, endorsed by his opponents the States of Brabant, that in her "Joyous Entry" of May 1477 Mary Duchess of Burgundy promised to suppress the "watch" on the Honte, and that in consequence "lon avoit laisse pour aulcun temps de lever ledict droict sur ladicte honte".[1] The Procureur-General went on to declare that neither the Duchess nor her consort, the Emperor Maximilian, had regarded this or their other concessions to popular clamour as binding and were determined to revoke them as soon as they had reasserted their authority. It was in 1486, on the occasion of the grant of the second lease of the toll to Middelburg, that Maximilian (Mary had died in 1482) ordered the re-establishment of the "watch" on the Honte. The Procureur's evidence on this point is confirmed by the inclusion, for the first time, in this lease of the Honte as one of the "watches" of the toll.[2] Then follows his most interesting revelation. It is that as soon as the "watch" was re-established the town of Antwerp made an agreement with the Emperor by which, in return for the payment of 500 florins a year for six years, "il leur promoyct les tenir quict du thonlieu pour la honte pour le mesme temps".[3] Such "compositions" had, of course, long been a feature of the administration of the toll of Iersekeroord, and this agreement had the further precedent of Antwerp's own acquisition of the shares in the Honte *geleide* in 1479.[4] What is remarkable, however, is that the town should have come so dangerously near to renouncing its cherished claim to exemption from the "watch". Doubtless Antwerp saw the transaction in a different light, not as a surrender of this claim but as a recognition of it for which the town expressed gratitude in the accustomed manner; the transaction nevertheless furnished the Procureur-General with a telling point in his argument ten years later, and one to which the States of Brabant do not seem to have found a reply.

Before the second Middelburg lease expired on 22 July 1496 Philip the Fair had formally denounced the concessions extorted from his mother in 1477[5] and had followed this up with the Reform Edict of May 1495. The application to the toll of Iersekeroord of the rule laid down in that edict was foreshadowed in a draft ordinance of 20 March 1496 which provided for the public auction of the toll on

[1] F. 14.
[2] Unger, 49.
[3] F. 14v. Middelburg appears to have kept a register of Antwerp ships passing the "watch" without payment and to have claimed compensation from Maximilian. De Stoppelaar, *op. cit.*, I, nos. 595, 605, 616, pp. 156, 159, 162.
[4] See above, pp. 44-5.
[5] In his own "Joyous Entry" of Sept. 1494. *Placcaeten van Brabandt*, I, 178-9.

the following 15 and 26 April. The toll was to be offered for three years at a commencing figure of £2500; the auction was to be by burning candle and by the casting of a " godspenning"; and only private individuals were to be allowed to bid.¹ If there was any real intention of keeping the toll out of the control of one of the towns it was not to be realized; indeed, the projected auction did not take place. A fortnight before it was due Philip the Fair granted to Middelburg a three-year extension of the expiring lease. But the town had to pay heavily for it: the new rent was half as heavy again as the old (£3000 against £2000), and the town had in addition to pay £36 a year towards the upkeep of the toll-house at Iersekeroord.² Even at this price Middelburg seems to have been glad to secure the extension, for it was duly grateful to " some good friends" who helped on this occasion.³

What must chiefly have influenced the town's decision was the prospect of a considerable increase in the trade of the delta, and thus in the yield of the toll, resulting from Philip's recent negotiation of a commercial treaty with England, the famous Magnus Intercursus of 24 February 1496. Yet it was this treaty which was to revive in acute form the old conflict over the " watch" on the Honte. The first English merchant fleet to resume trade with the Netherlands entered Zeeland waters in June 1496. The Middelburg authorities demanded toll on its cargo of cloth at the old rate of two groots Flemish a cloth and when this was refused detained fifteen of the ships. The Englishmen protested that as the cloth was only passing up the Honte to Antwerp it was not liable to toll; the Intercursus had provided that they might trade on payment of the same tolls as they had paid fifty years before, and the toll now demanded was not one of them. The dispute was patched up by an agreement for the release of the ships on payment of "caution-money", but the Englishmen's remonstrance to the Archduke elicited only a non-committal reply which cannot have satisfied them.⁴ By this time, however, the States of Brabant, doubtless inspired by memories of 1468, had entered the field, and to such purpose that on 11 August the Archduke's Council

---
¹ Unger, no. 29, pp. 51-7.
² Ibid., no. 30, pp. 57-9.
³ The town paid them £400. Kesteloo, H. M., " De Stadsrekening van Middelburg, 1450-99" in *Archief uitgegeven door het Zeeuwsch Genootschap der Wetenschappen*, VI, i (1885), i, 83.
⁴ De Stoppelaar, J. H., *Inventaris van het Oud Archief der Stad Middelburg, 1217-1581* (Middelburg, 1883), I, 199-202; Unger, *Bronnen*, II, 175-6. On the justice of the English complaint, see above, p. 51. The liability of English merchants to the toll during the years following 1496 is discussed by De Smedt, O., " De Engelsche Natie te Antwerpen en de Scheldetollen (1496-1582)", in *Antwerpsch Archievenblad* (2de reeks), IV (1929), 40-73.

instructed Middelburg as lessee of the toll to suspend the "watch" on the Honte and to abstain from levying toll on Brabanters and others "who did not touch the waters [*stroom*] of Holland and Zeeland", a confused, not to say dangerous, phrase meaning apparently those who used the Honte only to pass between Antwerp and the sea.[1]

All was now ready for another of those long-drawn-out inquiries into the applicability of the toll of Iersekeroord to the Honte, and for another lawsuit, this time between the States of Brabant and the town of Middelburg. But before either could be proceeded with Antwerp took the law into its own hands. On 22 September 1496 the town wrote to threaten Middelburg with reprisals for an alleged infraction of its market-rights; four days later came the news that an armed expedition from Antwerp had seized the "watch" on the Honte and had maltreated the eighty-year old collector and his staff, seven of whom had been taken prisoners to Mechlin. The imprisoned men were soon released through the intervention of the Middelburg agent at Mechlin, but one of them was again seized on his way home through Antwerp and was brought repeatedly before the municipal court to answer a charge of piracy.[2] It was now Middelburg's turn to invoke the aid of the law, and the town accordingly entered a cross-suit against Antwerp for its violent intervention in a matter then *sub judice*. It was these two suits which, after a hearing which lasted for eight years, were brought to a close by the celebrated verdict of the Great Council of Mechlin of 11 October 1504.[3]

The only record of the proceedings in this case is contained in the preamble to the verdict, and full as this record is—it covers eighty folios of manuscript—it gives practically no information as to their

---

[1] Unger, no. 32, p. 59.
[2] De Stoppelaar, *op. cit.*, 205-8.
[3] There are several MS. copies of this verdict, among them one belonging to the archives of the Chamber of Accounts of Lille (see Dehaisnes and Finot, *Inventaire sommaire des archives départementales antérieures à 1790. Nord. Archives civiles, Série B. Chambre des Comptes de Lille*, I, ii, B. 1452, no. 12, p. 393), another (in Dutch) to the town archives of Middelburg (Den grote Zeeuwsche thol, no. 9), and a third to the archives of Antwerp. It is the Antwerp copy, in the form of a photostat kindly made for me by the archivist, Fl. Prims, that I have used and to which all the folio numbers given in footnotes refer. None of these copies has been published *in extenso*. The best-known extract from the verdict is that printed by Kluit in his *Historia Critica Comitatus Hollandiae et Zeelandiae*, II, ii, 1081-2 (on this see below, p. 61 *n* 1); a different extract had previously been published by Smallegange in his *Nieuwe Cronyk van Zeeland*, I, 165-6. Both these extracts were taken from the Middelburg copy. In recent years M. J. Denucé has published a summary of, and two extracts from, the Antwerp copy in the text accompanying his reproduction of the contemporary map of the Scheldt-Honte (see below, p. 60 *n* 3), and Dr. Unger, using the Middelburg copy, the portion containing the verdict itself in his *Tol van Iersekeroord*, 69-71, but the greater part of the document remains unpublished.

chronology. But this deficiency is more than compensated by the generous length at which the arguments used on both sides are set out. Since these arguments were almost exclusively historical and related to episodes dealt with in preceding pages there is no need to reproduce them here; but on the main issues of the validity of the " watch " on the Honte and the exemption from it claimed by Antwerp they differed in some important respects from those employed in 1468. There was, for instance, no further discussion of the name Honte; if the Procureur-General remembered his predecessor's attempt to limit its scope he must have decided against reviving this argument, and throughout the proceedings it was taken for granted both by the parties and by the court that the Honte was the entire waterway between Hontemuide and the sea. More remarkable was the fact that, whereas in 1468 the Zeeland claim to this waterway had been met by a counter-claim on behalf of Flanders, in the present case the opposing claim was put forward on behalf of Brabant. The change may have been due to the fact that the deputies of Flanders had no part in this action as they had in the earlier one; or perhaps the recent troubles in Flanders made it impolitic to ground the case on Flemish rights. Although, surprisingly enough, the Procureur-General did not seize on this weakness, the Brabant claim must have appeared far less convincing in 1496 than the Flemish claim had done in 1468; indeed it is perhaps not too much to say that the change was fatal to the opposition's chance of success. The Brabant case must also have suffered from its association with the popular tumults of 1477. The Brabanters found themselves driven into the assertion, unlikely to commend itself in the opening years of the sixteenth century, that

Il nest licite aulx Princes de mectre [aucuns] nouveaulx tonlieux et augmenter les vieulx, sans le consentement du poeuple, et sans lauctorite du Pape, ou de Lempereur, et sans grande cognoissance de cause.[1]

With the important exception of the substitution of the Brabant for the Flemish claim, both sides had strengthened their arguments since 1468 and this time they came to closer grips with each other. This point is best illustrated by the Procureur-General's attack on the relevance of the documents of 1276 and 1343 which had always been the mainstay of Antwerp's claim to freedom on the Honte. He pointed out (and he was perfectly right) that the celebrated " arbitral decision " of 1276

nestoit que entre particuliers et[2] ladicte ville dAnvers, quy ne touchoit de Riens audict Conte, et sy estoit pour le droict de geleyde Inferee ausdictz particuliers Lequel se poeult vulgairement appeller tol ofte onghelt, ainsy

---

[1] F. 29v.
[2] The MS has " de ", which must be a clerical error.

quil faict en ladicte sentence, ou Il estoit dict Tol ofte geleyde Ainsy y avoit grande difference entre nostre thonlieu et ledict geleyde *Car le tonlieu est du vingtiesme denier, Et le geleyde de cincq solz trois deniers* anchienne monneye de flandres, . . . Et le tonlieu a tousiours appartenu au Conte de Zelande pleno Jure, sans Jamais avoir este Inferee a aultre en tout, ne en partie.[1]

In accordance with the usual procedure both parties, after presenting their case verbally in court, delivered their arguments in writing and the Great Council appointed commissioners to examine these written pleadings and the documents appended to them and to make independent investigation. It was probably these commissioners who drew up the memorandum on the administration of the toll which formed a supplement to the verdict.[2] They may also have been responsible for the production of the remarkable pictorial map of the Honte and Scheldt, the original of which is preserved at Brussels and a much finer copy at Antwerp.[3] Although of slight value as evidence of the size or character of the two waterways at the close of the century, this map is an important source of information on the place-names of the delta and on such landmarks as churches, fortresses and gallows which must have been familiar to its shippers.

The case had reached this stage when, in July 1499, the extension of the Middelburg lease expired. If the town hoped to secure a further extension it was disappointed, for this time the lease went to one of its rivals, Bergen-op-Zoom.[4] The new lease was for four years, at no less than £6000 a year, that is, twice what Middelburg had been paying. In conformity with the terms of the lease, and with the Archduke's express order, Bergen-op-Zoom re-established the " watch " on the Honte. This brought protests from the States of Brabant in the Great Council, and this new development, which for a time held up the progress of the main suit, as well as the Archduke's absence abroad between 1501 and 1503, help to explain the delay of five years in reaching a decision.

The decision was promulgated by the Archduke in letters patent of 11 October 1504. The Great Council found that
le Conte de Zelande a droict de lever et coeuiller par *Luy ses fermiers Recepveurs et Commis son thonlieu de Ghervliet et de yerskerort generale-*

---

[1] *Ff.* 34v-35. The words in italics are underlined in the original.
[2] Preserved with the Lille copy of the verdict. See above, p. 58 *n* 3.
[3] The Antwerp copy was first reproduced, with a commentary, by J. F. Willems in his *Mengelingen van Historisch-Vaderlandschen Inhoud* (Antwerp, 1827-30), 489ff. Willems dated it between 1461 and 1489 and concluded that it was the " veue de lieu " made in connection with the lawsuit of 1468 (see above, p. 54 *n* 2). But M. J. Denucé, late archivist of Antwerp, who published a photographic reproduction of the Antwerp copy, with an introduction which includes extracts from the Mechlin verdict, under the title of *De Loop van de Schelde van de Zee tot Rupelmonde in de XVe eeuw* (Antwerp, n.d.), shows that it must date from between 1494 and 1504.
[4] Unger, no. 33, p. 60; 156.

ment sans Riens excepter, par tout son pays et Conte de Zelande cours deauwes et strooms dIcelluy, Aussy bien le Honte que aultres quelz quilz soyent ou comment quilz se nomment, Et ce de touttes navires, denrees et marchandises telles quelles soyent, ou de quelles part quelles viennent, appartenants a marchants non francqz, quy en allant, venant, montant, descendant, et passant attouchent *aulcuns des cours deauwes et strooms dessusdicts La Honte ou aultre*, Et . . . de mectre ses Wachtes et *gardes par chascun des dessusdictz strooms et cours deauwes, aussy bien La Honte que aultres* . . . pour par le moyen desdictes Wachtes et gardes de tant mieulx et plus facilement Recouvrer Recevoir et faire entierement venir eus Les deniers et le droict dIcelluy son tonlieu.[1]

The States of Brabant were therefore liable for all losses sustained in this respect by successive Counts of Holland-Zeeland since 1443, a liability which the Archduke " reduced " to the sum of 18,000 Philippus gulden. He also levied a fine of 8000 Philippus gulden on the town of Antwerp for the exploit of 1496, besides suspending one of its officers and remitting him and all others involved to separate trial. Finally the Archduke reserved to the officers of the " watch " on the Honte at the time of its seizure their right of personal action for the injury which they had suffered.

So ended, with the complete vindication of the Count's right, this great " leading case " and with it the seventy-year old struggle over the " watch " on the Honte. For Brabant, and above all Antwerp, the verdict was a crushing defeat. True, the Great Council had, for reasons which are not altogether clear, confined its decision to the question of the legal validity of the " watch " on the Honte and had not ruled whether Antwerpers were to be numbered among the " marchants non francqz " who were liable to payment. There can be little doubt, however, that this was the effect of the decision, if only because Antwerp would hardly be prepared to embark upon the fresh suit which a last effort to save its claim would have involved. But if Antwerp had failed with its legal arguments, it could rely on another kind of argument to redeem what the law had declared to be a lost cause. This argument the town was now to bring into play, and to such purpose that the vindication of the " watch " on the Honte was but the prelude to its obliteration.

---

[1] *Ff.* 41-2. The wording in italics is underlined in the original. It is to be noted that the extract printed by Kluit (see above, p. 58 *n* 3), which includes the declaration, frequently quoted by later writers, " que ledict fleuve [namely, the Honte] du tout en tout estoit fleuve et stroom de zelande " saving only as far as the Count of Flanders could ride into it from his territory and touch the water with his sword, does not come, as Kluit and the writers who followed him believed, from the Great Council's verdict but from the argument of the Procureur-General. While the effect of the verdict was to establish the Zeeland right to sole jurisdiction on the Honte, this right was implied and not stated in this categorical manner.

CHAPTER THREE

The " Golden Age "

THE commercial and financial pre-eminence of Antwerp in the half-century preceding the Revolt of the Netherlands has been the subject of several classic accounts, from Guicciardini's contemporary description to the modern analyses of Pirenne and Ehrenberg. Guicciardini's figures of the main branches of Antwerp's imports at the height of its prosperity, about 1560, are a useful guide to the relative importance of the trade-routes which converged upon the town. The largest single item was English cloth, which accounted for almost one third of the total value; next came Italian luxury goods, amounting to nearly one-fifth; Northern foodstuffs accounted for rather more and German wine for rather less than one-tenth, French wine and Portuguese spices each for about one-sixteenth; Spanish wine and wool, German cloth, French dyes and salt, and English wool represented progressively smaller fractions.[1]

The great bulk of these imports entered Antwerp by way of the Lower Scheldt, and the conditions, both natural and man-made, governing the navigation of this waterway were thus of prime importance to the town. In the history of these conditions the period is one of transition; the new maritime navigation was yet far from having superseded the transit-trade as the principal means of communication between Antwerp and the sea; moreover, if it saw the last of the " watch " on the Honte, the period also saw the first tentative use of the new and deadlier weapon of compulsory transhipment. But neither of these obstacles constituted a serious limitation on the use of the waterway; for upwards of half-a-century the navigation of the Lower Scheldt was substantially " free ".

(i) *The Lower Scheldt.*

The evolution of the modern Scheldt estuary was virtually complete by the opening of the sixteenth century. If it was the inundations of the years 1530 to 1570 which effected the last major changes in the shape of the delta, the submergence of the land of Saeftingen and of the eastern coast of Zuid-Beveland, these catastrophes are to be viewed, like their forerunners, rather as the result of the previous broadening and deepening of the Scheldt and Honte than as the cause

[1] These " traditional " figures may now be supplemented and revised by those published by L. van der Essen in *Bull. de l'Acad. Roy. d'Arch. de Belgique*, 1920 (III), 39-64, and by J. A. Goris, *Etude sur les colonies marchandes méridionales* (Louvain, 1925), 317-37.

of their further enlargement. To us the main interest of these inundations lies in their effect on the location of the " control-points " on the waterways. The submergence of eastern Zuid-Beveland involved the destruction of the toll-house at Iersekeroord and was thus the immediate occasion of the transfer of the central collection and administration of the toll to Antwerp, while the loss of Saeftingen, by converting the hitherto still relatively narrow channel at the junction of Honte and Scheldt into a broad expanse of water, put a term to its usefulness as a key-point for the interception of traffic.

Both the size of the waterway up to Antwerp and the volume of traffic which it carried were the admiration and envy of foreign observers. A Venetian *relazione* of 1559 gave the width of the river at Antwerp as about 375 yards, that is, almost exactly its present width at low water.[1] While there appear to be no contemporary figures of its depth, all the accounts agree that it was capable of bearing large seagoing ships up to Antwerp, where at high water they could be moored at the quays.[2] The passage of the river was not without its dangers, especially in rough weather, and it demanded the services of a pilot, who, like his present-day successor, would be picked up off Walcheren. The volume of traffic on the river must itself have added considerably to the difficulty of its navigation. Scribani's figures of 2500 ships on the river at the same time and of 500 entering or leaving Antwerp every day are doubtless an exaggeration; but they are less incredible when it is remembered that the great majority of the vessels navigating the river were the small craft engaged in the local and transit-trade, and relatively few of them sea-going ships. The evidence of contemporaries as to the unprecedented number of " great ships " to be seen in the " road of Walcheren " shows that the practice of transhipment at the entrance to the delta was still common on the eve of the Revolt.[3] But there were so many more ships carrying cargoes bound for Antwerp than at any previous time that an increase in the number which ended their voyage off Walcheren did not exclude a simultaneous increase in the number continuing up the river to Antwerp.

While the accounts of the toll of Iersekeroord for 1570 afford the basis for a calculation of the number of ships unloading at Walcheren,[4]

---

[1] Wegg, J., *Antwerp, 1477-1559* (1916), 309.
[2] See, for example, Fris, V., " Tableau de la Flandre au début du XVI siècle, d'après Antonio De Beatis et Jacques de Meyere ", in *Bulletin der Maatschappij van Geschiedenis en Oudheidkunde van Gent*, XVIII^{de} jrg. (1910), 54, citing the description of Antwerp and the Scheldt written by Antonio de Beatis in 1517.
[3] Sneller, *op. cit.*, 2*ff*.
[4] Unger, no. 30, pp. 530*ff*.

those of the "anchorage duty" levied in Zeeland supply figures (although not complete ones) of the number making the direct passage to Antwerp during the years 1518-71.[1] These figures, which after a good deal of fluctuation during the first twenty years then settle down to a fairly steady total of between 200 and 300 a year, show that during the half-century before the Revolt the maritime navigation of the Lower Scheldt became a regular thing. The Venetian galleys, which had been visiting Antwerp for two hundred years, were now eclipsed by other foreign merchant fleets. Foremost among them were the Merchant Adventurers' fleets bringing the cloth which accounted for one-third of the total value of the town's imports; the English ships tended to be smaller than those making longer voyages and doubtless for that reason found the passage of the river relatively easy.[2] The first Portuguese ships to call at Antwerp appeared there in 1503, and thereafter they came regularly and in growing numbers; in 1525 there were upwards of fifty sail in the Iberian fleet which came up the river.[3] The third main group consisted of the Breton ships which handled the French trade, especially the trade in wine; in the fifteenth century they had anchored in the "road of Walcheren"; in the early sixteenth they began to pass up to Antwerp or Bergen-op-Zoom with their valuable cargoes.[4] Finally, Antwerp itself had some share, although never a large one, in this direct trade. From the beginning of the century the Antwerp shipyards began to build sea-going ships such as the one which, after making two voyages to the Levant under the enterprising Dirk van Paesschen, in 1515 went aground in the river below Antwerp and was lost.

(ii) *The "Watch" on the Honte.*

"Anno 1505. Those of Antwerp bought the toll on the Honte from Duke Philip, when he was to voyage to Spain, for 16,000 Philippus gulden". Thus the seventeenth-century Antwerp chronicler Bertrijn briefly recalled the transaction which opened a new chapter in the history of the "watch" on the Honte. Bertrijn was quite right to regard it as a deal between Antwerp and the Duke, although it was

---

[1] The annual totals are published by Unger in *Antwerpsch Archievenblad* (2de reeks), IV (1929), 159-69.
[2] But it is interesting to notice that one of the Merchant Adventurers' objections to Wolsey's proposed transference of their "mart" from Antwerp to Calais in 1527 was that Calais harbour could not accommodate the ships which went up to Antwerp. *Letters and Papers of Henry VIII*, III, ii, no. 2559; Wegg, *op. cit.*, 170.
[3] *Ibid.*, 175.
[4] On the wine-trade see the articles by Z. W. Sneller and W. S. Unger in *Bijdr. voor Vaderl. Gesch.*, VI, i (1924), 193-216, and VI, viii (1929), 225-44; also their volume of documents (see p. 76 *n* 1 below).

concluded in the name of the States of Brabant, but he was in error about the sum involved, which was 30,000 gulden.[1]

The opportunity was unique and Antwerp knew how to profit by it. The death in November 1504 of Isabella of Castile had made Philip the Fair, married in 1496 to Isabella's daughter Joanna, titular king of Castile. But Joanna was feeble-minded, and her father Ferdinand of Aragon intended to retain the government of her kingdom; Philip had thus no hope of asserting his authority unless he went to Spain, and in 1505 he devoted himself to preparations for the journey. Foremost among these was the raising of a large sum of money. The States-General assembled at Antwerp in 1505 granted 400,000 gulden towards the expedition and for the war with Gelders, which Philip brought to an end in July; but up to the time of his departure in January 1506 Philip was busy supplementing this from every possible source. One of the most lucrative was the sale or mortgage of ducal revenues, including the toll of Iersekeroord.

Antwerp's decision to neutralize the effect of the verdict of October 1504 by means of a financial " deal " probably dates from very shortly after that verdict was announced, and the project was doubtless mooted at the meeting of the States of Brabant in 1505. Whether political considerations dictated its postponement until the eve of Philip's departure we do not know, but it was not until November 1505, two months before the Archduke left the Netherlands, that the deal was concluded. Antwerp did not succeed in buying outright the " watch " on the Honte (such a complete alienation would in any case have been of doubtful validity) but only in obtaining its suspension " ledit transport durant ", that is, until its resumption by repayment of the capital sum. Nor was this suspension itself complete, for it applied only to ships which used the Honte for direct passage between Antwerp and the sea and which did not break cargo en route. (Ships were not, however, disqualified if they used the " road of Walcheren " for replenishing stores or equipment.) Since it was mainly, if not exclu-

---

[1] *Chronijck der Stadt Antwerpen toegeschreven aan den Notaris Geeraard Bertrijn* (ed. Ridder G. van Havre, Maatschappij der Antwerpsche Bibliophilen, Uitgave Nr. 5, Antwerp, 1879), 62. The Antwerp copy of the patent recording the agreement is listed in Verachter, F., *Inventaire des anciens chartes et privilèges . . . conservés aux archives de la ville d'Anvers, 1193-1856* (Antwerp, 1860), no. DCXXXV; the agreement was between the Duke and the States, and the sum was 30,000 gulden. Verachter gives the date as 14 November 1504, which, if correct, would mean that Antwerp took action immediately the Great Council gave its verdict. But the patent of 29 October 1507 confirming the agreement (see below, p. 67) gives its date as 10 November 1505. The discrepancy can only be cleared up by reference to the MS.; pending that, I prefer the later date, which, besides its greater probability on general grounds, connects this transaction more intelligibly with the others (see below, p. 66).

sively, foreign ships which made the passage to Antwerp direct, they were the principal beneficiaries, and one effect of the new arrangement must have been to increase the number of sea-going ships which berthed at Antwerp.

It was doubtless this aspect of the matter which prompted Middelburg to follow Antwerp's example. When Philip arrived there in December 1505 he was still in need of money, and on 2 January 1506 he sold to the town for 22,000 Rhenish gulden the " watch " of the toll maintained there, reserving his right to repurchase it for the same amount.[1] About the same time he sold the " watch " at Bergen-op-Zoom to that town for 15,000 gulden.[2] These two transactions differed from the recent one with Antwerp in that Middelburg and Bergen-op-Zoom did not propose, nor could they have afforded, to suspend the levy of the toll at their " watches ", although they doubtless intended to administer it as far as possible in the interests of their trade. But this did not alter the fact that when Philip the Fair sailed from Middelburg on 10 January 1506 he had mortgaged three of the principal " watches " of the toll, and it is against this background that we must set the toll-privileges which he conceded a month later in the commercial treaty, the Malus Intercursus, concluded with Henry VII during his enforced sojourn in England. The fifth article of that treaty provided that English merchants were to enjoy at Antwerp the privileged position accorded them by the " statute " of 1446, and that this was to include freedom from what the English called the " Sewesshe " or " Hounte " toll; they were also exempted, by clauses which leave something to be desired in clarity, from the Brabant toll when going to Middelburg or Bergen-op-Zoom, and the Zeeland toll when going to Bruges.[3]

If the first of these concessions was one of appearance only, since Antwerp had already bought it, the second was bound to provoke further trouble between the delta-towns. The Chamber of Accounts at The Hague had already protested against the sale of the " watch " to Middelburg on the grounds that the purchase-price was too low and that the other " watches " would suffer since traders would flock to Middelburg " pour estre affranchiez d'aultres tonlieux et gardes ".[4] The exemption of the English merchants there and at Bergen-op-Zoom

---

[1] Unger, no. 39, pp. 71-5, and 71 *n* 2, for references relating to the financing of this purchase by the town.
[2] This appears from the terms of Charles V's undertaking to Middelburg, of 19 Oct. 1515, to redeem this and the Antwerp mortgage (see below, p. 68).
[3] Rymer, *Foedera*, XIII, 134; the toll-article in Unger, no. 41, p. 76.
[4] Unger, no. 40, p. 75.

gave fresh grounds for both criticisms, and it is not surprising that the regency which Philip had left behind him decided to redeem the Middelburg "watch". This it succeeded in doing in July 1506 with the help of the banker Girolamo or Jerome Frescobaldi, who thus became the new lessee of the toll for four years at a (nominal) rent of £22,000 a year.¹ The fact that the Bergen "watch" was not redeemed suggests that the government's action was at least partly inspired by Brabant's jealousy of Middelburg.²

Two months later Philip the Fair's Spanish enterprise, which had such repercussions on the toll of Iersekeroord, was brought to a sudden end by his death at Burgos (25 September 1506). His son Charles, the future Charles V, was a child of six, and Philip's sister Margaret of Savoy came to the Netherlands as governor for her father, the Emperor Maximilian, upon whom devolved the regency. The first years of her governorship were troubled ones and during them the rivalry of the delta-towns found fresh outlet in disputes and recriminations over the toll of Iersekeroord. Antwerp began by securing the Duchess's confirmation of her brother's sale of the "watch" on the Honte.³ It is not clear whether the allegation that the lessee of the toll (this was the financier Frescobaldi) was still trying to levy it on the Honte is to be taken literally, or whether this was a form of words to justify the confirmation of the patent; but the object was plainly to forestall opposition seeking to profit by the change of regime. On the same date (29 October 1507) the Duchess issued an ordinance, also doubtless inspired by Antwerp, on the vexed question of the liability to toll of goods passing between Brabant, that is to say, Antwerp, and Bergen-op-Zoom; provisionally this traffic was to be exempt from toll.⁴

The confirmation of 1507 put the suspension of the " watch " on the Honte for the time being beyond the reach of effective attack, though not of criticism,⁵ and during the next few years Middelburg concentrated its attention on attempts to seduce the English Merchant Adventurers from their allegiance to Antwerp,⁶ and in preparing its campaign for the restoration of its staple-privilege. But the inaugura-

---

¹ *Ibid.*, no. 42, pp. 76-7, 157.
² This seems implied by the language of the preamble to the agreement with Frescobaldi, which also suggests that Middelburg's near neighbours and rivals, Veere, Flushing and Arnemuiden, had been campaigning against the sale of the " watch ". *Ibid.*, 77.
³ *Recueil des Ordonnances des Pays-Bas, 1506-1700*, I, 35-6.
⁴ The ordinance does not appear to have survived, but it is cited in a supplementary one of 3 Jan. 1509 on the same subject. *Ibid.*, 65-6.
⁵ The new lessee, Jan Willemszoon, complained of it in 1512 and secured a reduction of rent on account of it. Unger, 158.
⁶ Schanz, G., *Englische Handelspolitik gegen Ende des Mittelalters* (Leipzig, 1881), I, 53.

tion, early in 1515, of Charles as ruler of the Netherlands was the signal for a determined effort to have the "watch" restored. When Charles made his official entry into Zeeland he was met with a formidable list of grievances drawn up by the States. The list included three points relating to the toll of Iersekeroord. The first was a request that, in view of the continual disputes between the collectors and merchants, he would issue an ordinance stating clearly the incidence and amount of the toll and that a copy, "written on a board in plain letters", should be displayed at each "watch"; it was this request which led to the production of the great ordinance of 1519.[1] The second point related to the practice of the collector of demanding toll from Zeelanders, who were exempt, upon certain classes of goods which they bought in the Brabant markets on the ground that they were carrying these to "the highest markets, namely, Cologne, Wesel and Venlo"; this practice had been stopped by order of Duchess Margaret, but the petitioners wanted Charles to confirm its illegality. The third point concerned the "watch" on the Honte, which

> long has been and still is given over into the hands of those of Antwerp, contrary to the privileges of the land of Zeeland, for a small sum of money . . . to the prejudice of our gracious lord and to the destruction of the said land,

and concluded with a petition that Charles should remedy the situation "whether by redemption of the said toll or otherwise".[2]

To the first and second requests Charles replied by giving the promises desired; to the third he replied that he had sought and was still seeking the means to redeem the "watch" and that he hoped to be able to do so shortly.[3] In the event this last observation was not to remain merely the pious hope that it might have been. For what the States of Zeeland had petitioned for, the capital of Zeeland offered the means to realize. On 19 October 1515 Middelburg made an agreement with Charles by which, in return for a loan of 45,000 gulden, raised by the sale of annuities to the value of 3000 gulden a year, he undertook to devote this sum to the redemption of the "watches" of the Honte and of Bergen-op-Zoom.[4] By the end of the year Charles had redeemed the "watch" on the Honte from Antwerp, and it was reincorporated in the toll as leased from 12 January 1516.[5]

---

[1] See below, p. 69.
[2] Fruin, R., *De Keuren van Zeeland* (*Werken der Vereeniging tot uitgaaf der bronnen van het Oud-Vaderlandsche Recht gevestigd te Utrecht*, 2de reeks, No. 20, The Hague, 1920), 251-3.
[3] *Ibid.*, 255.
[4] *De Stoppelaar, op. cit.*, III, no. 1045, p. 5.
[5] Unger, 159. There are extant nine statements of receipts from the "watch" during the years 1518-20, totalling £3,281 13s. 7gr. Flemish. Fruin, R., *Rekeningen*, 307-13, 318-9.

Why was Antwerp prepared to forego in 1515 the privilege for which it had paid 30,000 gulden ten years before? The question is not an easy one, but there is one point which goes at least some way towards answering it. What Antwerp had purchased, or more correctly taken in mortgage, in 1505 was that part of the toll of Iersekeroord levied on ships using the Honte for direct navigation to Antwerp; the effect of the redemption was to render these ships again liable to toll. But in so far as they were English ships—and we know that many of them were—they were exempt from the toll under the treaty of 1506, concluded after Antwerp had made its original bargain with Philip the Fair. The renewal of this exemption as a result of the conference of Bruges in the summer of 1515[1] may thus have done something to reconcile Antwerp to the full re-establishment of the "watch". It is clear, however, that the town was not wholly satisfied with the new arrangement, for in 1518 it was envisaging the possibility of repurchasing the "watch".[2]

The "watch" on the Honte had not long been re-established when on 19 November 1519 there appeared the general ordinance on the administration of the toll promised by Charles V in 1515.[3] The ordinance falls into two parts. The first consists of an alphabetical list of goods, from "alum" to "vermilion", with the rate of toll by weight or quantity for every item, and concludes with a few general provisions, the first of which provides that any article not specified in the list is to pay at the rate of the one-hundred-and-twentieth penny (that is, about .8 per cent) *ad valorem,* "without prejudice to the right of the toil, which is based in the first instance on the twentieth penny." The other provisions confirmed Utrecht, Amersfoort and Kampen in their special privilege, fixed the rate of *roertol* at from one to eight groots according to the type of ship, reaffirmed the exemption from other Holland and Zeeland tolls conferred by payment of the present toll, ordered that the toll should be paid in Flemish money, and granted rebate on goods damaged by sea-water and on leakage of wine.

The second part of the ordinance, headed "Ordinance on Frauds", contains thirty-four clauses on the general administration of the toll. By the first clause all shippers, free or unfree, entering Zeeland with ships and goods were required, before unlading or breaking cargo, to anchor at the first principal "watch", declare their goods and obtain the collector's permission to proceed on their way. Clause two laid

[1] *Letters and Papers of Henry VIII,* II (1515-18), no. 723.
[2] Schanz, *op. cit.,* II, 244.
[3] Unger, no. 47, pp. 81-116.

the same duty on the masters of small craft receiving goods from "great ships". The penalty in both cases was the forfeiture of the ships and a fine of 50 gold "lions". Clauses 4 to 21 set out in detail the conditions governing the exemption of free goods from the toll. They were to be certified either by the production of their owner's *tolbrief* issued by his town, of which he must have been a resident citizen for a year and a day, or by his declaration; failing this, the amount of the toll due must be deposited and this would only be refunded upon the production within a specified time of proof that the goods were free. Clause 22 forbade shippers to seek out alternative routes with the object of avoiding the "watches" of the toll. Clauses 25 to 31 dealt with the conduct of the collectors; they were forbidden to demand more from shippers than was authorized by the present ordinance or to molest them in any way; they were not allowed to keep taverns or to sell wine or beer, and they were no longer to receive the presents of wine and victuals which they claimed to have had in the past, but were to pay for anything which they received. Clause 33 provided that in order to save merchants from being put to great costs in lawsuits against the collectors, the parties to any dispute arising out of the toll were in future to appear before the Rentmeester van Bewester Schelde or commissioners appointed by him. Save in special cases the decisions of this tribunal were to be final, and no other courts were to take cognisance of toll-cases. The final clause provided for the publication and observance of the ordinance.

The ordinance concluded with four supplementary sections. Two of these dealt respectively with certain weights and measures and with the rating of goods not listed in the "Zeeland tollbook"; the third enumerated 118 towns and 19 religious houses which were exempt from the toll; and the fourth comprised a special ordinance governing the collection of the *geleide* of Rooversberge.[1]

This great ordinance, which was to govern the administration of the toll during the next half-century and beyond that into the war-period, codified two hundred years' accumulation of ordinances and customs but did not itself introduce any notable change in the toll-regime. It did, however, include one provision relating to the "watch" on the Honte which may perhaps be regarded as the starting-point of

---

[1] This *geleyde van Rooversberge oft shertogen van Brabunt assyse* is a mystery which I do not pretend to be able to solve. I have met with no single reference to it outside this ordinance. The fact that it was levied on ships "commende uyt Schelt tusschen Eendracht of Tholensche gat ende Santvlietsche haevene" (De Stoppelaar, *op. cit.*, no. 1156) suggests that it may have been a relic of the medieval *geleiden* on the Scheldt.

a fresh development. Clause 3, after reciting that the principal "watches" were those of Iersekeroord, the Honte, Middelburg, Arnemuiden and Veere, declared that

those who navigate the Honte from the sea either upwards or downwards shall comply by speaking with and paying their toll at the "watch" on the Honte, unless in coming from the sea they meet with such stormy weather that they cannot without danger come to the tollhouse on the Honte nor the collector come in his boat to the ship, in which case the shipper, putting out a sign, may without penalty sail on to Antwerp, but may not break cargo there before he has given the collector on the Honte the information aforesaid [namely, as required by clause one] and acquitted himself of the toll . . . and if the shipper under colour of this shall commit any fraud or rebelliousness, sailing on when he might well anchor, he shall pay the same penalty as before.

It may be that this clause meant no more than it said. On the other hand it is at least possible that the otherwise remarkable silence which prevails during the next twelve years on the subject of the "watch" on the Honte is to be attributed to an interpretation of this clause which tacitly ignored its closing sentence. In that case, the final transference of the "watch" to Antwerp in 1532 would not have been so sharp a break with the existing situation.

There was a strong practical reason for the transaction of 1532. Since the end of the fifteenth century the north-eastern corner of Zuid-Beveland, where lay the toll-house of Iersekeroord, had been threatened with irreparable inundation. It is probable that the works in progress at Iersekeroord in 1496, towards the cost of which Middelburg agreed to make a yearly contribution, were undertaken to protect the toll-house against the waters.[1] Further repairs were in progress in 1530 on the eve of the final disaster.[2] On 5 November 1530 Holland and Zeeland experienced their worst inundation for fifty years. Both banks of the Scheldt suffered heavily; most of the villages between Bergen-op-Zoom and Lillo were submerged, and on the other side Reimerswaal was isolated and Iersekeroord had to be abandoned. Two years later another great inundation submerged for good the greater part of north-eastern Zuid-Beveland.

On 25 February 1532 the Emperor Charles V announced the transfer of the toll-house of Iersekeroord and of the "watch" on the Honte to Antwerp.[3] The change had doubtless been agreed upon in the course of the Emperor's visit to the Netherlands in the previous year,

[1] See above, p. 57.
[2] Fruin, R., *Rijks Archief-Depôt in de Provincie Zeeland. De rekeningen en andere stukken in 1607 uit de Hollandsche rekenkamer naar de Zeeuwsche overgebracht . . . 1433-1584* (The Hague, 1909), 332.
[3] Unger, no. 53, pp. 131-2.

but we do not know what inducement, if any, Antwerp had offered to secure it. On the face of it, the transfer was eminently justifiable. By far the greater part of the cargoes which contributed to the toll were being carried either to or from Antwerp, and it was the Antwerp money-market which was henceforward to raise the large annual rent of the toll. Antwerp thus had a strong claim to become the headquarters of the toll quite apart from any particular advantages which the town might expect to derive from the arrangement. Chief among these advantages was the transfer of the "watch" on the Honte to the town, although, as has been suggested, this may have been anticipated in practice during the previous decade. Here again the advantage was mutual, for it was probably becoming increasingly difficult to administer this "watch" on what was now the wide expanse of water at the eastern end of the Honte.

What is at first sight rather surprising is that the transaction apparently provoked so little opposition from Middelburg. The only recorded protest against it was made in 1548, on the occasion of the grant of a new lease of the toll. Then a deputation representing the three States of the island of Walcheren, and including the burgomasters and schepenen of Middelburg, represented to the Emperor

how it was understood that His Majesty had it in mind to lease the toll of Iersekeroord, with all its watches and dependencies, and to keep the principal bureau of the said toll at Antwerp, whereby it was to be expected that in course of time the toll would come to be reckoned as part of the domain of Brabant and thus alienated from the domain and revenues of Zeeland, which would be greatly to the prejudice and weakening of the land of Zeeland.[1]

The Emperor's answer, given on 16 October 1548, declared that the transfer of the headquarters of the toll to Antwerp had taken place in virtue of his own ordinance and that it should not operate to the disadvantage of Zeeland.[2] There the episode appears to have ended. What the States of Walcheren had raised was the constitutional issue involved in the transfer of the administration of a Zeeland revenue outside the borders of the County, and on this aspect of the matter the Emperor's reply could be regarded as satisfactory. But this was clearly the form rather than the substance of the complaint. Boxhorn, the editor of Reygersbergh's "Chronicle of Zeeland", in reporting the episode, reveals the true grounds of the Zeelanders' objection to the new regime when he adds that, since the toll was transferred, their trade had fallen by half because of the increase of direct navigation

---

[1] Smallegange, *op. cit.*, I, 166-7.
[2] Unger, no. 57, pp. 141-2.

to Antwerp.[1] Boxhorn was of course exaggerating both in his figure and in the importance which he attached to the transfer of the toll as a factor in the rise of this direct navigation, but so doubtless did the Zeelanders whose views he was expressing. This only makes it the more surprising that they did not clamour during these years for the re-establishment of the " watch " on the Honte.

The explanation seems to be that, after half-a-century of wasted effort, the Zeelanders had come to realize the futility of trying to use the " watch " on the Honte as a weapon against Antwerp. The campaign had, indeed, proved a conspicuous failure. The victory of 1504 had been largely neutralized by the mortgage of the " watch " in the following year, and even when Middelburg had succeeded in getting the " watch " fully re-established in 1515 the result had been disappointing. Moreover, if the " watch " was of little use as a weapon against Antwerp, it was of no use at all in the struggle against the rivals nearer home, the coastal ports of Walcheren, which were threatening to do to Middelburg what Middelburg would have liked to do to Antwerp. Since the early 1520's the Zeeland capital had been relying upon a new weapon in this struggle; it was a weapon which could also be turned against Antwerp. So it came about that the same year which saw the parting shot fired in the " battle of the Honte " saw a new battle joined, the " battle of the staple ".

The last of the major disputes over the toll of Iersekeroord presented the novel spectacle of Middelburg and Antwerp making common cause against a third party. Between 1547 and 1562 a new waterway was added to the network of the delta by the canalization of the Deurme, the river running north from Ghent and emptying into the Braakman west of the town of Axel.[2] This work, carried out by the magistracy of Ghent, was designed to fulfil the same purpose as the present Ghent-Terneuzen canal, that is, to provide a " short cut " between Ghent and the mouth of the Lower Scheldt in place of the long river-route through Antwerp and Dendermonde; the lock (*sas*) by which it was carried through the main dyke south-west of Axel took the name of the parent town and became known as Sas van Gent. In 1554, when the canal itself was finished but before the lock was built, Ghent petitioned Charles V to exempt its citizens' goods passing along the new waterway from all tolls, including the

[1] Smallegange, *op. cit.*, 167.
[2] The scheme is clearly described in the Emperor's patent of 26 May 1547 authorizing it. *Recueil des Ordonnances des Pays-Bas, 1506-1700*, I, 370-4.

toll of Zeeland.[1] Nothing came of this request, probably because of the Emperor's abdication the following year, but a few years later Ghent tried again. In spite of an adverse report by a commissioner appointed to examine the request, and the vigorous opposition of both Middelburg and Antwerp,[2] in August 1562 the Regent Margaret of Parma " par grace especiale " exempted those of Ghent from all tolls, including the toll of Zeeland, on goods brought in by way of the canal for distribution at Ghent. Foreign goods, and all goods passing down the canal, were, however, declared liable to toll, and a " watch " of the toll of Iersekeroord was established at Sas van Gent.[3] Middelburg and Antwerp continued to protest against the privilege thus granted, and Middelburg in addition objected to the constitutional impropriety of the collection in Flanders of a portion of Zeeland revenue.[4] But Ghent appears to have enjoyed the exemption until the outbreak of the Revolt deprived it of most of its value.

(iii) *The Middelburg Wine-Staple.*

Early in 1521 the magistrates of Middelburg addressed to the Emperor Charles V, then in the Netherlands, a doleful petition on the state of the town's trade. They reminded him that Middelburg had formerly been a flourishing town, able to support the Prince in his needs
tant en l'accord et payement de noz aydes comme au rachat du tonlieu de la Honte, pour lequel ilz ont baillé le seelle de la dite ville, et autrement en ce que leur a esté possible,
and in particular that when the town had held the lease of the toll of Iersekeroord it had been in a position to treat foreign merchants, especially those coming from the west,
gracieusement, et ou moyen de ce se rendoient plus enclins de hanter et frequenter la dite ville.
But, the petition went on, since the toll had passed out of the town's hands, the Western merchants had largely withdrawn, and had induced other foreign merchants to withdraw, from Middelburg to Veere, Antwerp, and elsewhere, and the town was " fère diminuée et amoindrie ". The magistrates asked the Emperor to restore Middelburg's fortunes by granting the town a right of staple over Western

---

[1] Unger, no. 59, pp. 143-4. This petition was evidently made on the expiry of the six-year exemption from toll on the new canal granted by Charles V to Ghent on 6 Feb. 1549. *Recueil des Ordonnances des Pays-Bas, 1506-1700*, I, 491-3.

[2] Unger, 146 *n* 2; De Stoppelaar, *op. cit.*, IV, nos. 2298-2300, p. 46.

[3] Unger, no. 61, pp. 146-7.

[4] *Ibid.*, 147, *n* 2.

goods, wine, wheat, iron, oil, and fruit, entering by the Wielingen or the Veergat, the channels on either side of Walcheren.[1]

The most significant feature of this petition is that, although it stressed the importance of the toll of Iersekeroord as a factor in driving trade from Middelburg, it aimed at bringing trade back, not by any fresh modification of the toll-regime, but by a device which was both older and newer; older, because Middelburg had once before exercised a right of staple over goods entering the Wielingen, newer, because the conditions in which the staple now demanded would operate would make it a very different institution from its predecessor. Foremost among these changed conditions was the navigability of the Honte, which allowed not only the foreign merchants but also their ships to abandon Middelburg in favour of Antwerp. The earlier staple had been designed to prevent transhipment off Walcheren without payment of toll; the staple now demanded would make transhipment compulsory for all Western cargoes going up to Antwerp. It therefore promised to be a much more effective weapon than the "watch" on the Honte had proved to be; moreover, unlike the "watch" it would serve to protect Middelburg not only against Antwerp but against the other Walcheren towns.

Middelburg had found fresh cause of complaint against these towns in the years before 1521 over the operation of the ordinance of 1508 instituting the compulsory measurement or "gauging" of imported wine. This ordinance had laid down that all wine brought into the Netherlands from Spain, France, or Burgundy must be measured by sworn officials before being sold, and that in the case of wine carried in foreign ships this was to be done at the port nearest to their place of entry. To the Spanish and Breton shippers who brought wine into Zeeland this was a most unwelcome innovation and they lost no time in exploiting the rivalry of the Walcheren towns by threatening to remove their trade elsewhere if it were not relaxed. Middelburg, which tried, or claimed to have tried, to enforce the ordinance, was soon complaining that it was losing its wine-trade to other towns, notably Veere and Flushing, which were less strict. Moreover, since wine was invariably brought in as part of a mixed cargo, the operation of the "gauge" system threatened to strike at the whole of Middel-

---

[1] De Stoppelaar, *op. cit.*, III, no. 1192, p. 48; Unger, *Bronnen*, III, no. 490, pp. 303-4. Middelburg supplemented the arguments used in the petition by distributing 1600 Rhenish gulden to persons about the court. Kesteloo, *loc. cit.*, VI, iii, 342.

burg's Western trade. The years 1510-20 were full of complaint and recrimination on the subject.¹

Middelburg's petition for a staple of Western wines, and of the other commodities which were usually carried with them, was thus partly conceived as a means of deliverance from the situation created by the ordinance of 1508. The demand must have been vigorously opposed from many quarters and the Emperor's decision to appoint a commission to consider it is probably to be regarded as a refusal.² Whether this commission reported or not, Middelburg did not secure the staple. Nor was the town to be any more successful when it revived the demand later in Charles V's reign.³ Yet, paradoxically, Middelburg was to find compensation for these failures in the evolution of the " gauge " system, which had originally operated so much to the town's disfavour.

From Middelburg's point of view the worst features of the ordinance of 1508 were the cut-throat competition to which it gave rise and the premium which that put on laxity in its enforcement. Both could be remedied by the designation of Middelburg as the sole port for the " gauge " of wines; secure in its monopoly, the town would then enforce the ordinance without fear or favour. It was this view which Middelburg pressed on the government during the years preceding the re-issue of the ordinance in 1523 and which the government, presumably in the belief that it offered the best prospect of enforcing the measure, appears to have accepted. Although the ordinance as re-issued merely repeated the stipulation that foreign wine must be measured at the " crane ", the instrument concerned, nearest to its place of entry, Middelburg proceeded with impunity to arrest a ship carrying wine for the household of the Lord of Veere which had not passed the " crane ", and followed this up by securing yet a further confirmation of the ordinance as a warning to any others who were disposed to challenge its new monopoly.⁴

Although such challenges would recur and even meet with some success, we may date from 1524 the establishment of Middelburg's right to be the sole town in Walcheren authorized to " gauge " foreign

---

¹ The ordinance for Zeeland, of 12 Oct. 1508, is no longer extant, but its tenor can be gathered from the ordinance for Flanders of 29 Sept. 1508 (*Recueil des Ordonnances des Pays-Bas, 1506-1700*, I, 56-7) and from the reissue of 25 June 1524 (Sneller, Z. W., and Unger, W. S., *Bronnen tot de geschiedenis van den handel met Frankrijk*, I (Rijks Geschiedk. Publ., 70, The Hague, 1930), no. 564, p. 323). For the disputes to which it gave rise see De Stoppelaar, *op. cit.*, II, pp. 263ff.
² *Ibid.*, no. 1192.
³ Unger, *Bronnen*, III, nos. 729, 731 (1555-6).
⁴ Sneller and Unger, *op. cit.*, I, nos. 562, 564, pp. 321, 323; De Stoppelaar, *op. cit.*, III, nos. 1235-6, 1264-6, 1269, 1276, pp. 61-73 *passim*.

wine. The town was now in a position to assert this right against the Brabant ports. It may have been the interruption of the wine trade arising from the war with France which postponed this next stage in the evolution of the " gauge " system; at all events it was the reopening of the French trade following the peace of 1537-8 which led to the first trial of strength. Middelburg seized the opportunity to enter into negotiatiation with La Rochelle, offering privileges in return for the exclusive handling of the French town's wine trade in the Netherlands. This offer La Rochelle declined by a letter of 4 October 1538, imprudently adding that it was already in negotiation with Bergen-op-Zoom.[1] Thereupon Middelburg decided to teach both towns a lesson about the wine-gauge. Having first secured from the Regent, the Emperor's sister Mary of Hungary, a provisional interpretation of the ordinance authorizing the arrest of any Rochelle ships which did not bring their cargoes to be gauged,[2] Middelburg stopped one of the ships as it sailed through the Roompot, the channel forming the mouth of the Scheldt, and brought it in to gauge its wine and to collect the duty (*craengelt*) payable.[3]

The first repercussions of this *coup* were eminently satisfactory to Middelburg. After a fruitless protest to the town itself, Bergen-op-Zoom brought a suit before the Great Council for the release of the ship. But in May 1539 the suit was withdrawn, presumably because it had no chance of succeeding, and in its place Bergen sued for a pardon, which was granted on 14 June, for its part in encouraging the Rochelle ships to ignore the gauge-regulations.[4] At this point Middelburg's victory seemed complete. But if Bergen was silenced, another town still had something to say. This was Zierikzee, which was the nearest port to the Roompot, as Middelburg was the nearest port to the Wielingen or Veergat, and which regarded that waterway with much the same proprietary air. Zierikzee had been almost as much disturbed by Middelburg's seizure of the wine-ship as Bergen itself, and it was Zierikzee which took the lead in 1540, on the occasion of Charles V's visit to the Netherlands, in pressing for the abolition of the gauge-privilege or, failing that, for an interpretation of it which would allow ships entering the Roompot to gauge their wine at Zierikzee. It was a petition to which the Emperor, fresh from his

---

[1] Unger, *Bronnen*, III, no. 567, p. 378.
[2] Sneller and Unger, *op. cit.*, I, no. 624, p. 362.
[3] Middelburg had also stationed a ship off Rammekens in case the Rochelle ships came in that way. Kesteloo, H. M., "De Stadsrekening van Middelburg, 1500-1549, in *Archief* . . . *uitgegeven door het Zeeuwsch Genootschap van Wetenschappen*, VI, iii (1888), 340-1.
[4] Sneller and Unger, *op. cit.*, I, nos. 626, 628, 629, pp. 363-5.

triumph over Ghent, the symbol of urban exclusiveness, might be expected to listen sympathetically. The Middelburg agent at Mechlin reported in October 1540 that he had been told that the Emperor " did not intend to make a staple of wine at Middelburg, like that at Dordrecht ".[1] Unfortunately there is no evidence how, or whether, Charles settled the question. The ordinance of 1508 was certainly not annulled, but whether the Emperor gave it any other interpretation than that which Middelburg had successfully upheld in 1539 we do not know.

Six years later, however, Zierikzee carried its point. On 12 May 1546 Charles V prohibited the import of French wine into the Netherlands without his special permission. Two months later he confirmed this ordinance, but gave French merchants leave to bring their wine into Zeeland on condition that they stapled it at Middelburg or Zierikzee and nowhere else, and then only at specified times and seasons. At the same time the Emperor informed the Schout of Antwerp that French wine would be allowed to enter Brabant by water provided it were stapled at Antwerp or Bergen-op-Zoom under similar time-restrictions.[2] The new ordinance was clearly intended as a compromise between the system of 1508 and the single-town system advocated by Middelburg; it is, however, noteworthy, in view of the coming legal battle between Middelburg and Antwerp, that what the new ordinance conferred on the two Zeeland and the two Brabant towns was a right of staple, that is, of the first sale of the commodity in question, and not merely the right of gauge which Middelburg (and perhaps Zierikzee) already enjoyed. But this did not redeem it in the eyes of Middelburg, which promptly objected both to the inclusion of Zierikzee and to the times and conditions laid down. This time, however, the Regent's interpretation of the ordinance was unfavourable to Middelburg; it confirmed Zierikzee in the right of staple over wine entering through the Roompot and confined Middelburg's right to wine passing before Arnemuiden.[3] Two years later Middelburg suffered a worse set-back. After gaining the verdict in a suit against the Lord of Veere over the compulsory unlading of some cargoes of wine at his towns of Veere and Flushing Middelburg had the mortification of learning that the Regent had provisionally allowed that nobleman (he was Maximilian of Burgundy, member of an illegitimate

---

[1] Unger, *Bronnen*, III, no. 583, p. 393.
[2] Sneller and Unger, *op. cit.*, I, nos. 670, 672, pp. 394-5; *Recueil des Ordonnances des Pays-Bas, 1506-1700*, V, 266-7, 320-1.
[3] Sneller and Unger, *op. cit.*, I, nos. 674-7, pp. 398-9.

branch of the ruling house) to have the wine-ships unladen in his ports without stapling their cargoes at Middelburg.[1]

These failures against its Zeeland neighbours must have made the town the more determined to assert its right against Antwerp and Bergen-op-Zoom. In 1548 Middelburg arrested off Flushing a ship laden with French wine belonging to a merchant of Paris and brought it in for "gauging". The ship itself belonged to Antwerp and it was carrying the wine there. Thereupon Antwerp brought a suit against Middelburg before the Great Council of Mechlin. The suit rivalled in importance that of 1504, and the Great Council took almost exactly as long to pronounce a decision.

Antwerp rested its case in general on the freedom which shipping coming up to its harbour had always enjoyed from any right of staple or gauge, and in particular on its designation, with Bergen-op-Zoom, in the ordinance of 1546 as the staple-place for wine entering Brabant. Middelburg began by citing the staple-right granted to it by William VI in 1405; the town admitted that this had been allowed to lapse, but pointed to the confirmations of its right of gauge in 1524, 1538 and 1546 as the basis of its present claim. Antwerp countered by asserting that Middelburg's right extended only to wine freighted for Zeeland and not to wine going elsewhere, as the cargo in question was; otherwise the Emperor's grant of a wine-staple to Antwerp would be meaningless. But Middelburg insisted that the ordinance of 1524 covered all wine entering the Zeeland waters, wherever bound, and supported this interpretation by referring to the expense which it regularly incurred in the upkeep of dykes and other works essential to the safety of the waterway to Antwerp. On 23 July 1556 the Great Council gave judgment in favour of Antwerp. Nothing daunted, Middelburg then pleaded error in the proceedings; the question at issue was not, as the verdict implied, whether Middelburg enjoyed a right of staple, but whether it had the right of gauge, over wine passing through Zeeland on its way to Brabant. After referring the case to a commission, the Great Council reversed its decision, declaring that Middelburg possessed the right of gauge and that Antwerp had therefore no legal grounds for proceeding against the arrest of the ship in question. The further pleading had occupied three years; the second verdict was pronounced on 25 October 1559.[2]

The legal distinction which had led the court to reverse its first decision is clear enough. The ordinance of 1508, confirmed in 1524,

[1] *Ibid.*, no. 688, p. 407, and *n* 2.
[2] *Ibid.*, I, no. 755, p. 455.

had made the gauging of foreign wine compulsory at the port nearest to the place of entry. In the case of the Wielingen, this port was Middelburg (that is, if Flushing was not to be recognized for this purpose); Middelburg's authority to gauge wine destined for Brabant had been upheld in 1538, and the final decision of 1559 accorded with this precedent. On the other hand, Middelburg had been granted the right of staple simultaneously with Antwerp, and the two grants were compatible only if the one were limited to wine freighted to Zeeland and the other to wine freighted for Brabant and merely passing through Zeeland to reach its destination.

Technically, therefore, the decision of 1559 confirmed Middelburg in the possession of two distinct rights over imported wine, a right of gauge over all wine entering the Wielingen or Veergat, and a right of staple over that part of it destined for sale in Zeeland. But in practice the two were indistinguishable. No sooner had Middelburg secured the verdict than it took steps to enforce the right of gauge.[1] It stationed a "pink", manned by 25 or 30 men, in the Wielingen with orders to stop and visit all ships entering from the West. Ships with no wine on board were allowed to go their way, but those carrying wine, no matter how small the quantity, had to have it gauged at Middelburg. The shallowness of the waterway, the Arne, leading to Middelburg prevented most of the ships concerned from coming up to the wharf where stood the "crane", so that the wine had to be taken out of the ships, carried in small craft to Middelburg to be gauged, and then, if it were destined for Brabant, brought back and reladen. This was inconvenient enough in any case; it was particularly so in the case of ships carrying only one or two vats of wine, usually in the form of ballast, because a large part of the cargo might have to be shifted before the wine could be taken out. In addition to the waste of time and energy, the process generally involved some loss of wine through damage to the casks; this loss might equal the loss sustained in the entire voyage from France or Spain.[2]

Few shippers, forced to discharge their cargo of wine at Middelburg, would have chosen to incur the further loss involved in relading it for carriage elsewhere; they would be content to leave it there to be sold and to carry the rest of their cargo up the Honte. It was for this reason that the confirmation of Middelburg's right of gauge was in practice equivalent to the grant to the town of a right of staple over all

---

[1] See the instructions to the "crane-master", of 2 Dec. 1559, in Unger, *Bronnen*, III, no. 768, p. 723.

[2] De Stoppelaar, *op. cit.*, IV, no. 2248, pp. 27-8.

wine entering the Wielingen. Middelburg had of course foreseen this result when in 1556 it shifted the issue in the suit with Antwerp from the right of staple to the right of gauge. What mattered was that all wine-cargoes should be forced to come to Middelburg; officially they might come there only to be measured, in practice they would remain there to be sold. The result fully justified the town's expectations. During the twelve years which were all that remained of the old regime in the Netherlands Middelburg remained the principal entrepôt for French and Spanish wines; and when the Zeelanders afterwards claimed that they had then enjoyed a wine-staple they were guilty of nothing more than a terminological inexactitude.

It was not to be expected that Antwerp would suffer in silence what was certainly its worst reverse in the "Scheldt question" since the verdict of 1504. Whether the town made any attempt to neutralize the effect of the decision by a "deal" similar to that of 1505 we do not know;[1] it certainly protested both against the decision and the way in which Middelburg carried it out.[2] Given time, Antwerp would probably have found the means of removing this obstacle to the freedom of the Lower Scheldt, as it had removed all others in the past. But within a few years Antwerp was facing dangers beside which the defeat of 1559 shrank into insignificance. The question seems to have been raised for the last time in the course of the trade-conference with England in 1565-6.[3] The Netherlands then already stood on the verge of revolution.

---

[1] In June 1561 the Regent was trying to solve the problem "par voye aymable". Sneller and Unger, *op. cit.*, I, p. 475 *n* 3.
[2] *Ibid.*, no. 757, p. 471.
[3] De Stoppelaar, *op. cit.*, IV, nos. 2376, 2389, 2392, 2416.

PART TWO
THE CLOSURE, 1572—1780

CHAPTER FOUR

The Eighty Years' War, 1572—1648

DURING the half-century preceding the Revolt of the Netherlands Antwerp had gone far towards solving the problem of securing its seaward traffic from interference or extortion. True, in the last years Middelburg had shown that it was still a foe to be reckoned with, and its wine-staple threatened to develop into a serious infraction of the freedom of the Scheldt. Given time, however, Antwerp would doubtless have proved as capable of disposing of this as of earlier hindrances to its navigation.

But Antwerp's enjoyment of unhindered use of the Scheldt, and of the commercial pre-eminence which went with it, rested upon one prime condition. In the words of Prims, " what ensured that, despite the stubborn particularism of the different communities which made up the united principalities, the sea-route to Antwerp remained substantially free, was the fact that the same ruler was master of the mouth of the Honte and of the lands higher up the river, including Antwerp itself ".[1] This political unity, then more than a century old, the men of the 'fifties and 'sixties took completely for granted; it did not occur to Guicciardini, for example, to make any reference to it in his survey. Yet when Guicciardini wrote its days were already numbered. Within a generation the political unity of the Scheldt delta was to be broken, and the power of the state, instead of serving to curb the economic feuds within it, was to be used to intensify and perpetuate them. In the conditions thus created Antwerp was to find herself facing dangers far graver than any which had threatened in the past and far beyond the power of the old remedies to dispel. Before the century was out the Scheldt was closed and Antwerp's long imprisonment had begun. The course and conditions of that imprisonment are the subject of this and the following chapter.

(i) *To the fall of Antwerp, 1572-85.*

To the historian of the Scheldt the two landmarks of the Revolt are the rebels' seizure of Flushing on 6 April 1572 and Parma's recovery of Antwerp on 17 August 1585. If the first gave the rebels that command of the mouth of the river which they were never to lose, the

[1] Prims, Fl., " De geschiedenis der Schelde ", in *Bull. Soc. Roy. de Géog. d'Anvers*, LVII (1937), 143.

second ordained that Antwerp was to be its chief victim. Between the two dates lies a confused period during which the future of the Scheldt, like that of the Revolt as a whole, hung in the balance.[1]

During the first four years, when the Revolt was confined to Holland and Zeeland, the situation on the river broadly anticipated that which was to follow the fall of Antwerp in 1585. Both sides did their best to prevent, or at least to control, the passage of supplies to the enemy or to enemy-occupied territory. Although these measures involved considerable interference with navigation, they did not put a stop to it, either on the Scheldt or elsewhere.[2] On the Spanish side they largely broke down before the determination of the traders, among whom sympathy with the rebels was strong and whose livelihood was at stake, to carry on "business as usual", while almost from the outset the rebel government aimed not so much at prohibiting trade with the enemy as at subjecting it to control and taxation.

In the first months of the Revolt the Zeeland rebels were able to maintain their fleet out of the proceeds of their privateering campaign at the mouth of the Scheldt. But this campaign soon defeated its own end by driving neutral trade off the river, and it then became necessary to find a permanent source of revenue. In the winter of 1572-3 the States of Zeeland therefore took over and regularized the "licences" previously levied by individual towns on exports to the enemy. The province of Holland similarly took over from its towns the "convoys" (their Dutch form, *geleiden,* reveals that, like the medieval tolls of that name, they were in theory levied in return for protection) and converted them into permanent duties. After an experimental period "convoys and licences" became in both provinces a dual system of import- and export-duties, "convoys" being levied on imports from neutral territory and "licences" on imports from and exports to enemy-occupied territory.[3] The rebels thus early accepted the necessity of trading with the enemy both as a means of livelihood and as a source of revenue. As far as the Scheldt was concerned, the decision sprang from a recognition of the essential economic unity of the delta-region. For in 1572 the internal and transit-trade was still, as it had been for two cen-

---

[1] Dr. J. H. Kernkamp has made the most detailed study of the trading relations between the rebel provinces and the remainder of the Netherlands in his two volumes entitled *De handel op den vijand, 1572-1609* (Utrecht, n.d.), on which I have drawn heavily for this chapter. The naval side of the story is dealt with in Grol, H. G. van, *Het Beheer van het Zeeuwsche Zeewezen 1577-1587* (Flushing, 1936).

[2] Nor did the Zeelanders' sole attempt at a physical "closure" of the Scheldt, by sinking ships in the channel opposite Lillo, in the winter of 1572-3. Mertens and Torfs, *Geschiedenis van Antwerpen,* IV, 481.

[3] Kernkamp, *op. cit.,* I, 26-32.

turies, the foundation of Zeeland's commercial position, and it was this trade which was to persist throughout the eighty years of war despite every obstacle, including the heavy burden of taxation.

But to Antwerp the transit-trade was only one part, and perhaps no longer the most important part, of her total trade. In the half-century before 1572 a large and growing proportion of Antwerp's overseas trade had been carried direct from the sea up the Scheldt.[1] It was to this direct trade that the Revolt dealt the heaviest, and as it was to prove the fatal, blow. The rebels' capture of Flushing and of the neighbouring ports put this trade at their mercy, and after their seizure in June 1572 of a Portuguese spice-fleet valued at half-a-million gulden it virtually came to an end. The foreign merchant communities who monopolized this trade were then compelled to accept the best terms they could get from the rebel government for its resumption, but since in doing so they came under the Spanish government's ban on dealings with the rebels the stoppage of direct trade lasted almost uninterruptedly until 1576. The alternative route through one of the Flemish sea-ports and then overland or by interior waterways through Flanders, although now, as later, it gave the rebels anxiety, was no substitute for the highway of the Scheldt.[2]

The autumn of 1576 brought a dramatic change in the situation. If for Antwerp this change was heralded by the awful convulsion of the "Spanish Fury", it also held the promise of deliverance from the slow strangulation of the last four years. The "Pacification of Ghent" of November 1576, by which the hitherto loyal provinces joined Holland and Zeeland in a programme of resistance to arbitrary rule, went far towards restoring the old political unity of the delta-lands and envisaged the re-establishment of freedom of traffic on the Scheldt. Temporarily traffic remained suspended owing to the presence of the Spanish troops at Antwerp, but when these were paid off and left the country in the spring of 1577 the prospects were brighter than at any time since 1572. The next two or three years did, indeed, bring something of a revival, especially of direct overseas trade. But even before 1582, when the triumphant progress of Parma's campaign for the recovery of the Netherlands first seriously menaced the town, the loss of most of its hinterland together with the general dislocation of trade had begun to spell its ruin. As late as 1582 large merchant fleets were still to be seen on the Scheldt—forty sail from Spain and

[1] See above, pp. 63-4.
[2] For the efforts of the Merchant Adventurers, supported by the English government, to maintain their trade with Antwerp, including the negotiation of the agreement of 15 March 1573 with Spain, see Kernkamp, *op. cit.*, I, chap. I *passim*.

Portugal came up to the Pinxtenmarkt of that year[1]—but it was the last year of anything resembling normal trading conditions. The next opened ominously with the " French Fury ", while the loss of Dunkirk in July, by leading Zeeland to intensify its measures against suspect trade, still further worsened Antwerp's commercial position. But by then the end was very near.[2]

Before 1583 was out Parma had taken Sas van Gent, Hulst and Rupelmonde, the last lying on the Scheldt only a few miles above Antwerp. Bruges fell in the spring of 1584, and by the early summer the enemy had appeared on both sides of the river below Antwerp; the States' unfinished fort of Liefkenshoek, on the left bank, fell in July, and Lillo on the opposite bank was closely invested. After his capture of Ghent (17 September) Parma established himself at Calloo and before the end of the month had begun his preparations to complete Antwerp's isolation. The story of the eleven months' siege has often been told, and there is no need to repeat it here.[3] The celebrated bridge across the Scheldt which sealed the town's fate was completed, in the face of every difficulty, in February 1585; Parma foiled all efforts to capture or destroy it and on 17 August 1585 Antwerp made its submission.

(ii) *The war, 1585-1648.*

The surrender of Antwerp left the twin forts of Lillo and Liefkenshoek,[4] lying on either side of the Scheldt some ten miles below the city, as the limit of the Northerners' control of the river. From here up to Antwerp it was commanded by several Spanish forts, among them the Kruisschans, on the right bank about one and a half miles above Lillo, and Forts St. Philip and St. Mary, on each side of the river between the Kruisschans and Antwerp. So the position remained until the armistice of 1607, which was concluded in a yacht lying off

---

[1] Mertens and Torfs, *op. cit.*, V, 305. The movement of shipping in the port during these years is described in the series of letters written from Antwerp to Cologne between 1581 and 1584 and published by J. F. Willems in his *Mengelingen*, 89ff.

[2] In 1581, after the marquisate of Flushing had been confiscated by decree of the Court of Holland, the Antwerp magistracy considered the possibility of acquiring it and thus securing an outpost at the mouth of the river. In the upshot, the marquisate was sold to the Prince of Orange; even if Antwerp had secured it in 1581, it would certainly have been confiscated again in 1585. See Hooft, *Nederlandsche Historiën* (A'dam, 1642), XVIII boek, 771.

[3] The most recent authoritative account is that by L. van der Essen in his *Alexandre Farnèse, Prince de Parme*, IV (Brussels, 1935).

[4] Liefkenshoek was recovered by the States in April 1585 after its loss the previous July. For the location of the forts mentioned in the text see map facing p. 96.

Lillo,[1] brought hostilities to an end. This was followed by the Twelve Years' Truce of 1609, which adopted the military line as a temporary political frontier. On the renewal of the war in 1621 the Scheldt again became a theatre of operations. In 1627 the States strengthened their position by building two more forts, Frederick Henry and Blauwgaren, some distance below Lillo and Liefkenshoek. Five years later William of Nassau opened his unlucky campaign for the capture of Antwerp by taking the Kruisschans, and this fort, surviving a Spanish attempt to recover it in 1640, remained the furthest outpost of the Northerners on the Scheldt for the remainder of the war. Between and around these forts stretched the waste of waters created by the breaching of the dykes during the siege of Antwerp; not until after 1648 were these dykes repaired and the river confined to its old limits.

Meanwhile the tide of war had ebbed and flowed on both sides of these key-positions. On the right bank the States' fortress of Bergen-op-Zoom had survived two strenuous sieges, but further east Breda was for twelve years in Spanish hands and a special squadron was then necessary on the interior waters to contain the enemy on this side. On the left bank thrust and counter-thrust followed one another more rapidly. In 1583, before the loss of Antwerp, the rebels had occupied Biervliet and Terneuzen; Biervliet was especially valuable for its command of the Braakman, the broad waterway which communicated, through Sas van Gent and the Gentsche Vaart canal with the town of Ghent and a broad stretch of Flanders, as well as with Antwerp by way of the Scheldt through Dendermonde. The States' fortification of Biervliet, begun in 1589, was finished in 1603. Meanwhile, in 1586, Prince Maurice had taken Axel and covered it by a fort, which took his name, on the Braakman opposite the Spanish fort of Philippine, half-way between Biervliet and Sas van Gent. In 1591 he took Hulst, only to lose it in 1596; but in 1603 he greatly strengthened the States' control of the approaches to Ghent by capturing Philippine, and in the following year he crowned his campaigns in this theatre by recovering Sluis, lost to Parma in 1587, and thus closing the Zwin. It was not until forty years later that his brother and successor Frederick Henry rounded off these conquests by capturing Sas van Gent and recovering Hulst. These successes secured for the Republic at the peace settle-

[1] Ermerins, J., " Eerste Stichting en Lotgevallen van sommige plaatsen ten oosten en westen der Schelde gelegen ", in *Verhandelingen uitgegeven door het Zeeuwsch Genootschap der Wetenschappen te Vlissingen*, V (Middelburg, 1776), 16. This article traces the history of all the forts mentioned.

ment a continuous strip of territory, States-Flanders or Zeeland-Flanders, on the left bank of the Scheldt estuary.[1]

For almost the entire period under review, therefore, the strong points of Lillo-Liefkenshoek on the Scheldt and Biervliet-Philippine on the Braakman were the keys of the States' position on this front. Here were concentrated their naval forces. After the fall of Antwerp they kept upwards of thirty ships, known as the " fleet " (a name inherited by the single guardship which replaced them after 1648), permanently stationed at Lillo, and a smaller squadron at Biervliet, both reinforced from time to time to meet threatened attack. For Parma, and after him Spinola, laboured to build up on the rivers a naval force powerful enough to break through the States' defences, which were only kept intact at the cost of such bloody conflicts as that of 29/30 November 1600 and the Battle of the Slaak of August 1631.[2]

It was across the watery " no man's land " above Lillo and Philippine that the bulk of the trade between the warring provinces had to be conducted. (The alternative route, through the Flemish sea-ports, was prohibited by the States-General to its subjects in view of the risk of capture and the impossibility of exercising any real control over it.) Of its vital importance to both sides the persistence of this trade in the face of every difficulty is proof enough. The Southern provinces could by no means dispense with the supplies, especially of foodstuffs, which came to them, however enhanced in price, from the North; even the temporary withholding of foodstuffs by the States-General could reduce the South to famine conditions, as in the winter of 1585-6, and seriously hinder military operations. To the Earl of Leicester, during his brief governorship of the United Provinces (1585-7), the situation seemed logically to demand the rigorous use of this potent weapon of blockade to harass the enemy. But this view ignored the fact that Holland and Zeeland were scarcely less dependent upon this trade than were Brabant and Flanders; if the goods themselves were essential to the South, the proceeds of their sale, both in the form of trading-returns and of state-revenue, were vital to the North. An English observer recognized this in 1588 when he wrote:

But herein doth appear their weakness and insufficiency of means, that they are constrained, for the levy of money, by licences to permit traffic with the

---

[1] See map facing p. 96. Strictly speaking, the name Zeeland-Flanders dates only from 1814, when this territory was incorporated in Zeeland (see below, pp. 160-1), but as it is much more familiar than " States-Flanders " I have used it throughout.

[2] For the naval organization on the Spanish side see Denucé, J., " De Admiraliteit van de Schelde te Antwerpen van de 16e tot de 18e eeuw " in *Antwerpsch Archievenblad* (2de reeks), VII (1932), 289-313; VIII (1933), 13-38.

enemy, and so to victual him to their own prejudice, that in a manner the money levied cannot do them so much good as the furnishing of the enemy with things necessary doth them harm.[1]

Although during the later stages of the war the expansion of Dutch overseas trade diminished the importance of trade with the Southern provinces, other factors, and notably the jealousy between Zeeland and Holland, then helped towards the maintenance of the policy of trading with the enemy.

It was the Spanish government which from time to time took the initiative in attempting to put a stop to this trade. The prohibitory ordinances of 9 February 1599 and 24 November 1600 remained in force until 5 April 1603 and were again brought into operation on 12 March 1605;[2] a similar ordinance issued on 29 July 1625 remained in force until 8 May 1629.[3] On the rebels' side the Earl of Leicester's severe placard of 4 April 1586 was quickly suspended by the States-General following his departure, but the Spanish ordinances of 1599 and 1625 both provoked retaliatory prohibitions from The Hague. None of these measures remained effective for more than a few months, after which it was either openly revoked or quietly forgotten. Alongside this series of ordinances, therefore, must be read the complementary series legalising and regulating trade with the enemy. On both sides the regulations laid down in this second series were designed to serve two purposes, to derive governmental revenue from the trade, and to prevent assistance to the enemy, either through traffic in those articles, such as munitions of war, which were always prohibited, or through treasonable relations under the cloak of business dealings.

On the side of the United Provinces, the fiscal motive was served by the system of " convoys and licences ". " Convoys " were levied *ad valorem* on the import and export trades with neutral countries, as well as on imports from the enemy, that is Spain (including Portugal) and the Southern Netherlands; since the volume of imports from the Southern provinces during the war was small, " convoys " were not of great importance on the Scheldt. It was otherwise with their counterpart, " licences ", which were *ad valorem* duties, payable at the port of lading, on all exports to enemy countries as well as to adjacent territories from which the enemy might seek to provision himself. On the principle that the enemy ought to pay dear for supplies, licences were

---

[1] *Cal. S. P. For., 1588 July-December,* 254.
[2] *Placcaeten van Brabandt,* I, 290, 298, 315, 321; on the earlier ordinances see Kernkamp, *op. cit.,* II.
[3] Brants, V., ed., *Recueil des Ordonnances des Pays-Bas . . . 1597-1621* (Brussels, 2 vols., 1909-12), I, 46-9, 115-7, 203-10, 262.

fixed at high rates, being generally four or five times as heavy as
" convoys "; this difference in rate, and the greater volume of trade on
which they were levied, made the " licences " on the Scheldt trade of
much greater account than the " convoys ".

It was under these " licences " that the export trade to the South
was resumed in 1587 and carried on, with brief intervals of suspension,
down to 1648. The working of the licence-system was greatly complicated by the fact that the entire Scheldt estuary as far as the military
frontier lay within the territory of the province of Zeeland. With the
day-to-day administration of trade-control at the frontier largely in their
hands the Zeelanders were under a perpetual temptation to advance
their own interests at the expense of the other provinces, and above all
Holland, of whose ascendancy they grew more jealous in measure as
it increased. Thus no sooner was trade reopened with the South in
1587 than Zeeland proceeded of its own accord to levy a licence on all
ships passing through its waters towards the enemy. To the
Hollanders, who had already paid licences on lading, this was an out-
rage, and there followed three years of recrimination and reprisals
between The Hague and Middelburg. Finally, in April 1590, by a
" provisional accord " for one year, afterwards regularly renewed,
although not without further crises, the two provinces agreed that
goods exported to enemy territory through Zeeland should pay half the
licence due at their port of lading and half on passing through the
Zeeland waters. This was the origin of the " Zeeland half-licence ",
which was later redeemed by Holland by an annual payment.[1] The
agreement of 1590 also provided for the appointment of Holland commissioners in Zeeland, and of Zeeland commissioners in Holland, to
supervise its operation.

During the war the States-General frequently suspended the issue
of licences for trade with any part of the Southern provinces in which
enemy troops were operating. Thus during the two Spanish sieges
of Bergen-op-Zoom in 1588 and 1632 trade with Brabant and Flanders
was prohibited, and the attempted relief of Breda in 1625 was supported by a suspension of licences for the export of victuals to Antwerp,
Ghent and Bruges. Such temporary prohibitions were as unwelcome
to the Colleges of Admiralty, which depended on the revenue from
convoys and licences to pay their way, as they were to the merchants
whose trade was thus periodically interrupted, and each College attempted to interpret them, within its area of jurisdiction, in a manner

---

[1] Kernkamp, *op. cit.*, II, 72-3; for the redemption of the " half-licence " see *Neder-landsche Jaarboek*, 1753, I, 277ff.

as little prejudicial as possible both to its own finances and to local commercial interests, at the same time condemning similar manœuvres by other Colleges. Here again the persistent rivalry of Holland and Zeeland provoked continual disputes, culminating in the violent denunciation by Holland of Zeeland's premature resumption of the issue of licences for the Antwerp trade in 1635 following their suspension for the siege of Schenkenschans. Thereafter Holland refused to countenance any further suspensions and trade with the enemy continued without interruption until the end of the war.

The trade between North and South was burdened with a similar system of licences levied by the Brussels government. Here the emphasis was on the import rather than on the export side. The ordinances of 6 December 1592 and 20 March 1593 allowed any subject holding a passport to trade with the rebels, except in certain goods, on payment of licence.[1] Revised by the ordinances of 12 and 14 August 1598[2] and reintroduced after each of the short-lived prohibitions, this system remained in operation, with periodical changes in the rates of duty, throughout the remainder of the war. Like convoys and licences in the North, licences soon became too important an item of revenue in the South to be lightly cast aside, and it was with obvious reluctance that Brussels followed Madrid in periodically prohibiting the trade which yielded them.[3]

On both sides these war-time duties were an addition to the tolls in existence in 1572, including the toll of Iersekeroord, or toll of Zeeland as it was now invariably called, which both governments continued to levy on the Scheldt trade. In the North this was now collected by the States of Zeeland, which in January 1597 issued a new set of regulations to improve its yield.[4] These provided for the stationing of collectors at Lillo, Fort Maurice and Hofstede (covering Sluis, then still in enemy hands), that is, at the posts already occupied by the collectors of licences, and the payment of toll before transhipment. The confirmation of all existing exemptions meant that the toll fell mainly on foreign goods, since natives were nearly all free of it. On the Spanish side the collection was similarly regulated by an ordinance of 1587. The Brussels government suspended the levy of the toll during the Truce but reimposed it on 1 July 1623.[5] In 1644 the towns

---

[1] Kernkamp, *op. cit.*, II, 99-101.
[2] Brants, *op. cit.*, I, 20-6.
[3] Lonchay, H. and Cuvelier, J., *Correspondance de la Cour d'Espagne sur les affaires des Pays-Bas au XVIIe siècle* (6 vols., Brussels, 1923-37), I, 18, 224; II, 142, 164.
[4] Hogendorp, *De Flumine Scaldi Clauso*, 68 n 68.
[5] *Placcaeten van Brabandt*, I, 442.

of Antwerp and Ghent, in an effort to revive trade by lightening the burdens upon it, purchased their freedom from the whole complicated system of tolls then in force;[1] but the malady which afflicted them was beyond the power of this traditional remedy to cure.[2]

If on both sides trade with the enemy on payment of heavy duties was much better than no trade with the enemy, the prospect of trading at war prices without paying those duties was still more attractive, and the smuggler was everywhere at work. On both sides every variety of fraud was practised to evade payment and to deal in prohibited wares. It was chiefly with the object of combating these widespread evasions, which assisted the enemy both directly, by provisioning him, and indirectly, by diminishing the resources out of which he was fought, that the United Provinces early introduced the compulsory transhipment of goods at the military frontier. In its inception a Zeeland measure directed against the alleged infraction by the Hollanders of the partial prohibition of trade in 1587, the system was adopted by the States-General on 1 September 1588 and remained in force throughout the war. It involved the concentration of trade at points on the military frontier where it could be enforced. Two such points presented themselves, Lillo-Liefkenshoek on the Scheldt and Biervliet-Philippine on the Braakman; commanding the waterways to Antwerp and Ghent, both positions were guarded by their forts and naval squadrons. The Zeelanders would have preferred to make Biervliet-Philippine, over which they had the greater direct control, the sole route, but the Hollanders would not forego the contact with the Antwerpers which the ascent of the Scheldt to Lillo afforded.[3] Thus there came to be stationed at Lillo and Biervliet the inspectors and controllers of convoys and licences appointed by the Zeeland Admiralty, together with the commissioner from Holland under the Accord of 1590. Their duties were to examine the certificates of shippers with cargoes from the United Provinces to make sure that their licences had been paid and in the case of those from Holland to receive the "Zeeland half-licence"; to collect the convoys due on goods brought in from the South; and to watch all the cargoes being transhipped in order to check them by their bills of lading and to detect any prohibited goods. Cer-

---

[1] Mertens and Torfs, *op. cit.*, V, 465; VI, 158.
[2] The Scheldt trade also had to bear local dues such as the 20 shillings per cargo levied by the shippers' guild of Arnemuiden, half of which went to the poor and half to the guild. "Regestenlist van het oud-archief der gemeente Arnemuiden", in *Verslagen omtrent 's Rijks Oude Archieven*, XLVIII, ii. (1925), 473.
[3] Kernkamp, *op. cit.*, I, 215.

tain goods, notably foodstuffs, were usually exempted from transhipment to avoid damaging them.[1]

Clearly this system could only be worked in collaboration with the Southerners, whose ships had to be ready at the transhipment-points to deliver and receive the cargoes; hence we find the Southern authorities arranging matters from their side. An Antwerp ordinance of 29 July 1595 regulated the participation of Antwerp ships in the transhipment at Lillo,[2] and this was followed, after the prohibition of trade from 1599 to 1602, by an ordinance of the Brussels government on the subject on 17 September 1602. This made transhipment at Lillo compulsory for all goods save those, like fresh herring, salt, silk and wine, which would suffer in the process. Antwerp shippers were to keep a sufficient number of well-conditioned vessels always at Lillo to receive the goods, including *waterschepen* for fresh fish and other perishables, and these were to leave for their destinations as soon as laden. Enemy ships carrying exempted goods up to Antwerp were to be visited at the Kruisschans and their masters were to pay caution-money for their good behaviour while in Southern territory.[3] When in May 1607 the Archdukes, at the urgent appeal of Bruges, gave that town leave to reopen trade with the enemy, forbidden since March 1605, it was on condition that goods were transhipped at the forts on the Zwin between Bruges and Sluis.[4]

The system of transhipment appears to have worked fairly successfully during the war. On both sides it facilitated control of the trade, so necessary from the political and fiscal standpoints. To the United Provinces it had the further advantage that the sudden prohibitory ordinances which Madrid, and following Madrid Brussels, from time to time launched against their trade did not expose their ships to confiscation in South Netherland ports. The shippers of Antwerp and Ghent profited by a system which gave them a share in the trade which would otherwise have fallen entirely into the hands of the Northerners. If anyone suffered, it was the importers on both sides who sometimes found that goods had been damaged through transhipment.

Throughout the war, save for brief intervals of prohibition, trade between the sundered Netherlands lived on. But of any resumption

---

[1] The concentration of traffic at Lillo and Biervliet also facilitated postal censorship; see Grotius' letter of 6 Aug. 1622 to the States of Zeeland complaining of the opening of his letters there. Molhuysen, P. C., ed. *Briefwisseling van Hugo Grotius* (Rijks Geschiedk. Publ., 64, 82, The Hague, 1928-36), II, no. 777, p. 234.

[2] *Index der Gebodboeken; berustende ter Secretary der stad Antwerpen, 1489-1620*, in *Antwerpsch Archievenblad*, I (1864), 407.

[3] Brants, *op. cit.*, I, 191-5.

[4] *Ibid.*, 327.

of direct trade between Antwerp and the outer world there could be no question. Cargoes destined for Antwerp had either to be shipped to one of the Zeeland ports, whence they would be carried up to Lillo and there again transhipped, or to run the Dutch blockade of the Flemish ports and thence pass through Flanders. The events of 1572-85 had in any case largely ruined Antwerp's overseas trade, and in the years that followed two of the main branches of that trade, the English cloth-trade and the Portuguese spice-trade, were both cut off by war. The peace of 1604 between England and Spain was, indeed, followed by the first of the series of attempts to secure some relaxation of the closure of the Scheldt in favour of English ships. It is to this, and to the more serious question raised by the advent of the Truce of 1609, that we must now turn.

(iii) *The Twelve Years' Truce, 1609-21,*

So long as the war lasted the obstacles raised on both sides to the navigation of the Scheldt could be regarded as exceptional measures dictated by military needs. What was to become of them when peace was restored? This question was not to be answered finally until after 1648; but it was raised, and provisionally answered, during the Truce of 1609-21, and the decisions then taken were an important precedent for what was to happen at the final settlement.

Even before the suspension of hostilities in 1607 the States-General had to meet a demand for concessions to neutral trade. The peace-treaty between England and Spain in August 1604, with its provision for the renewal of English commercial relations with the Southern Netherlands, revived the situation created by the Anglo-Spanish agreement of March 1573.[1] That agreement had been followed by the resumption, with the consent of the rebel government, of direct trade between England and Antwerp, and it was doubtless with this precedent in mind that the English government in the autumn of 1604 sounded the States-General on the possibility of some relaxation of the closure of the Scheldt in favour of English ships. Among various suggestions the most practical was that English ships

with all kind of merchandise [should] have free accesse to the forte of Lillo on the River of Scelde; and there to unlade the same, and to be transported from thence to Andwerpe: And lykewise all other commodities of Andwerpe, to be brought to Lillo, and there to be reladen into English or Scottish vessels, and so to be brought into his Majesty's dominions, without impediment. Provided also, that the commodities which shalbe brought

---

[1] See above, p. 84 *n* 2.

from his Majesty's dominions to Lillo, shalbe mere marchandise, and not extende to Vittle, Munition, or any Warlick provision.[1]

This proposal, and another made at the same time for the lifting of the blockade of the Flemish sea-ports, the States-General rejected by a weighty resolution of 16 November 1604 as tending to the "certain ruin" of the Republic, and the English government did not press them.[2]

Although this episode did not itself raise the issue of the maintenance of the closure on other than purely military grounds, there can be no doubt of its importance as part of the background of the negotiations of 1608-9. In Zeeland it must have revived memories of the time when so many ships had sailed straight up to Antwerp without touching at a Zeeland port; although no ship had done so for more than twenty years, clearly Antwerp had not yet lost its power of attraction. If for the present the war was a conclusive argument against allowing foreign ships to penetrate even as far as Lillo, the return of peace would both bring a renewal of the demand and deprive the States of the main argument for refusing it. It was this prospect which made the Zeelanders the most determined opponents of the policy leading first to the armistice of 1607 and then, through the abortive peace-negotiation of 1608, to the Truce of 1609, and which led them to assent to the Truce only in return for an undertaking which is a landmark in the history of the Scheldt.

The discussion of the Scheldt during the peace-negotiation of 1608 was notable for the bland assumption of the Southern envoys that peace would bring a reopening of the river, and even more for the fact that the States' representatives did not disillusion them. To the Southerners' demand that, while the war-time duties on both sides should be abolished, the pre-war duties should be confined to the trade between the two countries, leaving the direct trade between Antwerp and the sea entirely free, the Northerners did not retort that there would be no direct trade; their reply took the form of a demand that Middelburg (and Dordrecht) should retain their right of staple over wines imported into the Netherlands, and they studiously avoided the suggestion that this would involve any greater interference with traffic on the Scheldt than when it had been in force before the Revolt.[3] We need not share the credulity of the Southern envoys, and of Jeannin, their French colleague, who seem to have swallowed this whole; clearly

[1] P.R.O., S.P. For. 77/7 f.77v. Endorsed: "Overtures for trade with the Archdukes."
[2] This interesting episode deserves more attention than it has received. See Kernkamp, *op. cit.*, II, 303-4, and references there.
[3] See above, pp. 80-81.

in 1608, as later, the Middelburg wine-staple was only the historical cloak which was to be cast over something new and far more drastic. As the Northern envoys told Jeannin when he counselled moderation in their demands

etant souverains ils entendoient faire dans leur pays ce qu'ils jugeoient convenable, sans en demander l'avis et consentement des archiducs, lesquels auront la liberté d'en faire autant chez eux.[1]

But in 1608 the States-General had yet to decide how they would use their sovereignty over the Scheldt estuary, and in the event they did not have to commit themselves, for the negotiation broke down on a different point, the trade to the Indies.

When it was renewed the following year, it was no longer for a peace but for a truce. In the interval, however, the Zeelanders had forced the issue. Jeannin was wrong in thinking that there was no way in which they could protect their trade from the consequences of a peace or truce. During the early months of 1609 the States of Zeeland exacted from the other provinces, as the price of their assent to a truce, an undertaking that it should involve no relaxation of the closure of the Scheldt. Three of the Zeeland towns, Middelburg, Veere and Flushing, wanted a clause to this effect inserted in the truce itself, but yielded to the advice of the majority that this would be to provoke the enemy unnecessarily.[2] The enemy would doubtless have preferred to know the worst. As it was, the Brussels government was told nothing about this all-important reservation; on the contrary, the terms delivered by the States-General through the intermediary of the French and English envoys, Jeannin and Winwood, were designed to postpone the revelation as long as possible, for they concluded with an article referring the whole question of commercial relations to an ulterior negotiation, with the significant proviso that failure to reach agreement should not invalidate the truce. The Brussels government was reluctant to commit itself in this way, but the mediators spoke reassuringly, and the articles were accepted. The Truce was signed at Antwerp on 9 April and proclaimed there, to the general joy, five days later.

The Southern envoys were prompt to demand the opening of the

---

[1] *Les Négociations du President Jeannin* (Michaud et Poujoulat, *Nouvelle Collection des Mémoires pour servir à l'histoire de France*, 2me série, 10 vols., Paris, 1837-8, IV), 313. For Oldenbarnevelt's journal of the negotiation see Van Deventer, M. L., *Gedenkstukken van Johan van Oldenbarnevelt en zijn tijd* (3 vols., The Hague, 1860-65), III, 168-239, esp. pp. 195ff.

[2] Kernkamp, *op. cit.*, II, 338 and *n* 1; the entry in the "Notulen" of the peace-delegation recording the engagement is printed in Wagenaar, J., *Vaderlandsche Historie* (71 vols., Amsterdam, 1790-1811), X, Bylage B, pp. 123-4.

ulterior negotiation, and it was only then that they learned how little prospect there was that it would lead to the reopening of the Scheldt.[1] The Northerners would in any case do nothing before the Spanish government had ratified the Truce, and it was not until the following September that the supplementary negotiation was opened at The Hague. From the outset there was no possibility that the States-General would forego their right to keep the river closed. Outside the province of Zeeland and the town of Amsterdam there was, indeed, little disposition to enforce this harsh measure; but the other provinces were bound by their undertaking to Zeeland.[2] The entreaties of the Southern representatives were therefore as futile as their mild threats of retaliation against the trade of the North. Their final proposal that the matter should be referred to the Kings of France and Great Britain, under whose auspices the Truce had been concluded, was naturally declined by the States-General, for there can be little doubt that the royal decision would have gone against them. The agreement signed on 7 January 1610, which reaffirmed the principle of freedom of commerce between the two parties enunciated in the Truce, was therefore silent on the question. Even after the Brussels government had thus resigned itself to the continued closure of the river, Antwerp made repeated efforts to soften the hearts of the Zeelanders by missions to Middelburg. When appeals failed, the town's envoys warned the Zeeland towns that in the long run it was not they, but the Holland towns, and above all Amsterdam, which would profit by the ruin of Antwerp. It was both a shrewd argument and a sound prophecy, but it availed nothing, and Antwerp too eventually gave up the hopeless struggle.[3]

It might be expected that both the Spanish and South Netherland governments would have found powerful support among neutrals, and especially from England, in the campaign. There was, to be sure, some talk during the Truce of attracting the English cloth trade back to Antwerp, especially at the time of the trade-war between England and the Republic occasioned by James I's disastrous project for concentrating the finishing processes in England instead of exporting unfinished cloth to be dyed and dressed at Haarlem and Leiden.[4] But

[1] Spencer and Winwood to the Privy Council, 6/16 April 1609. Winwood, *Memorials*, III, 4.
[2] Winwood to Salisbury, 24 Dec. 1609/3 Jan. 1610. *Ibid.*, III, 100.
[3] Gielens, A., " Onderhandelingen met Zeeland over de opening der Schelde (1612-13) " in *Antwerpsch Archievenblad* (2de reeks), VI (1931), 194-221.
[4] Lonchay and Cuvelier, *op. cit.*, I, 445-455 *passim*, 478-9, 486, 496, 526, 534, 539, 587-8. The standard account of the project is Friis, A., *Alderman Cockayne's Project and the Cloth Trade* (Copenhagen and London, 1927), which contains a few references to suggestions for " procuring a vent " for English cloth at Antwerp.

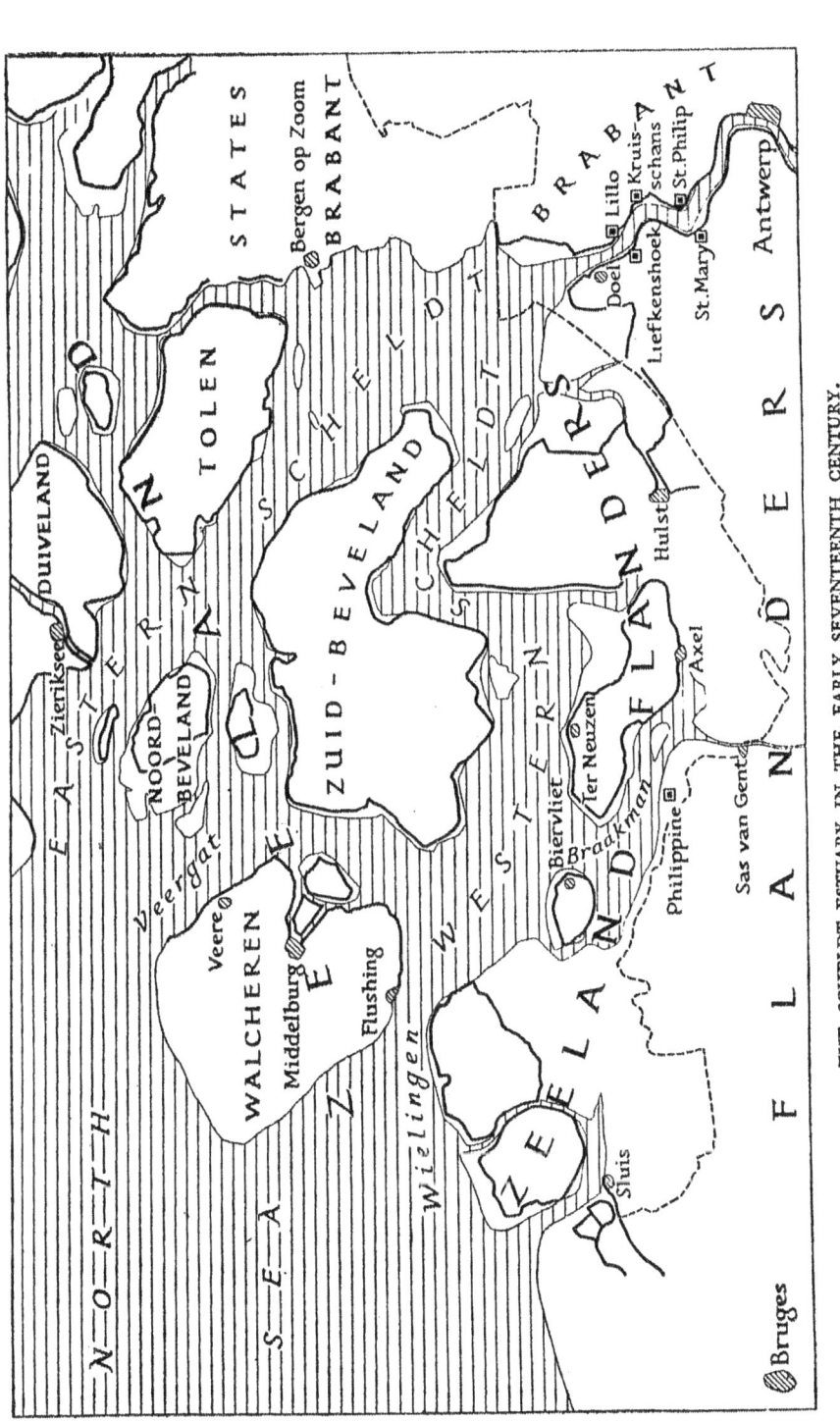

THE SCHELDT ESTUARY IN THE EARLY SEVENTEENTH CENTURY. ☐ Principal forts.

——— Main dykes beyond which there was much inundation.
······ Frontier between United Provinces and Southern Netherlands according to treaties of 1648 and 1664.

these schemes, which, like earlier and later ones, were conceived at least partly in the hope of embroiling England and the Republic in a dispute over the Scheldt,[1] did not have this result. Why this was so has yet to be fully explained. Had religious scruples not obstructed the promising scheme of 1615 to establish English clothiers at Antwerp, this might have induced the English government to intervene. But the fact that the Antwerp trade had always been in the hands of the Merchant Adventurers, who were now at loggerheads with the government over the cloth-finishing question, probably accounts for the government's relative indifference.[2]

If the Truce brought no reopening of direct sea-traffic on the Scheldt, it did lessen the hindrances to the internal and transit-trade using the river. Already in June 1608, during the peace-negotiation at The Hague, the Archdukes had shown their goodwill by suspending the system of transhipment on their side and allowing Northern ships free access to their ports, on payment of licence and tolls and on production of a certificate bearing some information about the ship and crew.[3] The States-General for their part did not relax the system until after the conclusion of the Truce; they then first allowed passenger-ships, and afterwards cargo-ships, to pass between their ports and Antwerp.[4] This was the end of transhipment until the renewal of the war. Its suspension was the signal for a "scramble" by the Northern towns to make agreements with the commercial centres of the South. Rotterdam was early in the field; the month of the Truce saw negotiations begun between Rotterdam and Antwerp which led to a provisional agreement in August 1610 and a definitive one in May 1612 for daily sailings from each port with passengers and non-perishable cargo. Rotterdam made similar agreements with Ghent (taking advantage of the improvements then being made to the Gentsche Vaart canal) and with Mechlin. Other towns to make agreements with Antwerp were Amsterdam, Middelburg and Gouda; in the last case the States-General sent representatives to attend the negotiation, among them no less a person than Oldenbarnevelt, the Grand Pensionary.[5]

[1] Lonchay and Cuvelier, *op. cit.*, I, 587-8.
[2] Had the English government chosen to take up the question it would doubtless have tried to profit by its occupation of Flushing, one of the three places (the others were Brielle and Rammekens) which English troops had garrisoned since 1585 as security or "caution" for the repayment of English costs in assisting the Republic against Spain. The States-General's anxiety to redeem these places, which they did in 1616, may not have been unconnected with their potential significance in this respect.
[3] Brants, *op. cit.*, I, 386-7.
[4] Kernkamp, *op. cit.*, II, 335, 342.
[5] Bijlsma, R., *Rotterdams welvaren, 1550-1650* (The Hague, 1918), 130-2; Kernkamp, *op. cit.*, II, 345-6; Génard, P., *Anvers à travers les âges* (2 vols., Brussels, 1888), I, 135-8; *Handvesten . . . Amstelredam*, III, 1506.

It would be an error to attach any political significance to these agreements; they were business contracts into which any sense of community between the sundered parts of the Netherlands can scarcely have entered. What they do reveal is the importance which the North still attached to the South Netherland market and to the navigation serving it. By cutting short Antwerp's career as a sea-port the closure of the Scheldt had, at least for the time being, increased rather than diminished the importance of the internal and transit-trade on the river. It was this trade which was to provoke increasing jealousy between Zeeland and Holland; their rivalry for it had begun during the war-years before 1609, and the alacrity with which Rotterdam opened negotiations with Antwerp in that year illustrates the Hollanders' determination not to let the Zeelanders steal a march on them in the new conditions.

The Truce also brought some lightening of the burden of duties on the trade between North and South. Nothing came of the Southerners' proposal of 1608 for the abolition of all war-time duties, and the Truce itself included no specific provisions on the subject. But the States-General went to work immediately upon a reduction of convoys and licences. They did so principally at the instance of Zeeland, which feared that the maintenance of the war-tariff on the Scheldt would drive trade to the Flemish sea-ports. After months of wrangling between the provinces a new tariff of incoming- and outgoing-duties was adopted on 13 October 1609; it represented a considerable reduction from the existing tariff of 1603, particularly on exports to the Southern Netherlands, and must have come as a relief to the Southern consumer.[1] The Archdukes had no such inducement to reduce their licences; they had no wish to encourage the river-trade with the North, on the contrary they aimed at developing the route through the Flemish ports. In their ordinance of 19 February 1610 the tariff of duties on goods entering or leaving Brabant was therefore kept at the level of 1597.[2] In 1616 these duties were said to bring in half-a-million gulden a year.[3]

The Brussels government did, however, agree to suspend the other principal tax on trade with the North, the Zeeland toll. The convention of 7 January 1610 provided that neither government should levy duties outside its territorial limits and that the subjects of each should enjoy their old freedom from tolls. These provisions were applied to

---
[1] Kernkamp, *op. cit.*, II, 343-4.
[2] Brants, *op. cit.*, II, 37-9.
[3] Lonchay and Cuvelier, *op. cit.*, I, 478-9.

the Scheldt by the first article of the supplementary convention of 24 June 1610, which stipulated that from 30 June following the Archdukes should cease to levy the toll of Zeeland on condition that the States of Zeeland assumed responsibility for the annual rents charged on the toll before 1572.[1] This was the beginning of the end of the famous toll of Zeeland which had played so large a part in the earlier history of the Scheldt; it would be revived during the later stages of the war, to disappear finally in 1648.

(iv) *The Evolution of Articles XIV and XV of the Treaty of Münster.*
If the Twelve Years' Truce furnished the first test of the Dutch Republic's determination and ability to maintain the closure of the Scheldt after the suspension of hostilities, the course of events after 1621 both hardened the resolution and increased the ability. This is well illustrated by the States-General's handling of the subject during the negotiations of 1632-3, the only ones which offered any real chance of success before those leading to the Treaty of Münster.

Since 1630 the Southern Netherlands had shared the misfortunes which everywhere beset the Habsburg cause, and Frederick Henry's capture of Maastricht (22 August 1632) was a further staggering blow. A malcontent movement was conspiring both with France and with the Republic to overthrow the Spanish regime, and when in September the Archduchess Isabella was forced to summon the Southern States-General she was met with a resolute demand for negotiation with the States-General of The Hague. The result was a preliminary discussion at Maastricht during September and October, followed by a full dress negotiation at The Hague. The preliminary talks led to the drafting of a series of nine articles providing for a renewal of the Truce of 1609 " in all its points and articles "; these were communicated to the Northern States-General early in October by deputies returning from the army at Maastricht, and that assembly then had to prepare its terms for the peace-negotiation which was to follow.

Although officially this negotiation was for a truce or peace between the Republic and the Southern Netherlands as a dependency of Spain, what was really at stake was the political future of the Southern Netherlands. There were two revolutionary plans afoot, one for a partition of the Southern provinces between France and the Republic, the other for their erection into an independent state under the patronage of

[1] Particulars of many of these rents will be found in De Waard, C., *Rijksarchief in Zeeland. Regestenlijst van de charters en bijbehoorende stukken van de Zeeuwsche Rekenkamer, 1525-1784* (Middelburg, 1918), 9ff.

England. The fate of both schemes largely rested with the three foreign governments concerned, and above all with the government at The Hague. Had Frederick Henry followed up the capture of Maastricht with a swift invasion of Brabant from the east the Brussels government would have had little or no chance of saving the Brabant towns, and among them Antwerp, which awaited his coming " with the keys in their hands ".[1] But although this opportunity was missed, and although the situation was already far less propitious when the Southern envoys arrived at The Hague early in December, the Northern government's attitude was still perhaps the most important single factor. It certainly lay with that government to offer such terms as would tend either to restore or to weaken still further the Southerners' fast-waning resolution to have done with Spanish rule.

It is against this background that we must set the Northerners' attitude on the Scheldt question. They had begun at Maastricht by proposing a revival of the situation during the Truce. This was not calculated to encourage the Southerners, especially those of Antwerp, who took the liveliest interest in the proceedings.[2] But worse was to follow. When the Southern delegation received the Northern States-General's terms at The Hague in December, they included the two following articles:

5. That the rivers of the Scheldt, item the channels of the Zwin and other waterways adjoining shall be navigated in the same manner as during the former Twelve Years' Truce and not otherwise.

6. With this understanding and express condition, that ships and goods passing in and out of the harbours of Flanders shall be charged with such and no less convoys, imposts, tolls, and other duties as goods passing up and down the Scheldt and the aforesaid channels, and that sufficient order shall be taken for the execution of the same.[3]

These two articles are the first version of the celebrated fourteenth and fifteenth articles of the Treaty of Münster. They were, as might be expected, of Zeeland origin. It was the Zeeland members of the commission entrusted with the preparation of the terms who had urged the inclusion of articles providing not only for the closure of the Scheldt but for the device, soon to be known as the "equalization" of the Flemish sea-ports, designed to prevent any diversion of the Scheldt

---

[1] Quoted in Geyl, *The Netherlands Divided, 1609-48* (1936), 101.
[2] Prims, Fl., *Stadsarchief Antwerpen. Inventaris op het archieffonds van Handel en Scheepvaart . . . Aanhangsel: inventaris op den bundel Jurisdictie op de Schelde* (Antwerp, 1925), 27-8. On 15 April 1633 Antwerp received a letter from the Hanse Towns asking to be included in the peace terms, which they hoped would lead to a revival of the old commercial relations.
[3] Aitzema, L. van, *Historie of Verhael van Saken van Staet en Oorlogh* (8vo, The Hague, 15 vols., 1647-71), III, ii. 76.

trade to a route which in peace-time would otherwise lie outside their control.[1] But if it was Zeeland which formulated these articles, it was Holland which ensured their incorporation in the States-General's terms. Holland's interest in the closure had increased notably since 1609; indeed, at times Holland appeared to be even more uncompromising on the subject than Zeeland.[2] The reason is clear enough: as the Antwerpers had prophesied in 1613, it was Holland, and within Holland Amsterdam, which had most profited by the fall of Antwerp and which therefore had most to lose if Antwerp should rise again. It was Holland moreover whose economic ascendancy in the Republic enabled it increasingly to dictate policy. By contrast, Zeeland had in both respects lost ground since 1609. If the Zeelanders still clung to the closure of the Scheldt, it was for fear of losing what trade yet remained to them, and from now on they must be content to rely upon Holland to secure its adoption in the States-General.

In their joint insistence on the necessity of these articles Holland and Zeeland made it clear to the Southerners that whether they made peace or remained at war, whether they continued under Spanish rule or won for themselves any measure of independence, they could expect no concessions from the North in the interests of their trade. There were some in both provinces who were disposed to go further and to regard the continuance of Spanish rule in the South as preferable to any form of independence, since it would give the measures which they were determined in either case to maintain a less fratricidal appearance. It was in accordance with this line of thought that Holland insisted on continuing the negotiation after the disillusioned Southern envoys had renounced all thought of independent action and had become merely the mouthpiece for Spanish demands. There was some opposition to this among the other provinces, but Holland and Zeeland harped on the danger of "diversion of trade, if the provinces now subjected should attain to freedom of government, religion, and commerce, especially on the Honte and Scheldt",[3] and the negotiation proceeded on the new footing, but with only a remote chance of success.

If Friesland and Groningen were moved to protest against the brutal realism of Holland's policy, to the Southerners it must have seemed even more abhorrent. The two Scheldt articles came in for

---

[1] The Zeeland recommendations, dated 11 November 1632, were later printed as one of the appendices of the *Deductie . . . tot Iustificatie van de Acte von Seclusie* published by the States of Holland in 1654 and inserted in the Resolutions of the States of Holland for that year at p. 306.
[2] Lonchay and Cuvelier, *op. cit.*, II, 36.
[3] Aitzema, *op. cit.*, III, iii, 43; quoted in Geyl, *op. cit.*, 106.

their bitterest criticism: they were "beyond all reason", they were "a new servitude, never used before the war, against the rights of all nations and the freedom of trade ".[1] But if the maritime provinces had felt no call to withhold them at a time when Southern independence was still a possibility, they were not likely to weaken when that possibility was removed, and from now on these two articles became an indispensable condition of peace. Had they been free agents the Southerners would have accepted them, along with the North's other demands, in 1633; but Spain was not yet ready for peace, and it was a purely Spanish demand, the restoration by the Republic of Pernambuco, which made any such sacrifice useless.

Twelve years later the victories of France and the Republic, in alliance since 1635, together with the revolt of Portugal, had brought Spain low enough to concede almost everything which the States-General demanded. Little need be said here about the general course of the negotiations leading to the Treaty of Münster, since as far as the Scheldt was concerned it was merely a question of Spain's accepting the articles of December 1632.[2] At first the negotiation was for a new truce; but by the close of 1646 both parties were thinking in terms of a definitive peace. This made no difference to the Scheldt articles; these were among the first to be settled, and by 8 January 1647 an agreed draft of the entire treaty was in existence. But more than a year passed before it was signed. The delay was chiefly due to the reluctance of the States-General to contravene their engagement with France by concluding a separate peace. As late as July 1647 they renewed the French alliance and with it this undertaking; but the prospects of a Franco-Spanish peace were slight, and in November the States-General resolved, by four provinces against three, to sign the treaty if a last attempt to bring France and Spain to terms should fail. It was in accordance with this decision that on 30 January 1648 the Peace of Münster was signed. Of the three provinces which had opposed the resolution, two (Utrecht and Friesland) had already been won over, but Zeeland, loth to renounce the lucrative privateering trade, withheld its assent until after the ratifications had been exchanged. The final act of pacification, the formal proclamation of the treaty, took place on 5 June 1648, eighty years to the day after the execution of Egmont and Hoorn.

[1] Aitzema, *op. cit.*, III, ii, 79; III, iii, 50, 60.
[2] It was doubtless in connection with these negotiations that the Dutch historian Vossius delivered to the States of Zeeland on 19 July 1645 " een Tractaatken aengaende het Recht dezer Provintie over de Rivier van de Hont ", of which, however, no copy appears to have survived. See Ermerins, J., *Eenige Zeeuwsche Oudheden*, VIII, i, 15-16.

Foremost among the general provisions of the treaty were those (Articles I and II) by which Spain recognized the sovereignty of the Republic within its existing frontiers. These frontiers, which were finally delimited by the boundary treaty of 28 September 1664, preserved for the Republic its strategic position athwart the estuary of the Scheldt. On the left, or south, bank of the river the Republic retained Zeeland-Flanders, the strip of territory including Sluis and Sas van Gent, commanding the waterways to Bruges and Ghent, as well as Axel and Hulst, now no longer ports. Eastward of this territory the frontier crossed the Scheldt south of the "submerged land" of Saeftingen to join the Brabant mainland north of Santvliet; thus both banks of the river from Antwerp down to Santvliet on the Brabant side and to the polder of Doel, the most northerly polder still intact on the Flemish side, was Southern territory. But within this territory there lay, on the right bank, the forts of Frederick Henry, Lillo and the Kruisschans, and on the left bank that of Liefkenshoek, and these the Republic retained and continued to garrison.[1] While Zeeland-Flanders was a "Generality land", that is to say, it was not incorporated in a province but was administered by the States-General, the Scheldt forts, which during the war had also been a concern of the Generality, were in 1648 handed over to the province of Zeeland. The estuary itself of course remained part of that province, as it had been before 1572.

It was on the sovereignty thus recognized that the States-General based the right to close the Scheldt. This right the Spanish government now conceded in the following terms:

Art. XIV. Les rivières de l'Escau, comme aussi les Canaux de Zas, Zwijn, et autres bouches de Mer y aboutissants seront tenues closes du côté desdits Seigneurs Etats.

Art. XV. Les Navires et denrées entrants et sortants des Havres de Flandres respectivement seront et demeureront chargés par ledit Seigneur Roi de toutes telles Impositions et autres charges, qui sont levées sur les denrées allants et venants au long de l'Escau, et autres Canaux mentionnés en l'article precedent; et sera convenu ci-apres entre les parties respectivement de la taxe de la susdite charge égale.[2]

The interpretation of these articles will be the chief topic of the next chapter, but one or two textual points may be mentioned here. The plural form "les rivières de l'Escau" (which dates back to 1632[3])

[1] See map facing p. 96. Liefkenshoek was only formally ceded by Spain in 1644, the other forts in 1648.
[2] This is the original French form of the articles; I take it from the official publication *Tractaten en Tractaatsbepalingen de Schelde betreffende sinds 1648* (The Hague, 1919). The treaty is of course to be found in all the standard collections of treaties.
[3] See above, p. 101.

was clearly designed to comprehend within the scope of the articles both the Scheldt proper and the Honte, and its use therefore marks the formal recognition of the Honte as a branch of the Lower Scheldt, just as the verdict of 1504 had recognized the Honte as the entire waterway between Hontemuide and the sea. The Honte, which two centuries before had eclipsed the Scheldt as a highway of trade, was now to take its name. At first it would be known as the Western Scheldt, while the Scheldt proper became the Eastern Scheldt; this is indeed still the official usage.[1] But in common speech the adjective was soon to disappear; the Honte would then become " the Scheldt " and the question of its navigation " the Scheldt question ".

The inclusion of the Zwin, the " canal de Zas ", that is, the waterway to Ghent which, since the capture of Sas van Gent, lay partly in Northern, partly in Southern, territory, and the channels adjoining them, was likewise intended to bring within the terms of the articles all the water-routes which crossed the frontier of Zeeland-Flanders between the Scheldt and the sea. By the fourteenth article the Scheldt itself, and all these waterways, were to be " tenues closes " on the side of the Republic, and borrowing the adjective all later writers have termed the effect of the article the " closure " (*clôture, sluiting*) of the Scheldt. Now it is clear that a river may be " closed " in a variety of ways: by a physical barrier placed across it (Parma had closed the Scheldt below Antwerp in this way during his siege of the city), by a simple declaration enforced by policing, or by some indirect means such as the imposition of exorbitant charges for its navigation. The fourteenth article said nothing as to the way in which the Scheldt and its confluents were to be " closed ". The omission might have meant one of two things: either that the negotiators and their principals knew so well what the term signified that explanation was unnecessary, or that they deliberately refrained from explaining it in order to secure latitude in its interpretation.

The States-General and their plenipotentiaries at Münster certainly knew what they meant by keeping the Scheldt closed. The term had been adopted in their original instructions for the negotiation in preference to the former provision for the re-establishment of the situation

---

[1] The earliest example which I have found of the use of the names " Eastern " and " Western Scheldt " occurs in a map of 1621 preserved in the archives at Brussels. See *Kataloog der Schelde Tentoonstelling, Antwerpen, 1925* (Antwerp, *n.d.*), 42. The recent application, on marine charts, of the name " Honte " to the most westerly reach of the West Scheldt represents an interesting, if unhistorical, new use of the name now that it is no longer needed as a synonym for " Scheldt "

during the Truce.¹ To the States-General, then, the "closure" of the Scheldt meant the prohibition of direct navigation between Antwerp (and Bruges and Ghent) and the sea by means of compulsory transhipment at the mouth of the river.² It did not imply the maintenance of the system of transhipment at the frontier, although the Zeelanders were later to confuse matters by describing the reintroduction of this measure as " closing " the Scheldt;³ nor, strictly speaking, did it include the levy of duties on traffic using the river, although such duties would in practice remain an important feature of the regime on the Scheldt, especially in view of the provisions of the fifteenth article.

Did the Spanish plenipotentiaries who accepted the articles understand what the term implied? Grandgaignage sought to show that they did not, and further that the fourteenth article as discussed and agreed upon at Münster could not legitimately be made to bear the construction which the States-General afterwards put on it.⁴ But this is a piece of special pleading which cannot be accepted. It was no new demand which the Republic brought forward in 1645-6; it had been advanced and debated at length in 1632-33 and there could have been little or no doubt as to what it meant.⁵ Moreover, the Spanish envoys were in no position to oppose it; peace they must have, and peace could only be secured at the price of accepting, among other things, whatever regime the States-General cared to maintain on the Scheldt. Such opposition as the Spaniards did offer was directed, less against the fourteenth, than against the fifteenth article, and even this they accepted without much difficulty, partly no doubt because it was to be the sub-

---

¹ These instructions are printed in Aitzema, *op. cit.*, VI, 109*ff*.
² Cf. the Zeeland deputies' recommendation of 11 November 1632 (see above, pp. 101-2, and n 1) " that the Scheldt . . . shall remain closed, in such manner that all incoming ships shall be required to discharge and tranship their cargoes ".
³ See below, p. 119.
⁴ Grandgaignage, E., *Histoire du péage de l'Escaut* (Antwerp, 1868), 76-8.
⁵ Article XIV (then numbered XIII) was included in the project of treaty in seventy-one articles delivered by the Dutch to the Spanish plenipotentiaries on 11 May 1646. On 17 May the Spanish plenipotentiaries declared themselves ready to accept the Article on the understanding that the words " tenues closes " should not exclude or hinder the use of the river by subjects of Spain and that the King of Spain should be free if he chose to apply the same condition to subjects of the United Provinces. In reply, the Dutch plenipotentiaries delivered a written statement on the closure, as founded upon the Zeeland right of staple, which ruled out any such exemption of Spanish or South Netherland subjects from its operation. It was with the full knowledge of the Dutch interpretation of the article derived from this statement that the Spanish plenipotentiaries accepted it. See " Correspondencia diplomática de los Plenipotenciarios Españoles en el Congreso de Munster, 1643 á 1648," in *Coleccion de Documentos inéditos para la historia de España* (112 vols., Madrid, 1842-95), LXXXII, 316-9, 323-4, 385-6; Le Clerc, *Négociations Secrètes touchant la Paix de Munster* . . . (4 vols., The Hague, 1725) III, 436, 468*ff*, and the *Deduction* of 1654 (below, pp. 120-121), which briefly reviews this episode in the negotiation of Article XIV.

ject of further negotiation. There was thus little motive and less opportunity for the States' envoys to have concealed the significance of Article XIV. Indeed, if either party allowed itself any *arrière pensée*, it is more likely to have been the Spaniards. In considering the article they would scarcely have overlooked the possibilities inherent in the position of " third States " in relation to it. These possibilities the Spanish government would soon set itself to explore, with results which will be described in the next chapter.

CHAPTER FIVE

The Münster Regime, 1648—1780

It seems to be commonly assumed among historians that with the signature of the Treaty of Münster the closure of the Scheldt became an accepted feature of the public law of Europe and that no question of its abolition arose until the very eve of the collapse of the *ancien régime*. If this were true, the century and a half which lie between the signature of the treaty and the attempt of Joseph II to free the river would be a practically blank page in the history of the " Scheldt question ", as indeed it tends to be in most versions of that history.

The shortest way of criticizing this view is to point to the length of the present chapter, and in particular to that part of it which treats of the first thirty years of the lifetime of Article XIV of the treaty. These thirty years were the " testing-time " of the closure of the Scheldt as embodied in that article; not only did they witness the evolution, by process of trial and error and in the face of considerable opposition, of the actual regime on the river, they were also marked by more than one challenge to the closure by interested " third States ". Each of these developments is the subject of a section of this chapter; the remaining section deals with the century from 1680 to 1780, during which a permanent regime was, with the assent or forbearance of the " third States ", established and maintained.

(i) *The Evolution of the Regime on the Scheldt, 1648-80.*

It was the Brussels government which took the first step towards lifting the war-time obstacles to the navigation of the Scheldt. On 19 March 1648, a few weeks after the signature of the treaty and some months before its formal proclamation, Northern traders were given safe-conduct to enter the Southern Netherlands and relieved of the obligation to tranship their goods at the frontier.[1] This step was doubtless taken, like the similar one in 1608, as a gesture of goodwill towards the Northerners; but the Brussels government soon found itself forced into a much greater concession to its own subjects. The proclamation of the treaty at Antwerp was followed by a violent popular demand for the abolition of licences on the Scheldt trade. Incoming licences were provisionally suspended at Antwerp on 10 June and less than a month later (4 July) the States of Brabant secured a similar suspension of outgoing licences. An official report of August 1648 spoke of the very name of these duties as being odious to the Ant-

---

[1] " Index der Gebodboeken ", in *Antwerpsch Archievenblad,* II, 63.

werpers and of their absolute refusal to pay them now that the war was over. Early in November the Archduke Leopold William, the new Governor of the Southern Netherlands, wrote gloomily to Philip IV of the danger of a fresh popular outburst; the Antwerpers had now added to their refusal to pay licences on trade with the North a refusal to pay either the similar duties on French goods (the South being still at war with France) or the old duty on the import of English woollens. These had to be provisionally withdrawn by the ordinance of 12 November which made definite the provisional suspensions of June and July. Early in December the King notified his consent to these surrenders by the Governor. Thus before the year was out the war-time hindrances to the navigation of the Scheldt from the Spanish side had been swept away.[1]

No such popular pressure made itself felt in the North, nor was the government of the Republic so fashioned as to permit of such swift decisions. But the mutual jealousy of Holland and Zeeland could on occasion make for celerity, and it did so now in the matter of transhipment. No sooner had the Brussels government suspended this than Zeeland allowed its own ships to take advantage of the exemption while continuing to enforce transhipment upon those of other provinces. To Holland, which had never liked the system because of the scope for interference which it gave Zeeland, this latest abuse was a final argument for getting rid of it, and on 15 July 1648 it was suspended by resolution of the States-General.[2] A few days later Antwerp was allotting berthing-places to Northern ships.[3] With transhipment gone, Zeeland now sought to turn convoys and licences into a weapon against Holland. Ten days after the States-General's decision, the town of Middelburg concluded with a number of Southern towns, Antwerp, Ghent and Bruges among them, an agreement for the " promotion and advancement of their mutual trade " by which, among other things, the Zeeland capital undertook to refund to the shippers of all goods passing between them two-thirds of the licence payable at Lillo, Sas van Gent or on the Zwin.[4] This was tantamount to the reintroduction, without the knowledge or consent of the States-General, of the " moderation " in force during the Truce. Holland was naturally furious, and there followed yet another long, confused and bitter conflict between the two provinces out of which there finally

[1] *Placcaeten van Brabandt*, III, 446-7; Lonchay and Cuvelier, *op. cit.*, IV, 84, 98, 105.
[2] See *Holland Staten Resolutiën*, 29 July/3 Aug. 1648.
[3] " Index der Gebodboeken ", in *Antwerpsch Archievenblad*, II, 64.
[4] Elias, *Schetsen uit de geschiedenis van ons Zeewezen* (3 vols., The Hague, 1916-30), II, 11-13.

emerged the new tariff of 1651; this tacitly sanctioned the virtual abolition of licences already put into effect by the two Admiralty Colleges in the course of the struggle.[1]

Zeeland's anxiety to relieve the Scheldt traffic of the war-burdens was largely inspired by fear of its diversion to the Flemish sea-ports. This danger the maritime provinces had sought to counter by Article XV. But Article XV proved far more difficult to carry into effect than Article XIV. Zeeland had first to convince the States-General of the urgency of the matter; notwithstanding it had the support of Holland, which hoped to use the requisite negotiation with the South as a weapon in the domestic conflict over convoys and licences, this preliminary campaign occupied three years, and it was only towards the close of 1652 that commissioners from the two governments, meeting as a " chambre mi-partie " at Mechlin, took up the question. The Spanish commissioners promptly delivered an ultimatum: they were authorized to consent to the equalization of the duties payable at the Flemish sea-ports with those on the Scheldt only if both were reduced to zero by the reciprocal abolition of all war-time duties. To the Brussels government this settlement would have involved little or no loss, since it had so far failed to reimpose the licences withdrawn under popular pressure in 1648. But for the Republic, already engaged in its first war with England and needing every penny of revenue it could raise, the proposition was out of the question. With the States-General's declaration of 13 January 1653 rejecting this interpretation of the article the talks were suspended; the first attempt to enforce the article had ended in complete defeat for the Republic.[2]

With the mutual suspension of transhipment in 1648 the only " closure " of the Scheldt consisted in the prohibition of direct traffic between Antwerp and the sea; in other words the barrier was laid, not at Lillo, the effective frontier between the Republic and the Southern Netherlands, but across the mouth of the river between Flushing and Cadzand. What took place at Lillo was nothing more than took place at any other river-frontier, the usual customs-formalities and the payment of convoys and licences,[3] under the eye of the Dutch forts and of the guardship (*uitlegger*) still known as the " fleet " (*vloot*) in

---

[1] Aitzema, *op. cit.*, VI, 565*ff*.
[2] *Ibid.*, VII, 581, 758, 765.
[3] And of the toll of Zeeland, whose collection was entrusted to the *licentmeester*. Thus Quirijn Bolle was appointed on 1 January 1670 to the receivership of convoys and licences at Philippine and on 2 February 1672 to the collectorship of the toll of Zeeland at the same place. *Verslagen omtrent 's Rijks Oude Archieven*, XXV (1902), 257.

memory of the powerful squadron which had once lain there.[1] At Sas van Gent, the frontier fort and lock on the canal running from the Scheldt to Ghent, and at Sluis, lying at the junction of the Zwin and the canal to Bruges, the situation and routine differed only in detail from those at Lillo.

But it was not long before the Zeelanders were agitating for the revival of transhipment at the frontier. The proposal was prompted by the increase of the tariff of convoys and licences made necessary by the war of 1652-4 with England. It was in March 1653 that the Zeeland deputies in the States-General proposed that all goods, save only those which it had been customary to exempt, should in future be transhipped " in the respective fleets ", that is at Lillo and Sas van Gent. As in the past the principal argument was the fiscal one: the financial burden of maintaining the navy at war-strength demanded a maximum yield from import and export-duties, and this was only possible with the aid of the control which transhipment afforded. But the Zeelanders could reinforce this with another argument. The war with England had given rise to rumours, not entirely unfounded, of an Anglo-Spanish campaign for the opening of the Scheldt. So long as the only " closure " of the river consisted in the prohibition of the passage of foreign ships beyond Flushing, it would, argued the Zeelanders, be difficult to give a convincing answer to an English demand for the free passage of the river, whereas if transhipment, which involved the unlading of all ships at Lillo and Sas van Gent, were brought into force again, the Republic would be in a much stronger position to refuse. For the time being, however, neither argument succeeded in shaking the States of Holland's determination, based on their past experience of transhipment, to have nothing more to do with it; the Zeeland proposal was accordingly exposed to all the delays which the Republic's constitution seemed deliberately designed to provoke, and twelve months passed before the States of Holland would so far humour the Zeelanders as to recommend the drafting of a regulation for transhipment, on condition that military and naval authorities should have no hand in its execution and that there was no danger of any diversion of trade to the Flemish sea-ports. Another four months elapsed before (July 1654) the regulation actually stood

---

[1] The *uitlegger* appears in the accounts of several contemporary travellers, for example, Hoogewerff, G. J., ed., *De Twee Reizen van Cosimo de' Medici Prins van Toscane door de Nederlanden (1667-69)* (Hist. Genootsch. Werken, 3de serie, 41, Utrecht, 1919), 123. A view of Lillo, with the *uitlegger*, appears in *Thoneel der steden en der stercҟten van 't vereenight Nederland* (Antwerp, 1674).

drafted.¹ It was at this point that the long-standing threat of English intervention became imminent. The Zeelanders redoubled their agitation, but the Hollanders stood firm and undertook to settle the matter without recourse to transhipment. Their successful handling of the affair is related elsewhere.²

The blowing-over of the threatened crisis really settled the fate of transhipment, although the States went on debating it for some weeks. Zeeland continued to urge its necessity on fiscal grounds, Holland to oppose it as a fresh burden which might well drive the river-traffic elsewhere.³ The draft regulation of July came back to the provinces early in August. A committee of the States of Holland made some amendments to it and on 8 August it was adopted as a " provincial advice ", that is, as a considered recommendation by the province to the States-General. The amended regulation comprised fifteen articles, nearly all of them designed to prevent abuses and to make transhipment as little hindrance as possible to trade. Several articles stipulated joint action by the Holland and Zeeland officers engaged in its administration; neither province was prepared to give the other a free hand. Other articles provided for a reduction of the cost of transhipment below its previous level. Finally, the regulation envisaged the adoption of the higher tariff of convoys and licences proposed by the Admiralties in July.⁴

Aitzema briefly describes the fate of this regulation, which had consumed so much time and energy during the preceding months, with his remark: " But it was again shelved and nothing came of it ".⁵ The reduction of the navy to a peace-establishment doubtless eased the financial position, while with the passing of the threat of an Anglo-Spanish *entente* transhipment ceased to be necessary as a defensive measure. Several years were to pass before the Zeelanders brought it forward again.

Before the end of 1654 the regime on the Scheldt had given rise to new difficulties between The Hague and Brussels. By ordinance of 12 October 1654 the Brussels government re-established on the Scheldt the licences, now renamed import- and export-duties, suspended since 1648.⁶ This step provoked determined opposition in the country, not-

---

¹ *Holland Staten Resolutiën* (H.S.R.), 26 March 1653, 4 March 1654, 18 July 1654; Aitzema, *op. cit.*, VIII, 261.
² See below, pp. 119*ff*.
³ Aitzema, *op. cit.*, VIII, 143.
⁴ *H.S.R.*, 7 and 8 Aug., 1654; Aitzema, *op. cit.*, VIII, 262-3.
⁵ *Ibid.*, VIII, 263.
⁶ Lonchay and Cuvelier, *op. cit.*, IV, 477-83, 491 and *n* 1.

ably at Antwerp. For nearly two years the government struggled to keep the duties in force, but in August 1656 it was again compelled to suspend them.[1] Meanwhile, to the opposition of Antwerp had been added that of the North, which challenged the duties as an infraction of Article XV of the treaty;[2] the question was referred to the "chambre mi-partie", but no ruling had emerged from that sleepy assembly before the duties were again suspended.

Several factors combined to produce the next major "incident" on the Scheldt, which occurred in 1665. The Southern Netherlands' chief contribution to it was their campaign to divert the trade of the Scheldt to the Flemish sea-ports. This involved the improvement of the interior waterways through Flanders; the work of canalization begun during the Truce was therefore taken up again, and in 1664-5 the completion of the two canal-systems between Ostend and Ghent and between Ostend and Bruges for the first time gave Antwerp an alternative route to the sea for small sea-going vessels. It was on 5 March 1665 that, amid great rejoicing, the first ship to reach Antwerp by way of Ostend and Ghent, a Biscay wine-ship, entered the port.[3] Having thus partially overcome the physical difficulties to the development of the new route, the Brussels government tackled the obstacles created by the rights of staple and of shipping monopoly still claimed by Ghent and Bruges, claims which if upheld would have subjected the route to a "closure" not dissimilar to that on the Scheldt itself. By a series of ordinances of 1663-4 these rights were suppressed or curtailed, and ships were enabled to pass direct between Ostend and Antwerp without detention or break of cargo.[4] Finally the Brussels government introduced a new tariff of duties at the Flemish sea-ports designed to attract trade to this route.[5]

It was not to be expected that the Northerners would view these developments without concern.[6] The danger of a diversion of the Scheldt trade to the Flemish sea-ports had never been out of their thoughts since 1648, and Article XV of the treaty, which had been designed to forestall it, had so far proved unenforceable. Meanwhile,

---

[1] *Ibid.*, 554-5. *Liste Chron. des Edits et Ordonnances des Pays-Bas . . . 1621-1700* (Brussels, 1910), no. 104 and references there.
[2] Aitzema, *op. cit.*, VIII, 266.
[3] "De Kronijk van Antwerpen door Andries van Valckenisse (1665-1698)", in *Bijdr. tot de Gesch.*, XXVII (1936), 95; Mertens and Torfs, *op. cit.*, VI, 39, giving the date as 5 May 1665; Génard, *op. cit.*, 526.
[4] *Edits et Ordonnances*, nos. 134-6 and references.
[5] *Ibid.*, no. 132.
[6] Aitzema (XI, ii. 1259) has a description of the new route and of Zeeland's jealousy of it.

they themselves had been preoccupied with another aspect of the question. In 1661 the States of Holland had recommended a bold solution of the problem of meeting the Republic's growing naval expenditure; they proposed that the tariff of convoys and licences, the chief source of the Admiralties' revenue, should be doubled. The plan naturally encountered opposition from the other provinces, especially the "landward" ones, which were less interested in the upkeep of the navy. The Zeelanders for their part were at one with Holland in recognizing the urgency of the need, but they would only consider the proposal on certain conditions; one of these was that the river-trade, in which they were particularly interested, should be exempt from at least part of the extra burden, another that the increase should be accompanied by the reintroduction of transhipment, and a third that renewed efforts should be made to prevail on the Spanish government to implement the terms of Article XV. For upwards of three years the two maritime provinces wrangled over these points, delegations made their leisurely way between The Hague and Middelburg, and at the beginning of 1665 little or no progress had been made.

The proposal for transhipment would doubtless have been " talked out " again as it had been in 1654 but for the outbreak of the second war with England. This made an increase of convoys and licences a matter of utmost urgency, and it was in the interest of securing Zeeland's speedy assent to such an increase that Holland at long last accepted the Zeeland scheme. On 16 April 1665, six weeks after the English declaration of war, the States-General resolved to bring into force the tariff of convoys and licences adopted during the first English war, and with it the regulation for transhipment approved by the Admiralties in November 1664 but since shelved. This regulation did not differ materially from that of 1654; it did, however, specify what goods were to be exempt from transhipment. Among outgoing goods millstones, Rhenish wine, salt, fresh fish and herring, and Liége coal were to be exempt, among incoming zinc, paving stones and lime. Both the increased tariff and the transhipment-regulation were to come into force on 10 May 1665, in the first instance for two years.[1] By the end of April copies had been printed and were being distributed to the authorities concerned.[2]

What followed must have been as great a surprise to contemporaries as it is to the present-day historian, accustomed as he is to thinking of

---

[1] *Groot Placaet Boeck*, III, 1377; Aitzema, *op. cit.*, XI, ii, 897ff.
[2] *H.S.R.*, 28 April 1655. For the detailed instructions issued by the Zeeland Admiralty see *Groot Placaet Boeck*, I, 1245ff.

the Southern Netherlands as the helpless victim of Dutch exploitation. No sooner had the regulation come into force than the Brussels government issued an ordinance prohibiting on pain of death the import of any goods which had been transhipped at Lillo or Sas van Gent.[1] It was a bold but also a well-calculated move. The Brussels government foresaw that, with their overseas trade temporarily at a standstill, the Dutch could not face a stoppage of the river-trade; the South, for its part, could take advantage of the new route through the Flemish seaports, which, while much inferior to the Scheldt route, would enable the country to maintain the boycott long enough for it to serve its purpose. The forecast proved correct. If the Dutch had at first entertained any thoughts of accepting the challenge these were dispelled by the defeat off Lowestoft (13 June), which left the English for the time being masters of the sea. A few days later the States-General were seeking the approval of Holland for the suspension of transhipment, approval which was quickly forthcoming,[2] and on 3 July the States-General resolved to instruct the Admiralty Colleges to allow ships past Lillo and the Sas without transhipment; the fact that this was to be done " by shutting eyes " (*by oochluyckinge*) and that the regulation was to remain nominally in force could not conceal the fact that the States had been successfully defied by the Southern government which they despised.[3]

Emboldened by their success the Brussels government proceeded to indulge in a series of aggressions which produced something like an economic war between the two Netherland governments during the next two years. In 1666 and 1667 the South took a number of measures against the entry of goods from the United Provinces, including a new and higher tariff of duties; Dutch shippers also complained of their treatment in Southern ports.[4] The French invasion of 1667 and the diplomatic revolution which followed brought the two states closer together in a common fear of France, but even this did not at first put an end to their economic quarrels. In the summer of 1668 the Brussels government again revised its list of duties; it also set up a new customs post at Fort St. Mary, on the Scheldt between Antwerp and Lillo, which mightily affronted the Zeelanders. Negotiations at The Hague

---

[1] The ordinance itself does not appear to be extant, but there is a similar ordinance of 13 Feb. 1666 (*Edits et Ordonnances*, no. 142). The first ordinance was reported to the States-General by its Resident at Brussels, Thomas Sasburgh, in a letter of 27 May 1665 (*H.S.R.*, 29 May 1665).
[2] *Ibid.*, 23 June 1665.
[3] Aitzema, *op. cit.*, XI, ii, 1266.
[4] *H.S.R.*, 25 Feb., 24 Aug., 12 Oct., 14 Oct., 1666, 10 and 11 Feb., 1667; Aitzema, *op. cit.*, XII, 671.

later in the year were without result, and the year ended with a spate of reprisals. The situation was aggravated for the Dutch by the fact that the war of 1665-7 (in which France had joined the Republic against England) had stimulated traffic through the Flemish sea-ports at the expense of the traffic on the Scheldt. This development the Brussels government continued to promote by removal of hindrances and lowering of duties;[1] protests from The Hague and demands for the " equalization " of duties in accordance with Article XV were without avail.

These commercial difficulties between the Northern and Southern Netherlands were, however, increasingly overshadowed by the economic war which France, under the leadership of Colbert, launched against the Republic, while in 1672 the Dutch found themselves fighting for their very existence as an independent nation. The South was not at first involved in this struggle, but in October 1673 Spain joined the European coalition against France and the two Netherland governments found themselves in an alliance which was to last, with hardly a break, until 1701. One result of this political *rapprochement* was to give the regime on the Scheldt a greater measure of stability. On the Dutch side there was no further talk of transhipment, while the Zeelanders carried their point about the exemption of the river-trade from the wartime increase of convoys and licences.[2] On the side of the South, the 'seventies saw a relaxation of the protectionist measures of the preceding years; this movement culminated in the low-duty tariff of 1680, a measure which, from being represented as the result of undue pressure by the Republic, is now seen to have answered to the demands of the trading elements in the South, especially at Antwerp, against the opposition of the industrial elements strong in Flanders.[3] Finally, if the Brussels government did not forget its earlier interest in the route through the Flemish sea-ports (a new sea-canal to Bruges was opened in 1676), the drain on the country's resources imposed by the recurrent wars fought over it was a serious check on all such enterprise. We are therefore justified in regarding the late 'seventies and early 'eighties as the turning-point in what may be called the " internal " history of the Scheldt regime. We shall find that there was taking place at about the same time an even more important change in its " external " history. It is to this aspect that we must now turn.

(ii) *" Third States " and the Closure, 1648-80.*

If during the quarter of a century following the Treaty of Münster

[1] *Edits et Ordonnances*, no. 159.
[2] *Groot Placaet Boeck*, III, 1272.
[3] Geyl, P., " Een historische legende. Het Zuid-Nederlandsch tarief van 21 December 1680 ", in *Mededeelingen der Kon. Akademie van Wetenschappen*, afd. letterkunde, LXXVI, serie B, no. 4 (1933).

the South Netherland government and people were by no means incapable of waging economic war against the Republic, their warfare was of the guerilla type, which, while it could on occasion (as in 1665) win a notable victory, could hardly achieve the overthrow of the regime established in 1648. But what the Southerners could not do for themselves might not be beyond the power of a foreign government. So long as the "closure" of the Scheldt consisted solely of the prohibition of direct traffic between Antwerp and the sea, it was "potential" rather than "actual"; it was a theoretical prohibition which would be made a reality only if a foreign ship attempted to pass up the river or an Antwerp vessel to gain the sea.

The first such attempt occurred in 1651, when ships bringing two thousand Spanish and Italian soldiers from Italy entered the mouth of the Scheldt with the object of passing up to Antwerp. The States of Zeeland refused them passage and they were forced to disembark at ports on the Flemish sea-coast. Although Zeeland justified its refusal, not by Article XIV, but by Article XXIII, which forbade the entry, except under stress of weather or other necessity, of large bodies of troops at the ports on either side, the episode was in fact the first test of the closure and may have been designed as such by the Spanish government.[1] This is the more likely as Spain was already inciting foreign governments to challenge the closure on their own account.

The Spanish government's attitude was that, although Article XIV of the treaty allowed the Republic to close the Scheldt to all foreign shipping, if other governments, not party to the treaty, were disposed to challenge the closure, the Spanish (and consequently the South Netherland) government was under no obligation either to hinder them or to deny their ships access to Antwerp or other Southern ports.[2] Officially the initiative must come from one or other of these "third States", but that would not of course prevent Spanish diplomacy from doing all in its power to persuade them to take that initiative. It was a game that Spain had played before,[3] both during the war and the Truce, but now there seemed a better chance of its success. Not only had the restoration of peace in the Netherlands deprived the States-General of their strongest argument for excluding foreign shipping from

[1] Aitzema, *op. cit.*, VII, 500. In January 1650 ships carrying half a million gold *écus* on government account from Spain to Antwerp had arrived in Zeeland, but in this case the cargo was evidently transhipped. Lonchay and Cuvelier, *op. cit.*, IV, 160, 163.
[2] This comes out most clearly in the comments made by Philip IV in November 1652 on a *mémoire* dealing with the execution of the Treaty of Münster. *Ibid.*, IV, 365 and n 1.
[3] See, for example, the instructions to the South Netherland agent Henri Teller, sent to England in 1631; he was to urge English merchants to attempt to make direct passage to Antwerp. Lefèvre, J., "Henri Teller, Doyen d'Anvers et diplomate (1598-1662)," in *Archives Bibliothèques et Musées de Belgique*, XIII, ii (1936), 89-104.

the Scheldt, but there were at least two governments which might be expected to listen favourably to Spanish promptings.

These two were England and Sweden. Their common interest in the newly reopened South Netherland market, and the political alignment which accompanied it, was well summed up by Aitzema. It was observed, he wrote,

that the Swedes would not let themselves be deprived of the trade with Flanders either by the Danes or by the Hollanders. . . . In summa, it was clear that Sweden, England and Spain would take a common line, Holland and Denmark another and contrary one. Flanders and Brabant, after being denuded of trade for eighty years, now hungered exceedingly for it; Holland and Zeeland had by contrast waxed fat on trade as Flanders and Brabant had done down to eighty years ago. Holland had therefore to look to it that this Helen, this bride was not torn from her.[1]

The outbreak of the first Anglo-Dutch war in the summer of 1652 both added importance to the South Netherland market and erected a fresh obstacle to it in the shape of the Dutch measures against what they regarded as contraband trade. The closure of the Scheldt was one of the many grievances brought against the Republic by England at the opening of the war,[2] and the war itself gave Spain an excellent opportunity of exploiting the position.[3] There could, of course, be no question of English goods reaching Antwerp by the Scheldt route during the war, but the English government could be encouraged to raise the matter during or after the peace-settlement, while something might be done with Sweden before then. As early as May 1652—within a few days of Tromp's first meeting with Blake off Dover—the Spanish government was giving a favourable reception to a Swedish proposal to establish commercial relations with Antwerp, at the same time recognizing the stumbling-block of the closure of the Scheldt.[4] Although nothing seems to have come directly of this, perhaps because of Christina's abdication, it may have encouraged Spain to persevere with England. The little trace that the campaign in London appears to have left suggests that its results must have been disappointing. There was some talk of the English government's demanding the opening of the

---

[1] Aitzema, *op. cit.*, VII, 742.
[2] Geddes, J., *History of the Administration of John de Witt* (1879), I, 119; for contemporary allusions see the references in Ballhausen, P. C., *Der erste Englisch-Holländische Seekrieg* (The Hague, 1923), 21 *n* 4.
[3] The English claim to navigate freely to Antwerp is mentioned with approval in a Spanish dispatch of 16 July 1652. Lonchay and Cuvelier, *op. cit.*, IV, 346.
[4] *Ibid.*, IV, 334-5 and *n*. It is possible that the letter from Christina to Antwerp, quoted in Génard, *Anvers à travers les âges*, I, 166-7, and ascribed by Verachter (*Inventaire*, 256) to about 1649, relates to this episode. Denucé, printing the letter in *Antwerpsch Archievenblad* (2de reeks), II (1927), 31-6, suggests 1650.

Scheldt in the negotiations of 1653,[1] and the Merchant Adventurers included it among the articles which they submitted to the Council of State in November of that year;[2] but it is doubtful whether the subject was raised with the Dutch and there is certainly no reference to it in the Treaty of Westminster of 15 April 1654.

But as we have seen the Zeelanders seized on the threat as a fresh argument in favour of their proposal of March 1653 for the revival of transhipment at the frontier. Aitzema reports them as saying in July 1653:

If the English claimed the free navigation to Antwerp it would be difficult to refuse them. But if the Scheldt were closed again (in accordance with the Treaty of Münster) one could refuse the English, saying *Pacta obstant*.[3] (It will be noticed that to the Zeelanders the " closure " of the Scheldt meant transhipment at Lillo-Liefkenshoek; it is this confusion of meaning which has led several writers astray in their description of the " closure " as it actually operated after 1648.) In the upshot the Hollanders managed to stave off the demand, with the result that a year later (July 1654) the regulation for transhipment was still in draft.[4]

Then came a disturbing piece of news. On 13 July 1654 the Dutch plenipotentiaries in London (they had remained there to settle points arising out of the peace-treaty of April) informed the States-General that some English merchants, " resolved to drive some kind of commerce from hence to Antwerp ", had laden one ship in the Downs and were lading another in the Thames, with the intention of sending them up the Scheldt. The Dutch envoys had immediately waited upon Thurloe, Cromwell's Secretary of State, and had explained the "jealousies and inconveniencies " which might arise from a prosecution of the plan; they told him that there was no likelihood that the States-General would allow the ships to pass up the Scheldt, " the same not being permitted to our own inhabitants ", and asked him to move Cromwell not to grant the passes necessary before they could leave.[5]

It appears that the Dutch had already got wind of the scheme before this letter was made public by being read in the States-General on 19 July, and a lively discussion followed. Aitzema records that the Zeelanders took an alarmist view, saying " periculum in mora " and urging the " closure of the Scheldt ", by which they meant " that there should be transhipment at Lillo and Sas as in time of war ".[6] They

---

[1] *Cal. S.P. Venetian, 1653-4*, 102-3.
[2] Birch, T., ed., *Collection of the state papers of John Thurloe* (7 vols., 1742), I, 569; Rymer, XX, 712.
[3] Aitzema, *op. cit.*, VII, 901.
[4] H.S.R., 26 March 1653, 4 March 1654, 18 July 1654; Aitzema, *op. cit.*, VIII, 261.
[5] *Thurloe Papers*, II, 429.
[6] Aitzema, *op. cit.*, VIII, 128.

were able to point to the draft regulation for transhipment which lay ready and only needed a resolution to carry it into effect. But the Holland deputies, and behind them their principals, the provincial States, were not to be stampeded. They jeered at the Zeelanders' shifts and turns: had they not first clamoured for the opening of the Scheldt when peace was made with Spain, hoping to get the lion's share of the trade, and then, when this hope proved vain, demanded the reclosure of the river? The Hollanders even went so far as to accuse the Zeelanders, with their Orangist leanings, of wanting to use the present episode to give fresh offence to England in the interest of their party.

It was the States of Holland which undertook to settle the matter by persuading the English government not to countenance the merchants' project. The document which they had drawn up for this purpose, the "Provisional Deduction serving to inform their High Mightinesses' Ambassadors Extraordinary touching the closure of the Scheldt", is of unique importance as being the only official declaration made on the subject for nearly a century and a half after 1648.[1] It sets out to prove

that inhabitants of England, having set course with their ships and goods towards Antwerp, may not come with them further from out the sea than into the ports of Holland and Zeeland; and having there paid the proper duties are required to break cargo and to carry their wares thence in other ships.

In justification of this assertion the "Deduction" points out that not only are the Scheldt and its neighbouring channels closed on the side of the United Provinces but also

the province of Zeeland possesses by good title the right of staple over all those ships which enter the rivers above-mentioned from the sea, which ships are accordingly required to discharge their wares in Zeeland and to lade them into other ships; of which right the States of Zeeland are in immemorial possession and which is in vigorous and living exercise to this day.

In defence of this right (on which, the "Deduction" adds, the welfare of the country largely depends) the States-General have from time to time taken important resolutions, such as that of 13 January 1609 on which was based the continued closure of the Scheldt during the Truce. In the case of the definitive treaty with Spain, however, the States determined to have the right confirmed by specific engagement, and the clause which eventually became Article XIV of the Treaty of Münster was therefore insisted upon by their plenipotentiaries from the

---

[1] It is printed in several places: *H.S.R.*, 24 July 1654; Aitzema, *op. cit.*, VIII, 129*ff*; *Verbael Gehouden door de Heeren H. van Beverningk . . . Als Gedeputeerden . . . aen de ·Republyck van Engelandt* (The Hague, 1725), 514-7.

outset of the negotiation. The Spanish representatives made a show of opposition to the clause but did not sustain it, and the article as originally drafted by the States-General was incorporated in the treaty. In conformity with this article

the practice (which had never been interrupted) has been maintained to the present day, without exception, and even with respect to the natural-born subjects and inhabitants of the States who come with their ships from out the sea carrying goods destined for the places and towns of the aforesaid King of Spain. There are thus no grounds for exempting the inhabitants of England from the practice or in any way relaxing it in their favour.

The "Deduction" concludes by refuting the argument that Article XVII of the Treaty of Westminster (which it was believed had given rise to the projected voyage) in any way prejudiced the States' right to keep the Scheldt closed. True, that article permitted the merchants of England, Scotland and Ireland to travel into and through the States' territory, and past their forts, in the course of trade, but the article itself expressly stated that it was applicable only in accordance with the country's laws. This point had already been made by the plenipotentiaries in their conversation with Thurloe and the "Deduction" approves their quickness in fastening upon it.

The chief importance of the "Deduction" lies in the clear distinction which it draws between the Zeeland right of staple and the recognition of this right by Spain in Article XIV of the Treaty of Münster. According to the "Deduction" the King of Spain, in accepting this article, had done no more than formally recognize a right of which the province of Zeeland had enjoyed "immemorial" possession; he had not conceded anything new or revolutionary, he had merely accepted something old and established. In this view, therefore, the "closure" of the Scheldt was nothing but a continuation of Zeeland's, or more strictly Middelburg's, right of staple. Historically, of course, this was absurd. Neither in the fifteenth nor in the sixteenth century had the exercise of the right of staple amounted to anything like a "closure" of the Scheldt. Middelburg had, it is true, succeeded between 1559 and 1572 in enforcing a right of staple over Western wines; but none of its attempts to extend this right to any other, much less all, of the foreign cargoes entering the Scheldt had come within measurable distance of success. The "Zeeland right of staple", of which the States made so much in the seventeenth century, was a fiction, not a fact, of history; at best, one can say that it represented what Middelburg would have liked to achieve, but conspicuously failed to achieve, a century before.[1]

---

[1] On the Middelburg staple, see above, pp. 39-40, 74-81.

This being so, it may at first sight appear strange that the States-General in its justification of the closure should have subordinated the legally irreproachable Article XIV of the treaty to a claim of such doubtful validity as the Zeeland staple. But in truth the States had no option in the matter. If they were to seek to ground the closure of the Scheldt upon any other basis than that of mere *force majeure* they must choose a form of prohibition which would operate indiscriminately against all potential users of the river. It was not enough to point to Article XIV, for this merely prevented Spanish or South Netherland ships from attempting the passage. Whether or no the now universal *pacta tertiis* rule was either clearly formulated or generally accepted in the seventeenth century[1], it would obviously have been foolish to oppose an English or Swedish subject's claim to navigate the Scheldt merely by citing a treaty to which neither England nor Sweden had been party. We have seen that in the official Spanish view (amounting to a recognition of the rule) it was no part of Spain's obligation under Article XIV to discourage "third States" from ignoring the ban or even to refuse their subjects entry if they succeeded. The States were well aware of the Spanish attitude and they were not likely to miss its legal implication.

The States-General's invoking of the "staple theory" (which, as we have seen, dates back to 1608[2]) was therefore not the gratuitous elaboration of their case which it has appeared to some historians but an integral and indispensable part of that case. In this way alone could they represent the closure, not as a legally indefensible outcome of the successful use of force which "third States" might be tempted to use force to overthrow, but as an established feature of their own municipal law which all friendly states were bound to respect. The modern text-book tells us that it was Article XIV of the Treaty of Münster which gave the Dutch the right to close the Scheldt; it is a proposition to which the authors of the "Deduction" would hardly have subscribed.

We for our part must guard against the error of attaching too much importance to the argument presented in the "Deduction". Whether the Dutch won or lost their case would be determined less by its intrinsic soundness than by the balance of the opposing forces and interests. The "Deduction" was adopted by the States-General on

---

[1] The historians of international law seem to be silent on this interesting point. Colbert's recognition of the rule is illustrated below, p. 126.
[2] See above, pp. 94-5.

23 July and sent to the plenipotentiaries in London (who had in the meantime heard nothing further about the scheme[1]), and was delivered by them to Thurloe. Of any official discussion of the question in London there is little or no trace; all we know is that Cromwell and his advisers, if they had ever considered giving the project their blessing, decided not to do so, and that in consequence nothing further came of it. It is not even clear whether the "Deduction" itself had any influence on the decision, although the determination which underlay it was doubtless an important factor. In any case, the decision is easy enough to understand. To Cromwell the issue at stake must have seemed a small, even a trivial, one; it was three-quarters of a century since Englishmen had taken their ships up to Antwerp, and during that time trade had found new routes and markets which lessened the value of a reopening of the Antwerp route.[2] But what was of little moment to England was of great, even vital, importance to the Dutch, whose immediate and unmistakable reaction to the news of the English project left no doubt that they would oppose it strenuously. Was Cromwell, who only a few months before had successfully carried through a difficult and delicate peace-settlement with them, to jeopardize that settlement, and all that hung on it, for the hypothetical advantages of the Scheldt navigation? That settlement, moreover, had only been made possible through the co-operation of De Witt and the States of Holland; to raise the issue of the Scheldt now would be to compromise the position of these allies and to present the anti-Republican and Orangist elements in the Republic with a welcome opportunity of making trouble.[3] Above all, we know that it was just at this time (July-August 1654) that Cromwell reached his greatest decision in the field of foreign policy, the decision to go to war with Spain. A decision to challenge the closure of the Scheldt necessarily involved an understanding with Spain; conversely, a worsening of relations with Spain would make the reopening of the river both more difficult and, if it should be achieved, less valuable. The outbreak of the Anglo-Spanish war in 1655 did, in fact, "settle" the Scheldt question as far as England was concerned for some years to come.

[1] *Thurloe Papers*, II, 454.
[2] For the commercial background of the project see Ashley, M.P., *Financial and Commercial Policy under the Cromwellian Protectorate* (Oxford, 1934), especially pp. 121*ff*.
[3] See the news letter of 31 July 1654 from The Hague printed in *Thurloe Papers*, II, 495: "The protector, in letting fall the design of keeping the Escault open, hath thereby obliged this state, and especially Holland, for already friends of the Pr. of Orange did expect thereby some new disturbance."

Here were reasons enough to deter Cromwell from meddling with the Scheldt in 1654. The historian of the river cannot but feel some professional disappointment at the tame ending of what might have been a *cause célèbre*. There seems to have been some surprise, as well as great relief, in the Republic that the Protector, who had displayed such obstinacy in the recent peace-negotiation, should yield the point so easily, a circumstance for which the Hollanders did not fail to claim the credit.[1] What would have happened if Cromwell had again proved obstinate it is difficult to say. It is inconceivable that he would have risked a resumption of the war for the sake of the few individuals who stood to gain by the opening of the river; it seems much more likely that the determined stand which the maritime provinces were clearly prepared to make would have kept the river closed.

Between the "attempt" of 1654 and the crisis of 1672 occurred an episode which showed how jealously the Dutch would in future guard their right. In February 1656 the States-General received a request from the town of Lübeck for permission to send three ships up the Scheldt to Antwerp with building materials for the repair of the Easterlings' House (*Oosters-huys*) at Antwerp. The deputies of Holland and Zeeland replied that they would report the matter to their principals, the provincial States, that is to say, adds Aitzema in reporting the episode, " they honourably excused themselves, for the decision would not come from Holland and Zeeland in a year and a day ".[2] It is in this connection that Aitzema makes clear that the Dutch did not, as they professed to the outside world, impose transhipment on themselves.

There is no evidence that the English government raised the question of the Scheldt during or after the war of 1665-7.[3] During the negotiations for the treaty of 1667 the Dutch plenipotentiaries did, indeed, profess to see in one of the English proposals an attempt to divert part of the trade between England and Germany through the Southern Netherlands, but the Englishmen explained it away.[4] If throughout the 'fifties and 'sixties England remained the most likely source of danger to the closure, a threat of another and more serious kind arose in connection with the French schemes for the political future of the Southern Netherlands. From 1648 until 1659 France

---

[1] *Cal. S.P. Venetian, 1653-4,* 248.
[2] *Op. cit.,* VIII, 660.
[3] It is interesting to notice that Thurloe mentioned the closure in the review of Anglo-Dutch relations which he drew up for the Restoration government. Firth, C. H., " Secretary Thurloe on the Relations of England and Holland," in *E.H.R.,* XXI (1906), 319-27.
[4] D'Estrades, G. L. Comte, *Lettres* (9 vols., The Hague, 1743), V, 430*ff*.

remained at war with Spain and continued to prosecute the conquest of the South; from 1657 she had the help of England. The prospect of the establishment of French domination in the South was one which the Republic could not view without misgivings; that England should be the partner of France made matters worse rather than better.

We should have [wrote John de Witt] to be prepared for the English, once masters of the Flemish ports and doubtless also of the chief trading towns of Brabant, to divert trade from our provinces and to establish it in those countries. They would not hold themselves (and in fact they would not be) obliged to observe the precautions stipulated between the Republic and Spain, such as the closure of the Scheldt, the equalization of the Flemish ports, etc.[1]

It was with the object of protecting the Republic from these dangers that De Witt lent his support to Mazarin's scheme of 1658 for the erection of the Southern Netherlands into an independent Republic, under the guarantee of its neighbours. Whether or no this was intended seriously, France soon afterwards made peace with Spain and the South remained under its old masters.

The question of its future came up again in 1663. As in 1632 there were two plans, one for "cantonnement" and another for partition. De Witt would have preferred the former, but had little hope of persuading Louis XIV to adopt it. In either case, he was prepared to demand guarantees that the new arrangements should not prejudice the closure of the Scheldt; Amsterdam wanted a specific engagement to this effect inserted in the treaty embodying the plan.[2] Whether any such clause would have been worth much once the French were masters of a large part of the Southern Netherlands is open to question. Fortunately for the Republic Louis XIV let the scheme drop. Soon he was claiming the whole of the Southern Netherlands as part of his wife's inheritance. In organizing the Triple Alliance, the coalition which helped to check his realization of this claim, the Republic took a leading part, and Pomponne, the French ambassador at The Hague, wrote that

Anvers seul et l'Escault décide de la succession de la reine et l'intérêt seul d'Amsterdam doit armer seul l'Angleterre, la Suède et les princes de l'Empire.

The years 1668-72 were noteworthy not only for the diplomatic preparation of the Anglo-French assault on the Republic but also for

---

[1] To Cornelis de Graeff van Zuidpolsbroek, 29 July 1658. Japikse, N., ed., *Brieven van Johan de Witt* (Hist. Genootsch. Werken, 3de serie, 18, 25, 31, 33, A'dam, 1906-13), II, 49-50; also printed in Dollot, R., *Les Origines da Neutralité de la Belgique* (Paris, 1902), 544.
[2] *Ibid.*, 171.
[3] To Louis XIV, 18 April 1669; quoted *ibid.*, 194-5.

the economic war with which Colbert prefaced that onslaught. It is interesting to find that among his numerous schemes for discomfiting the Dutch Colbert did not overlook a challenge to their closure of the Scheldt. There is preserved a minute in his own hand on the subject, dating from 1668.[1] He begins by declaring that the prosperity of Amsterdam is founded upon the ruin of Antwerp, which the Dutch compassed by means of the closure of· the Scheldt. After quoting Article XIV Colbert explains that it undoubtedly empowers the Dutch to prevent the passage of the Scheldt by subjects of the King of Spain; but (he continues)

ils n'ont pas ce mesme pouvoir à l'égard des vaisseaux françois, qui peuvent entrer sans difficulté, et, par ce moyen, le Roy peut restablir le commerce d'Anvers, puisque les sujets de Sa Majesté peuvent y porter toutes sortes de marchandises.

Colbert clearly grasped the fact that France, as a " third State ", was not bound by the Treaty of Münster (he evidently knew nothing of the " Deduction " of 1654, with its argument designed to bring " third States " under the ban), and he recommended the King to make full use of his liberty of action. Colbert was not naïve enough to believe that the Dutch would take this lying down, but, he concludes,

il faut de nécessité, ou que les Hollandois courent risque de voir le commerce sortir de leurs mains et passer en celles des François et des Flamands, ou qu'ils s'accommodent avec la France à des conditions avantageuses au service du roy et proportionnées à l'importance de ces avantages.

Nothing seems to have come of this suggestion, perhaps because Louis XIV, already plotting the downfall of the Republic, was unwilling either to be diverted from this object or to put the Dutch on their guard.

The Anglo-French alliance of 1670, and the war of 1672, threatened to put an end not merely to the closure of the Scheldt but to the very existence of the Republic. From the outset of the negotiations for the dismemberment of the Republic the English government laid claim to Walcheren and Cadzand, although the marquisate of Veere and Flushing was reserved for its legal owner, the Prince of Orange.[2] Charles II and his ministers, blind as they were to the larger interests of their country, were fully aware of the strategic importance of the mouth of the Scheldt and determined to secure a commanding position

[1] Printed in Clément, P., *Lettres, Instructions et Mémoires de Colbert* (10 vols., Paris, 1861-82), II, ii, 448; referred to in Cole C. W., *Colbert and a Century of French Mercantilism* (2 vols., New York, 1939), I, 438, but with little appreciation of its significance.

[2] The first draft of the treaty submitted by the English government on 18 Dec. 1669 is printed in Mignet, F. A. M. A., *Négociations relatives à la succession d'Espagne sous Louis XIV* (4 vols., Paris, 1835-42), III, 117-23.

there. They carried their point, and by the secret Treaty of Dover of 22 May 1670 it was agreed that the English share of the territory to be torn from the Republic should comprise Walcheren, Cadzand and the town of Sluis.[1] Six months later, in the " bogus " treaty intended to hoodwink the Protestant members of the English ministry, the English share was increased by the addition of the islands of Goeree and Voorne, commanding the mouth of the Maas.[2]

Had the Anglo-French attack on the Republic in the spring of 1672 gone according to plan, it is probable that England would have acquired, at least for a time, the territories named in this rogues' bargain. In that case, the Scheldt would almost certainly have been opened. Moreover, even if the Dutch had afterwards rallied to fight a second War of Independence and to recover the lost territory, it is doubtful whether they would have been in a position to close the river again. As it was, while the land-invasion carried out by the French struck deep into the heart of the Republic's territory,[3] the plan for a landing from the sea, for which England was chiefly responsible, failed completely in the face of De Ruyter's resolute naval defence. To this fact, and to the refusal of the young Prince of Orange to betray his country by lending himself to the enemies' schemes, the Republic owed its survival of the first shock of the assault and hence its ultimate emergence from the war with its territory and institutions intact and with the Scheldt still closed. Almost from the outset the failure to effect a landing on the Dutch coast deprived the English government of any real chance of obtaining the coveted territory. When an English embassy consisting of two of the ministry, Buckingham and Arlington, delivered the terms to the Prince of Orange, newly restored to the offices of his ancestors by the revolutionary movement within the Republic, they were met with a flat refusal to cede any towns or territory; the ambassadors' device of calling the towns " cautionary ", that is, redeemable by the Dutch (on the analogy of the towns so ceded in 1585), made no difference to the answer.[4] The ambassadors then moved on to Heeswijk, where Louis XIV had his headquarters, and there helped to formulate the final allied terms (6 July 1672). In these, while France was to annex nearly all the Generality lands, including Zeeland-Flanders, the left bank of the Scheldt, England's share was

---

[1] The treaty is printed in Mignet, *op. cit.*, 187-97, and in Lingard, J., *History of England* (10 vols., 1849), IX, 503-10, and summarized in Ogg, D., *England in the reign of Charles II* (2 vols., Oxford, 1934), I, 344-6.
[2] Mignet, *op. cit.*, III, 256-67.
[3] But the French attack on Zeeland-Flanders failed before Aardenburg (27 June 1672).
[4] Barbour, V., *Henry Bennet Earl of Arlington* (1914), 194-5; Trevelyan, M. C., *William the Third and the Defence of Holland, 1672-4* (1930), 254-5.

fixed at Walcheren, Goeree and Voorne to the north, and Cadzand and Sluis to the south, of the Scheldt estuary. From Antwerp on their return journey the ambassadors explained to their colleague Clifford the inclusion of Cadzand and Sluis:

although you gave us a direction from his Majesty not to insist upon having surrendered to him Sluse and Cadsand, but rather to gratify the French with yeelding them to them, not to retard the making the peace, yet the matter not coming to bear, wee upon advice forbore to owne it, neither have they called upon us to explaine ourselves thereupon, wherefore we humbly hope that his Majesty reflecting upon the importance of those places will bee pleased to retract his condescention therein, because what he is like to have besides will bee of little value without them for the opening the river to Antwerp, and consequently lessening the trade and value of Amsterdam, and this made us heretofore fight this battle so warmely with the ministers, that perhaps they thought it fitt to avoyde the coming againe to us in the same argument. . . .[1]

This despatch shows clearly not only that the ambassadors were intent on securing the opening of the Scheldt but, what is more significant, that they realized from which direction the opposition to the opening was likely to come. It was, and is, inconceivable that a Dutch Republic shorn of most of Zeeland and of all Zeeland-Flanders, and crippled by the huge war-indemnity which the allies proposed to exact, could have raised a finger to prevent the opening of the Scheldt. But a France which held territory on both banks of the river between Antwerp and the sea,[2] and which completely dominated, if she did not speedily annex, the Southern Netherlands themselves, might well attempt to close the Scheldt to English ships, and England find that she had helped to break the Dutch closure to no purpose.

Happily, this remains merely a speculation, since Europe did not yet have to suffer the eclipse of the Dutch Republic and the establishment of French power on the Lower Scheldt. When, two years later, England made a separate peace with the Republic, there was no question of any cession of Dutch territory or any relaxation of the closure of the Scheldt; nor, so far as we know, did the subject recur in the negotiations with France which eventually brought the war to a close in 1678.

It is clear that at no time during the quarter of a century following the Treaty of Münster was the closure of the Scheldt immune from

---

[1] Printed in Colenbrander, H. T., *Bescheiden uit vreemde archieven omtrent de groote Nederlandsche Zeeoorlogen* (Rijks Geschiedk. Publ., Kleine Serie, 18-19. The Hague, 1919), II, 169.

[2] Besides holding the left bank (Zeeland-Flanders) France would have held a strip of the right bank in the neighbourhood of Bergen-op-Zoom as a result of her annexation of States-Brabant.

challenge by one or other of the Republic's neighbours and rivals. In meeting such a challenge Article XIV of the treaty was of little value; hence the development of the "staple theory" as exemplified in the "Deduction" of 1654. But the real "sanction" of the closure of the river during these years was the determination and ability of the Republic to defend it. From shortly after 1680, however, the conditions of the problems were to undergo a change; instead of being based upon a dubious legal theory the closure was to become the subject of international guarantee and the responsibility for enforcing it would no longer rest with the Republic alone. This important development will be traced in the following section.

(iii) *The Closure under International Guarantee, 1680-1780.*

By about 1680 the closure of the Scheldt had withstood a number of crises, actual and potential, and the Dutch might feel reasonably confident that, so long as the Southern Netherlands remained under Spain, they could defend it against any further attack. But the days of the Spanish regime in the South were already numbered; the King of Spain, the weakling Charles II, neither had nor was likely to have issue, and the Southern Netherlands, in common with the rest of his dominions, were thus destined to pass to one or other of the claimants to the inheritance. In these circumstances the problem of keeping the Scheldt closed became merged in the larger problem of securing a settlement of the Southern Netherlands which would safeguard the interests of the Republic.

That such a settlement was ultimately secured was due almost entirely to the alliance between the Republic and England which resulted from the events of 1688. There had been anticipations of this alliance before that date, notably in 1668 and 1674-8, but they had been exceptions to the general trend of Anglo-Dutch relations during the period. From 1688, however, the two countries developed, under the common leadership of William III, an identity of outlook and policy which made the "Maritime Powers" virtually a unit in international relations. The major results of their collaboration, which bulk large in the history of the period, lie outside the scope of the present study; we are concerned only with a small by-product, the evolution of an international guarantee of the closure of the Scheldt.

For the closure the advent of the Anglo-Dutch alliance had both a negative and a positive significance. As we have seen, since 1648, as indeed earlier, England had been the chief potential danger to the closure; since the crisis of 1672 the danger had certainly diminished, but as late as 1685 Gastañaga, the Governor of the Southern Netherlands, could suggest using James II as an intermediary to secure the opening of the river.[1] After 1688 all danger from England vanished; it would not reappear for close on a century. But that was not the full extent of the change. By the very nature of her new relationship with the Republic England was led, not merely to desist from her own former opposition to the closure, but to discourage opposition to it from other quarters. For if, as the Dutch maintained, the closure was a prime condition of their security and strength, then England was bound in her own interest to defend it. In short, England recognized that—to adapt a phrase current in our own day—her frontier lay on the Scheldt.

The problem of the future of the Southern Netherlands, which had so long exercised both France and the Maritime Powers, entered on a new phase with the negotiations between them for a peaceful partition of the Spanish monarchy. By the First Partition Treaty (24 September/11 October 1698) the Southern Netherlands were allotted to the Electoral Prince of Bavaria, through his mother a great-nephew of the King of Spain and a grandson of the Emperor; the prince was a child of seven, and the actual government of the Southern provinces would have been vested in his father, the Elector Max Emmanuel, who since 1692 had governed them with wide powers from the King of Spain. From the point of view of William III, who in these negotiations spoke for both of the Maritime Powers, this was the most satisfactory solution, for the conversion of the Bavarian governorship into Bavarian sovereignty promised to raise few problems.[2] Unfortunately the death of the prince within three months of the treaty not only nullified it but made the negotiation of a new one far more difficult. However, the difficulties were overcome, and on 3 and 25 March 1700 the Second Partition Treaty was signed. This time the Southern Netherlands went, with all that had previously gone to the prince, to the Archduke Charles, younger son of the Emperor. Although the Maritime Powers had at that time no particular desire to see the house of Austria established in the Southern Netherlands, that prospect was greatly to be

---

[1] Cuvelier and Lefèvre, *op. cit.*, V, 470 *n* 2.
[2] The treaty said to have been signed by the Elector with the Republic in August 1698, by which, in return for certain concessions, including a strengthening of the Dutch position on the Scheldt, the Republic guaranteed him possession of the Southern Netherlands, is now generally considered spurious. See Legrelle, A., *La diplomatie française et la Succession d'Espagne* (4 vols., Paris and Ghent, 1888-92), II, 498-507, and Bussemaker, Th., in *Handelingen en Mededeelingen v.d. Maatschappij Nederl. Letterk.*, 1909-10, 147. The treaty is printed in Lamberty, *Mémoires pour servir à l'histoire du XVIIIe siècle* (12 vols., The Hague, 1724-34), I, 115, and summarized in Dollot, *op. cit.*, 317.

preferred to the only practical alternative, the establishment of a French prince there.

There is no need to describe here the well-known sequence of events which followed the signature of this treaty; its repudiation by both the Emperor and the King of Spain; the King's bequest of the entire Spanish monarchy to Louis XIV's grandson Philip of Anjou, and its acceptance by the French King; and finally, the proclamation of the new sovereign as Philip V at Brussels on 19 November 1700 and the occupation by French troops, early in February 1701, of the Barrier towns which since 1697 had, by agreement with Spain, been garrisoned by Dutch troops. Thus, within a year of the conclusion of the Second Partition Treaty, it had become a mere " scrap of paper ", and French power was installed from Antwerp to Gibraltar. Louis XIV's confirmation, in return for a defensive alliance, of Max Emmanuel's governorship of the Southern Netherlands (9 March 1701), made little difference to the reality of the situation there, especially as the Elector himself soon returned to Bavaria.

Legally, of course, there could be no question that in succeeding to the Spanish throne Philip V had inherited Spain's treaty-obligations, and among them those of the Treaty of Münster; he was thus no less bound to respect the closure of the Scheldt than his predecessors had been. But if his grandfather should choose to do now what Colbert had suggested he should do in 1668, namely, to assert the right of his subjects to pass freely up and down the Scheldt, was it likely that Philip V would do otherwise than Philip IV had resolved to do in such a case, which was " to receive them favourably "? Louis did, indeed, instruct his ambassador at The Hague to let fall a word about reopening the Scheldt in the event of hostilities and to add that " if commerce were once re-established there, it would not be safe to rely upon effecting a change in it at the conclusion of peace ".[1] If Louis did thus attempt to use the Scheldt to bully the Dutch, it was a tactical blunder comparable with his recognition later in 1701 of the Old Pretender as King of England. England and the Republic had both adopted a formally " correct " attitude by recognizing Philip V as King of Spain; for Louis to use the forms of diplomacy to challenge the Protestant Succession was a foolish gesture. From being indifferent or even hostile to William III's view of the situation opinion in both counties reacted sharply during the year, and on 7 September 1701 the

[1] Legrelle, *op. cit.*, IV, 115; Dollot, *op. cit.*, 330. A statement in Génard, *Anvers à travers les âges*, II, 530, suggests that French ships made a show of entering the mouth of the Scheldt in 1701, but I have been unable to establish the truth of this.

Grand Alliance came into being at The Hague. Among its aims was the recovery of the Southern Netherlands and their erection into a permanent barrier against France; it did not, however, envisage any change in the succession to Spain itself, provided the crowns of Spain and France were never united.

It was in accordance with the Grand Alliance that on 8 May 1702 the Republic declared war on France and Spain; England's declaration followed six days later. Since the Republic had recognized Philip V as lawful King of Spain, it appears to follow that, in the light of the then prevailing doctrine that all treaties are abrogated by the outbreak of war between the contracting parties, the Dutch declaration of war put an end to the Treaty of Münster. The point is not merely an academic one. Although as long as the war lasted it scarcely mattered whether or not Spain considered herself bound by Article XIV, it mattered a good deal to the Dutch whether they emerged from the war with or without any legal sanction of the closure. They were, of course, determined that whoever should succeed to the King of Spain's estate in the Southern Netherlands must accept that estate with all its encumbrances, but this only made it the more necessary to place these encumbrances upon a sound legal footing.[1]

The Dutch must have believed that they had gone a long way towards this objective with the signature in October 1709 of the First Barrier Treaty, commonly known as the Townshend Treaty from the name of its English negotiator. In return for a guarantee of the Protestant Succession the Republic secured the assent of England to virtually all its Barrier demands; moreover, Article XV of the treaty, after reciting Articles XIV and XV of the Treaty of Münster, concluded:

La reine de la Grande Bretagne promet, et s'engage, que Leurs Hautes Puissances ne seront jamais inquiétées dans leur droit et possession à cet égard, directement ni indirectement. . . .[2]

It was the first time that any "third State" had formally recognized and guaranteed the permanent closure of the Scheldt. It was the first step—although, as it turned out, a false one—towards giving the closure international status.

---

[1] The war in the Netherlands provoked trading-difficulties similar to those during the Eighty Years' War; for example, on 7 June 1706 the States-General forbade the detention by the Zeeland Admiralty at Lillo of Northern ships bound for Antwerp. *Recueil van alle de Placaeten . . . betreffende . . . Zeesaaken* (13 vols., The Hague, 1701-80), III, 483-5.

[2] Besides being included in the usual collections, the Townshend Treaty will be found, with the treaties of 1713 and 1715, as one of the appendices to Geikie, R., and Montgomery, Isabel A., *The Dutch Barrier, 1705-1719* (Cambridge, 1930), 377ff.

Unfortunately for the Dutch, whose waning enthusiasm for the war the Townshend Treaty, as it was intended to do, helped to revive, the following year brought a change of ministry in England and with it a radical change of policy. The new ministers were soon negotiating privately with France and, as soon as these overtures gave promise of success, they informed the Republic that the Townshend Treaty was now considered too unfavourable to England and would have to be revised. When, early in 1712, the ministry laid the treaty before Parliament and carried a resolution in the Commons declaring it "destructive of the trade and industry of Great Britain" and its authors "enemies to the Queen and Kingdom", the Townshend Treaty was dead. Thus when the official negotiation with France opened at Utrecht the Dutch found themselves not only dependent upon Britain for the terms of the new settlement of the Southern Netherlands but once again without any formal recognition of the closure of the Scheldt. The terms which they secured by the Second Barrier Treaty of January 1713 were far less favourable than those of 1709; among other advantages the Republic lost the English guarantee of the closure of the Scheldt. But although the English government refused the Dutch demand for the retention of this clause, its refusal sprang rather from the temporary urge to whittle down the obnoxious Townshend Treaty than from any significant change of outlook. English ministers might show intense jealousy of any concession calculated to perpetuate the Dutch trading-monopoly in Brabant and Flanders, but in the long run this was bound to be outweighed by the cogent political arguments which had for a generation enlisted English support for the closure.

By the Franco-Dutch Treaty of Utrecht (13 April 1713) Louis XIV, on behalf of his grandson, ceded to the Republic what remained to him of the Southern Netherlands; the Republic was to retain them until it had reached agreement with the Emperor on the terms of the Barrier to be established there, and they were then to pass under the sovereignty of Austria. By a separate article Louis also promised that

tous les avantages et utilités de commerce et de navigation et autres, portez par le traité de Munster, seroient accordez aux Etats Généraux.

Although this article related primarily to the terms of Dutch trade with Spain and the Indies, it could be construed as a Spanish, and indirectly also a French, recognition of the continued validity of Articles XIV and XV despite their abrogation or suspension since 1702, and hence as a contribution to the legal security of the closure. But what mattered far more was that Austria, as Spain's successor in the

Southern Netherlands, should accept the closure. Britain and the Republic were already agreed on the conditions to be demanded of the Emperor, but it was only after a difficult negotiation lasting for more than a year that the three governments reached agreement in the Third Barrier Treaty (15 November 1715). Article XXVI of this treaty, after dealing with the terms of British and Dutch trade in the Southern Netherlands, provided that trade between the Northern and Southern Netherlands was to be carried on

de la manière portée par les Articles du Traité fait à Munster les quels articles viennent d'être confirmés par le présent article.

It was by this loosely-worded clause that Austria (and Britain) formally accepted the continued closure of the Scheldt. The looseness may have been deliberate. The negotiation of the treaty, which took place at Antwerp, had been the occasion for a fresh campaign by the town against the closure,[1] and the signatories may have preferred the indirect form of recognition adopted in the article to a blunt restatement of Articles XIV and XV. It is in any case unlikely that the Emperor harboured any *arrière-pensée* on the subject, if only because he agreed at the same time to a frontier-revision which considerably strengthened the Republic's position on the river. By Article XVII of the Barrier Treaty the Republic acquired the polders of Doel, St. Anna and Keetenisse, a stretch of territory on the left bank running from south of Fort Liefkenshoek to the north-easterly " tip " of Flanders. As early as 1668 the States-General had considered the desirability of acquiring this territory as a cover to the fort,[2] and its possession undoubtedly strengthened their position on this side; on the other bank, however, their forts of Lillo and Frederick Henry remained isolated.

The significance of Article XXVI of the Barrier Treaty can best be appreciated if we glance back at the two previous phases of the closure. Throughout the first phase, from 1585 to 1648, the closure had remained a war-measure, which needed no other justification than that of national security. During the second phase, the phase of the Münster regime, from 1648 to 1702, the Republic had been forced to rely, in defending the closure against challenge by " third States ", upon the dubious " staple theory ". But if during this period the theoretical basis of the closure left a good deal to be desired, that weakness was compensated by the power which the Republic could wield in its defence. After 1715 this situation was to be reversed. The power

---

[1] Huisman, M., *La Belgique commerciale sous l'Empereur Charles VI. La Compagnie d'Ostende* (Brussels and Paris, 1902), 67 and *n* 3.
[2] Aitzema, *op. cit.*, XIV, 1008.

of the Republic, already drained by the exertions of the war-years, would undergo a steady decline during the next forty years, so that by the middle of the century the country would have fallen back into the second or even third rank of European states. It would have been difficult, if not impossible, for a state so weakened to have maintained the closure of the Scheldt, had it been left to do so alone. The importance of the treaty of 1715 was that it relieved the Republic of part of the burden by making the closure the subject of international recognition and guarantee.

Ironically, it was the two states which furnished this recognition in 1715 which were later to take the lead in attempting to abolish the closure, a fact which bears out the importance to the Republic of having so long enjoyed their acquiescence in it; but for the treaty of 1715 the campaign of the 'eighties might have come a good deal earlier. As it was, the Republic remained for nearly three-quarters of a century in peaceful possession of a right which alone it would have been scarcely capable of defending. True, it had to meet one serious attempt to upset the economic settlement confirmed by the treaty of 1715, namely, the establishment of 1722 of the Ostend Company. But that project did not involve any challenge to the closure of the Scheldt; on the contrary, like the earlier attempts to develop the route through the Flemish sea-ports, it was based upon an acceptance of the closure as being too established an institution to overthrow.

The failure of the Barrier Treaty to fulfil its primary function of providing a line of defence against France was devastatingly exposed during the War of the Austrian Succession. In two brief campaigns (1744-5) the French overran the greater part of the Southern Netherlands, and in June 1746 they occupied Antwerp. In the following year began the invasion of the Republic; during April and May the French conquered all Zeeland-Flanders and in September they captured the great fortress of Bergen-op-Zoom, together with the whole line of Scheldt-forts. By the beginning of 1748 Zeeland lay open to invasion. At Antwerp the French occupation again stirred hopes of the reopening of the Scheldt;[1] but fifty years were to pass before another French invasion brought this result in its train. Not only was France unable to raise this question, her losses elsewhere forced her to abandon all her conquests in the Netherlands. The allies were thus in a position to re-establish the regime of 1715. But Austria made no secret of her disgust with the whole Barrier system, which involved such inroads

[1] Mertens and Torfs, *op. cit.*, VI, 151.

upon her sovereignty in the Netherlands without materially contributing to their security. By the Treaty of Aix-la-Chapelle, therefore, although the Republic retained the right to garrison the Barrier fortresses, the treaty of 1715 was not formally confirmed. The Empress subsequently repudiated any intention of infringing it, but certain of its provisions, notably that governing the payment of the Austrian contribution towards the upkeep of the Barrier, she would observe only in return for commercial concessions which the Maritime Powers were unwilling to grant, so that these provisions became a dead letter.

If the Barrier Treaty, and with it the Austrian recognition of the closure of the Scheldt, therefore emerged somewhat shaken after 1748, a far more serious threat developed out of the Austrian decision to abandon the " old system " of alliance with the Maritime Powers in favour of an alliance with France. Completed by 1756, this aspect of the " diplomatic revolution " of that year, by removing the century-old French threat to the Netherlands, severed the chief remaining link between the former allies and destroyed whatever interest Austria retained in the Barrier system. Eventually, in 1780, the new Emperor Joseph II decided to demolish the Barrier fortresses, and two years later the Republic withdrew its last remaining garrisons from them. Since, in doing. so, the States-General explicitly reserved all their rights under the treaty of 1715, the winding-up of the Barrier system in 1782 did not constitute an abrogation of that treaty. But when one of the signatories had by unilateral action secured the suspension of its central provisions, the remainder of the treaty could not fail to be compromised.

The first rumours of a new attempt to open the Scheldt were already abroad. Paradoxically, they were prompted by the revival, from about 1760, of the traffic reaching Antwerp by way of Ostend and Ghent. During these years a small but regular traffic developed along this route. In 1776, for no very clear reason, this traffic suddenly increased, and it was then that the Antwerpers began to talk about the reopening of the Scheldt.[1] They were doubtless encouraged by the suggestions already current that the Emperor Joseph II, the heir to the Austrian throne, intended to raise this, and the question of the Barrier, as soon as his other preoccupations allowed. Thus even before 1780, when the death of Maria Theresa gave Joseph II a free hand with his multifarious projects, the Dutch had grounds for believing that they might soon be called upon to face a new challenge to the closure.

[1] Mertens and Torfs, *op. cit.*, VI, 156; Colenbrander, H. T., ed., *Dépêches van Thulemeyer, 1763-1788* (*Hist. Genootsch. Werken*, 3e serie, 30, Amsterdam, 1912), 158, 160.

In these circumstances the Republic might have been expected to turn for support to the third signatory of the Barrier Treaty. But since the middle of the century Anglo-Dutch relations had undergone a progressive deterioration. Not only did the decline of the Republic diminish the importance of the Dutch alliance to Britain, but within the Republic the anti-British " Patriot " party was getting the upper hand and appeared bent on effecting a minor " diplomatic revolution " by drawing closer to France. Thus the Dutch neither could nor would look to Britain for support. The climax came in 1780, when, as a result of growing friction over Dutch trade with countries already at war with Britain, the Republic found itself in the ranks of Britain's enemies. On 10 December 1780 Britain and the Republic went to war for the fourth and last time.

The outbreak of this war brought to an end the British recognition of the closure which had lasted in fact since 1688 and in law since 1715. Whether it simultaneously released the Emperor from his obligation in this respect is a question for the international lawyer; but since Joseph II had already (7 November) shown how he intended to take advantage of the rupture by repudiating the Barrier system, the question was, and remains, of purely academic interest.[1] Thus at the close of 1780 the Republic found itself, both in law and in fact, worse placed to defend the closure than ever before. Neither Austria nor Britain could be counted on to lift a finger to help keep the river closed; on the contrary, they might be expected to join forces in getting it opened. When, in addition, we remember how avowedly hostile was " the spirit of the age " to all such " unnatural " restrictions on the freedom of individuals and of nations, the odds against the survival of the closure in the early 1780's appear long indeed. That it withstood the initial crisis shows to what an extent it had become part of the established order of things. But what had been its salvation in 1784 was to prove its undoing in 1792, for it was as part of that established order that it was to be swept away in the onrush of the French Revolution.

---

[1] In this connection it is to be noted that the Emperor cited his treaty-obligations as the main obstacle to co-operation with Britain against the closure in 1781 (see below, p. 139); but they did not prevent his own attempt three years later.

PART THREE
THE REOPENING, 1780—1839

CHAPTER SIX

The End of the Closure, 1780—1830

THE story of the reopening of the Scheldt comprises four principal episodes. First came the unsuccessful campaign of the 1780's, culminating in the celebrated attempt of the Emperor Joseph II to compel tht Dutch Republic to open the river. Ten years later Revolutionary France overthrew the Republic and with it the closure of the Scheldt. But although the year 1795 marked the real end of the closure, it was not until 1815 that the reunion of the Netherlands under the ægis of the Great Powers promised to effect a permanent solution of the " Scheldt question ". This promise was not, however, to be fulfilled. In 1830 came the Belgian Revolution and with it the need to seek a settlement of the question along new lines. That settlement was ultimately achieved by the treaties of 1839.

The present chapter deals with the first three episodes and covers the years 1780-1830. The negotiations of 1830-39 and the resulting settlement are the subject of the three chapters which follow.

(1) *The Austro-British Campaign against the Closure, 1780-85.*[1]

The plan of the present chapter, according to which the attempts of 1781 and 1784-5 are treated as the first stage in the reopening of the Scheldt, implies that they introduced a new element into the " Scheldt question ". While this is true of the later and more famous of the two episodes, it is not true of the earlier, which was wholly traditional in character and which is placed here instead of at the end of the last chapter solely on grounds of convenience.

When the fourth Anglo-Dutch war broke out in December 1780 the Dutch ports were closed to English trade for the first time for over a century. Throughout that time Britain had acquiesced in, and for the greater part of it had formally recognized, the closure of the Scheldt as a necessary condition of the prosperity of the Republic, upon which she had formerly relied as the first line of defence against France. But now that the Dutch had thrown in their lot with France there was no reason why Britain should not seek to reopen the Antwerp route to the Continent. Accordingly, early in 1781[2] the British

[1] The standard account is Magnette, F., *Joseph II et la liberté de l'Escaut. La France et l'Europe* (Brussels, 1897).
[2] The first tentative approach had been made in Aug. 1780, before the outbreak of war, but received no reply.

government sounded Vienna on the subject. Joseph II, already imbued with the ideas which were to inspire his own attempt three years later, was not unsympathetic, but his old chancellor Kaunitz poured cold water on a scheme which, for the sake of Antwerp, would probably lead to a rupture with France and perhaps involve the Empire in another Seven Years' War. Joseph II allowed himself to be persuaded, and the British overture was killed by the reply that in this matter Austria was bound by treaty.[1] The same fate befell an attempt to bring pressure to bear at Vienna through Antwerp itself. When, on the outbreak of war, Sir Joseph Yorke, the British ambassador, quitted The Hague, he came home by way of Antwerp, where he improved the occasion by urging the trading community to agitate for measures to revive their trade, including the opening of the Scheldt. He succeeded in securing the presentation of a petition in this sense by the town's representatives to the States of Brabant, which in turn brought the matter before the government at Brussels. But there it was frowned upon as an unwarranted intrusion into the sphere of foreign policy and officially ignored; even if it had got as far as Vienna it would have made no difference to the Imperial government's attitude.[2]

The British government's decision not to pursue the matter in the face of Austria's *non possumus* shows how purely " political " its attitude was; both the raising and the shelving of the question were " prompted by the circumstances of the moment rather than by any considerations of general principle ", just as Cromwell's decision had been over a century earlier.[3] Accordingly the subject does not appear to have been broached during the negotiation of the peace treaty of May 1784; on the other hand, by that treaty the Dutch got nothing which in any way resembled the pre-war British recognition of the closure—they did not even succeed in restoring the historic defensive alliance of 1674—so that it remained legally most insecure.

Thereafter, the initiative passed from Great Britain to the Emperor himself. The Austrian decision not to raise the question in 1781, which came as a welcome relief to the Dutch, had been based upon the same opportunist considerations as had determined the British attitude and was no guide to the trend of future policy. It was after

---

[1] An account of this overture and of British policy in relation to Joseph's attempt, including extracts from diplomatic correspondence, will be found in Smith, H. A., *Great Britain and the Law of Nations* (in progress, 1932-), II, 279*ff*.

[2] Magnette, *op. cit.*, 30*ff*.

[3] Smith, *op. cit.*, 280. The reader of this book will, however, note with surprise Prof. Smith's statement in the preceding sentence that " it is at this point [*i.e.* 1780] that we find the first signs of any British interest in the Scheldt question ".

the conclusion of the Treaty of Versailles in September 1783 that Joseph II decided that the time had come to push forward his schemes for the revival of trade and industry in the Netherlands. A succession of "incidents" on and about the Scheldt at Doel and Liefkenshoek during the winter of 1783-4 served him for an excuse to take up the question of the river with the Republic, and on 4 May 1784 he presented an ultimatum in the shape of a *Tableau sommaire* of his demands. In this document the Emperor did not, as is often stated,[1] claim the free navigation of the river; he confined his demand to a recognition of his absolute sovereignty over the Scheldt from Antwerp down to the Dutch frontier opposite Saeftingen and, as a corollary of this, the withdrawal of the guardship at Lillo.[2] But it was clear that what he was really aiming at was the opening of the river, and on 23 August the Austrian plenipotentiary delivered a fresh ultimatum, by which the Emperor, in return for abandoning certain of his earlier demands, claimed entire liberty of navigation on the Scheldt, the restoration of the frontier of 1664 (which would involve the transfer of Doel and its neighbouring polders, ceded to the Republic in 1715[3]) and the evacuation of the Scheldt forts. The Emperor even went so far as to declare that "from the present moment" he regarded the river as "entirely and absolutely free" and that the least offence committed on it against his flag would be treated as an act of war.[4]

So it had come at last. In the one hundred and thirty-seventh year since the signing of the Treaty of Münster the King of Spain's successor at Brussels emphatically repudiated the closure of the Scheldt and announced his determination to treat its maintenance as a *casus belli*. Nothing illustrates more clearly the hold which Article XIV still exercised over the minds of all Dutchmen, Hollanders and Zeelanders, Orangists and Patriots, than the unanimity with which the States-General met the challenge. Declaring that the opening of the Scheldt would be a breach of incontestable rights and "an event upon whose issue would depend nothing less than the safety or destruction of the whole Republic and the security of its people", the States-General solemnly announced their intention of maintaining it by means of their "ancient and accustomed orders". A few days previously they

---

[1] Most recently by Prof. Smith (*op. cit.*, 285), despite the fact that he quotes the relevant clause of the *Tableau sommaire*.
[2] As a conciliatory gesture the States-General had already withdrawn the guard-ship from Lillo to the Hulstergat, that is, to within their own territorial water. Magnette, *op. cit.*, 73.
[3] See above, p. 134.
[4] Magnette, *op. cit.*, 88-9. A. Cauchie published extracts from the diplomatic correspondence relating to this episode in his "Le comte L.C.M. de Barbiano di Belgiojoso et ses papiers d'État conservés à Milan", in *Bull. Comm. Roy. d'Hist.*, LXXXI (1912), 177-200.

had resolved to restore the guardship to its position at Lillo and to station warships at the mouth of the river to stop any ship entering it from the sea.[1]

Thereupon the Emperor ordered two Austrian vessels to force the passage of the Scheldt, one from Antwerp and the other from Ostend. The brig *Louis*, which sailed down from Antwerp, was fired upon and captured by a Dutch cutter, while the other vessel was stopped and taken into Flushing (8-15 October 1784). Joseph II immediately withdrew his ambassador from The Hague, declaring that the Dutch had themselves commenced hostilities against him. For a short time war appeared probable, if not certain. It was left to France to pour oil on the troubled waters of the Scheldt and to reconcile the irate Emperor with the stubborn Dutch, a task which French diplomacy performed with consummate skill. So, instead of the threatened war, there came about the negotiated settlement of Fontainebleau (9 November 1785), the third in the long series of treaties and treaty-stipulations relating to the Scheldt.

The central article of the treaty, Article VII, was as follows:

Leurs Hautes Puissances reconnoissent le plein Droit de Souveraineté absolue et indépendante de S. M. Imp. sur toute la partie de l'Escaut depuis Anvers jusqu'au bout du Pays de Saftingen. . . . Les Etats-Généraux renoncent en conséquence à la perception et levée d'aucun Péage et Impôt dans cette partie de l'Escaut . . . de même à y gêner en aucune manière la Navigation et le commerce des Sujets de S.M. Impériale. Le reste du Fleuve . . . dont la Souveraineté continuera d'appartenir aux Etats-Généraux, sera tenu clos de leur côté, ainsi que les Canaux du Sas, du Swin et autres Bouches de Mer y aboutissans, conformément au Traité de Munster.[2]

It cost the Republic some sacrifices to keep the Scheldt closed. By Articles VIII and IX they agreed to cede Forts Lillo and Liefkenshoek and to demolish and surrender Frederick Henry and the Kruisschans;[3] they also accepted the frontier of 1664 in Zeeland-Flanders, thus losing Doel. Finally, the Emperor's magnanimity was acknowledged by a "pourboire" of ten million Holland gulden, of which nominally four and a half, in reality one and a half, millions were paid by France.

At this point it may well be asked in what way Joseph's attempt to open the Scheldt marked the opening of a new era in the history of the river. Had it not failed, as all previous attempts had failed? And was not its failure due ultimately to the same cause as theirs,

---

[1] *Ibid.*, 92, 94. For an interesting *mémoire* by Van de Spiegel, then Pensionary of Zeeland, on the closure, see Vreede, G. W., *Van de Spiegel en zijne tijdgenooten* (4 vols., Middelburg, 1874-7), II, 388-95.

[2] De Martens, G. F., *Recueil des principaux traités de paix* (Göttingen, 1791-1801), II, no. 134.

[3] To replace the lost forts the Republic built a new fort at Bath, on the south-east tip of Zuid-Beveland (see map facing p. 151).

namely, to the fact that, when it came to the test, Joseph II was as ready to tolerate the closure of the Scheldt as any of his predecessors, provided that his doing so could be made to serve another purpose? In his case, as Magnette has shown, that purpose was the exchange of the Southern Netherlands for Bavaria; the fact that the Emperor failed in his plan of using the Scheldt as a lever to procure French assent to the exchange-project does not affect the argument. Had Joseph II been as single-minded in his devotion to the cause as in 1784 he appeared to be, had he insisted on treating it as a question of principle which admitted of no compromise, who can doubt that he would have succeeded?

" To appreciate fully the importance of Joseph II's attempt to open the Scheldt ", says Magnette on the last page of his book, " we must leave Antwerp and even Belgium and visit the different capitals of Europe. It is there, after all, that the question is really fought out, it is there that the solution is found ". In these two sentences lies the clue to the whole book; Magnette (and the many later writers who founded their accounts on his work) treated the subject primarily as an episode in the diplomatic history of the time. But to us, who view the attempt of 1784-5 against a different background, its real importance lies elsewhere. If one result of the crisis was, as we have seen, to make the closure of the Scheldt the subject of a new international convention, far more precise than that of 1715, another was to make it for the first time the subject of vigorous public interest and discussion. The pamphlets of Linguet and Mirabeau are only the ablest and best-known of the many which dealt, *pro* and *contra*, with the Emperor's challenge to the Republic; the whole collection would repay detailed study.[1] Here we can do no more than make a general point about this pamphlet literature, and the public, as opposed to the " official ", controversy about the Scheldt to which it gave tangible and permanent expression. While the success or failure of the immediate attempt hung, as Magnette rightly says, upon the attitude of the European courts, and this in turn depended upon political considerations of purely temporary validity, the pamphleteers and essayists, whose views counted for little or nothing at the time, were yet helping to shape the future of the river. Linguet demanding the freedom of the Scheldt on the ground of natural law, or Mirabeau stressing the danger of

[1] A number of these pamphlets is listed in the bibliographical note appended to Terlinden, Ch., " The History of the Scheldt ", in *History*, New Series, V (1920), 1*ff*. In publishing one of these contemporary writings, Magnette mentions the principal pamphlets and clearly recognizes the interest of the question of principle, as distinct from the political or diplomatic interest. " Un mémoire inédit sur la liberté de l'Escaut ", in *Bull. Comm. Roy. d'Hist.*, LXIV (1895), 405-17.

opening the river without political safeguards, were not only contributing to that heritage of ideas whose power would long outlive that of the kings and statesmen of 1784, they were—it is not fanciful to say so—helping to ensure that the navigation of the Scheldt and of all other international waterways would one day be placed beyond the reach of the politician in the safer hands of the international lawyer. In this sense (but in this sense only) the " Scheldt question " itself may be said to date from 1784.

The Treaty of Fontainebleau was the high-water mark of French influence in the Republic; British efforts to take advantage of the crisis to reassert her own influence failed completely.[1] But where Britain failed in 1785, she succeeded in 1787, when the Orangist party returned to power and with it British influence became once again paramount in the Republic. The following year Britain and Prussia entered into an alliance with the Republic, by which they guaranteed her " Etats, Domaines, Villes & Places, franchises & libertés ", as well as the stadholderate as an essential part of her constitution.[2] Thus to the Franco-Austrian recognition of 1785 the Republic could now add what was in effect an Anglo-Prussian guarantee of the closure. Legally, the closure had never been more secure than during the last few years of its existence.[3]

(ii) *The French Revolution and Napoleon.*

On 16 November 1792 the Executive Council of the French Republic ordered Dumouriez, commander of the French armies invading the Netherlands, to take all the measures necessary
pour assurer la liberté de leur navigation et des transports dans tout le cours de l'Escaut et de la Meuse.
Dumouriez had already overrun most of the Southern Netherlands, and was planning to bring warships up the Scheldt to help reduce Antwerp. But, in addition to the immediate practical motive for this sudden threat to the closure, the Revolutionary government was eager to challenge so long-established and flagrant a limitation on the Rights of Man. The arguments used to justify the order included the declaration that le cours des fleuves est la propriété commune et inaliénable de toutes les contrées arrosées par leurs eaux, ... parceque la nature ne reconnait pas plus de peuples que d'individus privilégiés et que les droits de l'homme sont à jamais imprescriptibles.[4]

---

[1] Material for the study of British policy in the crisis of 1784-5 will be found in Colenbrander, H. T., *De Patriottentijd* (3 vols., The Hague, 1897-9), II *passim*, and in the *Diaries and Correspondence* of Sir James Harris, afterwards Earl of Malmesbury, who went to The Hague as British minister in Dec. 1784 (4 vols., 1844, especially II).
[2] Martens, *Recueil*, III, 127, 133.
[3] For references to the raising of the Scheldt question by the revolutionaries in Brabant in 1789 see Hubert, E., *Correspondance des Ministres de France accredités à Bruxelles de 1780 à 1790* (Brussels, 2 vols., 1920-4), II, 189 *n* 3, 204 *n* 1, 214 *n* 1, 482.
[4] *Réimpression de l'Ancien Moniteur* (31 vols., Paris, 1858-63), XIV, 535.

Along with the decrees of 19 November and 25 December, by which the National Convention promised support to all nations " struggling to be free ", the Scheldt decree was a challenge flung down to Europe. Only seven years before France had guaranteed the closure of the river; this and all her previous engagements in this sense her new government now proceeded to denounce.[1]

The Dutch government was paralyzed with fright. Totally unprepared for war and with an active " fifth column " at work in her midst, the Republic was helpless before the menace of invasion. The decree of 16 November was quickly followed by a demand from Dumouriez for the free passage of the river, which the Dutch government, under protest, was forced to concede; and on 21 November a French squadron sailed up to Antwerp, the first foreign ships to do so for more than two centuries.[2] In a review of the situation which he submitted to the Stadholder on 1 December the Grand Pensionary, Van de Spiegel, after boldly declaring that the opening of the Scheldt " belongs indubitably to those cases in which resistance is necessary and unavoidable ", tamely concluded that alone the Republic could do nothing and found in the approach of winter, when little use could be made of the Scheldt, an excuse for not opposing the French.[3]

Of the Powers which had guaranteed the closure Austria and Prussia were already at war with France. In England Dumouriez' conquest of the Southern Netherlands and the November decrees awoke the nation to a sense of its danger. By the end of November, when Maret, the French envoy in London, announced his government's determination to adhere to the decrees and to demand recognition, Britain was virtually committed to war. The opening of the Scheldt was too closely bound up with the general policy of defiance and aggression pursued by the French government in 1792 for British statesmen to be able to isolate it and treat it on its merits. There can be little doubt, however, that British public opinion would not have supported a crusade to maintain the closure of the river. It is significant that two men with such widely differing attitudes towards the

---

[1] The writer of a letter printed in the French *Moniteur* on 19 Feb. 1793 (*Réimpression de l'Ancien Moniteur*, XV, 490 b) drew attention to the English demand of 1652 for the opening of the Scheldt, to which he had found reference in two lives of Cromwell in the Bibliothèque Nationale.

[2] Their passage of the river is illustrated in documents published by L. Wichers in *Bijdr. voor Vaderl. Gesch.*, III, viii (1894), 269ff.

[3] Consideratiën van Van de Spiegel, 1 Dec. 1792. Colenbrander, H. T., ed., *Gedenkstukken der Algemeene Geschiedenis van Nederland, van 1795 tot 1840* (Rijks Geschiedk. Publ., The Hague, 10 parts in 22 vols., 1905-22), *1789-1795*, 238.

Revolution as Burke and Fox were at one in their conviction that the Scheldt question was no sufficient motive for war, while those who maintained in Parliament that England was bound to assist the Dutch confined themselves to invoking her treaty obligations and argued that the question whether the closure of the Scheldt was a natural and equitable arrangement did not enter into the matter.[1] In the upshot opinion on this question did not affect the main issue of peace or war. The initiative remained with the French government, and on 1 February 1793 the French Convention declared war on the " King of England " and the " Stadholder of the Republic ". A fortnight later Dumouriez crossed the Dutch frontier.

Two campaigns sufficed to put the Republic at the mercy of France. The Prince of Orange fled to England, leaving the country in the hands of the Jacobins and Patriots, who hailed the French as liberators. But when it came to settling the terms of the " liberation " they were quickly undeceived. France demanded, among other things, the cession of Zeeland-Flanders and the right to garrison Flushing; the French were determined to hold the keys of the Scheldt, not only to keep guard over Zeeland, always a stronghold of Orangism, but also pour opposer un jour l'Escaut à la Tamise, Anvers à Londres, et nos flottes de Flessingue à la tyrannie anglaise sur les mers d'Allemagne, du Nord et de la Baltique.[2]

The Dutch made a feeble protest, but the French were their masters, and on 16 May 1795 the terms were incorporated in the definitive treaty between the newly-forming Batavian Republic and France.[3] Article XVIII of the Treaty proclaimed the freedom of the Scheldt to its riparians:

La navigation du Rhin, de la Meuse et de l'Escaut, du Hondt, et de toutes leurs branches jusqu'à la mer, sera libre aux deux nations française & batave; les vaisseaux français & des Provinces-Unies y seront indistinctement reçus & aux mêmes conditions.

The Treaty of May 1795 converted the long-standing menace of French domination over the Netherlands into a reality. The Southern Netherlands, Antwerp and Flushing were in the hands of France, and so they remained until the overthrow of Napoleon in 1813-14. During these years Antwerp reaped little profit from the opening of the Scheldt,

[1] Burke's opinion will be found in *Parliamentary History*, XXX, 114, and in Prior, *Life of Burke* (3rd ed., 1839), 419; for Fox's see Malmesbury, *Diaries and Correspondence*, II, 474. References to the Scheldt in Parliament are in *Parl. Hist.*, XXX, 9, 11, 25, 50-1, 84, 88, 105-6.
[2] *Gedenkstukken, 1789-95*, 632.
[3] Martens, *Recueil*, VI, 532. For the negotiation see *Gedenkstukken, 1789-95*, 622ff., and Vreede, *Geschiedenis der Diplomatie van de Bataafsche Republiek*, I, 110-93, and Bijlage IX.

for the British navy kept close guard over the estuary, while the revival of trade was hampered by the heavy burdens imposed by the war. The Peace of Amiens and Napoleon's development of the port as a naval arsenal brought a brief period of activity.[1] Napoleon entertained grandiose projects for the future of Antwerp and himself paid a visit there in July 1803. In 1804 two new docks were built and a beginning made with the creation of a squadron of warships, which in eight years reached a strength of thirty ships.[2]

If the practical results of the French opening of the Scheldt remained small, both legally and morally the effect of twenty years' " freedom " on the river was decisive. Although the unilateral denunciation of the " closure " made by France in 1792 had, of course, no legal validity, the Batavian Republic's surrender of the right of closure by the Treaty of 1795 might be held to be binding on its successor. In any case, the treaties by which " third States " had guaranteed the closure were abrogated by the advent of a state of war between them and the Batavian Republic; in the case of Britain, Lord Stowell, the Admiralty judge, took this consequence for granted in pronouncing a prize-decision in 1801.[3] From the legal standpoint, therefore, it can be argued that the closure of the Scheldt came to an end in 1795 and could only have been revived in 1814-15 by means of a new treaty. Politically, such a revival was, of course, out of the question. It is certain that no settlement of the Southern Netherlands which involved the re-establishment of the Münster regime would have had the slightest chance of success, if only because the Antwerpers, once they had tasted the fruits, however meagre, of free navigation, would never have submitted to be deprived of them. No sooner had the French been driven out than Antwerp set to work to make this clear to those in whose hands its political future lay.

(iii) *The Settlement of 1814-15.*

Following the overthrow of Napoleon France made her peace with the Allies by the Treaty of Paris of 30 May 1814.[4] Annexed to the patent treaty was a series of secret articles explaining and amplifying its provisions and virtually constituting a second treaty. Article VI of

---

[1] In 1801 76 neutral vessels entered the port, in 1802 969, in 1803 2,006 and in 1804 2,718. Grandgaignage, *op. cit.*, 91-2.
[2] Charliat, " Le Prélude d'une Renaissance; Napoléon à Anvers ", in *Revue d'histoire moderne*, VI (1931), 268-74.
[3] The *Frau Ilsabe*. 4 C. Rob (4 Aug. 1801). The decision is cited in Phillipson, C., *Termination of War and Treaties of Peace* (1916), 252, and in McNair, (Sir) A. D., *The Law of Treaties* (1938), 532.
[4] Martens, *Nouveau Recueil*, II, 1.

the patent treaty stipulated that Holland, under the sovereignty of the House of Orange, should receive " un accroissement de territoire "; by the third secret article this was specified as comprising the whole of the Southern Netherlands. Article XV dealt with the disposal of the naval arsenals surrendered by France and concluded:
Dorénavant le port d'Anvers sera uniquement un port de commerce.
Finally, the last paragraph of the third secret article provided that
La liberté de navigation sur l'Escaut sera établie sur le même principe qui a réglé la navigation du Rhin dans l'article V du présent Traité.[1]

Of these three provisions of the Treaty the first two—the reunion of the Northern and Southern Netherlands and the demilitarization of Antwerp—marked the success of British policy in gaining two of its main objectives.[2] When, in the winter of 1813-14, after the Dutch had liberated themselves, the Allies could contemplate an invasion of the Southern Netherlands, British statesmen straightway began to occupy themselves with the problem of Antwerp. As Castlereagh wrote to Aberdeen:
I must particularly entreat you to keep your attention upon Antwerp. The destruction of that arsenal is essential to our safety.[3]
Antwerp must be taken out of the hands of France and secured against any future attempt on her part to regain it. By the end of 1813 Castlereagh had decided that the best means of doing this would be to give Antwerp, with a sufficient *arrondissement,* to Holland under the sovereignty of the Prince of Orange, and the third secret article of the Treaty of Paris represented the adoption of this solution. The demilitarization of Antwerp provided for by Article XV was an additional safeguard also inspired by Britain.

Since it was the British plan for the resettlement of the Netherlands which the Allies adopted at Paris, it might be concluded that the freedom of the Scheldt stipulated by the third secret article also originated in London. Alongside the great questions at issue in the negotiations of these months the navigation of the Scheldt must have seemed of small moment, and it is not surprising that the despatches of the period bear little trace of any concern on the part of British statesmen upon

---

[1] Article V was as follows:—
La navigation du Rhin, du point où elle devient navigable jusqu'à la mer, et réciproquement, sera libre, de telle sort qu'elle ne puisse être interdite à personne; et l'on s'occupera, au futur Congrès, des principes d'après lesquels on pourra régler les droits à lever par les Etats riverains, de la manière la plus égale et la plus favorable au commerce de toutes les nations.

[2] For British policy on the Netherlands question in 1813-15 see Renier, G. J., *Great Britain and the Establishment of the Kingdom of the Netherlands, 1813-15* (1930).

[3] 23 Nov. 1813. *Castlereagh Correspondence,* IX, 75; Webster, C. K., ed., *British Diplomacy, 1813-1815,* 114.

this point. What evidence there is, however, reveals little or no enthusiasm, but rather a certain reluctance, to press for the opening of the river. Wellington, away in the Pyrenees, found time to advocate a revival of the old system on the Scheldt,[1] and Liverpool, the Prime Minister, while sympathetic towards the claim of the Belgians as riparians to enjoy the use of the river, did not favour the extension of free navigation to other countries and in any case would have preferred to see the matter left aside until after the reunion of the Netherlands.[2] Renier has suggested that the inclusion of the clause in the Treaty was due primarily to the altruism of the Austrians in wishing to render their former subjects a last service.[3] Whether or no the initiative came from that side,[4] there can be no doubt that what made its adoption certain was the interest of the Allies, and particularly of Britain, in securing the support of the Belgians for the new regime. A Belgian deputation which proceeded to the Allied headquarters at Chaumont in March 1814 demanded guarantees that the Catholic religion should be respected and the freedom of the Scheldt secured; they were told that the Allies would maintain their religion and protect their commerce " contre toute entrave contraire à la raison et à la nature de sa position ".[5] This vague assurance did not satisfy Antwerp, and in May 1814 the Antwerp Chamber of Commerce proposed to send a deputation to Paris to press for the explicit abolition of the closure. The Austrian governor Vincent advised them to address their request to the Prince of Orange as their prospective sovereign, but the Dutch commissioner Van der Capellen would not authorize the deputation to proceed.[6] There was more behind Van der Capellen's caution than his ostensible desire not to anticipate the Allies' intentions. The Prince of Orange was well aware that neither his present nor his prospective subjects were enthusiastic for the Union, and he therefore wished to make the formal announcement of the opening of the Scheldt simultaneous with the declaration of the Union, so that the two things might be linked together in the minds of the people.[7] He also had a scheme to make the freedom of the river more palatable to his Dutch subjects by shifting part of the national debt on to the Southern Nether-

---

[1] To Bathurst, 10 Jan. 1814. *Gedenkstukken, 1813-15,* 27-8.
[2] To Castlereagh, 27 May 1814. *Ibid.,* 131.
[3] *Op cit.,* 249.
[4] Jonkheer W. J. M. van Eysinga has drawn attention to Talleyrand's proposals for the freedom of international rivers, including the Scheldt, in 1814. They are found in Dupuis, C., *Le Ministère de Talleyrand en 1814,* I, 374ff.
[5] *Gedenkstukken, 1813-15,* 92.
[6] *Ibid.,* 576-7.
[7] *Ibid.,* 584.

lands as the price of their economic freedom.[1] A premature announcement of the opening of the Scheldt would spoil these schemes.[2]

Castlereagh had himself heard the Belgians put forward their case at Chaumont and had urged them to look to reunion with Holland as the best guarantee of their religious and economic freedom. Should he leave it to the Sovereign Prince to declare the Scheldt free at the moment when the reunion became an accomplished fact, or should he incorporate this provision in the treaty? Since the main object was to turn the reluctant Belgians into loyal subjects of the Prince there was clearly something to be said in favour of giving him the benefit of making the announcement. On the other hand, Castlereagh may well have thought that a situation established by treaty should be formally and finally abolished by treaty, and that to leave it to the good pleasure of the Prince would be to put too powerful a weapon in his hands when it came to settling the terms of the Union. Castlereagh was aware, too, of the jealousy already displayed by the Dutch ports to their prospective rival, and he may have considered a treaty stipulation necessary to avoid all possibility of their bringing pressure to bear on the Prince, if not to withhold the freedom, at least to attach to it burdensome conditions.

The solution adopted in the treaty went some way towards satisfying both requirements. The navigation of the Scheldt was declared free, but the clause was included among the secret articles, so that the Sovereign Prince could still reap the benefit of appearing to bestow it on his new subjects. At the same time it was provided that the Scheldt, as an international river between France and the Netherlands, should be included among the rivers which were to be the subject of regulation at the coming Congress. Thus was the Münster regime finally abolished, at the same time as the political reunion of Antwerp with the mouth of the river obliterated the old frontier which had always been the root of the problem.

The Commission appointed by the Powers at Vienna to deal with the question of international rivers met for the first time on 2 February 1815.[3] The original Commission consisted of representatives of Austria, France, Britain and Prussia, but it straightway co-opted representatives of the Netherlands, Baden, Hesse-Darmstadt, Nassau and Bavaria as

---

[1] *Ibid.*, 128.
[2] For the indiscretion of Künigl, the Austrian commissioner in the Southern Netherlands, in issuing orders for the opening of the river, and its countermanding by Vincent, see *Gedenkstukken, 1813-15*, 124, 127-8.
[3] The work of the Commission can be followed in Chodzko, L. B. (*pseud.* Comte d'Angeberg), *Le Congrès de Vienne et les traités de 1815* (Paris, 2 vols., 1863).

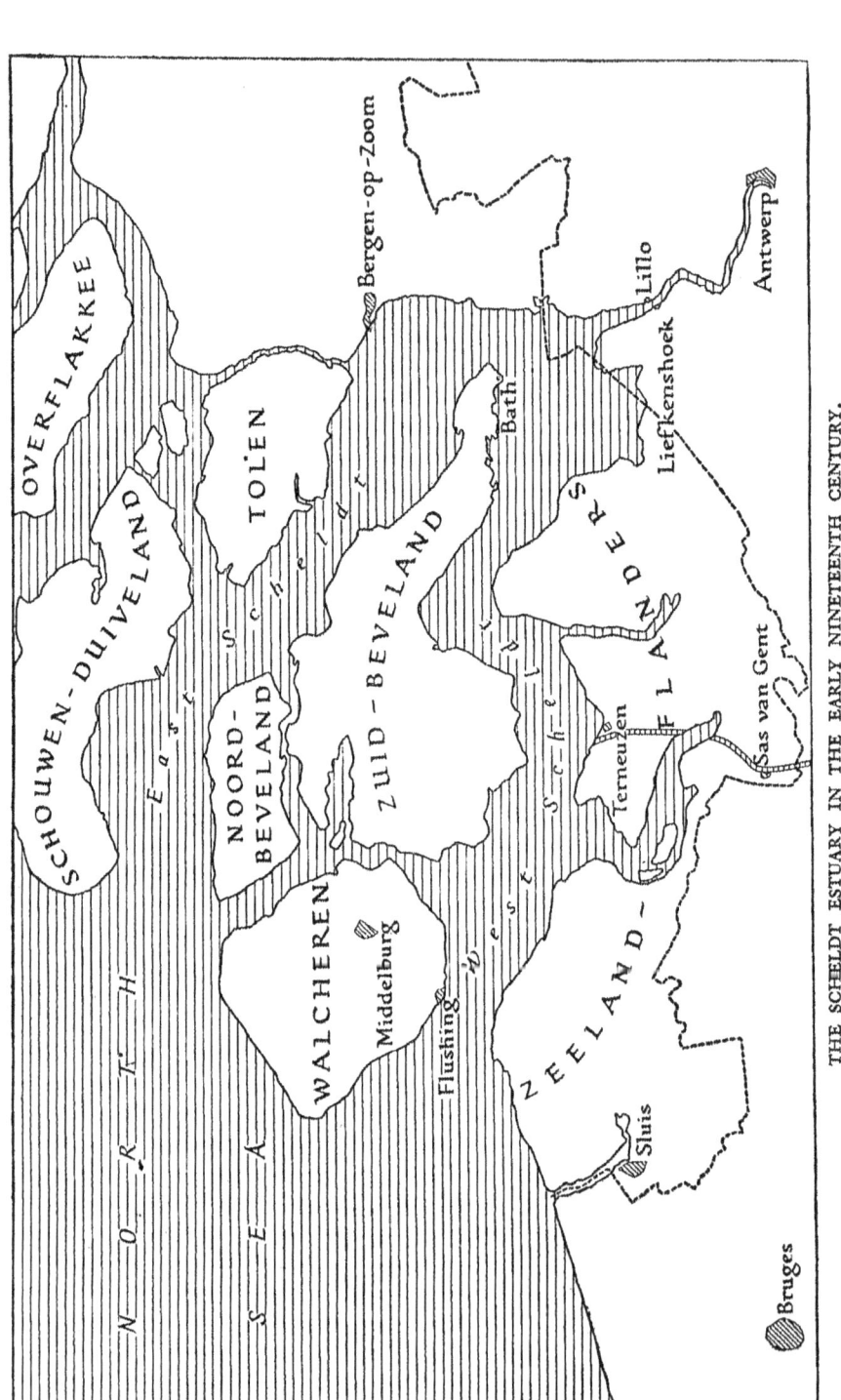

THE SCHELDT ESTUARY IN THE EARLY NINETEENTH CENTURY.

----- Frontier between Holland and Belgium since 1831.

riparians of the Rhine. The main task of the Commission was to establish the free navigation of the Rhine, but it was also charged with the task of formulating the general principles which should govern the navigation of all international rivers in Europe. The principles adopted by the Commission were set forth in ten articles incorporated in the Final Act of the Congress (Articles CVIII-CXVII). The most important was Article CIX:

La navigation dans tout le cours des rivières indiquées dans l'article précédent [namely, rivers which traverse or separate the territories of more than one state], du point où chacune d'elles devient navigable jusqu'à son embouchure, sera entièrement libre, et ne pourra, sous le rapport de commerce, être interdite à personne; bien entendu que l'on se conformera aux réglements relatifs à la police de cette navigation, lesquels seront conçus d'une manière uniforme pour tous, et aussi favorables que possible au commerce de toutes les nations.

Article CVIII laid an obligation on the riparian states of the rivers in question to appoint commissioners who should meet within six months of the conclusion of the Congress to work out a detailed regime in each particular case; and Article CXI stipulated that a tariff of duties, based approximately on that to be established for the Rhine and in no case exceeding the duties then in force, should be settled for each river and that once settled it should not be increased except with the consent of all the riparians.[1]

It had been clear from the outset that there were two views among the members of the Commission as to what constituted the " freedom " of international rivers. The British representative, Clancarty, championed the " liberal " view which demanded equal and favourable treatment for all users and not merely for riparians. Humboldt, for Prussia, saw in Clancarty's demand an attempt to make the Rhine a cheap route for British goods into the Continent and therefore fought for the restriction of the benefits of free navigation to riparians. It was this " restrictive " view which carried the day at Vienna and which found expression in the wording of Article CVIII.[2]

In his memorandum of 3 February 1815 Humboldt confessed that he did not know enough about the Scheldt to say how his general principles would apply to it, and the Commission apparently took no steps to remedy this deficiency. At its ninth meeting, on 16 March, the Commission dismissed the Scheldt by resolving

---

[1] Martens, *Nouveau Recueil*, II, ii, 434-5; d'Angeberg, *op. cit.*, II, 1430.
[2] For a discussion of the development of these two views see Kaeckenbeeck, G. F. S. C., *International Rivers* (Grotius Society Publications, No. 1, 1918), 40*ff.*; the most useful introduction to international river law is Eysinga, W. J. M. van, *Les fleuves et canaux internationaux* (Bibliotheca Visseriana, II, Leiden, 1924).

que la libre navigation sur cette rivière serait nommément exprimée, en abandonnant du reste à la France et à la Hollande le soin de prendre entre elles, sur ce point, des arrangements conformes aux principes généralement établis.[1]

At the following meeting Humboldt presented a new draft of the Articles and in this the articles relative to the Scheldt took their final form:

La liberté de la navigation, telle qu'elle a été déterminée pour le Rhin, est étendue au Neckar, au Main, à la Moselle, à la Meuse et à l'Escaut, du point où chacune de ces rivières devient navigable jusqu'à son embouchure. . .

Tout ce qui aurait besoin d'être fixé ultérieurement sur la navigation de l'Escaut, outre la liberté de la navigation sur cette rivière, prononcée à l'Article Ier, sera définitivement réglé de la manière la plus favorable au commerce et à la navigation, et la plus analogue à ce qui a été fixé pour le Rhin.[2]

These clauses, and in particular their final provision, were later to assume such importance in the evolution of the Scheldt regime that it is important to grasp what they involved in their context of 1815. Since the closure of the Scheldt was the classic example of those " unnatural " restrictions to free navigation which the Vienna Commission wished to abolish for ever, the inclusion of the river within the purview of the Commission must have appeared, even apart from the stipulation of the Treaty of Paris, altogether right and proper. Yet, as we have seen, the Commission was rather at a loss when it came to deal with the Scheldt. Why was this so? The answer is that it was not with the " Scheldt " of diplomatic fame, namely, the waterway between Antwerp and the sea, with which the Commission found itself called upon to deal. The Commission did not have to tackle the " Scheldt question ", because that question no longer existed. The reunion of the Northern and Southern Netherlands had made the navigation of the whole course of the river from the French frontier to the sea the domestic concern of the Kingdom of the Netherlands. (Although this Kingdom was not formally proclaimed until July 1815, it had in fact come into existence when on 1 August 1814 the Sovereign Prince took over the provisional government of the Southern Netherlands from Vincent.) Already on 21 June 1814 the Sovereign Prince had given Antwerp the duty-free navigation of the Scheldt by exempting Belgian ships from the operation of the duty (*lastgeld*) established in 1809.[3] Moreover, the third of the Eight Articles governing the constitution of the new state, which the Prince accepted on 21 July, secured the

[1] D'Angeberg, *op. cit.*, II, 924.
[2] *Ibid.*, 947-8.
[3] *British and Foreign State Papers, 1830-1*, 747 n.

Southern Netherlands from any economic discrimination by stipulating that

les différentes Provinces jouiront également de tous les avantages commerciaux et autres que comporte leur situation respective, sans qu'aucune entrave ou restriction puisse être imposée à l'une au profit de l'autre.[1]

If by the summer of 1814 the maritime navigation of the Scheldt had thus ceased to be international in character, the interior navigation of the river remained so, with France and the Netherlands as the two riparians, and strictly speaking it was solely in virtue of this fact that the Scheldt came within the purview of the Commission.[2] But the navigation of the Upper Scheldt across the Franco-Netherland frontier was a very different thing from the navigation of the Scheldt between Antwerp and the sea,[3] and its unimportance in the eyes of the Commission was reflected in the scant attention which it received. As we have seen, the Commission was content to declare the freedom of the Scheldt in general terms, leaving it to France and the Netherlands to take any steps necessary to carry this resolution into effect. It does not appear that these two governments did in fact take any action in the matter during the years 1815-30.[4]

Although the inclusion of the Scheldt among the rivers governed by the Vienna Articles was thus of little or no practical significance at the time, it was to assume a wholly unforeseen importance when the separation of Belgium from Holland brought up again the historic " Scheldt question ". Then the international character of the Upper Scheldt faded into insignificance beside the maritime navigation of the Lower Scheldt, which, from being a domestic affair of the Kingdom of the Netherlands, became once more an international matter. When the statesmen of Europe, finding a precedent in these stipulations of 1815 for the freedom of the Scheldt, applied them to the maritime navigation of the river, it was only to find that they could not be made to fit. The attempt revealed for the first time the contradiction inherent in the Vienna provision that all future arrangements on the Scheldt should be conceived " in a manner as favourable as possible to commerce and navigation and as alike as possible to what has been fixed for the Rhine."

[1] *Ibid.*, *1814-15*, ii, 141-2.
[2] I can find no evidence to justify Blondeau's statement that " en 1815, l'Escaut redevient un fleuve international, mais uniquement . . . parce qu'il constitue par les eaux intermédiaires un débouché du Rhin, fleuve international, vers Anvers ". *L'Escaut fleuve international* (1932), 16.
[3] See above, p. 2*ff*.
[4] De Rive, who covers the history of the interior navigation of the Scheldt during this period in his *Précis Historique et Statistique des Canaux et Rivières Navigables de la Belgique* (1835), 30*ff*, has nothing about any Franco-Netherland negotiations on the subject.

(iv) *The Years of the Union, 1815-30.*

During the brief interlude of the Union the "Scheldt question" ceased to exist. For the first time since 1572 Antwerp enjoyed the use of the river in peace-conditions and the town quickly began to regain something of its old commercial importance; while Amsterdam continued to handle most of the Baltic and Scandinavian, and Rotterdam most of the British trade, Antwerp attracted to itself a large share of the commerce of the Kingdom with Southern Europe, America and the colonies.[1] William I went out of his way to encourage the material prosperity of the Southern provinces, and Antwerp responded to his efforts; between 1818 and 1829 the annual tonnage entering the harbour more than doubled.[2] From these years, too, dates the establishment of some of the leading merchant houses in Antwerp, many of them by foreigners attracted by the favourable outlook. Among these were several British houses, whose representatives we shall meet playing a minor role in the negotiations of 1830-39.[3]

If there was no trouble over the Scheldt during these years, there was enough and to spare over the Rhine. After disputes lasting for fifteen years and giving rise to more than 500 protocols on the part of the Central Commission, the riparian states resolved to abandon the attempt to reach agreement on principle and to content themselves with a working arrangement. This arrangement was embodied in the Convention of Mainz of 31 March 1831.[4] Since this agreement was concluded just at the time when the navigation of the Scheldt was once more the subject of international discussion, it was perhaps natural that the parties to this discussion should seek in the terms of the Convention some guidance towards the establishment of a new regime on the Scheldt. It is therefore the more important for us to grasp that the Convention of Mainz, being founded, not upon the principles of the Vienna Act, but on the mutual agreement of the riparians, could not legally be held to form part of the Rhine regime for the purpose of being applied to the other rivers, including the Scheldt, specified in that Act.

The significance of this distinction becomes clearer if we recall the nature of the question most in dispute at Mainz, namely, whether the Vienna Articles were to apply solely to the internal or fluvial naviga-

---

[1] For some comparative figures of the movement of the three ports during these years see Van Mechelen, P. A. A., *Zeevaart en Zeehandel van Rotterdam in 1813-1830* (Rotterdam, n.d.), 181-91.
[2] Prims, F., *Antwerpen in 1830*, I, 112.
[3] See below, pp. 170, 176, 184-5, 186-8.
[4] B.F.S.P., *1830-1*, 1076.

tion of the lower part of the river. This question, summed up in the phrases "jusqu'à la mer" and "jusque dans la mer", was not the mere verbal quibble which it is sometimes represented to be. The Prussian demand for the inclusion of the maritime navigation within the purview of the Commission was in effect a demand for advantages which would enable Cologne to become a sea-port and a rival of the Dutch ports as a Rhine entrepôt; the Netherland government's championship of the opposite thesis was likewise dictated by the determination to prevent Cologne from realizing this ambition. Unfortunately for the government of The Hague, its stand in this matter, combined with the difficulties which its protectionist policy put in the way of the transit-trade across Dutch territory, gave it the reputation of being excessively obstinate and obstructionist in all that concerned the navigation of rivers, a reputation which was to stand it in ill-stead when the Scheldt question came up again in 1830.

CHAPTER SEVEN

The Belgian Revolution and the Treaty of November 1831

THE break-up of the Kingdom of the Netherlands resulting from the Belgian Revolution both revived the " Scheldt question " and led to the settlement which has endured substantially unchanged to the present day. The chief interest of the negotiations of 1830-39 therefore lies in the evolution, through the successive projects put forward to and by the Conference of London, of the terms of the ninth article of the treaties of 1839 which has since governed the navigation of the river. Of these numerous projects, four stand out as landmarks in that evolution; they are the " Bases de Séparation " of January, the Eighteen Articles of June, and the Twenty-Four Articles of October 1831, the last being incorporated in the treaty of 15 November 1831, and finally the " Theme " of Lord Palmerston of September 1832. The present chapter deals with the first three of these projects and carries the story down to May 1832; the " Theme " is the subject of Chapter Eight and the remainder of the negotiation, including the final settlement, of Chapter Nine.[1]

(i) *The Belgian Revolution and the " Bases de Séparation ".*

During the last week of August 1830 popular riots in Brussels heralded the Belgian Revolution. For about a month it seemed that an administrative separation of the Northern and Southern Netherlands might meet Belgian grievances, but after the failure of the royal forces to reoccupy Brussels (23-26 September) the revolutionary leaders established a provisional government there which quickly gained control of all the Southern provinces. On 4 October the provisional government proclaimed the independence of Belgium and summoned a national congress to frame a constitution, and by the end of the

---

[1] This and the two following chapters, being largely an abridgment of the writer's M.A. thesis (above, p. viii), are based upon researches in the archives of the Foreign Office, of the Foreign Ministries of the Netherlands and Belgium, and the Archives Générales, Brussels, as well as among the private papers of Lord Palmerston (by courtesy of the late Lord Mount-Temple). Since it would be impossible to give all the references necessary to support every statement in the text, I have confined myself to indicating the sources of quotations and of a few of the most important statements. A copy of the thesis, which includes the complete *apparatus criticus*, is preserved in the Library of the University of London, and a summary of it, with a detailed list of the MS. and chief printed sources used, will be found in the *Bulletin of the Institute of Historical Research*, XII (1934), 60-63. In the footnotes the archival sources appear in the following abbreviations: Records of the British Foreign Office, F.O., of the Netherlands Foreign Ministry (*Buitenlandsche Zaken*), B.Z., and of the Belgian Foreign Ministry (*Affaires Etrangères*), A.E.; the Palmerston Papers are abbreviated P.P.

month the only traces of royal power left in the South were the garrisons of the two citadels of Antwerp and Maastricht.

Clearly the King could not hope unaided to recover his Southern provinces. But by the terms of the settlement of 1814 his kingdom stood under the guarantee of the Great Powers, and accordingly on 5 October he called on the British, Prussian, Austrian and Russian governments for armed assistance in the task. The European situation did not, however, admit of any such concerted action to suppress the revolution; instead, the Powers concerned, together with France, resolved to meet in conference in the hope of finding a peaceful settlement. On the invitation of the British government London became the meeting-place of the Conference, and its first session was held at the Foreign Office on 4 November. It was composed of the ambassadors of Austria and France (Esterhazy and Talleyrand), plenipotentiaries from Prussia and Russia (Bülow and Matuszewic), and the British Foreign Secretary. The British representative at the opening of the Conference was Lord Aberdeen, but he was soon succeeded, on the advent of the Whig government of Lord Grey, by Lord Palmerston. The Conference's first task was to put an end to the fighting. Its first protocol ordered the combatants to suspend hostilities and to retire on either side of the line which before 30 May 1814 had divided the Northern and Southern provinces. It was in connection with this arrangement that the Conference had its attention drawn to the problem of the Scheldt.

Already on 20 October, before the Revolution had reached Antwerp, the King had taken "precautionary measures" affecting the river; Antwerp was declared to be in a state of siege and no ships were allowed up the Scheldt. On 26-27 October the rebels took possession of Antwerp, but to their demand for the surrender of the citadel the commander, General Chassé, replied with a bombardment which killed 85 people; a week later a local armistice left Chassé in the citadel and the revolutionary government in peaceful possession of the town.[1] Meanwhile the King had ordered two naval flotillas into the Scheldt, one off Flushing and the other at Antwerp; he also garrisoned Forts Lillo and Liefkenshoek. During the first half of November these forces allowed merchant ships to leave Antwerp, but since 20 October no ships had been allowed up the river, and by 6 November there were 25 detained at Flushing. On 23 November the Dutch government, in accordance with the Conference's first protocol,

[1] The fullest study of the course of the revolution at Antwerp is Prims, Fl., *Antwerpen in 1830* (2 vols., Antwerp, *n.d.*). For some additional information see the despatches of Larpent, the British consul, published by R. Demoulin in *Bull. Comm. Roy. d'Hist.*, XCVIII (1934), 417*ff*.

suspended all hostilities by land and water, but decided to keep in force the " precautionary measures ".

When the suspension of hostilities brought no opening of the Scheldt the Belgian provisional government began to bombard the Conference with protests, soon accompanied by threats of a renewal of the fighting. On 10 November, after hearing a statement by Falck, who as ambassador in London had become Dutch plenipotentiary to the Conference, the Conference issued a protocol (No. 5) requiring the King to withdraw the " precautionary measures " immediately. When this failed to produce any effect, the Belgian forces resumed their investment of Maastricht. The danger of a general resumption of hostilities, coupled with a French threat to force the opening of the river,[1] compelled the Conference to demand in still stronger terms the withdrawal of the measures. When this protocol was presented at The Hague on 2 January 1831 the Dutch Foreign Minister, Verstolk van Soelen, announced the King's intention to open the river on 20 January. But the value of this concession was impaired by the addition of a clause making it dependent on the adoption, by that date, of the articles governing the separation of the two countries; worse still, the Dutch government was not willing to allow Belgian ships on the river. It was this second reservation, with its calculated affront to Belgian national pride, which led Palmerston to reinforce the Conference's third protocol on the subject, which demanded " une dernière fois " the restoration of the freedom of navigation " sans autres droits de péage ni de visite que ceux qui étoient établis en 1814 ", by a characteristic move. On 13 January he informed the British consul at Antwerp, Baron de Hochepied Larpent, that the Scheldt would be opened on the 20th " and that no obstruction to its free navigation will be permitted by the five Powers after that time ".[2] This despatch the consul caused to appear in the Belgian papers. Not only did its reassurance materially contribute to the decision of the Belgian Congress to obey the Conference by withdrawing its troops from Maastricht, it left the King with no option but to comply. On 25 January the Dutch plenipotentiaries (Baron van Zuylen van Nyevelt had joined Falck towards the end of December) announced that the river had been opened since the 20th.[3]

---

[1] Sébastiani to De la Rochefoucauld, 23 Dec. 1830. *Gedenkstukken, 1830-40*, II, 115. From Sébastiani's reference to this threat in the French Chamber on 23 Feb. 1831 (*Archives Parlementaires, 1800-60*, LXVII, 168) it appears that this was one of the rare occasions on which France acted in the capacity of a riparian of the Scheldt.

[2] Shee, Under-Secretary of State, to Larpent, 13 Jan. 1831. F.O. Belgium/8.

[3] It was of this Note that Palmerston wrote to Bagot, ambassador at The Hague, that " hard words break no bones and Dutch is naturally a harsh language ". To Bagot, private, 26 Jan. 1831. P.P.

The struggle to secure the withdrawal of the "precautionary measures" was no more than a preliminary passage of arms. The "closure" of the Scheldt in October 1830 was a purely naval measure which had nothing whatever to do with the historic closure,[1] and the reopening of the river in January 1831 left untouched the main question of the permanent regime to be established on it. Since 1814 there had been no "Scheldt question", and so long as the Union existed, or was deemed to exist by the European Courts, that question could not arise. The Union in fact expired on 27 September 1830 with the establishment of the provisional government; in the eyes of Europe, however, it came to an end only on 20 December 1830, with the issue of the Conference's seventh protocol, by which the Powers formally recognized its dissolution and resolved to discuss

les nouveaux arrangemens les plus propres à combiner l'indépendance future de la Belgique avec les Stipulations des Traités, avec les intérêts et la securité des autres Puissances, et avec la conservation de l'équilibre Européen.[2]

Even after the issue of this historic protocol the Scheldt question need not necessarily have arisen, at least in its "classic" form, for the arrangements which the Conference envisaged might not have restored that political dualism on the Lower Scheldt which, as we have seen, is an indispensable element in the question. What was "Belgium" to consist of? Was it to include Antwerp, or would Antwerp be converted into a "free city"? Or again, was Belgium to acquire Zeeland-Flanders, in which case the question of a Belgo-Dutch co-sovereignty over the Scheldt estuary might arise? These questions the Conference was called upon to answer during the weeks following the issue of the seventh protocol.

The question of Antwerp was one in which all the Powers, and above all Great Britain, had a direct interest. When at the close of October 1830 the town threw in its lot with the Revolution the question which Castlereagh had sought to settle in 1814 was revived. In England even those who favoured Belgian independence were uneasy at the prospect of Antwerp's belonging to a state incapable of defending itself against France, and it is significant that the Dutch garrison was allowed to remain so long in unchallenged occupation of the citadel. From the outset Palmerston was determined that at least the

---

[1] Belgian writers are frequently in error about this. Thus in Van Bruyssel, E., *Histoire politique de l'Escaut* (Paris, 1864), we read (p. 190): "L'Escaut était bloqué par les Hollandais en vertu de l'article XIV du traité de Munster", and in Terlinden, Ch., "The History of the Scheldt", in *History*, New Series V (1920), 3: "King William kept the Scheldt closed on the excuse that this was a right which Holland had enjoyed previously, even in peace time".

[2] *British and Foreign State Papers, 1830-1*, 750.

demilitarization of Antwerp provided for in 1814 should be confirmed. Talleyrand, who wanted to see this clause abolished, had a scheme for making Antwerp and Ostend free towns or " villes hanséatiques ", for which there was support in those towns but which was coldly received in London.[1] Fortunately, the Belgians were quite willing for Antwerp to remain solely a commercial port, and in the Conference this was treated as a necessary corollary of the neutrality of the Belgian state.

The future of the left bank of the Scheldt was more controversial. The Belgian provisional government first advanced a claim to this territory in connection with the armistice-line adopted by the Conference on 4 November. Assuming, quite unwarrantably, that this line was to become the permanent frontier, the Brussels Comité Diplomatique laid claim to Zeeland-Flanders on the ground that on 30 May 1814, the date mentioned in the protocol, it still formed part of the Southern Netherlands, to which the French had joined it in 1795, and was not incorporated with Zeeland until 20 July of that year. The Belgians' anxiety to obtain Zeeland-Flanders is easy to understand. For two hundred years its possession had given the Dutch Republic the practical mastery of the mouth of the Scheldt, and the reopening of the river was identified in Belgian memory with its severance from the Republic by the French in 1795. The closing of the Scheldt in October 1830 only strengthened their conviction that the future of the river turned on the possession of the left bank, while the Dutch authorities' shutting of the sluices controlling the outflow of water from Flanders and the resulting inundation of large areas furnished them with an additional argument. Thus by the end of 1830 the claim to Zeeland-Flanders had become an *idée fixe* with Belgian opinion. On 31 December two Belgian envoys—one of them, Sylvain van de Weyer, was to become very well-known in London—arrived in London as envoys extraordinary. One of their first acts was to address to the Conference a Note in which, among other things, they demanded Zeeland-Flanders; without the left bank of the Scheldt, they declared,

la Belgique serait à découvert de ce côté, et la libre navigation de ce fleuve pourrait n'être qu'une stipulation illusoire.[2]

At a time when the Conference was hard at work trying to secure

---

[1] Pallain, G., ed., *Ambassade de Talleyrand à Londres, 1830-34* (Paris, 1891), I, 173, 186; *Gedenkstukken, 1830-40*, II, xix-xx; De Lannoy, Fl., *Les origines diplomatiques de l'indépendance belge. La Conférence de Londres, 1830-1* (Louvain, 1903), 114.

[2] Quoted in Juste, Th., *Le Congrès National de Belgique, 1830-1831* (Brussels, 1880), I, 195.

the withdrawal of the "precautionary measures" this argument was calculated to appeal to its members. But all the evidence, or rather the complete absence of evidence suggesting any conflict of opinion, points to the conclusion that in London there was no doubt as to what ought to be done. Historically, the Belgian claim was without foundation. When, after nearly two centuries, Zeeland-Flanders was taken from the Republic it had become part, not of Belgium, since no such state then existed, but of France, while the Belgian argument based on what had taken place in 1814, even if correct,[1] was vitiated by the fact that the Conference had cited that year solely in connection with the armistice. When, in addition, it is remembered that the population of Zeeland-Flanders had shown no sympathy with the Revolution, it is clear that neither legally nor politically had Belgium any claim to this territory.

The Belgian claim could, indeed, have been upheld solely on the ground that Nature had made Flanders one and that it was a mere accident of history which had drawn a frontier separating this northernmost strip from the rest of the Flemish plain. Had the Conference, either in virtue of some such "natural" right or simply as a matter of expediency, awarded Zeeland-Flanders to Belgium, what would have been the effect of this transfer upon the Scheldt question? The Belgians doubtless took it for granted that the acquisition of Zeeland-Flanders would not only strengthen their actual position with regard to the Scheldt estuary but also convey a certain legal right over the estuary. The Conference would certainly have found itself obliged to trace a frontier-line between the two riparians, and following recent precedent[2] it would probably have chosen the *thalweg* or fairway rather than an artificial line midway between the two banks. But in doing so it would have come up against the Dutch thesis—Frederick van Hogendorp's Latin dissertation of 1827 in which it appears would doubtless have been in demand—that the sovereignty over the Scheldt estuary, formerly the Honte, belongs to Zeeland independently of the possession of the southern bank, and the resulting tussle might have made an interesting chapter in the development of the law of territorial jurisdiction.

If the Conference avoided this knotty problem by confirming Holland in her possession of the left bank of the Scheldt, that decision

[1] For certain facts which tell against it see Ramaer, Ir. J. C., *De Fransche Tijd (1795-1815)* in the *Geschiedkundige Atlas van Nederland* (The Hague, 1926), 98.
[2] The *thalweg* rule had been adopted in the treaty of Lunéville of 1801 (Art. VI) and in the Second Treaty of Paris of 1815 (Art. VII); and the term was defined in the Convention of Strasburg between France and Baden of 30 Jan. 1227.

itself committed the Conference to tackling the Scheldt question in its classic form. The Belgians had attempted to persuade the Conference that so long as Holland remained master of both banks there could be no real freedom on the river; the Conference had to disprove this assertion by devising a settlement which should reconcile the territorial rights of Holland with the freedom of navigation required by Belgium. There was no possibility of a revival of anything resembling the Münster regime, if for no other reason than that it would conflict with existing treaties, treaties to which all the Powers represented in the Conference had been party. But that the Dutch government had no thought of trying to put the clock back so far appears from the fact that the first proposal for the freedom of the river came from The Hague. On 6 January 1831 the Dutch plenipotentiaries presented to the Conference, under the title " Bases principales de la Séparation ", a set of three propositions: first, that Holland should keep all the territory she had possessed in 1790, and Belgium comprise the remainder of the Netherlands; second, that each should assume responsibility for its own debts incurred before the Union and for half the debt incurred during the Union; and third, that if Belgium were willing to bear a larger share of the total debt she should enjoy freedom of trade with the Dutch colonies and freedom of navigation on the Scheldt.

It will be seen that the Dutch government regarded the freedom of the Scheldt, not as a Belgian right, but as a privilege which she must purchase by means of a financial concession. The Dutch government contended that the freedom of the Scheldt proclaimed in 1814-15 was linked with and dependent on the reunion of the Netherlands. At that time (so the argument ran), with the prospect of Antwerp's being brought within the boundaries of the Netherlands state, Dutch statesmen had not hesitated to grant the freedom of the river, which, by increasing the trade of Antwerp, would benefit the country as a whole. But now that the secession of Belgium was both to deprive Holland of the extension of territory secured in 1814 and to make Antwerp a foreign port, the question arose how far the freedom of the Scheldt must also be considered to have lapsed. There is certainly nothing in the treaty-stipulations themselves to bear out this view, but as we have seen the Powers had purposely left it to the Sovereign Prince to make the public announcement of the opening of the river in 1814 and it was this which had enabled him to meet potential Dutch opposition by giving the impression that it was linked with the extension of territory.¹ However, the adoption of this argument by the Dutch in 1830-31 did not mean that they had any intention of attempting to revive the closure of the river. When they asserted (it was in any case a questionable assertion²) that their right to do so remained unimpaired, it was merely with the object of bargaining that right away; their initial price was an addition to the Belgian share of the debt.³

It was from the Dutch Note of 6 January that the Conference's own " Bases destinées à établir la séparation de la Belgique d'avec la Hollande " of 27 January 1831 took both their name and certain of their provisions. These " Bases de Séparation " were divided into two groups, Articles I to IX being labelled " Arrangemens fondamentaux " and Articles X to XVIII " Arrangemens proposés pour le partage de Dettes et avantages de commerce qui en seraient les conséquences ".⁴ Article III is as follows:

Il est entendu que les dispositions des Articles CVIII, jusqu'à CXVII inclusivement, de l'Acte Général du Congrès de Vienne, relatifs à la libre navigation des fleuves et rivières navigables, seront appliquées aux rivières et aux fleuves qui traversent le Territoire Hollandais et le Territoire Belge.

It is noteworthy, in the first place, that this article does not mention the Scheldt by name. This omission is not difficult to understand.

¹ See above, p. 149.
² Even granted the Dutch contention that whatever was stipulated about the Scheldt in 1814-15 was dependent on the Union, it is still open to question whether the termination of the Union, and the concurrent lapse of the stipulations relative to the Scheldt, brought the closure of the Scheldt legally into force again. It has been suggested above that the renunciation of the closure by the Republic itself in the treaty of 1795 with France might be held to be binding on any subsequent Dutch government, and it is certain that the advent of a state of war between the Batavian Republic and " third States " which had recognized or guaranteed the closure released these from their obligation to do so (above, p. 146). This line of argument leads to the conclusion that the closure as recognized by the Treaties of Fontainebleau and (implicitly) by those of 1788 (the Triple Alliance) was abolished legally, as well as in practice, in 1795 and could not therefore be brought into force again by any subsequent change of conditions; even the closure as based upon the " Zeeland staple ", which was independent of any international recognition, could scarcely be held to have survived the treaty of 1795.
³ To establish the point, it is only necessary to cite the *mémoire* presented by the Dutch plenipotentiaries to the Conference on 14 December 1831, where it was stated: " Quant à la navigation de l'Escaut le gouvernement des Pays Bas n'a jamais eu l'intention de l'entraver si non lorsque la défense du Royaume pendant la guerre le commandoit temporairement; et bien que par la séparation de la Hollande et de la Belgique, l'Article 14 du Traité de Munster ait repris sa vigueur, la Hollande considère la liberté de l'Escaut comme la conséquence immédiate d'un Traité équitable de séparation ". *British and Foreign State Papers, 1831-2*, 65. The Dutch attitude is seriously misrepresented both in the *Cambridge History of British Foreign Policy*, II, 152, and by Prof. Terlinden in the second of his two articles in *History*, New Series V (1920), 5. It is gratifying to find it correctly stated by Prof. Smith in his *Great Britain and the Law of Nations*, II, 299, although in contrast to his full and reasonably accurate treatment of Scheldt history between 1780 and 1815 Prof. Smith's account of the infinitely more important period 1830-39 is disappointingly brief and weak.
⁴ *B.F.S.P., 1830-1*, 766. The " Arrangemens fondamentaux " had already been inserted in the eleventh protocol of 20 Jan. *Ibid.*, 759.

In the Vienna Articles the Powers had laid down the principle of freedom of navigation and had named the rivers to which it was to apply. It is clear, however, that as a result of frontier-changes a river may lose or acquire international status, and in the latter case it is necessary that the riparians should recognize the principle in its new application. While it would not be true to say that either the Scheldt or Maas acquired international status in 1830-1—they had both been named in the Vienna Articles as traversing the territories of France and the Netherlands—the advent of a third riparian had so modified the political situation as to render necessary a restatement of the principle of free navigation as applying to them. It has even been plausibly argued that since the Netherlands was already pledged to respect that principle, the real purpose of this article was to lay the same obligation upon Belgium. This was not, however, the full extent of its significance.

What the Conference intended by the article appears from a letter which Palmerston addressed to King William IV on 23 January in reply to the king's observations on the "Bases".[1] Palmerston first explains in answer to the king's surprise at finding no reference to the navigation of the Scheldt, that the freedom of that river is provided for by Article III; he also makes the point that since this article does no more than confirm the stipulations of 1814-15 the Dutch government can have no objection to it. He adduces another consideration in favour of the article:

The Conference felt that such having been the arrangement established by the Treaty of Vienna and it being of high & general importance for the tranquillity of Europe to uphold as much as possible the provisions of that Treaty it was expedient to recognise in this protocol that this arrangement remained in full force.

To the king's remarks on the importance of protecting Dutch commercial interests, Palmerston replies that, although Antwerp will of necessity be something of a rival to Amsterdam and Rotterdam, the King of Holland evidently entertains no serious fears on this score, since he himself offered the freedom of the Scheldt in exchange for a concession in the matter of the debt.

In Palmerston's exposition of the article it is possible to discern two guiding principles. The first is that the free navigation of the Scheldt, as established by the Vienna Articles, is the inalienable right not only of Belgium but of all the Powers who were signatory to those Articles; it is not a privilege within the power of the King of Holland to bestow

[1] P.P.

or to withhold, and hence there can be no question of giving Holland anything in exchange for it. That this was the principle adopted is shown by the fact that this article comes under the head of " arrangemens fondamentaux ", whereas the clause concerning freedom of trade between Belgium and the Dutch colonies, in which the Conference did admit the Dutch claim to compensation, is found among the " arrangemens proposés ". The second principle is that the freedom of navigation stipulated in the article goes no further than that sanctioned by the Vienna Articles and applies solely to the Scheldt and Maas. The Conference itself was at pains to make this clear; on 18 February Palmerston informed the Dutch plenipotentairies that the Conference had requested him to explain that Article III applied " only to rivers whose navigable course traverses the territories both of Holland and Belgium, and separates those Countries ".[1] It was, as we shall see, a significant proviso.

To his defence of the article on legal grounds Palmerston added the following sentence:

Viscount Palmerston begs also to submit that it appeared to the Conference that unless Belgium were to obtain that outlet for her Commerce which the free navigation of the Scheldt would afford she never could attain that degree of prosperity which alone can attach her to her national independence & wean her from her desire for French Connection.

In these words Palmerston epitomized the attitude to the Scheldt question from which he was never to deviate throughout the negotiation. To him it was an integral part of the problem of devising a system by which Belgium, separated from Holland, should not be absorbed by France. Political guarantees alone were not enough; what was also essential was the material welfare of the Belgian people. It was this line of reasoning which quickly brought Palmerston to grasp the political importance of the Scheldt question. The Belgian state which the Conference was helping to erect would possess but one first-class harbour, Antwerp; its welfare would thus be closely bound up with the prosperity of Antwerp, and this in turn depended upon free communication with the outer world by way of the Scheldt. In a political sense there were two possible views of the matter: one, that the greater the freedom on the Scheldt, the greater the prosperity of Belgium and the smaller the danger of its absorption by France; the other, that Antwerp could only prosper at the expense of the Dutch ports, and that Holland, the old and tried member of the anti-French coalitions, must not be sacrificed to Belgium, which would inevitably fall under

[1] *B.F.S.P.*, *1830-1*, 779.

French influence. It was round these two positions that the battle was joined in 1831; Palmerston had already made clear on which side he would be found.

From their close resemblance to the Dutch government's own ideas the "Bases de Séparation" could hardly fail to win the approval of The Hague, and on 18 February the King's unconditional acceptance of them was announced to the Conference. The Dutch government might have been expected to say something about the rejection of its principle that the freedom of the Scheldt was a privilege for which Belgium must be prepared to pay. That it made no reference to the subject was probably due to its belief that the application of Article III to the Scheldt would require a negotiation with its co-riparians, France and Belgium, similar to that which was still proceeding between the Rhine States at Mainz, and that, like the Mainz negotiation, this would be based on the principle of "reciprocity"; Holland would thus be able to demand reciprocal concessions in return for any demanded of her. This idea of "reciprocity" was indeed to become the watchword of the Dutch government throughout the negotiation. A question of more immediate significance was that of the levy of a duty on the Scheldt. There can be no doubt that from the outset the Conference recognized the King's right to a duty in virtue of his sovereignty, and that in specifically applying to the river in its protocol of 9 January the rule, based on Article CXI of the Vienna Articles, that the duties on international rivers should never exceed those in force in 1814,[1] the Conference had understood that there was a duty in force on the Scheldt in 1814. Unfortunately, it soon discovered that there had in fact been no duty levied on the river at any time during that year, so that its order to the King to allow navigation "sans autres droits de péage ni de visite que ceux qui étoient établis en 1814" really meant its exemption from duty.[2] It was an error which might prove costly to Holland, since the Belgians could be relied upon to use it as an argument for the permanent abolition of all duties, and the Dutch government was naturally anxious to secure prompt recognition of its right by imposing a provisional duty pending a definitive settlement. Such a duty was at hand. The Central Commission for the Rhine

---

[1] See above, p. 151.
[2] Palmerston to Adair, private, 27 July 1832: "With respect to Duties on the Scheldt when we summoned the King of Holland in 1830 to raise his Blockade and establish the Duties which existed in 1814 before the Union, the Conference believed from Information given in by Falck that in 1814 some duties had been levied. It turned out, however, that in 1814 no Duties were levied and so the Navigation has hitherto been entirely free". P.P.

had drawn up a tariff for that river which only awaited the consent of the riparian states to be put into force, and since the Vienna Articles themselves had laid it down that the future arrangements for the Scheldt should follow as nearly as possible those on the Rhine, the provisional application of this tariff to the Scheldt appeared the natural solution of the problem. The "tariff of Mainz" could hardly be applied to the Scheldt before it had been sanctioned for the Rhine, but in the meantime the Dutch government could seek the approval of the Conference to the plan. This was the origin of the "provisional application of the tariff of Mainz to the Scheldt", destined to provoke so much trouble in 1832.

The same reasons which made the "Bases de Séparation" acceptable at The Hague disposed the Belgian government to reject them. Moreover, any hope of their acceptance at Brussels was destroyed by the French government's decision not to participate in their communication there, in view of the known opposition of the Belgian government to certain of their clauses. This manœuvre was designed to secure the election of the Duc de Nemours, second son of Louis Philippe, as King of the Belgians, an object in which it succeeded. But it also provoked a fresh outburst against the Articles, especially in the matter of Zeeland-Flanders. Despite the united opposition of the Four Powers, France for a time felt constrained to support the Belgian claim; but when early in April Sébastiani began to talk about Belgium's securing this territory in exchange for the cession to Holland of a "corridor" to Maastricht, this tacit admission that the Belgians had no claim was a decided step towards the restoration of unity within the Conference. Although Palmerston had been for a moment tempted by the exchange-scheme,[1] he now, in concert with the other members, opposed it vigorously and pressed France to adhere to the protocol. This firmness was rewarded on 17 April, when Talleyrand announced that his government would do so. Thereupon the Conference resolved to present the "Bases" once more at Brussels and to declare that if they were refused the Powers would break off relations with the provisional government.

(ii) *The Eighteen Articles and the Ten Days' Campaign.*

Despite his election by the Belgian Congress Nemours did not become King of the Belgians. To Grey and Palmerston, no less

[1] On 25 January he wrote privately to Bagot at The Hague asking whether the King might be brought to agree to it. Bagot's replies of 28 and 31 January showed that it was out of the question, and Palmerston dropped the idea. P.P.

than to Wellington, his accession would have been tantamount to a reunion of Belgium to France, and they told France plainly that they would not have it. Louis Philippe was in no position to forfeit the entente, and he accordingly declined the crown for his son. But it was already clear that unless a candidate could be found acceptable both to the Belgians and to the Powers the independence of the new state would be compromised. It was this consideration which early in April impelled the Powers to unite in sponsoring Prince Leopold of Saxe-Coburg.

On 20 April a Belgian deputation arrived in London. Its members told the Prince that Belgium would not accept the territorial clauses of the "Bases", to which he replied that unless the "Bases" were accepted he would not take the crown. From this impasse there at first appeared to be no escape. But although Belgian public opinion, further aroused by a succession of "incidents" on the river, was as violent as ever on the subject of Zeeland-Flanders, the government soon showed signs of weakening, and on 5 May the Foreign Minister for the first time hinted that it was not a *sine qua non*.[1] When the government carried a motion that the Congress should proceed to the election, leaving outstanding questions to be settled by negotiation, the first part of the battle was won. On 4 June Leopold was elected; a mission straightway set off for London bearing the offer of the crown, and at the same time two new envoys, Devaux and Nothomb, were appointed to treat with the Conference. The negotiation which followed turned largely on the attitude of Leopold. As king-elect his position was a strong one, and he and Palmerston used it, on the one hand to whittle down the demands of the Belgian envoys and on the other to overcome the opposition of the plenipotentiaries of the three Eastern Courts to any modification of the "Bases". For some modification there clearly had to be if Leopold and his future subjects were to be brought to agreement. The principal changes eventually made were territorial ones, although Zeeland-Flanders was not affected by them. But the negotiation also marked an important stage in the evolution of ideas about the Scheldt.

There emerged in the course of it what were in effect two conflicting conceptions of international river-law. The first, to which the Dutch government adhered, was based upon two principles or postulates: one, that the rights and duties of the riparian states should be determined by a strictly legal interpretation of the Vienna Articles,

[1] Lebeau to the Belgian Deputation, 5 May 1831. A.E., Correspondance Politique. Conférence de Londres, II, no. 42.

and the other, that the application of these Articles would require a separate negotiation, based on "reciprocity", between the riparians alone. Both principles were well illustrated by the project for a new Article III which Bülow, the Prussian representative, drew up in conjunction with the Dutch plenipotentiaries and presented on 15 July. Bülow's draft repeated Article III of the "Bases" and added:

Les cinq puissances seront invitées à interposer leurs bons offices pour obtenir l'application à la navigation de l'Escaut des réglemens arrêtés en dernier lieu à Mayence pour la navigation du Rhin.[1]

The principle of "legality" was represented here both by the proposed application of the Convention of Mainz (which had been concluded since the formulation of the "Bases") to the Scheldt, and by the tacit exclusion from the scope of the article of any waterways other than the Scheldt and Maas; the other principle, that of "reciprocity", was implicit in the provision that in the further handling of the matter the role of the Powers should be limited to "good offices". Both principles flowed naturally from Dutch interests in the question. It was Holland which was called upon to make the sacrifices; hence the Dutch government's determination to limit those sacrifices by insisting on a literal interpretation of the Vienna Articles. Again, the Conference already manifested a disturbing tendency to give its protocols the character of binding decisions, and the Dutch government was far from wishing to see the whole Scheldt problem submitted to such a body; a separate negotiation would secure it from this danger and would give it scope to maintain the position which, in the words of Falck and Zuylen, it "had defended not unsuccessfully in the case of the Rhine".[2]

The Belgians were simultaneously feeling their way towards a radically different conception. To reduce this also to two basic principles, we may say that it postulated, first, that the Vienna Articles must be interpreted in a liberal sense and with due regard for the peculiar nature of the problem to be solved, and second, that the London Conference, as the "trustee" of the Vienna Act, was not only competent but was in duty bound to regulate its detailed application to the Scheldt. The first of these principles sprang from the liberal spirit which supplied the Belgian Revolution at once with its justification and its creed; it was the same spirit which had animated the French Revolutionaries when in 1792 they decreed the opening of the Scheldt. The Belgians argued that from the moment they

[1] Quoted in Juste, *op. cit.*, II, 257.
[2] To Verstolk, 24 Jan. 1831. B.Z., 1695.

achieved their independence they entered as a nation into possession of certain fundamental rights, and among them the right to unhindered use of the communications essential to their national welfare. In general, no ancient law or custom could be allowed to infringe the inherent right of a nation to live and thrive; nor, in particular, must too literal an observance of the Vienna Articles deprive Belgium of the advantages which their spirit intended her to enjoy. It was to the Conference that the Belgians looked for support and hence their second principle. Their faith in the omnipotence of the Powers is reflected in the letters of the Antwerp merchants appealing to the Conference to secure to them what they regarded as their rights. It followed that the Belgians wanted the whole question of navigation settled by and in the Conference, for there alone, they believed, would their demands receive proper consideration.

With the abandonment of the demand for Zeeland-Flanders in May 1831 Belgian interest in Article III increased notably. The Belgian demands were finally embodied in a project presented by Devaux and Nothomb to the Conference on 19 June. In this project Article III added to the original Article of the "Bases" the following clauses:

Les cinq grandes Puissances interposeront leurs bons offices pour que la Belgique participe librement à la navigation du Rhin par les eaux intérieures.

La Belgique conservera le libre usage des canaux de Gand à Terneuse et du Zuid-Willems-vaart, construits pendant l'existence du royaume des Pays Bas. L'écoulement des eaux des Flandres sera réglé de manière à prévenir toute inondation.

L'art. 3, relatif à la liberté de la navigation des rivières et des fleuves, recevra immédiatement son exécution.[1]

The question of the admission of Belgian ships to the free navigation of the Rhine had been raised by a group of Antwerp merchants in a letter to the Conference of 24 December 1830. They requested the Conference to "donner des ordres" (a revealing phrase) for the inclusion of Belgium in the arrangements then approaching completion at Mainz on the ground that the freedom of the Rhine was essential to the transit-trade between Germany and Antwerp.[2] The question of the "intermediate waters" between Rhine and Scheldt arose naturally from that of the Rhine. Their navigation had already been the subject of discussion at Mainz before the break-up of the Netherlands,

[1] Nothomb, J.-B., Baron, *Essai historique et politique sur la Révolution Belge* (4th ed., Brussels, 1876), I, 205.
[2] Comité de la Réunion Commerciale d'Anvers to the Conference, 4 December 1830. A.E., I, annexe 3 to no. 55.

and when it was agreed there that each state should designate certain ports on the Rhine as entrepôts the Netherlands government had named Amsterdam, Rotterdam, Dordrecht, and Antwerp (the last, although not on the Rhine, being included to avoid discriminating between North and South), and had agreed in effect that the Rhine States should navigate the intermediate waters on the same terms as the Rhine itself. After the separation of Belgium the Dutch government proposed that Antwerp should be struck out of the list of entrepôts; the other Rhine States were unwilling, however, to relinquish the freedom of the intermediate waters which its inclusion had given them, and they agreed to its deletion only on condition that its readmission as an entrepôt should be made the subject of future negotiation and under reserve of their right to navigate freely between it and the Rhine.[1] The Belgian demand of June 1831 thus represented an attempt to profit by this situation. The claim to the freedom of the Ghent-Terneuzen and Zuid Willemsvaart canals (the latter linking Antwerp with Maastricht) was a claim to the continued enjoyment of rights which Belgium ran the risk of losing now that she had no hope of securing the territories through which they passed, namely, Zeeland-Flanders and Limburg. The remaining demands do not call for comment.

The divergence between the Dutch and Belgian conceptions as formulated in these two projects comes out most clearly in connection with the Belgian demands relative to the intermediate waters and canals. The Dutch government had already sought and obtained a ruling from the Conference limiting the operation of Article III of the " Bases " to the rivers named in the Vienna Articles.[2] Bülow's draft was therefore silent on the other waterways, natural and artificial, which formed part of the great network of the Rhine-Maas-Scheldt delta. This was undoubtedly the correct legal view. But to the Belgians it was a matter of elementary justice that the Conference should ensure to Antwerp not merely freedom of communication with the ocean trade-routes but also, what was hardly less vital, freedom of communication with its hinterland and above all with Germany.

In deciding between these two projects of Article III the Conference was really deciding between the two conceptions which underlay them. It was the powerful support of the British Foreign Secretary which contributed more than any other factor to the adoption of the Belgian project. The first part of the battle was won by 20 June, when Bülow's project was abandoned, the second by 23 June, when the

[1] Rhine Protocol no. 512 of 30 March 1931. *B.F.S.P., 1831-2,* 88.
[2] See above, p. 165.

Belgian article, slightly toned down, was incorporated in the new preliminaries. Three days later these were formally adopted by the Conference; they are known to history as the Eighteen Articles. The article on navigation, now become Article VII, was as follows:

Il est entendu que les dispositions des Articles CVIII, jusqu'à CXVII inclusivement, de l'Acte Général du Congrès de Vienne, relatifs à la libre navigation des fleuves et rivières navigables, seront appliquées aux fleuves et aux rivières qui traversent le Territoire Hollandais et le Territoire Belge.

La mise à exécution de ces dispositions sera réglée dans le plus brief délai possible.

La participation de la Belgique à la Navigation du Rhin, par les eaux intérieures entre ce fleuve et l'Escaut, formera l'objet d'une Négociation séparée entre les Parties intéressées, à laquelle les 5 Puissances prêteront leurs bons offices.

L'usage des canaux de Gand à Terneuse et du Zuid-Willemsvaart, construits pendant l'existence du Royaume des Pays Bas, sera commun aux habitans des deux Pays; il sera arrêté un réglement sur cet objet. L'écoulement des eaux des Flandres sera réglé de la manière la plus convenable afin de prévenir les inondations.[1]

If it is the first step that matters, then from Article III of the Bases to Article VII of the Eighteen Articles was the decisive step in the evolution of the modern Scheldt regime. The difference between them was more than the difference between one paragraph and four (although this increase in length was indeed symptomatic); it was the difference between a mere restatement of principle and the first stage in its detailed application, and this in a liberal sense. The Eighteen Articles thus marked the initial victory of the " Belgian " over the original " Dutch " conception of what the article on navigation should comprise; the conflict between them would be renewed when the Conference returned to the subject after the Ten Days' Campaign.

The plenipotentiaries set their hands to the Eighteen Articles on 26 June. For the representatives of the Eastern Powers it was indeed, as Princess Lieven said, a " sacrifice ". In giving their assent to the new articles they were parting company with the Dutch government, which was determined to cling to the " Bases ", previously declared " irrevocable ". The Conference tacitly admitted the difficulty by sending the articles to The Hague by one of its own number, Wessenberg,[2] whose personal friendship with the King his colleagues hoped might smooth their reception. Wessenberg carried private instructions from the Conference, which included a not unimportant *éclaircissement* of Article VII; by this the Conference repudiated any intention of

[1] *B.F.S.P., 1830-1*, 804.
[2] Second Austrian plenipotentiary.

dragooning the Rhine States into giving Belgium the freedom of the Rhine.[1] From the outset there was little chance of Wessenberg's succeeding, but what finally destroyed it was the acceptance, after a magnificent speech by the Foreign Minister, Lebeau, of the articles by the Belgian Congress on 10 July. By painting the settlement in such colours as to convince his fellow-countrymen that they were getting the best of the bargain, Lebeau only confirmed Dutchmen in the view that they were getting the worst. The day after Lebeau's speech the Dutch government rejected the articles.

The Dutch Note, which the Conference received on 25 July, dealt briefly but trenchantly with Article VII. The proposal to admit the Belgians to the intermediate waters it virtually ignored, and although the King declared his readiness to negotiate about the Scheldt, he declined the " good offices " of the Powers, the more so as some of them were interested parties; finally, the Note stated that since the use of canals both in Holland and Belgium was " free ", there was no point in a special provision to this effect. The Note was not less severe on the other modifications, territorial and financial, of the " Bases ". The Conference's reply was to invite the King to furnish his representatives in London with full powers to negotiate a treaty with Belgium; a rider was added to meet any reluctance which the King might feel to committing the whole affair to a negotiation under the eye of the Conference. This invitation the King immediately accepted, and on 3 August Zuylen told Palmerston that he and Falck had the necessary full powers. But he gave no hint of a fact which robbed his announcement of most of its meaning, namely, that the Dutch army was at that moment crossing the Belgian frontier. The King's threat to treat as an enemy a Prince who accepted the sovereignty of Belgium without first adhering to the " Bases " was not the form of words which everyone in London had taken it to be. Within a few days the Dutch army, ably led by the Prince of Orange, did what was required of it. It not only vindicated the national honour and avenged the defeats of 1830; it exposed the defencelessness of the state which the Conference was erecting on the frontier of France. Only the arrival of a French army, summoned by Leopold and hastily authorized to act in the name of the Conference, saved Brussels from occupation. But by then the Prince of Orange had completed his task; on 13 August he concluded an armistice, and within a few days the Dutch Army was back in Holland.

[1] A copy of these instructions, entitled " Notice confidentielle pour M. le Baron de Wessenberg ", is in P.P.

It did not prove quite so easy to persuade the King to raise the obstacles which he had at the same time placed on the Scheldt, and there was a repetition in miniature of the struggle of the previous winter to get the river open again.[1] Not until the end of August were ships allowed up or down the river. It took even longer to get the French troops out of Belgium. But early in September they too were withdrawn, and the Conference was free to gather up the threads of the negotiation where they had been left a month before.

(iii) *The Twenty-Four Articles and the Treaty of November 1831.*

One of the effects of the Ten Days' Campaign on the Belgians was to make them far less amenable to the authority of the Conference. France had saved them, and it was on France that they determined to rely in the resumed negotiation. At first they were confident of French support for their claim, now brought forward again, to Zeeland-Flanders. This time the argument was one of expediency rather than of justice; as Belliard, French ambassador at Brussels, put it, " quand vous avez fait un enfant, il faut le nourrir ".[2] But single-handed France proved, as she had proved six months before, unequal to the task. The most that Paris could, or would, do was to put in a strong plea for the transfer to Belgium of the strip of Zeeland-Flanders in which lay the sluices which regulated the outflow of water from Flanders. It was to this demand, therefore, which would have given Belgium Sluis and Sas van Gent, that the Belgian government limited its territorial claim when replying, on 23 September, to the Conference's invitation to submit its ideas on the three principal questions at issue, those of the frontier, of Luxemburg, and of the debt. As was to be expected, the Dutch reply to the same invitation demanded the retention of the frontier of 1790.

The wide divergence between these replies, and between the observations which each party made on the other's (Falck and Zuylen in theirs waxed almost poetic over Zeeland-Flanders, " arrosé du sang et de la sueur de ses industrieux habitans "), convinced the Conference that it must abandon the Eighteen Articles, as it had previously abandoned the " Bases ", and embark on yet another attempt to draw up terms acceptable to both. The Conference accordingly asked the two

[1] The idea of using the British squadron under Codrington which had been assembled in the Downs on the outbreak of hostilities to force the passage of the river was soon abandoned. On 5 Aug. Palmerston wrote privately to Granville, ambassador at Paris: " Our Naval Men say it would be too hazardous to risk a Fleet up the Scheldt unless it was supported by Troops, and therefore a Blockade is the only practicable Measure ". Granville Papers (Public Record Office)/14.

[2] Reported in Adair to Palmerston, private, 23 Aug. 1831. P.P.

parties to supplement their observations on the principal points by communicating their ideas on all other questions, including navigation. In reply the Dutch plenipotentiaries handed in a project of which Article II consisted of one sentence:

Il sera ouvert sans délai une Négociation pour régler la libre navigation de l'Escaut, aux termes de l'Acte du Congrès de Vienne.[1]

Since this article tallies in every respect with what has already been said of the Dutch view, it does not call for comment. If its chief merit, or defect, lay in its brevity, the same cannot be said of its Belgian counterpart, which consisted of seven paragraphs drawn up by Van de Weyer, back in London as Belgian plenipotentiary, and a further five added by the new Foreign Minister, De Muelenaere.[2] Among its clauses a number deserve mention either by reason of their novelty or because they were later to assume importance. First among these is a provision that the pilotage, buoying, policing, etc., of the Scheldt should be submitted to a " surveillance commune ", that is, to joint Belgo-Dutch supervision, and linked with it is a demand for a separate Belgian pilotage establishment on the river. The stipulation that the duties on the Scheldt should never exceed those in existence in 1814 is doubtless to be read as an indirect claim to a duty-free navigation; whereas it was normally in the interest of the Belgians to support a liberal construction of the Vienna Articles, they were ready, when it suited them, to stand on the letter of those Articles. The confidence with which, in another clause, they demanded the free navigation of the Rhine suggests that they had not grasped the significance of the Conference's ruling on this point, as exemplified in the instructions to Wesenberg. But what is far more surprising is the discovery that Belgium is a riparian of the Rhine!

Riveraine du Rhin par l'enclave de Zevenaer, la Belgique a droit de participer aux avantages du réglement sur ce fleuve.

Originally part of the Duchy of Cleves, Zevenaar had been ceded to the Netherlands by Prussia in 1815. Thus, in accordance with the " rule of 1790 " laid down in the " Bases ", Zevenaar certainly fell to the lot of Belgium and by reason of its position on the Lek, one of the branches of the Rhine, conferred riparian status on her. But—and here was the " catch "—Article IV of the " Bases " had expressly provided for the exchange of any *enclaves* resulting from the application

---

[1] B.F.S.P., *1830-1*, 882.

[2] Van de Weyer had drawn up the first seven paragraphs himself to avoid delay in replying to the Conference, but he reserved the right to supplement them by a further communication, which he made on receipt of De Muelenaere's additions. The original Note is printed in B.F.S.P., *1830-1*, 883, and the " Complément " in Guillaume, P., Baron, *L'Escaut depuis 1830* (2 vols., Brussels, 1903), I, 36.

of the rule, so that Belgium would lose Zevenaar and its unique advantage. The advancement of the claim here should not, I think, be taken seriously, although it testifies to Belgian persistence and ingenuity. The same readiness to seize on every possible point is evident in the revival of the argument that Belgian ships should enjoy the freedom of the intermediate waters on the ground of the former designation of Antwerp as a Rhine entrepôt.

While the Conference was receiving this official information Palmerston was collecting fresh data from a different source. This source was the group of Antwerp merchants, some of them British subjects, who had already addressed both him and the Belgian government, and as before the intermediary was the Antwerp consul, Larpent. The merchants' observations were the more valuable as coming from men who had no political axe to grind—theirs was the " politique du florin "—and who possessed first-hand knowledge of their subject. In general, their proposals agreed with those of the Belgian government, but it is noteworthy that they did not hesitate to demand the exemption of the Scheldt from all duty, and that they supported the claim for a separate Belgian pilotage by charges of discrimination in this respect against Antwerp during the Union. From the many pencillings in the margins of these documents it is clear that the Antwerpers had not wasted their time in sending them.[1]

Palmerston went into the Conference, then, well supplied with ammunition. Over against him were ranged the three plenipotentiaries of the Eastern Courts, primed by Falck and Zuylen. The first important decision was reached on 6 October, when the Conference settled the division of the debt. After arriving at a figure of 7,800,000 florins as the amount payable annually by Belgium, the Conference decided that

eu égard aux avantages de navigation et de commerce dont la Hollande est tenue de faire jouir les Belges, et aux sacrifices de divers genres que la séparation a amenés pour elle,

Belgium should be called upon to bear an additional sum of 600,000 florins.[2] As we shall see, the Conference had already agreed upon the particular " avantages de navigation " which were to cost Belgium at least part of this sum. Writing to Brussels on 7 October Van de Weyer was able to report notable gains, but on some points, especially

---

[1] Larpent had enclosed the first memorial, from the British merchants, in a despatch of 6 Sept. In reply to Palmerston's own request for more detailed information upon one point, two further ones arrived at the Foreign Office on 6 Oct., just in time for the debate in the Conference. F.O. Belgium/8.
[2] B.F.S.P., *1830-1*, 889.

the provisions for ensuring the practical freedom of the Scheldt, he was still somewhat speculative. It was, indeed, when these provisions came up for discussion that the real fight began. Palmerston himself used the military metaphor in relating the story:

It was only by a most obstinate Battle single-handed, that I obtained for the Belgians from the Conference, the joint Fishery, Pilotage and Buoyage, the use of the Internal Channels, the Free Road through Maestricht and the Right of making a Canal or Railway through Sittart; But if these things had not been stipulated I could not have concurred in undertaking to compel the Belgians to accept our Terms, nor have agreed to award to them so large a portion of the Debt.[1]

Belgian gains on this part of the front were offset by disappointments elsewhere. Besides a less favourable settlement in Limburg and Luxemburg, they suffered the rejection of their claim to the sluices in Zeeland-Flanders. The Palais Royal had done its best here, but Talleyrand was lukewarm and Palmerston hostile. The articles were given their final form on 14 October and annexed to the forty-ninth protocol of that date. In this project of treaty, the Twenty-Four Articles, the article on navigation reached the position it was to retain in all subsequent versions, becoming Article IX. It was as follows:

Les dispositions des Articles CVIII—CXVII inclusivement de l'Acte Général du Congrès de Vienne, relatives à la libre navigation des Fleuves et Rivières navigables, seront appliquées aux Fleuves et Rivières navigables qui séparent ou traversent à la fois le Territoire Belge et le Territoire Hollandais.

En ce qui concerne specialement la navigation de l'Escaut, il sera convenu que le pilotage et le balisage, ainsi que la conservation des passes de l'Escaut en aval d'Anvers, seront soumis à une surveillance commune; que cette surveillance commune sera exercée par des Commissaires nommés à cet effet de part et d'autre; que des droits de pilotage modérés seront fixés d'un commun accord, et que ces droits seront les mêmes pour le commerce Hollandais et pour le commerce Belge.

Il est également convenu que la navigation des eaux intermédiaires entre l'Escaut et le Rhin, pour arriver d'Anvers au Rhin, et vice versa, restera réciproquement libre, et qu'elle ne sera assujettie qu'à des péages modérés, qui seront provisoirement les mêmes pour le commerce des 2 Pays.

Des Commissaires se réuniront de part et d'autre à Anvers dans le délai d'un mois, tant pour arrêter le montant définitif et permanent de ces péages, qu'afin de convenir d'un réglement général pour l'exécution des dispositions du présent Article, et d'y comprendre l'exercice du droit de pêche, et du commerce de pêcherie, dans toute l'étendue de l'Escaut, sur le pied d'une parfaite réciprocité en faveur des Sujets des 2 Pays.

En attendant, et jusqu'à ce que le dit réglement soit arrêté, la navigation des fleuves et rivières navigables ci-dessus mentionnés restera libre au commerce des 2 Pays, qui adopteront provisoirement à cet égard les Tarifs de la Convention signée le 31 Mars, 1831, à Mayence, pour la libre navigation du

---

[1] To Bagot, private, 18 Oct. 1831. P.P.

Rhin, ainsi que les autres dispositions de cette Convention, en autant qu'elles pourront s'appliquer aux fleuves et rivières navigables, qui séparent ou traversent à la fois le territoire Hollandais et le territoire Belge.[1]

This article, which was to be the basis of all subsequent negotiations at least until September 1832, when it was to some extent superseded by Article IX of Palmerston's Theme, deserves to be examined in some detail. Its first paragraph followed the previous articles, but with the addition of the words " à la fois " designed to establish beyond all doubt that it applied only to rivers common to both states and not, for example, to the intermediate waters, which lay wholly in Dutch territory. In so far as paragraph 2 established a " surveillance commune " on the Scheldt it bore a striking resemblance to the corresponding paragraph of Van de Weyer's project of 30 September; but it was Palmerston's insistence alone which had secured its inclusion and he was to remain its leading advocate. This " surveillance commune " was strictly limited in scope; it was to apply to pilotage, buoying, and the maintenance of the navigable channels, and to nothing else. A claim was made from the Belgian side during the 'thirties, and has been repeated since,[2] that this clause (or its equivalent in the treaty of 1839) gave Belgium co-sovereignty with Holland over the Scheldt estuary. To dispose of this contention it is only necessary to point out that Palmerston, the " father " of this clause, never gave the slightest hint that he regarded it in this light but on the contrary made it abundantly clear that he considered Holland's sovereignty over the estuary unimpaired. The only other point of interest about this paragraph is its omission of the separate pilotage service on which the Belgians had laid such stress.

Leaving paragraph 3 aside for the moment, we come to paragraph 4 with its provision for the meeting of Dutch and Belgian commissioners. This was the " négociation séparée et ultérieure " for which the Dutch showed such an affection and the Belgians an equally strong aversion. The terms of reference of this commission represented a compromise between the two views, for if most of the questions which the Dutch wanted left to it had already been settled in the article, the Belgians might still argue that to leave to it such an important matter as the permanent duty on the river was to ask for trouble. The fact that Matuszewic could number the " commission mixte " among the

---
[1] B.F.S.P., 1830-1, 896-7.
[2] Thus, writing in 1868, Grandgaignage could say (Histoire du péage de l'Escaut, 100): " Cette article nous admettait donc à la propriété commune de l'Escaut. . . " See also below, pp. 193, 212.

precautions against Belgium's entering too quickly and easily into enjoyment of the article proves that the Belgian contention was not unfounded.[1] The last paragraph held a further disappointment for the Belgians with its provision that pending the introduction of the permanent scale of duty (a prospect rendered more distant, they would argue, by reason of paragraph 4) the navigation of both Scheldt and Maas should be subject to the tariff of Mainz. Not only would it put an end to the existing situation by which the Scheldt was duty-free, it established beyond doubt that the Conference recognized the King's right to a duty and so destroyed the Belgian illusion that the freedom of the Scheldt meant freedom from duty. True, the Conference had never—apart from the misunderstanding about the situation in 1814—shown any disposition to enter into the Belgian view; the clause was nevertheless a blow to Antwerp, which felt strongly on the subject. But no one yet realized what a monstrosity the Conference had created in this innocent-looking clause.

To return now to paragraph 3, which dealt with the intermediate waters, it is clear that the Conference had not taken cognizance either of the Belgian claim to be a riparian of the Rhine or of the " entrepôt argument ". On what ground then did it propose the admission of Belgian ships to these channels subject to a moderate duty? The answer seems to be that the Conference, while adjudging this facility essential to Antwerp's welfare, could find no basis for it in existing treaties or agreements; the clause thus constituting a special unilateral privilege, the Conference required Belgium to pay for it by a concession elsewhere, and hence the addition of at least part of the 600,000 florins to the Belgian share of the debt. The arrangement was thus essentially another compromise; Palmerston and Talleyrand were determined to give Belgium this facility, the Eastern plenipotentiaries wanted the most favourable terms for Holland in the matter of territory and debt, and on this basis the bargain was struck. Theoretically, it was not beyond reproach;[2] in practice, the 600,000 florins had proved a powerful argument in overcoming the opposition to Palmerston's idea of what the ninth article should include.

If the article did not give the Belgians nearly all they asked for, and in some respects made concessions to the Dutch point of view, it clearly marked a further long step along the road which the Conference

---

[1] Matuszewic to Gourieff, " confidentielle ", 16 October 1831. *Gedenkstukken, 1830-40*, III, 502.
[2] Even Grey confessed himself unable to understand why Belgium had to bear the additional charge. To Princess Lieven, 31 Oct. 1831. *Correspondence of Princess Lieven with Earl Grey* (2 vols., London, 1890), II, 292.

had begun to travel the previous June. The Conference had confirmed its earlier decision not merely to state principles but to apply them and it had carried the application a stage further. The result was an article which, although far from perfect—and time alone would reveal its worst defect—constituted the strongest guarantee so far devised of Belgium's enjoyment of the substance, as well as the form, of the benefits envisaged in the Vienna Articles. There is abundant proof that what the Belgians had obtained, they owed entirely to Palmerston.[1] It is equally clear that if he had fought " a most obstinate Battle singlehanded ", it was not out of any particular affection for them nor yet in obedience to any dictates of doctrinaire liberalism, but solely because he conceived it to be in the interest of his own country that he should do so. " It was our duty ", he wrote to Bagot,

so to constitute Holland as to form her into a second Line of Defence, should the Neutrality of Belgium at any time be violated by France. For this purpose West Flanders [that is, Zeeland-Flanders] on one side, and Maestricht and the Right Bank of the Meuse on the other, became necessary for Holland. . . . But if a Military Position were necessary for Holland, Commercial Prosperity is equally required for the existence of Belgium, since without it, she must sooner or later be driven into the arms of France. This Prosperity we have secured to her the means of attaining. . . .[2]

It was the general opinion in the Conference that, taken as a whole, the Twenty-Four Articles represented a settlement advantageous to Holland. It was thus hardly a surprise when Van de Weyer declined to sign them, although he agreed to bear them to Brussels himself. There the terms at first produced an unfavourable impression, but on 7 November the Chambers authorized the King to sign a treaty embodying them, under such reserves as he considered desirable. Van de Weyer accordingly reappeared in London with his full power, but before signing he made a last effort to secure, among other changes, the duty-free navigation of the Scheldt. Only after the Conference had declared that it would admit no change did Van de Weyer signify his readiness to sign. On 15 November 1831 he signed with the five plenipotentiaries a treaty by which the Powers recognized the independence and neutrality of Belgium within the limits and upon the conditions specified in the articles. The treaty was greeted with enthusiasm in London and Paris as the first and decisive step towards a settlement; as Palmerston told William IV, " even the Refusal of the King of the Netherlands to accept these Articles could not now

[1] See, for example, the verdict of Stockmar. *Memoirs* (London, 2 vols., 1872), I, 201-2.
[2] Private, 18 Oct. 1831. P.P.

prevent the establishment of the Km. of Belgium upon the Basis of these Articles ".[1]

The King of Holland's refusal was, indeed, already certain. In the country itself the first impression was not unfavourable, but it soon became clear that approval was limited to the territorial and financial terms, and that the ninth article was everywhere condemned. It could hardly be otherwise. Taken by itself the article was bound to appear " unequal "; it was Holland alone which had to make the concessions, for the simple reason that Belgium had nothing to concede. But the real issue before Dutch opinion transcended the limits of this one article; it was whether the settlement as a whole was equitable, in other words, whether the territorial and financial advantages did not counterbalance the admitted sacrifices of Article IX. It was in this sense that Falck and Zuylen both approved the articles.[2] Unfortunately, in the circumstances what mattered was not this measured approval but the condemnation, especially in the Dutch ports, of Article IX. For it was this which gave the King his opportunity. There can be little doubt that what he objected to most strongly was not the terms themselves but the prospect of losing half his kingdom involved in their acceptance. It therefore became his policy to rally his people round him in opposition to the ninth article by representing it as an unwarranted encroachment upon Dutch sovereignty and a mortal blow at Dutch trade. In this he was completely successful, and on the strength of the support thus gained he was able to maintain a " wait and see " attitude for upwards of six years.

It was the conviction that no amount of persuasion would produce any different answer from The Hague which eventually led the Conference to break off the negotiation in 1833. But until that point was reached the plenipotentiaries strained patience and ingenuity in an attempt to find a " formula " which would meet the objections to the ninth article. This process began as soon at the Dutch Note conveying the expected refusal reached the Conference on 16 December 1831, and it was assisted by the reluctance of the Eastern Courts, especially Russia, to ratify the treaty. The British government, strengthened by a successful debate on the Belgian question in the Lords on 26 January 1832 (notable as the only occasion on which the Scheldt was discussed at any length in Parliament),[3] joined the French

---

[1] To William IV, 16 Nov. 1831. P.P.
[2] Falck to Van Lennep, 3 Nov. 1831. *Brieven, 1795-1843* (The Hague, 1861), 324. Zuylen to Van der Hoop, 25 Oct. 1831. *Gedenkstukken, 1830-40*, IV, 582-4.
[3] *Hansard*, 3rd series, IX, 834-890.

in taking a firm line with regard to ratification. On 31 January Palmerston and Talleyrand exchanged their ratifications with Van de Weyer. But it was not until after the mission of the Russian envoy Orloff to The Hague, which failed to shake the King's determination not to recognize Leopold, that the other Powers could bring themselves to ratify, Austria and Prussia on 18 April and Russia on 5 May, and even then their ratifications all contained reserves, those of Austria and Russia declaring specifically that Articles IX, XI and XII would require modification " de gré à gré " in a fresh negotiation to be opened between Holland and Belgium.

CHAPTER EIGHT

The Theme of Lord Palmerston

Accounts of the diplomacy of the Belgian Revolution tend to dismiss rather summarily the long drawn-out negotiations which separate the treaty of November 1831 from those of April 1839. In works of a general scope this diminishing scale of treatment is both legitimate and understandable; the international recognition of the kingdom of Belgium settled the major questions provoked by the Revolution, and the student's interest naturally wilts under the continuing spate of projects and protocols which in the end made no difference to the main lines of the settlement. But what is true in general does not apply to the particular case of Article IX; indeed, it was only after the great questions of territory and debt had been settled by the treaty that the question of navigation really came into its own. To the historian of the Scheldt, therefore, the negotiations subsequent to the treaty, and in particular those of 1832, are of much greater interest than is generally supposed, and it is for this reason that they are dealt with in considerable detail in the following pages.

(i) *The Background of the Theme.*

If, like the Powers, the Belgian government looked on the ratification of the treaty chiefly as a guarantee of Belgian independence, the Belgian people regarded it in the first place as a means to an end, the final liberation of their territory from the authority of their late sovereign. In particular, the cumulative effect of nearly eighteen months of vexation and distress at Antwerp was to give that unfortunate city a significance symbolic of the whole Revolution, and the Belgians had come to believe that, treaty or no treaty, they would not have achieved their independence until the last Dutch soldier was out of the citadel. The Belgian government lost no time in giving expression to the popular demand. Van de Weyer paid the penalty of accepting the Russian ratification with its reserves, and thereby suggesting that Belgium was willing to negotiate with Holland without first obtaining the citadel, by being immediately recalled from London. He was succeeded by General Goblet, whose instructions ordered him to state categorically that Belgium would do no more negotiating with anybody until the non-controversial articles of the treaty, including the territorial division, should have been put into force. To this position the Belgian government clung tenaciously throughout the weeks that followed. The Foreign Minister, De Muelenaere, was himself the

most uncompromising advocate of " no negotiation before evacuation ";
he was soon to reach the position of ordering Goblet to insist upon this
principle even if Holland accepted the Conference's revised terms, and
before the end of July he was officially urging the immediate declaration of war on Holland as the sole resource left to Belgium.

So long as the Belgian government insisted on " the treaty, the
whole treaty, and nothing but the treaty ", the Conference was forced
to rely, in its attempt to carry out the Austro-Russian programme of
modifications " de gré à gré ", upon the goodwill and general desire
of King Leopold and the " moderates " for a settlement. Belgium
had acquired rights under the treaty and it was only by an act of grace
on her part that any of its clauses could be modified. But as soon as
the Belgians themselves began to demand changes in the treaty their
position lost half its strength, for in doing so they gave the Conference
a lever with which to bring pressure on them to accept such other
changes as might satisfy the Dutch. This is what happened in the
summer of 1832, and the result was the next stage in the evolution of
Article IX, the Theme of Lord Palmerston.

Since the signing of the treaty the Belgian government had never
wavered in the view, expressed in Van de Weyer's Note of 12 November, that only by the exemption of the Scheldt from all duty could its
navigation be rendered really secure. But it was not until the early
summer of 1832 that there developed in Belgium a campaign for the
duty-free navigation of the river which, first threatening to wreck the
efforts of the Conference to reach an agreement " de gré à gré ", afterwards gave Palmerston the opportunity to keep the negotiation alive
in the face of what seemed a complete deadlock. The origin of this
campaign may be traced to a fresh effort by the merchants of Antwerp
to convert Palmerston to their point of view. For the most part the
arguments put forward in the two memorials which they sent, through
Larpent, to the Foreign Secretary in February 1832,[1] were unworthy of
serious attention. The writers were, indeed, attempting the impossible;
they were trying to put into the mouth of the Conference something
which the Conference had never said and was never likely to say,
namely, that there was to be no tonnage-duty on the Scheldt, and the
attempt led them into absurd misrepresentations. But when they exchanged theories for facts, they were, as usual, worth listening to, and
on one point in particular what they had to say was a revelation.

This point was the effect of the application of the tariff of Mainz

[1] Enclosed in Larpent to Palmerston, 29 Feb. 1832. F.O. Belgium/15.

to the Scheldt. There is no evidence that when the Conference inserted this clause in the ninth of the Twenty-Four Articles there was any discussion of the amount of the duty which it would lay upon the river; the plenipotentiaries doubtless assumed that what had been agreed upon by the Rhine States only after fifteen years of argument could do no harm if extended temporarily to the Scheldt, and it evidently did not occur to them that a tariff devised for the exclusively interior or fluvial navigation of the Rhine might be unsuitable for the almost exclusively maritime navigation of the Scheldt below Antwerp. Just how unsuitable it was the Antwerp merchants now made clear. They calculated that the tariff of Mainz was equivalent to 2 centimes per quintal per league for the inward, and $1\frac{1}{3}$ centimes for the outward journey, which for the 52 leagues from Flushing to Antwerp and back would amount to $17\frac{1}{3}$ francs per ton. The effects of such a duty would be disastrous:

Most of the vessels arriving at Antwerp with goods leave the Port in Ballast, and therefore mostly [*sic*] of this tax would fall on the " inward " freights, so that a vessel of 200 Tons burthen passing up the Scheldt from London to Antwerp would be subject to pay for every voyage not less than frs. 3466, being equivalent to 75 per cent of the usual freight paid on the average from the British ports, 35 to 40 p. Ct. on those from the Baltic and medit[errane]an & 15 to 25 p. Ct. on those from the new world, a tax which Your Lordship will at once see, is tantamount in its operation to the closing of the Scheldt.[1]

The truly staggering scale of duty which this harmless-looking clause had prescribed for the Scheldt fully justified the merchants' contention that it would nullify the freedom of navigation which the ninth article was designed to secure; the fact that it was only to operate pending a permanent settlement made matters worse rather than better, for starting from such a favourable point Holland would have no inducement to agree to such a settlement, which must of necessity be less favourable to her. But however important the revelation, it was both belated and untimely; belated, because the treaty had been signed and already ratified by three of the parties, and untimely, because it was not for Britain or France, at this moment doing their utmost to persuade the others to ratify, to give the slightest hint that Belgium was not content to abide by it. It is not surprising therefore to find no immediate trace of the effect of this representation on Palmerston's policy. But when on 11 June he submitted his first proposal since the resumption of the negotiation, a set of three supplementary articles

[1] This extract is taken from the memorial of the British merchants to Palmerston; the memorial of the Antwerp Chamber of Commerce sent with it made the calculation a different way but with almost the same result.

to be annexed to the Twenty-Four, one of them, providing for a separate Belgo-Dutch negotiation on Articles IX and XII, concluded with the stipulation that

provisoirement la libre navigation des fleuves et rivières navigables qui séparent ou traversent à la fois le territoire Hollandais et le territoire Belge restera soumise aux droits et péages qui y sont perçus maintenant de part et d'autre.[1]

This is the first indication that the Antwerp memorials had borne fruit. It soon became clear that Palmerston had taken up the question with the Eastern plenipotentiaries and had persuaded them that some modification of the existing clause was essential. The proposal of 7 July in which Matuszewic developed their ideas retained the provisional application of the tariff of Mainz, but added the words " avec diminution de   per cent "; in reporting it to The Hague, Zuylen said that they spoke of three per cent, which here as elsewhere meant three florins per ton, a reduction of the original tariff by at least a half.[2] In the circumstances the reappearance of the original clause in the Conference's project of 10 July—the last, the Conference declared, that it would send to The Hague—must be regarded as a real attempt on Palmerston's part to remove the only reasonable objection which the Dutch government could entertain against the article as it now stood. If the King could be persuaded to accept it and to sign the treaty, even the provisional application of the tariff of Mainz would be a small price to pay. If, as was far more likely, he rejected it as he had rejected all its predecessors since the " Bases ", the re-insertion of the clause would still have served its turn, for it would have reminded the Belgians that they were dependent upon the Conference for its suppression and that patience and moderation must still be the keynote of their policy.

It was, indeed, this project, coupled with the Dutch one of 5 July to which it was the answer, which stung the Antwerpers into vigorous protest against what they regarded as its sacrifice of Belgian interests. The leader of the new campaign was Jean-Baptiste Smits, a native of Antwerp, who had since 1814 filled various posts in the municipal administration and who was now in addition secretary of the Chamber of Commerce.[3] Smits had taken a large share in producing the various memorials of the Chamber, including those sent to Palmerston, and it was he who now drew up the new Antwerp manifesto. This appeared simultaneously in three forms; there was a memorial

[1] *B.F.S.P.*, *1831-2*, 121.
[2] To Verstolk, 7 July 1832. B.Z., 1698.
[3] *Académie Royale de Belgique. Biographie Nationale* (Brussels, 27 vols., 1866-1938), *sub* Smits, Jean.

addressed directly to Palmerston by the British merchants, another from the Chamber to the Belgian government, and finally an "open letter" from Smits himself to Baron Osy, one of the deputies for Antwerp, which was published under the title *Lettre à un Représentant sur la partie Commerciale et Maritime du Nouveau Projet de Traité proposé à la Conférence de Londres par le Cabinet de la Haye*.[1] It is unnecessary to analyse in detail the argument developed in these documents. The basis of the argument is that Articles CVIII to CXVII of the Vienna Act constitute an exception to the general principle of free navigation to meet the particular case of the Rhine and are in no wise applicable to the Scheldt, which presents an entirely different problem. It was a theory remarkable alike for its originality and for its total disregard of fact. The memorials reached firmer ground with their statement of the four indispensable conditions: a duty-free navigation of the Scheldt, a separate pilotage-system, practical safeguards on the river, and the freedom of the intermediate waters subject to the tariff of Mainz. But, just as the importance of the February memorials had lain in their exposure of the weight of the tariff of Mainz when applied to the Scheldt, so the present ones brought to light an even more alarming fact about that unfortunate clause. This is what the British merchants had to say about it:

By the application of the dispositions of the Convention of Mayence to the navigation of the Scheldt, all commerce to Antwerp by Foreign Flags (and since 1815 it has formed 4/5th of the whole) would be excluded, to the advantage of that of Holland. As the powers of Europe, who were parties to the Treaties of Vienna of 1814 & 1815, & then stipulated "that the navigation of the Scheldt & other European Rivers should be free to all nations", would thereby sanction the modification of this liberal principle, by admitting the more restricted views of the parties to the Convention of Mayence, by which "no Flags will be permitted to participate in the priviledges, stipulated by its provisions, but such as belong to the States whose Territories are traversed or separated by the scheldt", consequently, none but Dutch & Belgian & possibly French Vessels would be allowed to come up to Antwerp, even on the payment of the heavy duties levied. All vessels under other Flags, must land their cargoes at Flushing & have them forwarded by one of the priviledged flags; but from the power Holland would have to exempt her own vessels from the tax . . . it is No exaggeration to say that the Dutch would be the *only* Flag to be seen in the Scheldt.

We can dismiss—as Palmerston could dismiss—out of hand the fantastic conclusion that the application to the Scheldt of the terms and tariff of the Convention of Mainz would authorize the Dutch government to re-establish a modified Münster regime; even if the Dutch had

---

[1] The two memorials were enclosed in Larpent to Palmerston, 13 July 1832. F.O. Belgium/15. A copy of the "Lettre" is in the Bibliothèque Nationale, Brussels.

thought of it, they were debarred by one of those very Articles which the Antwerpers wished to repudiate.[1] But if the conclusion was false, the premise was sound. It was perfectly true that as a result of the victory of the " restrictive " principle at Vienna in 1815, the practical benefits of the freedom there enunciated had been reserved, as far as the Rhine was concerned, to the riparians. It was to the riparians alone that the terms of the Convention of Mainz therefore applied; if non-riparians navigated the Rhine they did so under whatever restrictions (short of actual prohibition) and on the payment of whatever duties the several riparians cared to impose. Now in the case of the Rhine no great hardship resulted from this limitation, since in practice the navigation was performed almost entirely by riparians, that is to say, it was carried on under the terms of the Convention. But if the application of the Mainz regime to the Scheldt, in whose maritime navigation the merchant navies of all countries took part, did in fact mean, as the merchants maintained, the extension to the Scheldt of this discrimination between riparian and non-riparian ships, the consequences would be grave indeed. One result would be to make the tariff of Mainz, high as it was, a " privilege " enjoyed solely by Belgian and French ships; all others (save, of course, Dutch, which would hardly fail to enjoy preferential treatment even to the extent of complete exemption) would be subject to a tariff at the discretion of the Dutch government, and in stating that they carried four-fifths of Antwerp's sea-borne trade the merchants were certainly not exaggerating.[2]

When Bligh, British *chargé* at The Hague, raised the question with the Dutch Foreign Minister, this was the reply he received:
In the first place he begged that I would quiet any apprehensions which you might entertain, that the Dutch Gov[t] ever imagined the exclusion of every Flag but the Belgian and their own from the Scheldt by any arrangement which they might either propose or be willing to agree to; he acknowledged however that by adopting for that River the Convention of Mayence as a Basis for its navigation other Nations might not be quite so favored as them though in the instance of the Rhine the difference was inconsiderable between the Duties leviable upon the Commerce of the Etats Riverains and of Strangers, below Krimpen, and above that place the Duties were he believed the same for all.[3]
If, then, the Antwerp merchants had drawn on their imaginations in depicting a new Münster regime, they had not invented the principle.

---

[1] See above, p. 162.
[2] In 1832 only 158 Belgian ships out of a total of 1,265 entered Antwerp, in 1833 only 103 out of 1,032; French ships are not listed separately, but the number could not have been large.
[3] Bligh to Palmerston, private, 13 Sept. 1832. P.P.

Whether or not, as Verstolk suggested, non-riparians would be admitted on a footing only slightly inferior to that of riparians, the fact remained that in the Dutch view they would be excluded from the scope of the arrangement. It is equally certain that both Palmerston and the Belgian government had always taken it for granted that whatever regulations the Conference laid down would apply to all who used the river, and that the Dutch plenipotentiaries had never hinted that they were not justified in doing so.

There can be no doubt as to the effect of this further revelation on Palmerston: it hardened his determination to get the clause suppressed. Only if the King, *per impossibile,* were to accept the Articles now would he be willing to pay even this price; at least, that was the threat he held over the Belgians.[1] But in his own Theme the clause disappeared, and he never afterwards tolerated its reappearance. Further than that, however, he did not go; it was left to the Belgians to use the " iniquities " of the clause as one more argument for the exemption of the river from duty.

In Belgium the " Lettre " and the memorials (which also appeared in print) fell on fruitful ground. For nearly nine months the Belgians had watched Holland bargaining for changes in the Articles while they themselves were denied their rights under the treaty. In their present mood they were ready to believe any evil of the Dutch and what they were now asked to believe had some truth in it. Forgetting that the provisional application of the tariff of Mainz to the Scheldt was the work of the Conference the Belgians now followed Smits and his collaborators in branding it as an insidious Dutch manœuvre to ruin their trade; to the popular demand for the citadel there was now added the cry: No duties on the Scheldt! It was a demand which the Belgian government was little disposed to resist, and by the middle of July the no-duty principle had become part of the official Belgian programme. Not content with Smits' presentation of the case, De Muelenaere brought out and refurbished the earlier argument based on the error about duties in 1814.[2] So strong was the feeling in the Cabinet that Leopold himself, always a friend of moderation, was forced into acquiescence; even more significant, perhaps, was Van de Weyer's conversion.[3] Thus by the beginning of August Belgian diplomacy had two immediate objectives: to secure the evacuation of the citadel and to obtain recognition of the no-duty principle. In practice the two

---

[1] See below, p. 202.
[2] Adair to Palmerston, 30 July 1832. F.O. Belgium/13.
[3] To Palmerston, private, 15 July and 3 Aug. 1832. P.P.

were closely linked. In order to secure the citadel Belgium had to make further negotiation impossible, and nothing seemed more likely to do this than a demand to which, as the Belgian government well knew, the Dutch would never agree. It was in this spirit that Leopold and his ministers set out for Compiègne, where on 9 August Louis Philippe's eldest daughter became Queen of the Belgians. The marriage celebrated, Leopold applied himself to the task of extracting from it all the advantages expected by his people. That he accomplished little made hardly any difference to the effect produced either in Belgium or elsewhere. It was generally believed that the meeting made the immediate coercion of Holland inevitable.

The word "coercion" had been freely used since it became known that on 30 June Britain and France had informed the other Powers that if the negotiation had achieved no result by 30 August they would proceed with the execution of the treaty. But since the Eastern Courts declined to sanction the use of force against Holland, for the two governments to prepare to substantiate this threat would have as its first result the break-up of the Conference. And, beyond that, no one could say where coercion might not lead; if, as was widely believed, the King of Holland was hoping to bring about a collision, the measures necessary to procure the evacuation of the citadel might well give him his opportunity. The British government, for its part, had neither the measure of support at home nor the degree of confidence in the French regime to make light of the risks involved. Palmerston himself had long since been driven to use two languages on coercion: he had been threatening Zuylen with it since the end of June, while continuing to preach patience to Goblet. His real attitude was one of expediency. The great object was still, as in '30 and '31, to avoid war, and coercion might lead to war; but Belgian patience was nearly exhausted, and now the French alliance held the threat of independent action. It was a challenge to the Foreign Secretary and his Fabian methods. Could he keep the negotiation alive now that one party refused to negotiate and the other rejected every proposal made to it? It was in answer to this challenge that Palmerston produced his Theme.

(ii) *The Theme and its Reception.*

Palmerston's reply to the meeting at Compiègne was to set about collecting the data necessary for a final effort at negotiation. In the first days of August he had sent Stockmar to Brussels to persuade Leopold to abandon the categorical demand for the citadel and to discover on what terms he would negotiate; Stockmar called it "a useless errand", as indeed it proved. But Palmerston did not have to depend on Brussels. On 10 August he summoned Larpent from Antwerp with all the information he could bring; the consul was to explain his trip as due to urgent private affairs.[1] Three days later Adair[2] was sending in a memorandum from two Antwerp merchants, De Lisle and Jollie, in which they gave their opinion that commerce on the Scheldt would not be prejudiced by a duty of from 75 cents to 1 florin per ton, provided it were treated solely as compensation to Holland for the maintenance of the river-channels and buoys and did not involve any interference with navigation.[3]

Two pieces of good fortune also came Palmerston's way. On 30 July the Rhine Commission, meeting at Mainz, issued a protocol deprecating the suggestion implied in a Dutch mémoire of 30 December 1831 to the Conference that the intermediate waters were the exclusive concern of Holland and recalling the right of the Rhine States to their free navigation; and on 5 August the Bavarian Minister in London, acting on the Commission's behalf, addressed a Note to the Foreign Secretary soliciting the support of the Conference for this protocol.[4] This document not only answered the Dutch objection to admitting the Belgians to these waters, it opened up the possibility of using this question to weaken the Prusso-Dutch connection. A few days later De Muelenaere played straight into Palmerston's hands by authorizing J.-B. Smits to visit London on behalf of the Antwerp Chamber of Commerce and recommending Goblet to put him in touch with the Foreign Secretary.[5] The Belgian Foreign Minister doubtless considered that so doughty a champion of the no-duty principle would be useful in London at this crisis; what he forgot was that with Smits in London Palmerston had all the materials for another attack on the problem, together with the knowledge that, through Smits, he had the support of Antwerp.

Larpent was the first to arrive, bearing a mass of information; he was quickly followed by Smits and, a few days later, by Van de Weyer, whose instructions forbade him to listen to any further proposals before the evacuation of the citadel. On 20 August the Conference met and faced a complete deadlock. Its own resolution of 10 July prevented it from making any further proposals; Belgium would neither make nor

[1] Bidwell to Larpent, secret, 10 Aug. 1832. F.O. Belgium/15.
[2] British ambassador at Brussels.
[3] Adair to Palmerston, 13 Aug. 1832. F.O. Belgium/13.
[4] *B.F.S.P., 1831-2*, 181.
[5] De Muelenaere to Goblet, 10 and 13 Aug. 1832. A.E. VIII, nos. 10, 13.

listen to any, and nothing acceptable could be looked for from The Hague. It was at this meeting that the question of the tariff of Mainz, hitherto kept decorously in the background, was first given official notice; Mareuil, who deputized for Talleyrand, raised it "with real warmth", and Palmerston himself cited the Antwerp memorials.[1] The following day Palmerston opened his campaign. He treated Van de Weyer and Smits to a long lecture on the present state of the Belgian question. De Muelenaere's idea of a war with Holland as the sole resource left to Belgium was absurd; Belgium would be going to war in defence of the Twenty-Four Articles, including Article IX and the tariff of Mainz. How much more sensible to seize the opportunity of rectifying this and other defects of the article. Palmerston then explained how this could be done. He proposed to exploit the reluctance of the King to unveil the mysteries of the *syndicat d'amortissement* by abandoning the clause of the treaty (Article XIII § 5) which provided for its liquidation by a Belgo-Dutch commission; in return the provisional application of the tariff of Mainz would be suppressed and replaced by a fixed annual payment by Belgium which could be capitalized and incorporated in the financial settlement. He himself suggested the rate of 1 florin per ton offered by De Lisle and Jollie, which on the basis of the most active year of trade would amount to 145,000 florins a year. He wound up by exhorting the two Belgians to give him their assistance in drawing up the new article.[2]

There is scarcely any evidence to illustrate the evolution of the new project from this broad outline to the finished product as it emerged on 6 September. Fortunately, the one piece of direct evidence is of the utmost interest. It is a set of observations by Smits on the ninth article of a draft submitted to him on 1 September. The article in question provides for the free navigation of the Scheldt by the ships of all nations, without visit or detention, at a uniform rate of 1 florin per ton, and for a free pilotage on the river at the same rate as that obtaining on the Maas; the maintenance and buoying of the channels is to be entrusted to separate Dutch and Belgian commissions for the respective portions of the river; Belgian vessels are to navigate the intermediate waters on the "most favoured nation" footing and under a tariff not exceeding that of Mainz, while the questions of fishing in the Scheldt and of the navigation of the Maas are referred to a joint Belgo-Dutch commission. Smits was far from satisfied with this article.

[1] Zuylen to Verstolk, 25 Aug. 1832. B.Z. 3241.
[2] Van de Weyer to King Leopold, 21 Aug., and to De Muelenaere, 21 Aug. 1832. A.E. VIII, nos. 24, 25.

After a "general observation" describing the whole article as "inadmissible", he criticizes it clause by clause. The first paragraph meets the same objection as Smits had advanced in his "Lettre", namely, that the freedom of the Scheldt cannot be based upon the Vienna Articles, because these authorize the levy of duties as well as visits and detentions; if, however, it must be retained, Smits would add a rider exempting the river from anything of this nature not specified in the article. He suggests some minor alterations to paragraph 2, which fixes the rate of duty, as well as an important addition empowering Belgium to redeem the duty by an annual payment of 100,000 florins or a capital payment of two millions. The use of the term "Escaut Néerlandais" in paragraph 3 moves Smits to declare that there is only one Scheldt and that Holland and Belgium are co-sovereigns of it; he also has criticisms of the pilotage and river-maintenance provisions. But his most important suggestion was the addition to paragraph 5, governing the intermediate waters, of the following:

et que si les eaux venaient à être supprimées de manière à empêcher les Belges de naviguer librement vers le Rhin et vice versa, le Gouvernement des Pays Bas s'engage à les rétablir ou à les remplacer convenablement.

Smits explains that this is necessary owing to the various projects afoot for connecting Walcheren and Duiveland with the mainland. Here, then, is the origin of the similar clause of Article IX of the treaty of 1839.[1] In this connection Smits also revives in a modified form the old Belgian claim to the freedom of the Rhine.[2]

A comparison of Smits' suggestions and the final version of the article shows to what extent his ideas were adopted, and leads to the conclusion that he played only a subordinate part in its evolution. His advice on points of detail was in the main followed, but when he tried to deal with matters of principle he carried little weight. The evidence of the "Observations" destroys the theory that Smits came over to London and dictated his terms to Palmerston.[3]

Palmerston showed the Theme to Lieven[4] on 5 September, presumably in its final shape. The following day he handed a copy to Zuylen and on the 8th Goblet set out with it for Brussels, while Palmerston communicated it to Britain's foreign representatives. The Theme is a project of treaty between Holland and Belgium in twenty-four articles.[5] The first seven articles are taken straight from the treaty, but Article

[1] See below, pp. 223-4.
[2] A copy of the "Observations" is in A.E. VIII, annexe A to no. 70.
[3] As is suggested, for example, in the article on Smits in the *Biographie Nationale de Belgique*.
[4] Russian ambassador in London.
[5] B.F.S.P., *1831-2*, 157-65.

VIII of the treaty is replaced by an article proposed in the Dutch project of 30 January 1832. By far the most sweeping changes occur in Article IX. The new article is as follows:

1. Les dispositions des articles CVIII-CXVII inclusivement de l'Acte Général du Congrès de Vienne, relatives à la libre navigation des Fleuves et Rivières navigables, seront appliquées aux fleuves et rivières navigables, qui séparent ou traversent à la fois le Territoire Belge et le Territoire Hollandais.

2. En ce qui concerne spécialement l'Escaut, la navigation de ce Fleuve dans tout son cours, tant dans sa branche orientale que dans sa branche occidentale, restera libre au Commerce et aux Navires de toutes les Nations; et Sa Majesté le Roi des Pays Bas s'engage à ne faire prélever sur les Navires qui remontent ou qui descendent ce Fleuve, soit en allant de la pleine mer en Belgique, soit en allant de Belgique en pleine mer, quel que soit le Pavillon qu'ils portent, qu'un droit de tonnage calculé sur la capacité des dits Navires, sans que ces Navires ne puissent jamais, soit en remontant, soit en descendant, soit à cause de ce droit, ou sous tout autre prétexte, être assujettis à aucune visite, ou à aucun examen de leur Cargaison.

3. Ce droit, qui ne pourra jamais et en aucun cas excéder 1 florin par tonneau, la remonte et la descente comprises, sera provisoirement fixé à 60 cents par tonneau pour les Navires qui, de pleine mer, remontent l'Escaut, se rendant en Belgique par Bathz, et à 40 cents pour ceux qui descendent l'Escaut, se rendant de Belgique par Bathz en pleine mer.

Quant aux Navires qui se rendent de la pleine mer, ou de la Belgique, par l'Escaut au Canal de Terneuse, ou vice-versâ du Canal de Terneuse en Belgique, ou en pleine mer, ils ne seront assujettis qu'à la moitié des droits fixés ci-dessus pour la remonte et pour la descente.

Ce droit de tonnage sera annuellement acquitté par Sa Majesté le Roi des Belges à Sa Majesté le Roi des Pays Bas, moyennant une somme de 150,000 florins, qui servira d'acquit pour tous les Navires indistinctement, et Sa Majesté le Roi des Belges aura en outre la faculté de se libérer pour toujours de ce payement au moyen d'une capitalisation.

4. Le Gouvernement des Pays Bas s'engage à fixer les droits de pilotage pour les bouches de l'Escaut, depuis la pleine mer jusqu'à Flessingue, et de Flessingue à Bathz, et vice-versâ, d'après le Tarif existant en 1829 pour les bouches de la Meuse, depuis la pleine mer jusqu'à Helvoet, et de Helvoet à Rotterdam, en proportion des distances.

Ces droits seront les mêmes pour les Navires de toutes les Nations. Le dit Gouvernement s'engage aussi à baliser ses côtes aux embouchures de l'Escaut, et à assurer la conservation des passes navigables de ce Fleuve, jusqu'à l'extrémité de son Territoire.

Le Gouvernement Belge prend un engagement pareil, pour la partie de l'Escaut qui traverse la Belgique.

De part et d'autre, le taux des droits de pilotage sur l'Escaut sera publié immédiatement après la Ratification du présent Traité.

Il sera toujours facultatif à tout Navire remontant ou descendant l'Escaut, de prendre tel Pilote qu'il voudra, et il sera loisible, d'après cela, aux 2 Pays d'établir, dans tout le cours de l'Escaut, et sur les Côtes des 2 Pays entre Ostende et l'Ile de Schouen, les services de pilotage qu'ils jugeront convenables pour pouvoir fournir les pilotes.

5. Chacun des 2 Gouvernements désignera, l'un à Flessingue, l'autre à Anvers, des Fonctionnaires ou des Commissaires, ad hoc, qui seront chargés de se concerter sur toutes les mesures qu'exigeront la conservation des passes de l'Escaut, et le placement, ainsi que l'entretien des balises qui les indiquent.

Ces mesures seront immédiatement mises en exécution, le cas échéant, par les Fonctionnaires ou Commissaires Néerlandais ou Belges, pour les parties du Territoire qui les concernent respectivement.

6. Il est convenu que la navigation des eaux intermédiaires entre l'Escaut et le Rhin, pour arriver d'Anvers au Rhin, et vice-versâ, restera libre pour le commerce Belge, et qu'elle ne sera assujettie qu'à des péages qui ne pourront jamais excéder ceux établis pour la navigation du Rhin, proportion des distances gardée. Il est convenu en outre que les Belges seront toujours admis à la navigation de ces eaux, sur le pied de la Nation la plus favorisée.

7. Des Commissaires se réuniront de part et d'autre à Anvers, dans le délai d'un mois, afin de convenir d'un réglement général pour compléter tout ce qui a rapport à l'application des Articles CVIII à CXVII de l'Acte Général du Congrès de Vienne, à la navigation de la Meuse, et de comprendre dans ce réglement l'exercice du droit de pêche et de commerce de pêcherie, dans toute l'étendue de l'Escaut, sur le pied d'une parfaite réciprocité en faveur des Sujets des 2 Pays.

En attendant, et jusqu'à ce que le dit réglement soit arrêté, la navigation de la Meuse et de ses embranchemens, restant libre au commerce des 2 Pays, sera assujettie aux dispositions de la Convention signée à Mayence, le 31 Mars, 1831, pour la navigation du Rhin, en autant que ces dispositions pourront s'appliquer à la dite rivière.

With the exception of paragraph 1, this is an entirely new article. Paragraph 2 is in some ways the key to the whole. Article IX of the treaty had not attempted to fix a duty on the Scheldt; indeed, the principle of a duty was only expressed by implication in the clause applying the tariff of Mainz provisionally. The new paragraph remedied this deficiency. But its real significance lay in the insertion of the phrase " without distinction of flag ". The Dutch statesman Van Hogendorp was right when he detected in this phrase the real motive behind the Theme, although he went on to draw a false conclusion.[1] A minor point of interest is the express designation, under the name " Scheldt ", of both the eastern and western branches of the river; the Eastern Scheldt (once the only " Scheldt ") no longer served for maritime navigation, but was still of importance as part of the route between Antwerp and the Rhine, and its treatment as part of the Scheldt, to be navigated under a duty of 1 florin per ton, instead of as part of the intermediate waters, which were to bear the tariff of Mainz, was thus a concession to Belgium. It had originated with Smits.

Paragraph 3 fixed the rate of duty at 1 florin per ton, the maximum suggested by De Lisle and Jollie, but raised Smits' equivalent of

[1] See below, p. 202.

100,000 a year to 150,000; on the basis of existing trade the higher figure was the more correct. The paragraph also adopted the suggestion that this yearly payment might be capitalized, but without naming a sum; the option to redeem the annual rent was strongly supported by d'Argout, the acting French Foreign Minister, who feared that Orangists might otherwise make political capital by contrasting this burden with the freedom enjoyed during the Union.[1] Paragraph 4 contained provisions to which Palmerston attached the highest importance. The disappearance of the " surveillance commune " made it necessary to introduce safeguards of a free and efficient pilotage; Palmerston's were four in number, the fixing of the dues by reference to those on the Maas, the provision that they were to be the same for all ships, the prompt publication of the tariff, and finally the freedom of each country to organize its own service. We have seen how strongly the Antwerp merchants had urged this " pilotage facultatif " as an indispensable condition of a really free navigation.

The substitution, in paragraph 5, of separate commissions for the " surveillance commune " of Article IX of the treaty represented a major concession to the Dutch point of view. Palmerston had first made it in his " confidential project " of 31 July, the immediate predecessor of the Theme,[2] and Sébastiani's criticism of it, with which Palmerston himself agreed, had not caused him to withdraw it now. Paragraph 6 dealt with the vexed question of the intermediate waters. The original Dutch objection to the corresponding clause in the treaty had been that it struck at Dutch sovereignty over these waters by making their navigation dependent on the will of foreign states, but in their last project[3] they appeared to have waived the point of principle and confined their objection to the footing on which the Belgians were to be admitted. They themselves had offered " most favoured nation " treatment, but without indicating what this would mean in practice. Palmerston himself had fought for a maximum tariff, and this now appeared in slightly modified form; in adding the " most favoured nation " proviso he was clearly thinking of the Rhine States, which might otherwise eventually enjoy better terms than Belgium. The final paragraph of the article left to a joint Belgo-Dutch commission two questions neither of which raised any special problem.

All the clauses had one thing in common, the utmost clarity and precision of drafting. It is this feature, combined with the wide scope

---

[1] Granville to Palmerston, 27 Aug. 1832. F.O. France/448.
[2] Enclosed in Zuylen to Verstolk, 31 July 1832. B.Z. 3241.
[3] Delivered to the Conference on 25 July. *B.F.S.P., 1831-2,* 179.

of its provisions, which accounts for the remarkable length of the article: it contains more than 800 words, compared with the mere 345 of Article IX of the Twenty-Four, and is almost as long as the final Article IX of 1839. The reason is self-evident: Palmerston had seized the opportunity to recast the article not merely so as to include every essential clause but so as to render every one of those clauses proof against misinterpretation. It was chiefly, though not exclusively, with an eye to Dutch tactics that he had done so; and if the Dutch government objected that all these repetitions and " vice-versas " were in themselves a reflection on Dutch good faith, he would doubtless reply, as he had recently replied to Zuylen: " Que voulez-vous, la plupart des traités sont basés sur la méfiance!"[1]

It was to Goblet that Palmerston entrusted the delicate task of communicating the Theme to Leopold and his ministers. In lending themselves to Palmerston's scheme Goblet and Van de Weyer had flatly disobeyed their official, and far exceeded their unofficial instructions, and what Brussels would think of the result of their disobedience was a subject of nervous speculation. Leopold himself showed little hesitation about accepting the Theme, but his ministers, although conceding that it represented a satisfactory settlement, declared that they could not take part in the new negotiation and therefore offered their resignations. The King persuaded them to continue to administer their departments, with the exception of De Muelenaere, who would not remain at the Foreign Ministry. Goblet himself therefore took over this department *ad interim,* and his first act was to send Van de Weyer full powers to convert the Theme into a treaty with Holland. The King and those who supported him had thus staked their political reputations on the project, and they could not fail to regard it as their " ultimatum ", their last effort to reach a settlement by negotiation. Much has been made of this use of the word " ultimatum " by the Belgians with reference to the Theme. What it really meant was that Leopold had gone as far as, if not indeed some way further than, his constitutional position allowed in the interests of a peaceful settlement; if he tried to go further then he and the Powers might be confronted with another Belgian Revolution.

During the time which Palmerston was devoting to the preparation of the Theme the three Eastern plenipotentiaries were bringing increased pressure to bear on Zuylen, and through him on the Dutch government, to yield on the two points which now dominated the

[1] Zuylen to Verstolk, 31 July 1832. B.Z. 3241.

negotiation, the tariff of Mainz and the intermediate waters. This fact goes far to disprove the assertion that in deciding to revise these clauses of the treaty Palmerston was parting company with his colleagues of the Conference; on the contrary, but for its own resolution to make no further proposals the Conference would probably have drawn up a new project in this sense. Palmerston was therefore quite justified in stressing the unofficial approval by the Conference of the ideas embodied in the Theme when on 6 September he handed it to Zuylen. After a tactless attempt to maintain the "correct" attitude that, since he was accredited to the Conference, he could not accept propositions from any other source, Zuylen expressed his astonishment at some of the features of the Theme, notably the disappearance of the provisional regime on the Scheldt. He immediately sought out his "friends", only to find them confused and hesitant, at once disposed to criticize the Theme in detail and to approve it in general as a conciliatory move.

The Theme reached The Hague on 10 September and was considered on the following day. To Bligh, the *chargé d'affaires,* Verstolk spoke of it with such a mixture of anger and sarcasm as to leave him in no doubt that

Resistance to any further material concession as to the Scheldt is the order of the day here and that upon that point, at least, little will be yielded except on compulsion.[1]

In its Note of 16 September to the Conference, however, the Dutch government chose to ignore the Theme, harking back to its own projects of July. This may have been good diplomatic form, it was scarcely good diplomacy. The Dutch Note, presented on 21 September, moved even the Eastern plenipotentiaries to indignation, and the Conference's reply was to invite Palmerston to communicate his Theme officially to it and to explain his motives in drawing it up. This Palmerston did on the 24th. His apology traversed what is to us familiar ground. Opening with a lucid analysis of the deadlock at the end of July, he described how he determined, as an individual member of the Conference, to make a last effort to overcome it. He therefore prepared the project in question, and in handing it to the Dutch plenipotentiary stated his belief "that this Arrangement, or something closely resembling it", if accepted by Holland, would lead to a settlement. He then analysed the Theme in detail, defending its departures from the treaty, and drawing attention to the concessions it made to the Dutch point of view.[2]

[1] To Palmerston, private, 13 Sept. 1832. P.P.
[2] *B.F.S.P., 1831-2,* 153-7.

This was really the end, although the Conference made a despairing attempt to stave off the inevitable by presenting Zuylen with a series of questions designed to elicit the Dutch government's last word. Zuylen's answers merely proved what everybody already knew, and five days later the British and French plenipotentiaries announced to their colleagues their governments' decisions to apply coercive measures to secure the evacuation of the citadel. Palmerston had, then, decided to throw in his lot with France and Belgium. While there can be no doubt that his pride was wounded by the treatment of his Theme at The Hague, and that he was in any case convinced that the King would not sign a treaty, whatever the terms, the salient fact was that the rejection of the Theme made coercion inevitable. A month ago, by his clever exploitation of the difficulty over the tariff of Mainz, Palmerston had wrung the reluctant consent, first of the Belgian plenipotentiaries in London, and afterwards of King Leopold himself, to his project. But it had cost Leopold his ministry, and the Belgian press and people still clamoured for the citadel and welcomed the prospect of war with Holland. And behind Belgium stood France, where the ministry of Casimir Périer, struggling on without its leader, had lost the confidence of both King and country. Already before the end of September Louis Philippe was negotiating with the "Doctrinaires" with a view to its reconstruction. They, too, made it clear that the adoption of vigorous measures against Holland was an essential condition of their taking office. By the end of September, therefore, the political stability of France, as well as of Belgium, depended in no small measure upon the prospect of the speedy evacuation of the citadel; it was these facts, not anything that Palmerston himself thought or felt, which made coercion inevitable.

(iii) *The Motive and Significance of the Theme.*

It remains to refer briefly to two widely-held views of the Theme which are sharply opposed to the view put forward above. The first of these sees the Theme as no more than a skilful diplomatic manœuvre, alleging that Palmerston meant it to be rejected at The Hague in order to throw on Holland the responsibility for the breakdown and thus pave the way for coercion. Originally sponsored by Charles White in his "Belgic Revolution" of 1835,[1] this thesis was adopted with characteristic vigour by Louis Blanc in the "Histoire de dix ans".[2] The Dutch historian De Bosch Kemper repeated it in his history of

[1] Vol. II, 351*ff*.
[2] Fourth ed. (1844), II, 452.

the period,[1] and the idea is still widespread that the Theme was no more than an "intrigue". The natural corollary of this view is that, to make certain of its rejection at The Hague, Palmerston incorporated in it every demand which the Belgians cared to bring forward, in other words, that the Theme was a Belgian "ultimatum" which owed little to Palmerston save the use of his name to conceal its real authorship.

Now it is undeniable that Van de Weyer and his associates, notably Smits (whose part is sometimes overlooked), did play a part in the making of the Theme. Their co-operation was both desirable and necessary. The first condition of Palmerston's attempt was that it must satisfy Belgium, not only because she had her treaty-rights to fall back upon but because of the danger of her emulating Holland by an appeal to force. Palmerston's first task, therefore, was to convince Belgium that the resources of diplomacy were not exhausted, and to win such men as Goblet, Van de Weyer and Stockmar over to his way of thinking was a prime condition of success. Moreover, their collaboration placed at his disposal the practical knowledge upon which any workable settlement had to be based. In view of the trouble caused by the shortcomings in this respect of Article IX of the Twenty-Four, it is not surprising that Palmerston went out of his way to secure the most detailed and reliable information as the basis of his Theme. But all this is not to say that the Theme was just a string of Belgian demands. Juste calls the Theme the Belgian "ultimatum", but it was an ultimatum in the sense of the "lowest" as well as the "last". To test the justice of this contention it is only necessary to compare the ninth article of the Theme with the Belgian government's demands of July and August or with the article proposed in Smits' "Lettre". Both had insisted on the freedom of the Scheldt from all duties other than those for pilotage and buoying; the Theme laid a tonnage-duty upon every ship using the river. Again, to the Belgians the "surveillance commune" was perhaps the most cherished feature of the original article, not merely for its own sake, but because through it they glimpsed the mirage of "co-sovereignty"; yet in the Theme the "surveillance commune" disappeared. Palmerston himself enumerated the modifications in favour of Holland in his statement of 24 September to the Conference. These De Bosch Kemper dismisses as "insignificant points of drafting";[2] if they were, the Dutch government had been wasting its own, as well as everybody's else's time, by

[1] *Geschiedenis van Nederland na 1830* (5 vols., Amsterdam, 1873-82), II, 272-3.
[2] *Ibid.*, 276.

offering such determined resistance to them. In any case, they would not have appeared in the Theme if the Belgians had had their way.

Again, if Palmerston had wanted the Theme to be rejected at The Hague, would he have gone to such pains to get the backing of the Eastern plenipotentiaries to it? On the contrary, his language to Zuylen, his stream of private letters to Jerningham[1] at The Hague, his delight at hearing that the Prussian Foreign Minister had approved the substance of the Theme, all testify to his hope that it might carry the day. Finally, there is the evidence of Goblet, who had been in close contact with Palmerston throughout these weeks and who himself bore the Theme to Brussels. On 25 September Goblet wrote to Van de Weyer:

Jusqu'à quel point l'engagement pris par le ministre anglais lui pèse-t-il aujourd'hui? Jusqu'à quel point a-t-il été trompé dans ses espérances? Ne s'était-il pas fait illusion sur les dispositions du gouvernement Néerlandais? Avait-il bien prévu les nécessités qui naîtraient d'un refus absolu de la Hollande? Ne serait-il pas tenté de les prévenir en se dégageant peu à peu lui-même. . . . Je n'ai aucune défiance contre Lord Palmerston, qui depuis trois mois est presque notre seul ami à Londres . . . mais je juge les hommes d'après ce que je crois être leur intérêt; et je pense que l'intérêt de Lord Palmerston est plutôt de voir la négociation ouverte et engagée que de recourir aux mesures coërcitives; que peut-être il se repent même d'avoir arrêté avec vous des bases qui le lient aujourd'hui. . . .[2]

The other view of the Theme is an "economic interpretation", which sees it, in common with the rest of Palmerston's Scheldt policy, as dictated by commercial motives. This is only part of the general view, widely held on the Continent both at the time and since, that Britain used the Belgian Revolution to destroy the Netherlands Kingdom, in which she found she had created a serious commercial rival and barrier, and to set up a petty and dependent state through which she could pour her cheap goods into the Continent.[3] It was, indeed, the general opinion, not less among her friends than her enemies, that Britain's insistence on the freedom of the Scheldt and the intermediate waters sprang less from her interest in Belgium's welfare than from solicitude for her own; it was this opinion which Le Hon, the Belgian ambassador at Paris, was voicing when, in conversation with Adair, he took it for granted

that the benefit to English commerce from settling the terms of the navigation of the Scheldt would of itself be sufficient to induce an English Parliament to risque even a war for its attainment.[4]

[1] *Chargé d'affaires* on the departure of Bligh.
[2] A.E. VIII, no. 62.
[3] This view has been given its most recent expression in Steinmetz, R., *Englands Anteil an der Trennung der Niederlande, 1830* (The Hague, 1930).
[4] Adair to Palmerston, 25 Sept. 1832. F.O. Belgium/13.

Applied to the particular case of the Theme this view saw in Palmerston's determination to suppress the provisional application of the tariff of Mainz the removal of a serious handicap to British trade. The Dutch "elder statesman" G. K. van Hogendorp, without sharing the violent animosity of some of his countrymen towards Britain, gave this view a special "twist" by declaring that it was only when Palmerston discovered that the tariff, high as it was, would apply solely to riparians that he took up his stand against this clause.[1]

Now it is indisputable that, after the two parties themselves, Britain had the greatest interest at stake in the matter. Of the 354 ships (totalling 48,675 tons) which entered Antwerp in 1831, 151 (of 19,622 tons) were British; and although in 1832 and 1833, largely owing to the operation of the Dutch embargo in reply to the coercive measures, the British share of the Scheldt trade dropped sharply, in 1834 Britain still had the largest national tonnage on the river (26,376 tons out of a total of 134,000).[2] In seeking to protect the Scheldt traffic from interference or excessive taxation Palmerston was thus promoting a British, as well as an international, interest, and as a British minister he could not, without neglect of duty, ignore this aspect of the matter. But it is quite another thing to argue that he allowed his duty to his country to override his duty as a member of the Conference. He himself rebutted the assertion in a despatch to Adair which has the genuine Palmerstonian "ring":

Y.E. states that M. Lebeau seems to fancy that Great Britain would never allow the establishment of the Tariff of Mayence on the Scheldt, because it would be injurious to British commerce. It is essential that you should fully undeceive Monsr. Lebeau upon this point.

In the first place, be that tariff injurious or not to British commerce, established on the Scheldt it would be at once if Holland were to accept the 24 Articles; and it would continue in operation until the Dutch Gov^t. should have consented, as a river-bordering State, to a different Regulation. . . .

In the next place Monsr. Lebeau is much mistaken in fancying that the free navigation of the Scheldt is of such paramount importance to the interest of British commerce. No doubt this additional channel of communication with Germany is of importance to Great Britain, as being advantageous to her commerce; but trade will always find its way where an effective demand exists. If the Scheldt were obstructed by heavy duties, British commerce would go by Rotterdam, and the one road would be nearly as convenient as the other.

It is not for British commercial interests that H.M.'s Gov^t. have made such a point of securing the free navigation of the Scheldt, but because the political interests of Great Britain require that Belgium should be an inde-

[1] *Brieven en Gedenkschriften na 1813* (The Hague, 3 vols., 1901-3), 273-4.
[2] *Tableau général du commerce de la Belgique avec les Pays Etrangers, 1831-4* (Brussels, 1836), table IV.

pendent State, and because it is felt that she cannot continue to be so, unless she has that free scope for the employment of her industry, and for the development of her resources, which the useful navigation of the Scheldt will afford her. But this is only an indirect interest, and if the mistaken views and erroneous course of the Belgian Gov^t. should render impossible a satisfactory arrangement on this point, it would be Belgium, and not Great Britain, that would be the first and principal sufferer.[1]

Palmerston's own explanation of his policy is borne out by all the facts. It was a political reason which had led him to confirm Holland in her possession of the left bank of the Scheldt, the cession of which Belgium had long represented as the only real solution of the problem; it was on the same ground that he rejected what was, short of the acquisition of Zeeland-Flanders, indisputably the best safeguard of the security of navigation, the abolition of all duties on the river. Hard as Palmerston fought for the economic independence of Belgium, it was only on the grounds and within the limits of political necessity.

No consideration of its motive can alter the fact that the settlement of the Scheldt question which Palmerston proposed in the Theme was, with negligible changes, the settlement which was embodied in the treaty of 1839 and which, pending revision by mutual consent, still governs the river. In the evolution of Article IX, therefore, the Theme marked the last decisive stage. That evolution may be summarized thus. From the original Article III of the " Bases ", which merely reaffirmed the application of the Vienna Articles to the Scheldt and Maas, each successive project and article (other than those emanating from The Hague) had marked a step in the direction of " liberalizing " that application by means of detailed provisions appropriate to the particular case. But this process had not gone so far but that Article IX of the Twenty-Four could exhibit marked traces of the " restrictive " view, above all in the provisional application of the terms and tariff of the Mainz Convention, with its discrimination between riparians and nonriparians. What Palmerston did in the Theme was not merely to save the Scheldt from the consequences of this provision; he boldly asserted (and in so doing ultimately established) the undiluted " liberal " principle, and with it emancipated the Scheldt from the false analogy with the Rhine. To put it another way, we may say that down to 1832 the Conference was still struggling in the toils of the Vienna stipulation that any future regime on the Scheldt was to be both " la plus favorable au commerce et à la navigation " and " la plus analogue à ce qui a été fixé pour le Rhin ". It was left to Palmerston both to demonstrate that these requirements were mutually inconsistent and to ensure that of the two it was the first which should prevail.

[1] To Adair, 18 Aug. 1833. F.O. Belgium/23.

CHAPTER NINE

The Convention of May 1833 and the Treaties of April 1839

ALTHOUGH the Theme of Lord Palmerston failed in its immediate object of saving the negotiation, it set a standard by which all subsequent projects of Article IX came to be judged. In one sense, therefore, the only important question which the Theme left unanswered was how long it would take to bring the King of Holland to accept an article framed on these lines. But the negotiations of 1833 and 1838-9, if they lack the interest of those which had gone before, both served to clarify the issues at stake and to contribute some minor points of their own; moreover, they derive an adventitious importance from the fact that it was during them that many of the *minutiæ* of the final settlement were elaborated.

(i) *The Coercive Measures and the Convention of May 1833.*

When, on 1 October 1832, Palmerston and Talleyrand declined their colleagues' suggestion to refer the question of coercion to the Court of Berlin, they committed their governments to joint action to secure the evacuation of the citadel. The negotiations between them which led to the convention defining this joint action testify to the doubts which still beset the British government. At first the British ministers had tried to limit the measures to a blockade of the Dutch coast, but the advent of the Soult ministry on 11 October, with De Broglie as Foreign Minister, made a direct attack on the citadel inevitable; even then Grey and Palmerston had to conquer the aversion of the King and the reluctance of their cabinet colleagues, and it was not until 22 October that the convention was signed. It stipulated that the two governments should call on Holland and Belgium to give an undertaking by 2 November to evacuate each other's territory within ten days. If Holland refused, Britain and France would lay an embargo on Dutch commerce and blockade the Dutch coast, and if the citadel were not evacuated by 15 November a French army would enter Belgium and achieve that result by force. The citadel would then be immediately handed over to Belgium.

The convention was ratified on 27 October and notified to the other members of the Conference. The Russian plenipotentiaries immediately signified their withdrawal, and the Conference therefore dissolved after nearly two years of continuous labour, enshrined in seventy protocols. On 2 November the Dutch government announced its refusal to comply with the joint demand, and four days later the embargo and blockade came into force. The Dutch government showing no disposition to yield, on 15 November a French army under Gérard entered Belgium and a fortnight later laid siege to the citadel. After a heroic resistance, Chassé capitulated on 22 December, and the Belgian army, which had been allowed no part in the operation, took possession. The garrisons in Forts Lillo and Liefkenshoek were left undisturbed, chiefly on account of the time required to reduce them, and Gérard's army marched back to France. It was a triumph for the entente; the coercive measures had passed off according to plan, and Belgium had the citadel.

Palmerston and Talleyrand had always held the view that, once the coercive measures were over, the Conference might reassemble. But early in December the Russian government informed its plenipotentiaries that their powers to take part in it, previously suspended, were now withdrawn, so that its reassembly was impossible. In this situation Talleyrand was disposed to settle the future of the negotiation in much the same way as Gérard's army was settling the future of the citadel; with De Broglie's approval he drew up a plan for presenting a fresh project, on the lines of the Theme, to the Dutch government as an " ultimatum " and for using the continuance of the embargo to procure its acceptance. Such a procedure could scarcely have recommended itself to Palmerston, who was of opinion that the time for "ultimatums" had gone by and that what was now needed again was a certain latitude for negotiation. As it was, the receipt shortly afterwards of the news of the fall of the citadel caused the two statesmen to concentrate on regularizing relations with the Dutch government and to shelve for the time being the main negotiation. On 30 December they completed and sent off a draft of a preliminary convention with Holland. In addition to providing for the removal of the embargo and the reduction of the Dutch and Belgian armies to a peace-footing, this draft dealt with the question of navigation; it required the King to open the Maas and its branches (a term probably intended to include the intermediate waters[1]) subject to the tariff of Mainz, and stipulated with regard to the Scheldt that

Jusqu'à la conclusion d'un Traité Définitif entre la Hollande et la Belgique, la navigation de l'Escaut restera libre et sans aucune entrave; comme elle a été depuis le 20 Janvier, 1831, conformément à la déclaration faite par Sa Majesté le Roi des Pays Bas aux 5 Puissances le 25 Janvier, 1831.[2]

[1] Palmerston to Wessenberg, private, 31 Dec. 1832. P.P.
[2] B.F.S.P., *1831*-2, 888.

It is clear that Palmerston was determined to be rid of the tariff of Mainz, indeed of any provisional regime on the river other than the complete freedom which had obtained since January 1831, and the more so since threats of a fresh closure were again in the air.¹

To the Anglo-French draft the Dutch government replied with a Note and a counter-project. The Note advanced two main objections to the draft: first, that a separate convention between Holland and the two Powers might be the excuse for those two Powers to edge the others out of the main negotiation, and second, that the terms proposed would place Holland in an unfavourable position compared with Belgium and thus prejudice her prospects in that negotiation. In particular, the indefinite continuance of the present situation on the Scheldt could not fail to encourage the Belgian demand for a permanent duty-free navigation. Accordingly the counter-project, which took the form of a convention to be signed by all Five Powers, not only provided for the commencement from 1 January 1833 of a Belgian debt-payment of 8,400,000 florins a year, but for the levy of a provisional duty on the Scheldt; the amount of this duty was not specified, but it would be the same for all ships, and it would be collected at Flushing " without visit or formality ".²

Simultaneously with the delivery of the counter-project the Dutch authorities attempted a partial closure of the Scheldt. During the siege of the citadel all traffic had been temporarily suspended, and it now appeared that the Dutch naval commander had decided to maintain the prohibition with respect to British, French and Belgian ships. At Brussels this report provoked intense excitement, and a leading minister proposed that the army should take advantage of the hard frost to invade Zeeland-Flanders; in London even the peace-loving Grey was moved to anger. While the continued closure of the river to British and French ships was a legitimate reprisal for the embargo (and in any case made no difference in practice, since they were already prohibited from entering Dutch territory), there was no justification for extending it to Belgian ships, since Belgium had taken no part in the coercive measures. Palmerston and Talleyrand were agreed that this question must be cleared up before they could go further. ' Tant que l'Escaut sera fermé ", declared Palmerston to Zuylen, " ma bouche sera close ".³ The French government may have welcomed what

¹ D'Eyragues, French *chargé d'affaires* at The Hague, to De Broglie, 5 Dec. 1832. *Gedenkstukken, 1830-40*, II, 335. Palmerston drew up a memorandum on the subject, dated 20 Dec. 1832. F.O. France/450.
² B.F.S.P., *1832-3*, 42-5.
³ Zuylen to Verstolk, 18 Jan. 1833. B.Z. 1700.

might prove an excuse for further hostilities, but the British ministers saw the matter in a different light. The embargo had already cost them enough in support at home and any further action might compromise their position when Parliament reassembled at the end of January. Palmerston therefore did his utmost to persuade the Dutch government to put the matter right, at the same time holding off Talleyrand and Van de Weyer with promises of decisive action in the event of a refusal. When, on 28 January, the Dutch reply came, it was not wholly satisfactory, for the Dutch government harped on the impossibility of recognizing the Belgian flag on the river; however, Palmerston and Talleyrand waived the formal point on Zuylen's assurance that no practical difficulty would be put in the way, and the negotiation was resumed.

It was already clear that the Dutch counter-project of 9 January would not do; who, indeed, could imagine that the King of Holland, drawing eight million florins a year from Belgium and levying duties on both Scheldt and Maas, would ever exchange such a position for a definitive settlement? Palmerston signified his view of the proposals by drawing a pencil through them.[1] All the same, the Dutch project did serve to raise the question of the scope of the arrangement to be negotiated with Holland. Was this arrangement to deal only with the questions arising out of the coercive measures, or should it embrace the points still in dispute between Holland and Belgium? The Dutch project not only fell between the two, being in Palmerston's phrase " either too little or too much ",[2] it also revealed the difficulties in the way of arriving at any provisional arrangement likely to pave the way to a permanent one. In the matter of the Scheldt, for instance, while Palmerston was determined that no mere provisional arrangement should authorize the levy of a duty, the King appeared just as determined not to accept an indefinite continuance of the existing situation which left the river free of duty. To Palmerston and Talleyrand the obvious way out of this difficulty was to cease discussing provisional terms and to negotiate for a permanent arrangement which should give the King his duty and the Belgians their free navigation. It was this consideration which led to their second project of 1 February; this envisaged the insertion in the preliminary convention of an article embodying a definitive agreement on all outstanding questions, including navigation.[3]

[1] Zuylen to Verstolk, 7 Feb. 1833. B.Z. 1700.
[2] B.F.S.P., 1832-3, 45.
[3] Ibid., 17.

This was the first of a spate of projects and counter-projects, some for a provisional, others for a definitive, arrangement, which appeared during the first two weeks of February. It is not difficult to see, through the mass of detail, what the two parties were striving for. Palmerston and Talleyrand, for their part, were trying to use the weapon of the embargo, which was producing a considerable effect on Dutch trade and, through it, on Dutch commercial opinion, to compel the Dutch government to agree to one of two things: either a provisional arrangement distinctly less favourable to Holland than she might expect under the permanent settlement and in any case leaving the Scheldt entirely free, or—and this they would have preferred—a negotiation with Britain, France and Belgium on the main question, with the other three Powers kept out of the way. The Dutch government was not deceived; in a long despatch of 13 February Verstolk dealt eloquently with this attempt by the two Powers to supersede the Conference and to sweep Holland into the web of " Gallo-British revolutionary designs ".[1] The Dutch government appealed to the Eastern plenipotentiaries to rally to its defence, but they were tired of Zuylen's intrigues and did little or nothing to help.

At this point the negotiation underwent two successive interruptions. The first arose from a report that the Dutch government was about to impose a duty on the Scheldt; the episode is an obscure one, but the two likeliest explanations (they were Jerningham's) are that the Dutch government was merely " flying a kite " to observe the reaction produced or that it had decided to introduce a duty should the negotiation break down.[2] Verstolk eventually denied the report and nothing more was heard of the matter. The second interruption arose from the receipt of a much more welcome piece of news, that of the nomination of Zuylen as Minister of State and of his recall from London. Zuylen's position in London had become exceedingly difficult, both by reason of the trend of events and owing to the increasing personal friction between him and Palmerston; to both the order of recall must have come as a great relief.[3] Palmerston and Talleyrand tried to turn the occasion to advantage by demanding that Zuylen's successor should

---

[1] To Zuylen, 13 Feb. 1833. *Gedenkstukken, 1830-40*, V, 193.
[2] Jerningham to Palmerston, 26 Feb. 1833. F.O. Holland/186.
[3] Zuylen told Wellington that the British government had asked for his recall on the ground of his too intimate relations with the Opposition, and Wellington expressed astonishment that the government should have done so " on account of communications between yourself and Lord Aberdeen and me " (Wellington to Zuylen, 19 March 1833. B.Z. 1700). The only piece of evidence which I have found in support of this is the fact that in Zuylen's recredential from William IV the customary paragraph expressing approval of the departing envoy's conduct was omitted (King William IV to King William I, 15 March 1833. F.O. 95/669).

come with full powers to sign a convention on the lines of their project of 2 February, but the Dutch government clung to the distinction between a preliminary convention with the two Powers and a definitive settlement with the Five, and since Palmerston at least was not prepared to risk a breakdown on this account, he signified that so long as the new plenipotentiary came with powers and instructions " dictated in the sincere spirit of an arrangement acceptable to all the Parties concerned " he would be welcome in London.[1] The new plenipotentiary, Salomon Dedel, arrived on 13 March. Not only was he an excellent choice,[2] but he carried instructions and a project which marked a distinct advance towards agreement. The new project, which he handed in on 23 March, included a provision for an armistice between Holland and Belgium until 1 August 1833—the date was not without significance!—and the maintenance during that period of the existing situation on the Scheldt.

The initial reception of this project was not encouraging. Palmerston and Talleyrand not only criticized its substance, especially the limited duration of the armistice, they made a final effort to persuade the Dutch government to negotiate with them for a permanent settlement. It was with the same object that Matuszewic now undertook, on his own responsibility, a mission to Berlin, where he urged the Prussian government to join in the presentation of a joint Note at The Hague recommending this course to the King and suggesting possible terms. At first it seemed that Matuszewic would succeed, and the joint Note, which mentioned, among other terms, a duty of $1\frac{1}{2}$ florins on the Scheldt, by far the lowest figure that the Russian or Prussian representatives had yet countenanced, was on the point of signature when the Prussian Foreign Minister, Ancillon, executed a characteristic volte-face and refused to sign it. Thereupon Matuszewic abandoned his first aim and substituted for it the presentation of a joint Note urging the King to conclude a provisional convention. On 3 May he won a hard-earned victory, when an Austro-Prusso-Russian memorandum in this sense was signed. Among its provisions was one for an armistice, and for the maintenance of the *status quo* on the Scheldt, until the conclusion of the definitive treaty; the three Powers warned the King that if he ignored their advice they would leave him to get the best terms he could from Britain and France.

Even before the presentation of this memorandum on 10 May the

---

[1] To Zuylen, 5 March 1833. *B.F.S.P., 1832-3*, 28-9.
[2] He had been educated at Eton and St. John's College, Cambridge, Palmerston's own college, and spoke perfect English.

Dutch government had made a further concession by offering to restore, with regard both to the armistice and to the Scheldt, the situation existing before 1 November 1832. The only difference between this offer and the terms of the memorandum was that whereas by the former the King would have reserved his right to renew hostilities, by the latter he would have to renounce it. This, then, was the extent of the final concession which the King made on 14 May, when he decided to act on the advice of the Three Courts. Two days later Dedel announced the decision in London, and in less than a week the convention was signed.

The Convention of 21 May 1833 between Britain, France and Holland provided for the re-establishment of friendly relations and for the resumption without delay, in conjunction with Austria, Prussia and Russia, of the negotiation for a final settlement. Article III of the convention, which was taken over unchanged from the collective memorandum, was as follows:

Tant que les relations entre la Hollande et la Belgique ne seront pas réglées par un Traité Définitif, Sa Majesté Néerlandaise s'engage à ne point recommencer les hostilités avec la Belgique et à laisser la navigation de l'Escaut entièrement libre.

An explanatory article (added at the instance of Van de Weyer) clarified the last two words by stipulating:

Il est également entendu que jusqu'à la conclusion du Traité Définitif dont il est fait mention dans le dit Article III de la Convention de ce jour, la Navigation de l'Escaut aura lieu telle qu'elle existait avant le 1 Novembre 1832.[1]

(ii) *The Negotiation of 1833.*

The hope held out by the convention of a speedy resumption of the work of the Conference was quickly dispelled by the news that the King of Holland had addressed himself to the Three Courts with a view to reaching agreement with them on the policy to be pursued. In the light of this fact the plenipotentiaries of these Courts would not commit themselves without fresh instructions, and this meant a delay of several weeks. As it turned out, the delay did not greatly matter, for the negotiation, if resumed, would certainly have been promptly interrupted by another of the recurrent and seemingly inevitable disputes over the situation on the Scheldt.

There had been some trouble about pilotage on the river before the signature of the convention, but the restoration, by that agreement, of the state of affairs existing before 1 November 1832, involved the re-

---

[1] *B.F.S.P.*, *1832-3*, 282; Martens, *Nouveau Recueil*, XIII, 97.

establishment of a " pilotage facultatif ", with both Dutch and Belgian pilots at liberty to operate between Antwerp and the sea. From early in June, however, reports began to come in that the Dutch authorities were insisting on an exclusively Dutch pilotage up to the frontier and that for this service they were making exorbitant charges.[1] The Antwerp authorities retaliated by refusing admittance to Dutch pilots, and the conflict was soon involving vexatious delay in the passage of the river. On 21 June Jerningham read Verstolk an angry despatch from Palmerston demanding the immediate cessation of this " arbitrary interference ", which constituted a " positive violation " of the convention, and to Verstolk's suggestion that the present arrangement should be mutually convenient the *chargé* replied that he conceived " the best way of avoiding the possibility of a dispute to be a *verbatim* execution of the Convention ".[2] But it was a week before Jerningham could report, along with a complaint by Verstolk of Palmerston's " severity " over a " trivial matter ", that the local authorities had been instructed to restore the previous state of affairs.[3]

If this episode did not augur well for the success of the negotiation, there were not lacking signs that the signature of the convention did in fact reflect some change of disposition at The Hague. Dedel was " very graciously received " by the King when he returned there, and the appointment of Verstolk himself as Dedel's co-plenipotentiary for the coming negotiation seemed to indicate that the King at last meant business. Verstolk himself drew up the instructions which he and Dedel carried to London, where they were formally received on 10 July. The Belgian plenipotentiaries, Goblet and Van de Weyer, were given their instructions on 13 July and were in London two days later.

A comparison of the two sets of instructions shows how close, in one sense, the two parties had been brought, and how widely, in another, they were still separated. The Dutch instructions[4] were accompanied by a project in which Article VII dealt with navigation; this article was identical with the corresponding one of a project, originally emanating from Berlin, which Zuylen had presented to Grey in the course of their conversations in November 1832,[5] with the in-

[1] Goblet to Van de Weyer, 11 June, 1833. A.E. XI, nos. 53, 54.
[2] Palmerston to Jerningham, 18 June 1833. *Gedenkstukken*, 1830-40, I, 328; Jerningham to Palmerston, 21 June 1833. *Ibid.*, 329.
[3] Jerningham to Palmerston, 28 June 1833. F.O. Holland/187.
[4] *Gedenkstukken, 1830-40*, V, 268-71.
[5] Printed in *B.F.S.P., 1831-2*, 761. For a detailed discussion of this project and of the Grey-Zuylen conversations, here omitted for reasons of space, see the writer's thesis, pp. 456*ff*.

sertion of 3 florins (1½ in each direction) as the duty for the return passage between the sea and Antwerp. The instructions authorized the plenipotentiaries to reduce this to 2 florins if necessary, and even to 1¾ if the negotiation depended on it, but in no circumstances were they to go lower. They were to insist on the restriction of this duty, and of the other provisions of the article, to the Western Scheldt as the only maritime waterway to Antwerp, and on the payment, or at least the declaration, of the duty at Flushing. In return for concessions on any of these points they were to secure equivalents elsewhere.

The Belgian instructions[1] laid stress on the favourable position in which Belgium now found herself, and which she must not lightly exchange for a permanent settlement. In the matter of navigation the Belgian demand was simple: it amounted to the substitution of Article IX of the Theme for Article IX of the treaty. The plenipotentiaries were, indeed, instructed in the first instance to demand the duty-free navigation of the Scheldt, but the conditions which they were authorized to accept if this demand failed, as it was bound to fail, namely, a maximum duty of 1 florin for the double journey, payable as an annual rent and redeemable by means of a capitalization, had all appeared in the Theme. This part of the instructions concluded with a significant sentence:

Dans tous les cas les plénipotentiaires du Roi éviteront d'exprimer que la souveraineté sur l'Escaut ou une partie de l'Escaut appartiendrait à la Hollande.[2]

Save in so far as the Belgians still clung to the no-duty principle and also cherished aspirations to "co-sovereignty", for neither of which they could expect an atom of support from the Conference, the two parties were no longer separated by those conflicts of principle which had dominated the earlier stages of the negotiation. But in detail they were still far enough apart. While King William put forward 1¾ florins per ton as the extreme minimum which he would accept, the Belgian government refused to go higher than 1 florin, and then only on condition that it should be paid annually, an arrangement which the King of Holland was unlikely to accept. The Dutch government insisted on the collection of the duty, or at least a declaration of the amount due, from every vessel at Flushing, while the Belgians would not hear of any stoppage of ships at Flushing or of the collection of the duty elsewhere than at Antwerp. There were similar conflicts over the detail of almost every clause. Finally, both parties expected equiva-

---

[1] A.E. XII (I), no. 17.
[2] In the MS. the words "la souveraineté sur l'Escaut ou une partie de l'Escaut" have been underlined, but this was doubtless done at some later date.

lents elsewhere in the articles for any concessions they might make in Article IX, although there was nowhere in the articles where any such adjustment could be made; and the nearer they approached agreement the more obstinate each became, and the greater the difficulties at every step of the way.

After the two parties themselves the person whose opinion mattered most was Palmerston. With the Belgian project, since it was to all intents his own, Palmerston could be expected to agree, although not as an "ultimatum" but only as a basis for negotiation. What he thought of the Dutch project is made clear by his pencilled comments on the copy given him confidentially by Dedel on 14 July.[1] Wherever the word "provisoirement" appeared he marginated "omit", and nearly every clause provoked some criticism, while clause 10, dealing with the intermediate waters, after being being dismissed as "nonsense" was further characterized—the writer's good humour having reasserted itself—as "pure matuzevity".[2] These comments fully bear out the view that Palmerston's criterion of any new project of Article IX was his own Theme, in which he had sought to define everything with a precision which defied cavil, and in which the word "provisoirement" had appeared only once, and then with a very limited application.[3]

The first meeting of the Conference on 15 July was devoted to a discussion of the plan of campaign. It was resolved that the Conference should negotiate verbally and secretly with each party at a time, and that when an article was agreed the plenipotentiaries should initial it, but without binding themselves until the whole treaty had been negotiated.[4] Thus the Conference was to resume its original role of mediator; there were to be no more protocols or "irrevocable" propositions, but each party would be free to get the best terms it could. The first week the Conference spent in giving a final form to those of the Twenty-Four Articles which the King of Holland had previously accepted and on which, therefore, the two parties were at least nominally agreed. It was not until 24 July that Article IX was reached.

---

[1] It is preserved in the volume F.O. Belgium/29. "Conferences in London, July-Aug. 1833", which contains the minutes of the Conference during this period, together with miscellaneous papers.
[2] Matuszewic prided himself on his skill as a *rédacteur*.
[3] In clause 3. See above, p. 194.
[4] Verstolk and Dedel to Zuylen, acting Foreign Minister, 16 July 1833. *Gedenkstukken, 1830-40*, V, 284.

According to the "Récit"[1] the primary aim of the Conference was to reach agreement on the principles of the article, leaving aside details of drafting, but in practice, so bound up were principles and wording, this differentiation proved impossible. A pragmatic division of the article into four parts, namely, the general principle of freedom, the duties to be levied, the navigational services, and the regime for the intermediate waters, proved more workable and materially assisted the negotiation along its difficult path. The first part, that is, the application of the Vienna Articles to the Scheldt, was adopted without trouble, by the Dutch on 24 July and by the Belgians five days later.

On the second part the plenipotentiaries also made initial progress. Verstolk and Dedel accepted the three general propositions that the Scheldt regime should apply to all vessels irrespective of flag, that there should be no visit or inspection of cargo, and that all ships should pay a single duty calculated on their tonnage. But when it came to the details, the prospect of agreement receded. The Dutch plenipotentiaries demanded 2 florins per ton ($1\frac{1}{2}$ for the upward and $\frac{1}{2}$ for the downward passage), which they represented as a notable concession, seeing that the Twenty-Four Articles had provisionally adopted the tariff of Mainz, variously estimated at from 3 to 6 florins per ton. Palmerston, who from the beginning acted as the spokesman of the Conference in the matter of navigation, merely replied that the Belgians had offered a single florin. The definition of the name "Scheldt" raised a fresh difficulty. Instead of arguing, on the lines of their instructions, that the regime should be limited to the Western Scheldt as the only maritime waterway to Antwerp, Verstolk and Dedel tried to prove that the Eastern Scheldt, although bearing the name, was not part of the river at all but part of the intermediate waters. But Palmerston was ready for this; producing a folio of Grotius and a number of maps, he discoursed at some length on the historical geography of the Scheldt and established, what we already know, that the Eastern Scheldt was

---

[1] One of the main sources for the history of this phase of the negotiation is the "Récit secret de la négociation hollando-belge". After the breakdown in September 1833 the Conference felt the need of an official version of the negotiation and entrusted its compilation to Bülow. His account was adopted at the Conference's final meeting on 15 November 1833 under the title "Récit secret". His original draft is in F.O. Belgium/29, and the official copy, signed by the plenipotentiaries, in F.O. Belgium/21. When, shortly afterwards, Verstolk delivered a report on the negotiation to the States-General, in the course of which he exhibited the work of the Conference in an unfavourable light, the plenipotentiaries considered the advisability of defending themselves by publishing the "Récit"; they decided against publication, and the "Récit" remained secret until it was published in the Belgian *Histoire parlementaire du traité de paix du 19 avril 1839* (Brussels, 1839). The "Récit" must be compared with the Dutch version of the story contained in the despatches of Verstolk and Dedel published in *Gedenkstukken, 1830-40*, V, 274-377.

the original river and the Western Scheldt a later creation. Verstolk and Dedel, however, professed themselves unconvinced.[1]

The question of where the duty was to be collected also provoked long discussion. The Dutch plenipotentiaries argued that since the duty was a recognition of Dutch sovereignty it must be collected on Dutch territory, that is, at Flushing; against this Palmerston maintained that its collection at Flushing would violate the rule of " aucune visite ni examen de cargaison " and wanted to substitute Antwerp. (It was an echo of the old battle over the collection of the toll of Iersekeroord.) Finally, there was the question whether ships using the Scheldt to enter Terneuzen should pay the same as those which went up to Antwerp; Verstolk and Dedel claimed that the amount of duty should be independent of the distance travelled, but they did not convince Palmerston.

The following day the Conference tackled with the Dutch plenipotentiaries the third and fourth parts of the article, the navigational services on the Scheldt and the regime for the intermediate waters. The former included the vexed question of pilotage. Palmerston defended the dual system, and a free choice of pilots, as the only satisfactory way of implementing the pilotage stipulations of the Twenty-Four Articles; the Dutchmen declared this system an encroachment upon the sovereignty of Holland and suggested that if Belgium were dissatisfied with any other arrangement which might be adopted she could always appeal to the Powers. After a long argument the question had to be postponed. There was more progress with regard to the intermediate waters, for although the Dutch plenipotentiaries still challenged the principle of Belgian admission they were ready in practice to admit Belgian ships under a tariff not exceeding that of Mainz, " proportion des distances gardée ".

It was now the turn of the Belgians. After spending 27 July in criticizing the clauses provisionally agreed upon by the Conference with the Dutch, the Belgian plenipotentiaries two days later presented their own ideas for a new Article IX. These included a duty of 1 florin for the double journey, to be collected—failing an arrangement for its payment annually by the Belgian government—at Antwerp; vessels bound for Terneuzen were to pay only half the duty, and the name " Scheldt " was to include both branches of the river. There should be a dual pilotage and a free choice of pilots, and the tariff of dues

---

[1] This dispute, originating in the Conference, was taken up by publicists in Holland and Belgium; Marshall and Bogaerts, publishing their Scheldt documents in the *Bibliothèque des Antiquités Belgiques* (Antwerp, 1833), refer to it, p. 12, *n* 1.

would be that in force on the Maas in 1829, " proportion des distances gardée ". Finally, Goblet and Van de Weyer accepted the application of the tariff of Mainz to the intermediate waters, from which, however, as already noted, they excluded the Eastern Scheldt.

The problem was now how to adjust the differences between these two sets of proposals. The differences had been narrowed to four main points: the rate of duty on the Scheldt (including the rate for Terneuzen), the place of its collection, the status of the Eastern Scheldt, and the system of pilotage. In several interviews with Goblet and Van de Weyer, Palmerston and Talleyrand tried hard to extort some concession; they represented that if Belgium could offer a duty of $1\frac{1}{2}$ florins, the Conference might in return secure its collection at Antwerp, adding that the Conference was unanimous that international law entitled the Dutch government to collect the duty within its frontiers. The plenipotentiaries could do nothing on their own responsibility, but they promised to refer to Brussels and in doing so they urged the Foreign Minister, De Mérode, to procure them the latitude demanded. This request came as an unpleasant shock to the Belgian government, which having made what it persisted in regarding as a major concession in agreeing to any duty, was waiting for the Dutch government to reciprocate. Even more disturbing was the news that J.-B. Smits, whom the government—rather naïvely, one thinks, in view of what had happened before—now sent to London again to stiffen the plenipotentiaries, straightway went over to the enemy by expressing astonishment that the government should boggle at a mere 75,000 florins a year as the price of ransoming the Scheldt from the tariff of Mainz.[1] But for the moment the Belgian government would not budge; on 8 August De Mérode forbade the plenipotentiaries to reduce the terms. Two days later, therefore, Palmerston wrote privately to Leopold urging him to authorize the extra half-florin and promising in return to do all in his power to carry the other points; this letter the King submitted to the Cabinet, which, after a long debate, decided to accept its assurance and to make the concession. On 13 August De Mérode instructed the plenipotentiaries to agree to $1\frac{1}{2}$ florins, but only on condition that they secured all the other demands; as an additional precaution they were not to initial the article until it had been approved at Brussels.

The Belgian government was, indeed, determined to sell its assent so dearly as to make the additional half-florin of little value in the negotiation. While he was extorting this from Brussels Palmerston had been hammering away at Verstolk and Dedel in an effort to obtain

[1] Van de Weyer and Goblet to De Mérode, 5 Aug. 1833. A.E. XII (I), no. 46.

something similar from them, and when his frontal assault failed completely he might well have given up the fight as hopeless. A fortnight of almost daily conferences, each lasting for anything up to five hours, had yielded negligible result; true, the Dutch government remained optimistic, but then, as Jerningham put it, " notions of celerity must be different in London and at The Hague ".[1] But that government, too, had an exposed flank, and this Palmerston now resolved to turn. At the meeting of the Conference on 30 July he asked the Dutch plenipotentiaries whether the King had taken steps to obtain the assent of the Germanic Confederation and of the Agnates of Nassau to the partition of Luxemburg, which was a state of the Confederation and a part of the Nassau patrimony, proposed in the Twenty-Four Articles, and, receiving a negative answer, urged the necessity of his doing so before the Diet adjourned at the beginning of September. Wessenberg and Bülow, who were in the secret, supported Palmerston by declaring that neither Austria nor Prussia, as members of the Confederation, could sign a treaty affecting Luxemburg unless the Diet had signified its assent. It was an once an excellent test of the King's intentions and a useful instrument for extracting concessions on Article IX. If the King really wanted to settle, then the application would be a mere formality, a request for the confirmation of an arrangement which he as Grand Duke had already accepted; but if he were still playing for time, then he would hardly be prepared to make it, for it committed him in advance to a recognition of Belgium as constituted by the Twenty-Four Articles.

The success of the manœuvre was soon evident. Jerningham pressed Verstolk hard on the subject during the first half of August, only to receive evasive replies. As Palmerston at the same time secured an adjournment of the meetings with the Dutch plenipotentiaries, ostensibly to devote himself to obtaining further concessions from the Belgians but in reality to await the effect of Jerningham's efforts at The Hague, the Dutch government was faced with the alternatives either of seeing the negotiation lapse or of making some positive gesture towards keeping it in being. The first result of the manœuvre was thus to wring from The Hague concessions on two of the four points at issue. On 14 August Verstolk and Dedel were authorized to agree to the collection of the duty at Antwerp, after a declaration at Flushing, and to propose an arrangement whereby Dutch pilots should take the up-river and Belgian the down-river traffic. But if the King believed that this would serve to prolong the negotiation, he was soon unde-

[1] To Palmerston, 2 Aug. 1833. F.O. Holland/187.

ceived. At a private meeting on 19 August Bülow and Wessenberg informed the Dutch plenipotentiaries of the result of Palmerston's latest efforts with Goblet and Van de Weyer. The Belgians agreed to a duty of $1\frac{1}{2}$ florins, to the exclusion of the Eastern Scheldt and to the payment of the full duty on the passage to Terneuzen, but they demanded the collection of the duty at Antwerp, a free choice of pilots, and the right to share in the Scheldt fishery. When Verstolk and Dedel revealed that while they could reduce their figure of 2 florins they could not accept $1\frac{1}{2}$, Bülow and Wessenberg expressed amazement and declared that in all their bargainings with Palmerston they had taken this figure for granted, and that nothing could now save the negotiation.

The end came on 24 August, when the minutes of the Conference ended with the words "Ajournement *sine die*". After a long discussion, Palmerston posed the following four points as an ultimatum: a duty of $1\frac{1}{2}$ florins, its collection at Antwerp, a free choice of pilots, and the Belgian right to fish in the Scheldt. He then asked the Dutch plenipotentiaries whether their government had approached the Diet and the Agnates on the question of Luxemburg, and when they replied that it had not, declared that the Conference would adjourn until notified of the assent of those bodies to the partition.

In thus breaking off the negotiation, Palmerston and Talleyrand were profiting by the favourable position in which Belgium now found herself and which enabled them, and her, to view with equanimity the prospect of its indefinite continuance. Palmerston at least would have been happier if he could have converted the provisional into a permanent settlement, as his efforts to bring the two parties together clearly proves. But those efforts had not been wasted, for they had led to the formulation of the "four points" with which the negotiation closed. While he was not prepared, once the negotiation was suspended, to treat these four points as an ultimatum in the sense that he would admit no modification of them, he did regard the principles they embodied as the *sine qua non* of a satisfactory settlement. When at the end of September Ancillon proposed that the Conference should concentrate on the single point of the rate of duty and leave the rest to ulterior negotiation, Palmerston's reply was that the four points were inseparable and that to settle one without the others would be to destroy their meaning. In substance, if not in detail, the four points had already appeared in the Theme; it was the same four points which Palmerston was to champion again in 1838. It was imperative, then, that the King should yield on them if he wanted a settlement. Verstolk and Dedel were emphatic on this point in their despatches, and when the King showed no such disposition Verstolk admitted the hopelessness of the situation by asking for his recall. He returned to The Hague early in September and presented a report to the States-General which was a veiled indictment of the King's attitude. In October Prince Schwarzenberg, in the name of the Three Courts, tried in vain to coax the King into a settlement, and when in December the States-General voted the budget for 1834 all hope of an early conclusion vanished.

During the four and a half years which passed before the King surrendered, Belgium enjoyed the advantages of the convention and among them the duty-free navigation of the Scheldt. It would have been too much to expect, however, that the river should cause no trouble during that time. In June 1835 Admiral Gobius, who had figured in previous disputes, tried to enforce a rule that Belgian pilots who had come down the river might not return along it but must go back by land. Palmerston, back at the Foreign Office after the fall of the Tory government in April, instructed Jerningham to take the matter up, but the complaints had ceased before the *chargé* could get an answer. Twelve months later the Antwerpers were protesting at the insufficient buoying of the river; it appeared that several of the marks had not been replaced since their removal in the days of the coercive measures. Representations from Disbrowe, the new British minister, at least coincided with, if they did not produce, an improvement. A dispute as to whether the Belgian right to fish in the Scheldt applied to shellfish, with Palmerston for once in agreement with the Dutch contention, closes the tale of these incidents. Small in themselves, they helped to point the moral that until it was founded upon precise treaty-stipulations the freedom of the Scheldt must remain more or less precarious.

(iii) *The Treaties of April 1839.*

On 14 March 1838 Dedel handed Palmerston a Note announcing that King William was ready to accept the Twenty-Four Articles and to convert them into a treaty with Belgium. The King made it clear that he expected the Powers to abide by the protocol of 15 October 1831, by which the Conference had declared the Articles " final and irrevocable " and incapable of modification.

In Belgium the news provoked an immediate outburst. For nearly five years Belgium had enjoyed a situation considerably more favourable than she had to expect under the treaty; released from the annual debt-payments, and occupying parts of Limburg and Luxemburg assigned by the treaty to Holland, the Belgians had no wish to be reminded of the treaty's existence, and the "audacity" of the King of Holland in proposing to convert it into a final settlement aroused great indignation. The Belgian government could not ignore the popular feeling and early in April Leopold let it be known in London that he would not accept the Articles. Belgium looked instinctively to France for support, and the government of Louis Philippe, inclining more and more towards an adventurous foreign policy, seemed disposed to support her protest. On the other side stood the three Eastern Courts, on whom the King of Holland relied to support his demand for the maintenance unchanged of at least the territorial and financial provisions of the Articles. Both parties immediately began to court the British government. Palmerston appears from the first to have regarded the maintenance of the Articles as impossible, if only because that would be to ignore the reserves contained in the ratification of the treaty by the Three Courts; at the same time he was by no means disposed to encourage extravagant Belgian demands, especially in the matter of territory.

The wide divergence of views threatened to break up the Conference as soon as it reassembled unofficially. The initial question of what answer to give the King's Note led to endless disputes over his right to demand the maintenance of articles which he had waited more than six years before accepting, as well as over the validity of the agreement reached on particular points in the course of the negotiations of 1832 and 1833. When Dedel, reading the Dutch Note, came to the words "aux conditions de séparation que les Cours d'Autriche, de France, &c. &c., ont declaré finales et irrévocables", Palmerston interjected: "Oui, mais il y'a de cela près de sept ans, et bien d'autres déclarations ont été fait depuis".[1] In the upshot, the King did not get his answer until December. The intervening eight months were a time of unrelieved difficulty and tension, with the King demanding a reply to his Note, with Belgium trying to force the Conference's hand, and with the Powers eyeing one another uneasily. Much statesmanship went to the adoption, on 6 December 1839, of a protocol embodying a unanimous decision. Belgium obtained a reduction of her share of the debt and some other concessions, notably in Article IX, but otherwise the Twenty-Four Articles remained intact. Even then Sébastiani, the French plenipotentiary, signed only *ad referendum*, and it was not until 23 January 1839 that the Notes communicating the terms to the two governments were despatched.

[1] Dedel to Verstolk, 17 March 1838. B.Z. 1703.

It was King William himself who had put forward the first project for a revision of Article IX. When Verstolk sent Dedel his full power on 13 July he announced that the King was offering, with the approval of the Courts of Berlin and Vienna, three " facilités " or modifications to the articles. The first related to the financial settlement; the second proposed to add to Article IX a clause fixing the duty on the Scheldt at 1½ florins (1.12 for the upward and .38 for the downward passage); and the third envisaged a meeting of Dutch and Belgian commissioners to settle questions arising out of the treaty, with a final arbitration by the Conference on any question not settled within three months. These proposals had been drawn up in concert with Count Senfft, who visited The Hague on his way to London as Austrian plenipotentiary. Senfft arrived in London on 15 July, and in an interview with Palmerston two days later he told the Foreign Secretary about these " facilités ". Palmerston at once raised two " insuperable " objections to the third of them: not only would the commissioners be discussing principles instead of applying them, as they should do, but the condition laid down by the Three Courts themselves in ratifying the treaty that all future modifications must be " de gré à gré " would prevent the Conference from arbitrating between them.[1] The proposals were, in fact, merely a revised version of Ancillon's plan of September 1833,[2] and Palmerston was as determined now as then that if the Belgians were to pay the extra half-florin they should get their money's worth in precise stipulations and not be left to bargain with the Dutch.

The Belgian government early placed its views on navigation before the British and French governments, and in Paris it found some support for its new campaign for the suppression of all duty on the Scheldt. But when on 3 August Van de Weyer and Sébastiani, now French ambassador and plenipotentiary in London, saw Palmerston on the subject they found him strangely reserved. Van de Weyer took particular exception to the Dutch proposal to leave the pilotage and buoying to commissioners and wanted everything settled in the treaty; Palmerston could not help but agree with this, but he added that any changes in the original article, beyond the fixing of a rate of duty, would meet with opposition from the Eastern plenipotentiaries, and his only encouragement was to ask Van de Weyer to draw up a " rédaction definitive " for his use.[3] During the next few weeks Senfft and

[1] Memorandum by Palmerston, 17 July 1838. F.O. 96/19.
[2] See above, p. 218.
[3] Van de Weyer to De Theux, 4 Aug. 1838. *Histoire parlementaire*, I, 37; Guillaume, *op. cit.*, I, 100; De Ridder, A., *Histoire diplomatique du traité de 19 avril 1939* (Brussels and Paris, 1920), 115.

Bülow were busy converting the King's " facilités " into a project of treaty consisting of the original Twenty-Four Articles with a series of additional articles dealing with finance and navigation; their proposals for the Scheldt included a tonnage duty of 1½ florins to be collected by Dutch agents at Antwerp and Terneuzen, and the reference of other questions to a Belgo-Dutch commission.[1] When Van de Weyer raised the subject again with Palmerston, the only reply he received was that the remedy lay in his own hands and that he should put his own ideas on paper for submission to Senfft and Bülow.[2]

Palmerston's unwonted coolness did not mean that he had changed his mind about the Scheldt since 1833; it was simply a move in his campaign to overcome the refusal of the Belgian government to discuss any other question until a satisfactory financial settlement had been reached. The Belgian ministers were naturally afraid that the Conference would attempt to bribe them into accepting a less favourable verdict on the debt-question with concessions in other articles. Van de Weyer's request to be allowed to begin discussion of Article IX thus elicited from the Foreign Minister, De Theux, only the reply that the financial question must come first. It was, in fact, the situation of July 1832 over again, with De Theux in place of De Muelenaere and the debt-settlement in place of the evacuation of the citadel. But this time the King of Holland really wanted a settlement, and Senfft and Bülow were anxious to push ahead with the modifications. If Belgium would not co-operate, then Palmerston would have to do his best without her; he was clear in his own mind as to the defects of the Austro-Prussian plan, and accordingly in October he set to work with Senfft and Bülow to give it a different shape.

It is possible to follow the evolution of the last Article IX much more closely than that of its predecessors. There are six drafts of it, dated between 19 and 25 October, among the papers of the Conference.[3] The first occurs in a draft treaty handed by Senfft and Bülow to Palmerston on 19 October, and bears modifications in Palmerston's hand. This is essentially the original Austro-Prussian project; Article IX follows very closely Article IX of the Twenty-Four, the only significant change being the insertion of a paragraph fixing the rate of duty at 1½ florins. Of Palmerston's modifications, the most important is the substitution, in the paragraph stipulating equal pilotage dues, for the words " pour le commerce Hollandais et pour le commerce Belge " of " pour les

---

[1] A copy of these " Articles explicatifs et additionnels " is in F.O. Belgium/64.
[2] De Ridder, *op. cit.*, 161-2.
[3] F.O. Belgium/64.

navires de toutes les nations"; it was one of the changes he had incorporated in the Theme. In the new paragraph fixing the rate of duty he struck out the adjectives "'Néerlandais" and "Belge" applied to the Scheldt, and added the clause

et que les dits navires ne puissent être assujettis à aucune visite ni à aucune retard ou entrave quelconque, soit en remontant l'Escaut de la pleine mer, soit en descendant l'Escaut pour se rendre en pleine mer.

Palmerston's next care was for pilotage. A second draft prepared by Senfft, and dated in Palmerston's hand 22 October, adopted his first set of modifications and added the stipulation that Holland must maintain an efficient pilotage service at Flushing. To this Palmerston made the following addition:

mais si par des causes quelconques ce service devenait incomplet il serait loisible à la Belgique d'établir dans le cours du Fleuve et à ses embouchures des services de pilotage à l'usage des navires de toutes les nations.

Senfft and Bülow opposed this as derogatory of the King's sovereignty but Palmerston was adamant and they included it in their next draft of the article.

At this point Van de Weyer's loyalty to his instructions was overcome by his fear of seeing the whole article take shape without his concurrence. Unable to take a direct share in the negotiation, he persuaded Palmerston to accept in lieu of himself the projects of Article IX which he had submitted on behalf of Belgium in 1831 and 1832. With these before him, the Foreign Secretary now prepared a new draft not only incorporating all but one of the former modifications but introducing some important new ones. Of these two were outstanding: first, the suppression of the existing pilotage clause, including Palmerston's own proviso, in favour of the dual system and a free choice of pilots; and second, the introduction of a new paragraph (numbered 8):

Si des événements naturels ou des travaux d'art rendraient par la suite impracticables les voies de navigation indiquées au présent article, le Gouvernement des Pays Bas assignera à la navigation Belge d'autres voies aussi sûres et aussi bonnes, en remplacement des dits voies de navigation devenues impracticables.[1]

The first of these had long been a staple demand of Palmerston's and its reappearance was not surprising; but once again it was stoutly opposed by Senfft and Bülow, and as vigorously defended by Palmerston, who declared that Belgium would never accept an Article IX which did not include it.[2] The eighth paragraph was not a new idea

---

[1] Van de Weyer to De Theux, 25 Oct. 1838, enclosing the draft. A.E. XIV, no. 37.
[2] Same to same, 26 Oct. 1838. A.E. XIV, no. 38; Dedel to Verstolk, 27 Oct. 1838. B.Z. 1703.

either; it had originally appeared in Smits' " Observations " upon a draft of the Theme,[1] but it had not been adopted in that project, and its reappearance now suggests that either Palmerston or Van de Weyer had been doing some research among their papers. At any rate, Smits himself could take no further credit for it, since when he saw it again he failed to recognize it as his own child and protested that it would give the Dutch the right to close any channel at will![2]

During the next few days there was some stiff fighting over these latest modifications, especially the new pilotage clause, but by 27 October Palmerston had won his last battle for the freedom of the Scheldt. On that day Van de Weyer was able to send to Brussels the new agreed draft of the article, which with one or two verbal changes was to become Article IX of the Conference's official project of 23 January and so of the treaty of 19 April 1939. De Theux's reply was to protest against the action of the Conference in discussing matters of the highest importance without consulting the Belgian plenipotentiary.[3] If this had been true, De Theux would have had only himself and his colleagues to blame; in fact, Van de Weyer had played a not unimportant part in shaping the article, but only by overstepping his instructions. As late as 28 December De Theux, in forwarding to Van de Weyer a note from Smits on the subject, was careful to add that it was " purement officieuse ", since " le moment de la discuter n'est point encore arrivé ".[4] By then the moment had already passed.

On 6 December the Conference, now officially reassembled, issued the protocol to which were annexed the Articles of Separation.[5] Article IX was as follows:

Les dispositions des articles 108 jusqu'à 117 inclusivement de l'Acte général du Congrès de Vienne, relatives à la libre navigation des fleuves et rivières navigables, seront appliquées aux fleuves et rivières navigables qui séparent ou traversent à la fois le territoire Belge et le territoire Hollandais.

En ce qui concerne spécialement la navigation de l'Escaut et de ses embouchures, il est convenu que le pilotage et le balisage, ainsi que la conservation des passes de l'Escaut en aval d'Anvers, seront soumis à une surveillance commune, et que cette surveillance commune sera exercée par des commissaires nommés à cet effet de part et d'autre; des droits de pilotage modérés seront fixés d'un commun accord, et ces droits seront les mêmes pour les navires de toutes les nations.

[1] See above, p. 193.
[2] Smits to De Theux, 9 Nov. 1838. A.E., XIV, enclosure in no. 158. Although the sense of the new clause was the same as Smits' of 1832, it was quite differently worded, the new wording having clearly been borrowed from Article III of the Convention of Mainz, which envisaged the blocking of one of the channels of the Lower Maas.
[3] To Van de Weyer, 30 Oct. 1838. A.E. XIV, no. 58.
[4] A.E. XIV, no. 158.
[5] Martens, *Nouveau Recueil*, XV, 486-501.

En attendant, et jusqu'à ce que ces droits soient arrêtés, il ne pourra être perçu des droits de pilotage plus élévés que ceux qui ont été établis par le tarif de 1829 pour les bouches de la Meuse, depuis la pleine mer jusqu'à Helvoet, et de Helvoet jusqu'à Rotterdam, en proportion des distances.

Il sera au choix de tout navire se rendant de la pleine mer en Belgique, ou de la Belgique en pleine mer par l'Escaut, de prendre tel pilote qu'il voudra; et il sera loisible d'après cela aux deux pays d'établir, dans tout le cours de l'Escaut et à son embouchure, les services de pilotage qui seront jugés nécessaires pour fournir les pilotes. Tout ce qui est relatif à ces établissements sera determiné par le règlement à intervenir conformément au § 6 ci-après. Le service de ces établissements sera sous la surveillance commune mentionnée au commencement du présent paragraphe. Les deux gouvernements s'engagent à conserver les passes navigables de l'Escaut et de ses embouchures, et à y placer et y entretenir les balises et bouées nècessaires, chacun pour sa partie du fleuve.

Il sera perçu par le gouvernement des Pays-Bas, sur la navigation de l'Escaut et de ses embouchures, un droit unique de fl. 1-50 par tonneau, savoir : fl. 1-12 pour les navires qui, arrivant de la pleine mer, remonteront l'Escaut occidental pour se rendre en Belgique par l'Escaut ou par le canal de Terneuzen; et de 0-38 par tonneau des navires qui, arrivant de la Belgique par l'Escaut ou par le canal de Terneuzen, descendront l'Escaut occidental pour se rendre dans la pleine mer. Et, afin que les dits navires ne puissent être assujettis à aucune visite, ni à aucune retard ou entrave quelconque dans les rades hollandaises, soit en remontant l'Escaut de la pleine mer, soit en descendant l'Escaut pour se rendre en pleine mer, il est convenu que la perception du droit susmentionné aura lieu par les agents néerlandais à Anvers et à Terneuzen. De même, les navires arrivant de la pleine mer pour se rendre à Anvers par l'Escaut occidental, et venant d'endroits suspects sous le rapport sanitaire, auront la faculté de continuer leur route sans entrave ni retard, accompagnés d'un garde de santé, et de se rendre ainsi au lieu de leur destination. Les navires se rendant d'Anvers à Terneuzen, et *vice-versâ*, ou faisant dans le fleuve même le cabotage ou la pêche (ainsi que l'exercice de celle-ci sera réglé en conséquence du § 6 ci-après), ne seront assujettis à aucun droit.

La branche de l'Escaut, dite l'Escaut oriental, ne servant point, dans l'état actuel des localités, à la navigation de la pleine mer à Anvers et à Terneuzen, et *vice-versâ*, mais étant employé à la navigation entre Anvers et le Rhin, celle-ci ne pourra être grevée, dans tout son cours, de droits ou de péages plus élevés que ceux qui sont perçus d'après les tarifs de Mayence du 31 mars 1831, sur la navigation de Gorcum jusqu'à la pleine mer en proportion des distances.

Il est également convenu que la navigation des eaux intermédiaires entre l'Escaut et le Rhin, pour arriver d'Anvers au Rhin, et *vice-versâ*, restera réciproquement libre, et qu'elle ne sera assujettie qu'à des péages modérés qui seront les mêmes pour le commerce des deux pays.

Des commissaires se réuniront de part et d'autre à Anvers, dans le délai d'un mois, tant pour arrêter le montant définitif et permanent de ces péages, qu'afin de convenir d'un réglement général pour l'exécution des dispositions du présent article, et d'y comprendre l'exercice du droit de pêche et du commerce de pêcherie, dans toute l'étendue de l'Escaut, sur le pied d'une parfaite réciprocité et égalité en faveur des sujets des deux pays.

En attendant, et jusqu'à ce que le dit réglement soit arrêté, la navigation de la Meuse et de ses embranchements restera libre au commerce des deux pays, qui adopteront provisoirement, à cet égard, les tarifs de la Convention signée, le 31 mars 1831, à Mayence, pour la libre navigation du Rhin, ainsi que les autres dispositions de cette Convention en autant qu'elles pourront s'appliquer à la dite rivière.

Si des événements naturels ou des travaux d'art venaient, par la suite, à rendre impracticables les voies de navigation indiquées au présent article, le gouvernement des Pays-Bas assignera à la navigation belge d'autres voies aussi sûres et aussi bonnes et commodes en remplacement des dites voies de navigation devenues impracticables.

Palmerston had done his best for the Belgians. On some points he had yielded: nothing was said about the annual payment of the duty or about its redemption; there was to be no reduction of duty on the passage to Terneuzen; and the Eastern Scheldt was after all to be treated as part of the intermediate waters. But all the essential points were there: equality of treatment as between riparians and non-riparians, a fixed and moderate tonnage-duty to be collected on Belgian territory, the "surveillance commune", the dual pilotage system, the free navigation of the intermediate waters, and, last but not least important, the same standard of precision in drafting as had characterized the Theme. It is, indeed, with the Theme that the present article must in the first place be compared. The comparison is not unfavourable, and Palmerston might well be satisfied with his last attempt to solve the Scheldt question.

So greatly had conditions changed that it was the King of Holland who now accepted the articles promptly and without reserve, and the King of the Belgians who refused. Dedel had received a copy of the new project confidentially from the Eastern plenipotentiaries on 13 November, and sent it to The Hague, where Verstolk drew up for the King a careful comparison between it and the Twenty-Four Articles. On Verstolk's showing the new project passed the test quite well. In Article IX the least acceptable feature was the dual pilotage, which was certainly a "servitude" and might be burdensome, but elsewhere the Foreign Minister found little ground for serious criticism.[1] It was otherwise at Brussels. Already at the beginning of January 1839, before the terms had been officially communicated, the Belgian government addressed a memorandum to the Conference setting forth its argument against the principle, amount and method of collection of the proposed duty, and demanding at the very least an arrangement for

[1] Verstolk to the King, " zeer geheim ", 30 Nov. 1838. *Gedenkstukken, 1830-40*, V, 663.

its annual payment as provided in the Theme.[1] The appeal to the Theme was, as might be expected, a marked feature of the whole Belgian campaign against the new article. Palmerston could, and did, reply that he had done his best for Belgium single-handed, and that if she had put forward her case six months before she might have enabled him to do better.[2] He did, in fact, sound the Dutch government on the possibility of its accepting some additional articles giving Belgium the privileges now asked for, but the reply was that, although the King was not averse from negotiating on these points, he would do so only after the treaty had been signed.[3]

On one point alone did the Belgian government ever look like being satisfied, namely, in its demand for the measurement of steamships, for purpose of duty, by their carrying-capacity instead of by their total tonnage. In this the Belgians had the support of the influential City of London Shipowners' Society, which on 12 March sent a deputation to the Foreign Office to urge the justice of their contention. Palmerston explained the difficulties in the way, but he decided to approach the Dutch government on it, a step which Senfft approved, as he thought that there was a better chance of success if Britain alone made the request. The King answered that he could accept no change in the articles, but intimated that he would be willing to come to an agreement with Britain alone in the matter.[4]

On 19 March the Belgian Chamber passed the *projet de loi* authorizing the King to sign the Articles, and the Senate accepted it a week later.[5] But for another month the government struggled on in its efforts to secure some modification of Article IX, and it was only on 18 April that the King sent Van de Weyer his full power. Dedel had been in possession of his for two months, and so at six o'clock on 19 April 1839 the three treaties, between Holland and Belgium, the Five Powers and Holland, and the Five Powers and Belgium, were signed. Article IX of the treaty between Holland and Belgium reproduced the ninth of the Articles of Separation, which has been given *in extenso* above. The same evening Palmerston wrote to Granville:

---

[1] Guillaume, *op. cit.*, I, 101-4.
[2] Van de Weyer to De Theux, 5 March 1839. De Ridder, *op. cit.*, 324-6. Same to same, 5 April 1839. A.E. XVIII, no. 20.
[3] Same to same, 2 April 1839. A.E. XVIII, no. 3.
[4] Disbrowe to Palmerston, 2 April 1839. F.O. Holland/215. Belgium eventually secured this concession by the convention of May 1843. See below, p. 229.
[5] For the debates in the Chamber and Senate see the *Histoire parlementaire du traité de 1839*; extracts relating to the Scheldt provisions from the speeches in the Chamber are printed by Guillaume, *op. cit.*, I, 110-45.

At last the Belgian affair is finished—we got through the signature of the Treaties at six o'clock this afternoon. This is indeed a capital Job, and has been at length arranged in a Manner which ought to be satisfactory to both Parties.—The Belgians have gained a good deal during this last negotiation, and they might probably have obtained even better Terms on some Points if they had chosen to negotiate instead of trying to prevent a settlement by sitting with their arms across and refusing to help us on a step. However all parties concerned will now I think be pleased with the settlement, and it was difficult to say today whether Vandeweyer or Dedel exhibited most satisfaction at the conclusion of the matter.[1]

THE treaties of 19 April were ratified by Holland, Belgium and the Five Powers in the course of the following month, and the ratifications were exchanged in London on 6 June 1839. The way was then clear for the various mixed commissions provided for in the main treaty to set to work to elaborate its details. The ninth article called for the appointment of two such bodies: there was to be a permanent commission to exercise the "surveillance commune" of the pilotage, buoying, and maintenance of the Scheldt estuary, and a temporary one to settle the tariff of duties on the intermediate waters, to regulate the Scheldt fisheries, and generally to deal with any problem of interpretation of the article.

The second of these commissions began work at Antwerp within the month's interval prescribed by the treaty, and by 25 October 1839 it had produced three provisional arrangements governing the "surveillance commune", the pilotage services, and the levy of the duty on the Scheldt; these were accepted by the two governments and came into force before the end of the year.[2] But this encouraging start was followed by a period during which the work of the Antwerp commission (as well as of the three others established under the treaty) encountered growing difficulty, chiefly because it was called upon to tackle problems on which there was insufficient preliminary agreement between the two governments. It was to remove these obstacles that the Belgian government proposed a direct Belgo-Dutch negotiation; this proposal was accepted at The Hague, and it led to the treaty of 5 November 1842. Of the 72 articles of this agreement, fifty were con-

[1] Granville Papers, G.D. 29/14.
[2] They are reprinted from the Dutch *Staatsblad* in *Tractaten en Tractaatsbepalingen de Schelde betreffende sinds 1648* (The Hague, 1919), 83-112, and in Lagemans, E. G. *Recueil des traités et conventions conclus par le royaume des Pays-Bas* (22 vols., The Hague, 1858-1926), I, nos. 173-5; and from the Belgian *Gazette* in Garcia de la Vega, D. de, *Recueil des traités et conventions concernant le royaume de Belgique* (in progress, Brussels, 1850-), I, 150-7.

cerned with navigation. The Scheldt itself accounted for only four articles (Arts. 16-19); by one of these Belgium accepted an addition of three cents per ton to the duty in consideration of additional buoying facilities to be provided by Holland, and by another Belgium secured the right to maintain a pilotage establishment at Flushing. Articles 20-37 dealt with the Ghent-Terneuzen canal, articles 38-49 with the intermediate waters and articles 50-55 with the Maas.[1] Simultaneously with this treaty there was signed a commercial convention by which each party undertook to admit the ships and goods of the other on the same terms as those of its own nationals; this was a notable contribution not only to commercial intercourse but to " good neighbourly " relations between the two countries.[2]

The treaty of 5 November envisaged the completion of the work of the mixed commissions within three months of its ratification, and the Antwerp commission for its part exceeded this allowance by only two weeks. The convention of 20 May 1843, which embodied its work, consisted of seven separate arrangements covering different aspects of the subject. The first of them, comprising 40 articles, regulated the payment of the Scheldt duty and the exemption of shipping from customs formalities; it included the provision that steamships should be liable to the duty only in respect of their cargo-carrying capacity. The second dealt, in 74 articles, with pilotage, health regulations, and the " surveillance commune ", and included, as an appendix, the tariff of pilotage dues; the third, of eight articles, covered the payment and use of the additional three cents authorized by the treaty of 5 November; and the remainder dealt with the fisheries, the intermediate waters, the Maas, and the Ghent-Terneuzen canal.[3]

It was under the detailed regulations thus fitted into the framework of the treaty of 1839 that the Scheldt and its neighbouring waters were to be navigated during the next twenty years. Of almost precisely the same duration was another arrangement supplementing the treaty, namely, the reimbursement by the Belgian treasury of the Scheldt duty to all vessels paying it. Introduced into the Belgian Chamber within a fortnight of the signing of the treaty, the law authorizing this concession was promulgated on 5 June 1839.[4] It was to cost Belgium sums rising from 600,000 francs in its first full year of operation to nearly two millions in its last, and a total expenditure over the whole

[1] Lagemans, no. 194; Garcia de la Vega, I, 234-53; Arts. 16-37 in Guillaume, *op. cit.*, I, 183-9.
[2] Lagemans, no. 195; Garcia de la Vega, I, 255-6; Guillaume, *op. cit.*, I, 198-9.
[3] Lagemans, no. 197; Garcia de la Vega, I, 259-323; Guillaume, *op. cit.*, I, 200-290.
[4] Guillaume, *op. cit.*, I, 157-81.

period of 28 million francs.[1] But from the outset the Belgian government made it clear to the beneficiaries that their exemption from the duty was a privilege, not a right, and from 1857 Belgium adopted the practice of seeking reciprocal concessions from their governments whenever occasion offered. The same principle underlay the final redemption of the duty in 1863; but that important transaction lies outside the scope of the present study.

To what extent Antwerp would have been handicapped by the Scheldt duty if the Belgian government had not thus shouldered the burden it is difficult, if not impossible, to estimate. But with the proviso of this unanswered question, it can be said that both the absence of any serious conflict over the Scheldt during the remainder of the century, and the fact that the renaissance of Antwerp did not work the ruin of Rotterdam, bear convincing testimony to the essential fairness of the settlement. Indeed, we may go further and claim that the ease and rapidity with which Belgium settled down to work out her own destiny and the vitality which has brought her intact through two great ordeals in our own time alike owe something to the far-sighted wisdom which led Palmerston to fight so stoutly for Article IX. Nor do the controversies which assailed that article a generation ago really impugn this verdict, for they were the product of changes in the political and economic terms of the problem which could in no wise have been foreseen or provided against a century ago. In so far as the Scheldt question was capable of solution in 1839, the treaty may fairly claim to have solved it. No one who has followed the six hundred years of Scheldt history traced in these pages will be disposed to make light of that achievement.

---

[1] *Ibid.*, 367-72. It is interesting to compare these figures with the 150,000 florins (or about 317,000 francs) proposed in Palmerston's Theme as an annual payment in lieu of the toll. See above, pp. 194-6.

APPENDIX

A LIST OF THE PRINCIPAL WORKS ON THE SCHELDT QUESTION TO 1839.

Hogendorp, F. van, *Disputatio Historico-Politica Inauguralis de Flumine Scaldi Clauso.* Leiden, 1827.
Bruyssel, E. van, *Histoire politique de l'Escaut.* Paris, 1864.
Grandgaignage, E., *Histoire du péage de l'Escaut.* Antwerp, 1868.
Magnette, F., *Joseph II et la liberté de l'Escaut. La France et l'Europe.* Brussels, 1897.
Guillaume, P., Baron, *L'Escaut depuis 1830.* 2 vols., Brussels, 1902.
Saint-Vincent, L. de, *L'Escaut. Histoire d'un fleuve international.* Paris, 1913.
Question of the Scheldt. Handbooks prepared under the direction of the Historical Section of the Foreign Office, No. 25, December, 1918.
Rotsaert, A., *L'Escaut depuis le traité de Munster (1648).* Les Cahiers belges, Brussels and Paris, 1918.
Terlinden, Ch., Viscount, " The History of the Scheldt ", in *History,* New Series IV (1919-20), 185-97, and V (1920-1), 2-10.
De Bas, F., " Another Version of the Scheldt History ", in *ibid.,* V, 159-70.
Pierrard, A., *La question de l'Escaut de 1648 à 1930.* Brussels, 1930.
Blondeau, A., *L'Escaut fleuve international et le conflit hollando-belge.* Paris and Bordeaux, 1932.
Smith, H. A., *Great Britain and the Law of Nations.* 2 vols., London, 1932-5. Esp. vol. II, pp. 279-301.

INDEX

Aberdeen, earl of: *see* Gordon, George Hamilton
Adair, Sir Robert 191, 201, 202
Agger, Den 9-10, 24 and *n* 5
Agusto, Francisco de, marquis de Gastañaga, governor of the Southern Netherlands 130
Aitzema, Lieuwe van 112, 118, 119, 124
Aix-la-Chapelle, treaty of (1748) 136
Albert, archduke of Austria, governor of the Southern Netherlands 92, 99
Albert of Bavaria, count of Holland-Zeeland 48
Amersfoort 69
Amiens, treaty of (1802) 146
Amsterdam 27, 96, 98, 102, 125, 126, 128, 154, 164, 171
Ancillon, Johann Peter Friedrich von 201, 209, 218, 221
Anne, queen of Great Britain 132, 133
Anthony, duke of Brabant 18, 37
Antwerp 1, 2; rise of, 3-4; 5, 7, 9, 10, 15-16; as part of Flanders, 18; exemption from *geleiden*, 26, 48, 52, 59-60; 60; becomes a sea-port, 34; growth of trade, 35-6; 37, 38; and *haringtol*, 40-43; purchases *geleiden* on Honte, 44-6; and "watch" on Honte, 50-61; "golden age" of, 62-4; purchases "watch" on Honte, 64-6; 74-5; and wine-staple, 78-81; 82; during the Revolt, 84-5; siege and capture by Parma, 85; 86-7, 89-90, 91; transhipment of goods for, 92-3; English attempts to reopen trade with, 93-4, 96-7, 118-23, 128, 139; truce of 1609 and, 94-6; makes commercial agreements with Dutch towns, 98-9; 101, 102, 105; secures abolition of licences, 108-9, 113; agreement with Middelburg, 109; receives ships *via* Ostend, 113, 136; 115, 117, 124, 125; Colbert and, 126; 134; occupied by France (1746-8), 135, 136, 141; French Revolution and, 143, 145-6; in settlement of 1814, 147-8, 149, 152; during Union, 154; in 1830, 157-8; merchants of, 154, 170, 176 and *n* 1, 184-5, 186-8, 191, 196; question of future of, 159-60; citadel of, 157, 183-4, 189-90, 204-5; 162, 165, 171, 177, 179, 187-8, 195, 202, 211, 212, 215, 216, 217, 224-5, 228-9
Archdukes, the: *see* Albert *and* Isabella
Argout, Antoine-Maurice, count d' 196
Arlington, earl of: *see* Bennet, Henry

Arne, the 80
Arnemuiden 15, 49, 67 *n* 2, 71, 78, 91 *n* 2
Austria 144, 149; and Conference of London, 157, 182, 209, 210, 217, 221. *See also* Emperor
Axel 73, 86, 104

Baden 149
Baerland 13
Bagot, Sir Charles 158 *n* 2, 167 *n* 1
Barrier, the Dutch 131, 132-7; Treaty of 1709, 132-3; of 1713, 133; of 1715, 134-5, 136-7
Bath, fort 141 *n* 3, 194
Bavaria 142, 149, 191; elector of: *see* Maximilian Emmanuel; electoral prince of: *see* Joseph Ferdinand
Beatis, Antonio de 63 *n* 2
Belcour 1
Belgiojoso, L. C. M. de Barbiano di, count 140 *n* 4
Belgium, revolution of 1830 in 156-7; provisional government of, 156, 158, 159; claims Zeeland-Flanders, 160-1, 167, 168, 170; rejects "Bases", 167; conception of river law, 169-70; demands on Scheldt, 174-5; treaty of 1831 with, 180-1; and citadel of Antwerp, 183-4, 189-90, 205; demands duty-free navigation, 184, 189-90; and negotiation of 1833, 211-9; and negotiation of 1838, 219-24; and Articles of Separation, 226-7; treaties of 1839 with, 228; and supplementary negotiation, 228-30
Belliard, Augustin-Daniel, count 174
Bennet, Henry, earl of Arlington 127
Bergen-op-Zoom 10 and *n* 1, 14, 15, 16, 18, 20, 30, 31, 34, 35, 36, 46, 48, 49, 60, 64, 66, 67, 68, 71, 77, 78, 79, 86, 89, 128 *n* 2, 135; lordship of 18
Bertrijn, Geeraard 64-5
Betkensveer 27, 28
Biervliet 11, 41 *n* 3, 43 *n* 3, 86, 87, 91-2
Blake, Robert, admiral 118
Blanc, Louis 199
Blauwgaren, fort 86
Bligh, Hon. John Duncan 188, 198
Bock, Jan de 51
Borchvliet, *geleide* of 27, 43
Bornesse, the 13, 30
Borssele, island of 13, 14
Borssele, Claes van 31 and *n* 7
Borssele, Frank van 37
Bouchain 1
Boxhorn, Marcus Zuerius 72-3

Braakman, the 6 *n* 1, 17, 73, 86, 91
Brabant 1, 9, 16-17, 31, 40-3, 49, 50, 52; duchy of, 11, 37, 47-8, 87, 89, 99, 101, 104, 118, 125, 133, 143 *n* 3; dukes and duchesses of, 17-18, 20, 23-5. *See also* Anthony, Henry 1, Johanna, John III, John IV, Philip the Good, *and* Burgundy, dukes and duchesses of; States of, 51-3, 57-61, 65, 108, 139
Breda 86, 89; baron of: *see* Raas van Liedkerke; barony of, 18; lords of: *see* Godfrey *and* Henry van Schooten; lordship of, 17-18, 18-19, 20, 23-4
Brielle 98 *n* 2
Broglie, Achille-Léonce, duke de 204, 205
Brouwershaven 31
Bruges 15-16, 17, 32, 34, 35, 50, 66, 69, 85, 89, 92, 104, 106, 109, 111, 113, 116
Brussels 156, 173
Buckingham, duke of: *see* Villiers, George
Bülow, Heinrich Wilhelm, baron 157, 169, 171, 214, 217-8, 222-4
Burgundy, dukes and duchesses of 32, 35, 36. *See also* Charles the Bold, Charles V (Emperor), John the Fearless, Margaret (1), Margaret (2), Mary, Philip the Fair, Philip the Good
Burke, Edmund 145 and *n* 1

Cadzand 10, 11, 12, 110, 126, 127-8
Calloo 40, 85; *haringtol* levied at, 40-43
Cambrai 1, 2
Capellen, Godert Alexander, baron van der 148
Castlereagh, viscount: *see* Stewart, Robert
Cats 14, 15, 49, 51
Charles V, emperor 67-9, 71-2, 73, 74, 76, 77-8
Charles I, king of England 126
Charles II, king of Spain 129-31
Charles, archduke of Austria 130
Charles the Bold, duke of Burgundy 42, 44, 52-3
Chassé, David Hendrikus, general, 157, 205
Chaumont, conference at (1814) 148
Christina, queen of Sweden 118 and *n* 3
Clancarty, earl of: *see* Trench, Richard Le-Poer
Cleves, duchy of 175
Clifford, Thomas, lord 127
Codrington, Sir Edward 174 *n* 1
Coesant 13
Colbert, Jean-Baptiste 116, 126, 131
Cologne 68, 155
Compiègne 190
Copenhagen, treaty of (1441) 50
Cromwell, Oliver 119-24

Dedel, Salomon 209, 210, 211-219, 220, 221, 226-8
Delft, Pacification of (1428) 37

Dender, the 1
Dendermonde 1, 73, 86
Deurme, the 73
Devaux, Paul 168, 170
Dirk VII, count of Holland-Zeeland 19, 30
Disbrowe, Sir Edward Cromwell 219
Doel 104, 134, 140, 141
Dordrecht 78, 94, 171
Dover, battle off (1652) 118; treaty of (1670), 127
Dudley, Robert, earl of Leicester 87, 88
Duiveland 10, 193
Dumouriez, Charles François, general 144, 145
Dunkirk 85

Emperor, the 17, 22, 59. *See also* Charles V, Frederick I, Henry VI, Joseph I, Joseph II, Leopold I, Maximilian
Empress: *see* Maria Theresa
England 16, 49, 55, 57, 62, 64, 66, 69, 81, 109, 118, 125; and " watch " on Honte, 51, 57, 66, 69; and opening of Scheldt, 93-4, 119-24; wars with Dutch Republic, 110, 111, 114-6, 118, 127-8; in alliance with Republic, 129-33. *See also* Great Britain; kings and queens of: *see* Anne, Charles II, James I, James II, William III, William IV
Esterhazy, Paul Anton, prince 157

Falck, Anton Reinhard 158, 166 *n* 2, 169, 173, 174, 176, 181
Farnese, Alexander, duke of Parma 5, 82, 84, 85, 87, 105
Ferdinand V, king of Castile and Aragon, 65
Flanders 6, 7, 12, 15, 20, 21, 31, 38, 40, 43, 161; counts and countesses of, 17-18, 21, 25, 44, 53. *See also* Louis de Male, Margaret, *and* Burgundy, dukes and duchesses of; county of, 11, 13-14, 37, 41-3, 59, 84, 86, 87, 89, 93, 101, 104, 113, 118, 134; sea-ports of, 113, 116, 117, 125. *See also* Dunkirk, Ostend; States of, 51-3; outflow of water from, 170, 172, 174
Floris III, count of Holland-Zeeland 30
Flushing 1, 14, 49, 67 *n* 2, 75, 78, 79, 80, 82, 84, 95, 98 *n* 2, 110, 111, 141, 145, 157, 185, 187, 194, 195, 223, 228; question of collecting Scheldt duty at, 206, 212, 215, 217, 218; marquisate of Veere and, 85 *n* 2, 126
Fontainebleau, treaty of (1785) 141, 143
Fox, Charles James 145 and *n* 1
France, as riparian of Scheldt 1, 4-5, 152-3, 158 n 1; 4, 16, 49, 62, 64, 75, 77, 96, 100, 103, 115-6, 125-9, 130-3, 135-7, 138-9; and Scheldt in 1784-5, 141-2; reopens Scheldt (1792), 143-4; occupies

Netherlands, 145-6; 149, 152, 153; and Conference of London, 157, 158 and *n* 1, 164, 165, 166; supports Belgian claim to Zeeland-Flanders, 167, 174; and treaty of 1831, 181-2; and coercive measures, 190, 199; and convention of 1833, 205-10; and negotiation of 1833, 213-9; and negotiation of 1838, 220-7; kings of: see Henry IV, Louis XIV, Louis Philippe
Frederick I, emperor 30
Frederick Henry, prince of Orange 86, 100, 101
Frederick Henry, fort 86, 104, 134, 135, 141
Frescobaldi, Girolamo 67
Friesland, county of 37; province of, 102, 103

Gastañaga, marquis de: see Agusto, Francisco de
Geervliet, toll of 15, 16, 29-30, 48, 60-1
Gelders, duchy of 65
Gérard, Etienne-Maurice, count 205
Germany 15, 16, 62, 124, 170, 171, 202; Confederation of, 217-8
Ghent 1, 2, 4, 6 *n* 1, 17, 41 *n* 3, 73-4, 78, 85, 86, 89, 91, 92, 98, 104, 109, 113; canal to Scheldt estuary, 73-4, 98, 104-5, 106, 111; canal to Ostend, 113, 136; canal to Terneuzen, 2, 4, 170-1, 172, 194, 215-6, 225, 229; Pacification of (1576), 84
Gobius, Otto Willem, admiral 219
Goblet, Albert Joseph, count 183-4, 190, 191, 193, 197, 200, 201, 211, 214-8
Godfrey van Schooten, lord of Breda 18, 23
Goeree, island of 127-8
Goes 15, 51
Gordon, George Hamilton, earl of Aberdeen 147, 157, 208 *n* 3
Gouda 98
Gower, George Granville Leveson, earl Granville 174 *n* 1, 227
Granville, earl: see Gower, George Granville Leveson
Great Britain, war with Dutch Republic (1780-84) 138-9; sounds Austria on reopening of Scheldt, 138-9; again guarantees closure, 143; and reopening of Scheldt (1792), 144-5; and settlement of 1814-15, 147-53; and Conference of London, 157; and Antwerp, 159-60; commercial interest of, 201-2. See also Temple, Henry John
Grey, Charles, earl 157, 167, 179 *n* 2, 204, 206, 211
Groningen, province of 102
Grotius, Hugo 92 *n* 1, 214
Guicciardini, Lodovico 52, 82
Haarlem 27, 96

Hague, The 100-1; treaty of (1795), 145
Hainaut, county of 1, 4, 37
Hanse, merchants of the 15, 16, 44, 50, 51, 52, 101 *n* 2, 124
Heentrecht (Eendracht), the 15, 19, 70 *n* 1
Heidensee, the 13-14
Helvoet 194, 225
Henry VI, emperor 30
Henry VII, king of England 66
Henry IV, king of France 96
Henry I, duke of Brabant 19, 23
Henry van Schooten, lord of Breda 23 *n* 3
Hesse-Darmstadt 149
Hinkele, between Honte and 9, 11-12, 12 *n* 1, 18-19, 24
Hofstede 90
Hogendorp, Gijsbrecht Karel van 195, 201
Holland, county of 13, 15. See also Holland-Zeeland, counts and countesses of; province of, 83, 84, 87, 88, 89, 90, 91, 99, 102, 109-15, 119, 120, 123, 124; States of, 111-2, 114, 120, 123
Holland-Zeeland, counts and countesses of 15, 17-19, 20, 24, 29ff., 37, 44, 47-61. See also Albert of Bavaria, Dirk VII, Floris III, Jacoba, Margaret, William III, William IV, William V, William VI, *and* Burgundy, dukes and duchesses of
Honte 7, 8; connotation of name at different periods, 10-13, 34-5, 53-4, 105 and *n* 1; as early trade-route, 15-17; jurisdiction over, 20-1; *geleiden* on, 24-5, 28-9, 43-6; transformation of, 32-4; navigation on, 35-6, 40, 48-9, 62-4; "watch" on, 49-61, 64-73
Hontemuide 7, 9, 12, 13, 15, 17-18, 23, 35, 48, 53, 54, 59
Hulst 85, 86, 104
Hulsterhaven 11, 53
Humboldt, Karl Wilhelm, baron von 151-2
Humphrey, duke of Gloucester 37
Iersekeroord, toll of 29-31, 46-61, 64-74, 90-1, 110 *n* 2; tollhouse of, 30, 57, 71; "watch" of, on the Honte, 21, 36, 49-61, 64-74
Isabella, queen of Castile 65
Isabella Clara Eugenia, archduchess of Austria, governor of the Southern Netherlands, 92, 99, 100

Jacoba, countess of Holland-Zeeland 37, 48
James I, king of Great Britain 96
James II, king of England 130
James Stuart, the Old Pretender 131
Jeannin, Pierre 94-5
Jenkinson, Robert Banks, earl of Liverpool 148

Jerningham, Hon. George Sulyarde Stafford 201, 208, 211, 217, 219
Joanna, queen of Castile 65
Johanna, duchess of Burgundy 37
John III, duke of Brabant 18
John IV, duke of Brabant 37, 48
John the Fearless, duke of Burgundy 37
Jollie, Antwerp merchant 191, 192, 195
Joseph I, emperor 133-4
Joseph II, emperor 136-7, 138-9; attempts to get Scheldt reopened (1784-5), 139-43
Joseph Ferdinand, electoral prince of Bavaria 130
Julius Cæsar 6 and n 1
Juste, Théodore 200

Kampen 50, 69
Kaunitz, Wenceslas, prince 139
Keetenisse, polder of 134
Kemper, Jeronimo de Bosch 199, 200
Kruisschans, fort 85, 86, 92, 104, 141
Künigl, Hermann Peter, count 149 n 2

La Rochelle 77
Larpent, John de Hochepied, baron 157 n 1, 158, 176 and n 1, 184, 191
Lebeau, Joseph 173, 202
Le Catelet 1
Le Hon, Charles Amé Joseph, count 201
Leicester, earl of: *see* Dudley, Robert
Leiden 96
Lek, the 175
Lemmel, the 14
Leopold I, emperor 130-1
Leopold I, king of the Belgians 168, 173, 180, 182, 184, 189-90, 197, 199, 216, 220, 226-7
Leopold William, archduke, governor of the Southern Netherlands 109
Liefkenshoek, fort 85 and n 4, 86, 87, 91-2, 104 and n 1, 119, 134, 135, 140, 141, 157, 205
Lieven, Christophe, prince 194, 204
Lieven, Dorothea, princess 172, 179 n 2
Lillo 71, 83 n 2; *geleide* of, 27; fort, 85, 86, 87, 90, 91-2, 93, 94, 104, 109, 110, 111, 115, 119, 134, 135, 141, 157, 205; *uitlegger* at, 110-111 and n 1, 140 and n 1
Limburg, county of 37; province of, 171, 177, 219
Linguet, Simon Nicolas Henri 142
Lisle, De, Antwerp merchant 191, 192, 195
Liverpool, earl of: *see* Jenkinson, Robert Banks
London 185; Conference of (1830-9), 157; and closure of Scheldt (1830), 157-8; and Belgian independence, 159; and Antwerp, 159-60; draws up " Bases de Séparation " (Jan. 1831), 163; draws up Eighteen Articles, 168-172; draws up Twenty-Four Articles, 174-180; and treaty of Nov. 1831, 180; faces deadlock, 191-2; and Palmerston's Theme, 198-9; is dissolved, 204; conducts negotiation of 1833, 213-8; suspends negotiation, 218-9; draws up Articles of Separation, 219-226; concludes treaty of 1839, 227; Shipowners' Society of, 227
Looyve, the 14, 15-16, 35, 48
Louis XIV, king of France 125, 126, 127, 130-132, 133
Louis de Male, count of Flanders 18, 37
Louis Philippe, king of the French 167-8, 190, 199, 220
Lowestoft, battle of (1665) 115
Lübeck 124
Lunéville, treaty of (1801) 161 n 2
Luxemburg, duchy of 174, 177, 217-8, 219

Maas, the 6, 7, 14, 15, 34, 152, 164, 165, 169, 179, 180, 192, 194, 195, 196, 203, 205, 207, 216, 225-6, 229
Maastricht 100, 101, 157, 158, 167, 171, 177, 180
Main, the 152
Mainz, convention of (1831) 154, 169, 187-195, 224 n 2; tariff of, 166-7, 177-8, 184-95, 205-6, 214, 215, 216, 226
Mareuil, Durand de 192
Margaret, countess of Flanders 18
Margaret, countess of Holland-Zeeland 37
Margaret, duchess of Burgundy (1), 37
Margaret, duchess of Burgundy (2), 37
Margaret, duchess of Parma, regent of the Netherlands 74
Margaret, duchess of Savoy, regent of the Netherlands 67, 68
Maria Theresa, empress 136
Mary, queen of Hungary, regent of the Netherlands 77, 78
Mary, duchess of Burgundy 25, 44, 56
Matuszewic, Adam, count 157, 178-9, 186, 204, 209, 213 n 2
Maurice, prince of Orange 86
Maurice, fort 86, 90
Maximilian, emperor 25, 44, 56, 67
Maximilian of Burgundy, lord of Veere 76, 78-9
Maximilian Emmanuel, elector of Bavaria 130 and n 2
Mazarin, Jules, cardinal 125
Mechlin 53, 58, 78, 99; chambre mi-partie at, 110-111, 113; Great Council of, 38, 77; its verdict of 1504, 11-12, 20, 21, 51, 55-6, 58-61; its verdict of 1559, 79-80
Merchant Adventurers of England 64, 67, 84 n 2, 98, 119
Mérode, Felix Philippe, count de 216

INDEX

Middelburg 15, 31 n 7, 34, 36, 49, 55-60, 66-8, 71, 72-81, 82, 95, 96, 98, 109; right of staple, 39-40, 49, 74-81, 94-5, 121-2, 163 n 2
Mirabeau, Honoré Gabriel Riquetti, marquis de 142-3
Moselle, the 152
Muelenaere, Félix Amand de 175 and n 2, 183-4, 189, 191, 192, 197, 222
Münster, treaty of 101, 103-7, 119, 126, 132-4, 140-3, 149, 159 n 1, 162; Art. XIV, 101, 104-6, 117, 119, 120-23, 126, 132-4, 140-3, 159 n 1, 163 n 3; Art. XV, 101, 104-6, 110-11, 113, 116, 132-4; Art. XXIII, 117

Napoleon I 2, 145-6
Nassau 149; Agnates of, 217-8
Neckar, the 152
Nemours, Louis-Charles, duke de 167
Netherlands, kingdom of (1815-30) 152-5; break-up of (1830), 156*ff.*; kingdom of (since 1830), 162, 180; and freedom of Scheldt, 162-3, 168-9, 173, 175, 181; war with Belgium, 173. See also William I
Noord-Beveland 10, 14, 15
Nothomb Jean-Baptiste, baron 168, 170

Oldenbarnevelt, Johan van, grand pensionary 98
Orange, princes of: see Frederick Henry, Maurice, William the Silent, William III, William V, William VI and William (VII)
Orloff, Alexis Fedorovitch, count 182
Ossendrecht 23-4
Ossenisse 12
Ostend 113, 136, 141, 160, 194: Company, 135
Osy, baron 187
Oudenaarde 1
Overvest, Lourijs van 46 n 2

Paesschen, Dirk van 64
Palmerston, viscount: see Temple, Henry John
Paris, first treaty of (1814) 146-7; second treaty of (1815), 161 n 2
Parma, duke of: see Farnese, Alexander; duchess of: see Margaret
Partition treaties, the 130
Pels, Gerard 53-4
Périer, Casimir 199
Philip IV, king of Spain 109, 117 n 2, 131
Philip V, king of Spain 131-2, 133
Philip the Bold, duke of Burgundy 37
Philip the Fair, duke of Burgundy 43, 54-61, 64-7, 69

Philip the Good, duke of Burgundy 37, 39, 40-2, 45, 48, 49-52
Philippine, fort 86, 87, 91-2
Pomponne, Simon Arnauld, marquis de 125
Portugal 62, 64, 85, 88
Portvliet 15, 16
Prussia 143, 144, 149, 151, 155; and Conference of London, 157, 175, 182, 191, 204, 209, 210, 211, 217, 221
Putten, lordship of 15, 30

Raas van Liedekerke, baron of Breda 19, 24
Rammekens 77 n 3, 98 n 2
Reimerswaal 10, 15, 16, 31, 33, 71
Reygersbergh, Johannes 72
Rhine, the 4, 6, 13, 14; freedom of navigation on, 147 and n 1, 151-5, 187-8, 203; admission of Belgian ships to, 170-1, 172, 173, 174-5, 177, 179, 193, 195, 225; Central Commission for, 154-5, 166-7, 185, 191. See also Mainz, convention *and* tariff of
Rilland 12 n 1, 24, 25 n 1; geleide of, 28-9, 43
Roompot, the 77, 78
Rooversberge, geleide of, 70 and n 1
Rotterdam 98, 99, 154, 164, 171, 194, 202, 225
Rupel, the 1, 2
Rupelmonde 1, 18, 85
Russia, and Conference of London 157; and treaty of Nov. 1831, 181-2; withdraws from Conference, 205; 209, 210
Ruychrock, Jan 45; Mary, 45; Nicolas, 50
Ruyter, Michiel Adriaanszoon de, admiral 127

Saeftingen 9 n 2, 11, 12, 25 n 1, 62-3, 104, 140, 141
St. Anna, polder of 134
St. Mary, fort 85, 115
St. Philip, fort 85
Santvliet 1, 4, 18, 70 n 1, 104; geleide of, 24, 27, 43
Sas van Gent 73, 74, 85, 86, 104-5, 109, 111, 115, 119, 174
Scenairt, Jan 31
Schakerloo 23-4
Schenkenschans 90
Schouwen 10, 15, 194
Schwarzenberg, Felix, prince 219
Scott, William, lord Stowell 146
Sébastiani, François-Horace, count 167, 196, 220
Senfft, Friedrich Christian Ludwig, count 221-4, 227
Sittard 177
Slooceters 27, 28
Sluis 86, 90, 92, 104, 111, 127-8, 174

Smits, Jean-Baptiste 186-7, 189, 191-3, 195, 200, 216, 224 and *n* 2
Soult, Nicholas-Jean, duke de Dalmatie 204
Spain 16, 62, 65, 67, 75, 84, 88, 93, 100, 103-6, 116, 117-23, 129-33; kings of: *see* Charles II, Philip IV, Philip V
Spiegel, Laurens Pieter van de, grand pensionary 144
Spinola, Ambrosio 87
Spruyte, Gillis 43
States-Flanders: *see* Zeeland-Flanders
States-General, of the Burgundian Netherlands 65; of the Dutch Republic, 86-8, 89-90, 91, 93-6, 98-102, 103-6, 109-10, 111, 112, 114-5, 119, 120-1, 122, 140-1; of the kingdom of the Netherlands, 214 *n* 1, 219
Stavoren 51
Steenvliet 27
Stewart, Robert, viscount Castlereagh 147-9, 159
Stociatech 10 and *n* 1
Stockmar, Christian Friedrick, baron 180 *n* 1, 190-1, 200
Stowell, lord: *see* Scott, William
Strasburg, convention of (1827) 161 *n* 2
Striene, the 14-15, 23
Sweden 118, 122, 125; queen of: *see* Christina

Talleyrand-Périgord, Charles-Maurice de, prince 148 *n* 4, 157, 160, 167, 177, 179, 182, 192, 204, 205-10
Teller Henri 117 *n* 3
Temple, Henry John, viscount Palmerston 157; and closure of Scheldt (1830), 158; and Antwerp, 158-9; on the " Bases de Séparation ", 164-5; view of Scheldt question, 165-6; 171; and Twenty-Four Articles, 176-180; on treaty of Nov. 1831, 180-1; 182, 184, 185-6, 187, 189; and coercive measures, 190, 199, 204-5; prepares his Theme, 190-8; responsibility for Theme, 200-1; motive of Theme, 201-3; negotiates convention of 1833, 205-10; and negotiation of 1833, 213-19; and negotiation of 1838, 220-7; 230
Terneuzen 2, 11, 86, 222, 225. *See also* Ghent
Theux, Barthélemy-Théodore de 222, 224
Thurloe, John 119-23, 124 *n* 3
Tolen, island of 10; town of, 16
Tournai 1, 2
Townshend, Charles, marquess 132; treaty: *see* Barrier treaty
Toxandria 6
Trench, Richard Le-Poer, earl of Clancarty 151
Tromp, Maarten Harpertszoon 118

Utrecht 51, 69; province of, 103; treaty of (1713), 133
Valenciennes 1, 2
Valkenesse 12 *n* 1, 24; *geleide* of, 28-9
Veere 16, 49, 55, 67 *n* 2, 71, 74, 75, 78, 95; marquisate of: *see* Flushing, marquisate of
Veergat, the 14, 15-16, 75, 77, 80
Venlo 68
Versailles, treaty of (1783) 139
Verstolk van Soelen, Johan Gijsbert, baron 158, 188-9, 198, 208, 211; Dutch plenipotentiary in London, 211-219; 214 *n* 1, 221, 226
Vienna, congress of 149; commission on international rivers, 149-53; Articles CVIII-CXVII, 151, 163-5, 166, 167, 168-9, 170, 172, 175, 177, 187-8, 193, 195, 203, 214
Villiers, George, duke of Buckingham 127-8
Vincent, Karl, baron 148, 149 *n* 2, 152
Vlaamsche Stroom 21, 39
Voorne 30, 127-8
Vortvuremuiden 17 and *n* 2, 19
Vossius, Matthæus 103 *n* 2
Vosvliet, the 15
Vosvlietshille 19

Walcheren 1, 10, 12, 13, 14, 15, 39, 63, 72, 73, 75, 126, 127-8, 193; " road " of, 34, 36, 39, 63, 65
Wellesley, Arthur, duke of Wellington 148, 168, 208 *n* 3
Wellington, duke of: *see* Wellesley, Arthur
Welsinge, the 14
Wesel 68
Wessenberg, Johann Philipp, baron 172-3, 175, 217-8
Westminster, treaty of (1654) 119, 121
Weyer, Sylvain van de 160, 175 and *n* 2, 176-7, 178, 180, 182, 183, 184, 189, 191-2, 197, 200, 201, 207, 210, 211-8, 221-5, 227-8
White, Charles 199
Wielingen, the 1, 12 and *n* 4, 14, 15, 21, 34, 39, 75, 77, 80, 81
Willemszoon, Jan 67 *n* 5
William IV, king of Great Britain 164, 180, 208 *n* 3
William I, king of the Netherlands 154; and Belgian Revolution, 157; takes " precautionary measures " on Scheldt, 157-8; 164; accepts the " Bases de Séparation ", 166-7; rejects Eighteen Articles, 172-3; rejects Twenty-Four Articles, 181; 189, 190; rejects Theme, 198-9; 204, 205, 207, 209; accepts convention of 1833, 210; and negotiation of 1833, 212-9; accepts Twenty-Four Articles, 219-20; accepts Articles of Separation, 226

William III, count of Holland-Zeeland 19, 24
William IV, count of Holland-Zeeland 25
William V, count of Holland-Zeeland, 31
William VI, count of Holland-Zeeland 37, 39, 79
William the Silent, prince of Orange 85 n 2
William III, prince of Orange and king of England 123 n 3, 126, 127, 129, 130, 132
William V, prince of Orange 144, 145
William VI, prince of Orange 147, 148, 149, 152, 162. *See also* William I, king of the Netherlands
William (VII), prince of Orange, afterwards king William II, 173
William, count of Nassau-Siegen 86
Winwood, Sir Ralph 65
Wissenkerke, Henry Janszoon van 53
Witt, John de, grand pensionary 123, 125
Wolfardsdijk 10
Worighezant (Orizand) 10
Wulpen 12, 13

Yorke, Sir Joseph 139

Zeeland 1, 12, 13-14, 20-1, 37, 38, 47-8, 49, 52-61, 64. *See also* Holland-Zeeland, counts and countesses of; province of, 83, 84, 85, 87, 88, 89, 90, 91, 94, 95, 99, 101-2, 103, 109-29, 135, 145, 160; staple: *see* Middelburg staple; States of, 68, 72, 83, 90, 95, 100, 117; toll of: *see* Iersekeroord, toll of
Zeeland-Flanders 87 and n 1, 104-5, 127 and n 3, 128 and n 2, 135, 141, 145, 206; question of future of (1830-1), 159, 160-1, 167, 171, 174, 177, 180, 203
Zevenaar 175-6
Zierikzee 15, 77-8
Zuid-Beveland 1, 9 and n 2, 10, 13, 14, 30, 62-3, 71
Zuidvliet, the 14
Zuylen van Nyevelt, Hugo van, baron 158, 169, 173, 174, 176, 181, 186, 190, 193, 197-8, 199, 201, 207, 208; recalled, 208 and n 3, 211
Zwake, the 14, 15-16, 32, 35, 49
Zwin, the 35, 86, 92, 101, 104-5, 109, 111

For Product Safety Concerns and Information please contact our EU
representative GPSR@taylorandfrancis.com
Taylor & Francis Verlag GmbH, Kaufingerstraße 24, 80331 München, Germany

www.ingramcontent.com/pod-product-compliance
Lightning Source LLC
Chambersburg PA
CBHW071825300426
44116CB00009B/1448